BACKSTAGE ON BROADWAY

★

MUSICALS AND THEIR MAKERS

MARTY BELL

NICK HERN BOOKS
London

A SUE KATZ & ASSOCIATES, INC., BOOK

Backstage on Broadway first published in Great Britain
as a paperback original in 1994 by Nick Hern Books Limited,
14 Larden Road, London W3 7ST by arrangement with
Sue Katz & Associates, Inc., New York, U.S.A.

First published in the United States of America under the title *Broadway Stories*
in 1993 by Broadway Cares/Equity Fights AIDS

Printed in the United States of America

British Library Cataloguing in Publication Data
A catalogue record for this book is available from the British Library

ISBN 1 85459 226 2

BACKSTAGE ON BROADWAY

★

MUSICALS AND THEIR MAKERS

The Broadway Musical is legendary for the sheer number of creative talents and artistic processes involved in its making.

Citing specific case histories from a whole raft of well-known recent Broadway musicals, this book takes us on a journey through the making of this complicated showbiz confection. Starting, of course, with the writers—in this case the authors of *City of Angels*—the author goes on to examine the various vital contributions made to the show on its way to the stage . . .

So, for example, he introduces us to the producer of *Jelly's Last Jam*, the director of *Guys and Dolls*, the choreographer of *Crazy for You* and the leads in *Most Happy Fella* and *Phantom of the Opera*. But he also looks at the crucial role played in the process by workshops, auditions (for *Five Guys Named Moe*), previews (of *Grand Hotel*) and—yes—by critics. And for those shows that make it through this series of ordeals, there is the headiness of award ceremony and the pleasures and pains of the long run . . .

'Marty Bell, one of the theatre's most plugged-in insiders, has come up with a spellbinding look behind the scenes at Broadway musical-making . . . The chapter on producer Margo Lion's odyssey in bringing *Jelly's Last Jam* to Broadway is alone worth the price of the book.' *Variety*

Marty Bell is the founder and president of the organisation called BROADWAY CARES/EQUITY FIGHTS AIDS, which will benefit from a proportion of the proceeds from the sale of this book.

BOOKS BY MARTY BELL

Breaking Balls
Carnival at Forest Hills
The Legend of Dr. J.
No Hard Feelings

For Charlie Willard, who got me started;
Susan Myerberg, who wouldn't let me quit;
and the cast, crew, and staff of
Kiss of the Spider Woman at New Musicals,
who allowed me to share the joy of the process

ACKNOWLEDGMENTS

One of my favorite sections of the *Playbill* magazine you receive when attending a Broadway show is the page set in agate type that appears at the end of the "Who's Who in the Cast" section and lists all the credits. Scanning the page, you get a sense of how many people there are who you never get to see but who are nevertheless instrumental in putting on a show. Every producer derives a sense of satisfaction compiling that list, which affords an opportunity to thank everyone. As the author of a book, I am delighted to have such an opportunity.

Thank you to Rodger McFarlane, executive director, and Tom Viola, managing director, of BROADWAY CARES/EQUITY FIGHTS AIDS, for approaching me with the request to publish this book, thus affording me the unique opportunity to have the majority of the revenue from my work go directly to providing care for people with AIDS. I have worked as a volunteer for the organization since its inception six years ago, and its participation here makes the experience of writing and publishing all the more meaningful.

Thank you to Sue Katz and her staff at Sue Katz & Associates, Inc., for providing BROADWAY CARES/EQUITY FIGHTS AIDS with the necessary publishing expertise. And to Mel Zerman and the staff of Limelight Editions for partnering with BC/EFA in this venture and thereby expanding the book's availability.

My editor, Jonathon Brodman, asked all the right, tough questions, and always provided focus. Thanks to Joel Avirom for his brilliant design and to Martha Swope, Joan Marcus, and the other photographers for illustrating these stories.

Thank you to Randy Lutterman for her persistent research; to Mark Olshaker, David Fisher, and Jay Acton, who, as always, were early readers and strong-minded critics; and to Harold Prince for always making sure I keep my eye on the ball.

Thank you to Susan Myerberg, David Bell, and Danny Bell for remaining patient while their husband and father was locked in his study all those nights and weekends when he should have been giving them his attention.

Thank you to the producers, press agents, and stage managers of all the shows visited in this book for providing me with the access to the shows and events that permitted me to search out these stories.

And, finally and most importantly, thank you to the seventeen talented and gracious artists whose stories are included here, for your time and your candor and your thoughtfulness. I am deeply honored that each of you permitted me to tell your story. And I eagerly look forward to seeing your work in the theatre in the future.

MARTY BELL
New York City
June 27, 1993

CONTENTS

★

OVERTURE

"Fasten Your Seat Belts"

★

Within the big city of New York, there sits a small town called Broadway. Like all small American towns, it has its gathering places, its peculiar customs, its annual celebrations, its lore. And gossip is a favorite pastime.

Broadway is a one-industry town, that industry being theatre. People from all across the country and around the world who aspire to make a name for themselves in theatre converge on the town with a résumé and a dream. Like all one-industry towns, the mood at any particular moment reflects the current state of the business.

Broadway has seen better days than today. The costs of doing business there have continued to escalate, and as a result the number of productions has diminished. Consequently, the initiative for originating plays, once a staple of Broadway, has largely been assumed by the regional theatres that have sprung up throughout the country over the past 30 years. Broadway has primarily become the home base for musicals, the place where a show comes to establish its credentials so it can then tour the United States and beyond. But production of musicals has declined as well, from about sixteen a season just a decade ago to half that or less in the past few years.

Even in the best of times, working in the theatre is an irrational occupational choice. It's not an endeavor encouraged by most parents or job counselors. The profession attracts people who are either tempted by risk or adept at denying its existence. It comes with all the drawbacks of any free-lance occupation—most notably, lack of security—as well as many drawbacks unique to the industry. Everyone who has worked in the theatre for any length of time has, on occasion, failed, and that failure is always very public. Probably the most quoted quip among theatre folk is playwright Robert Anderson's: that you cannot make a living in the theatre—but you can make a killing. In recent years, where commercial production has been significantly curtailed by economics and most of the work is in the not-for-profit theatre, where salaries are below what most people need to live on, the killings are fewer and farther between.

So why does anyone seek a *career* in theatre?

Well, I'm not sure that people do.

I was once at a gathering where a television theatre critic predicted the death of Broadway—a prognosis voiced all too frequently—to which Gene Klavan, a radio humorist, responded, "There will always be Broadway theatre because there are always people who want to put on shows." And I think that's the heart of the matter. As children, many of us daydream about becoming firemen or policemen or doctors or nurses—but I think the dream is different for those who fantasize about the theatre. Theatre is not so much about what we want to be as about what we want to do. Few rallying cries are as enticing as Mickey Rooney saying to Judy Garland, "Let's put on a show." It may be the results that keep you working—but it's the process that makes you want to keep working. The joy is in doing it.

I worked as a sports journalist and magazine editor, wrote books and produced a documentary film, before I ventured into the theatre to produce in my early thirties. A decade later, I've yet to have anything resembling a hit show. I've had my own share of disappointments, but this has not prevented me from experiencing a joy beyond anything I had ever known previously in the workplace. Joy that turns instantly to heartbreak, or vice versa, seems to be the rhythm of Broadway. And yet I know this is where I'm going to be spending my time from here on in. Like the romantic lead in a musical who has just discovered love, I have the urge to climb on top of a table or a mountain and sing about my passion, for all to hear. But I can't sing very well, so this is my song.

This is a book about putting on shows. From September 1991 to July 1992, I spent as much time as possible as a fly-on-the-wall wherever musicals were being created or performed. My intent was to submerge myself in the subculture of Broadway musical theatre and to write about how the business works and what it is like to work in it.

I hung out at sixteen shows in all, eight that had opened in the previous year and continued their runs into the 1991–92 New York theatre season, seven as they prepared to open during that season, and one in an early stage of development for a future season. The 1991–92 season provided a framework for the journey, but the stories told here could have been told in any season; though the specific events might change, the nature of the incidents described here would not.

At each show, I selected one participant—either an actor or a member of the creative team—and attempted to view the experience of doing the show through that person's eyes. I was also interested in the life and career history that had led each person to this opportunity.

The people I interviewed were selected because as an individual each could both provide an important perspective and had a good story to tell, and as a group their stories balanced to give an overview of the art form and business in which they work. The stories are told here in the usual order in which the participants get involved in the process of making musicals, beginning with the writing of a show and ending with the Tony Award ceremony honoring the best work of the season.

Most of the people you are about to meet are not well known—though some of them became a great deal better known over the course of the season. Many of them are friends of mine or people with whom I have worked. I will not pretend to be objective about these people; I like and admire them. The intent here is not to play critic. The critic looks at shows from an omniscient perspective; the stories herein are related from a different point of view—from deep down in the trenches. Except where necessary, the focus is not on how shows look from out in the house, but how they appear looking out from the proscenium.

With a few exceptions, the stories in this book are about people who are my contemporaries—people in their thirties and forties, my own generation of performers and creators. We're a generation that became adults after the so-called Golden Age of Musicals—which, depending on whom you talk to, was either the 1920s and 1930s of Gershwin, Kern, Porter, Berlin, and Rodgers, or the period that ran from the opening of *Oklahoma!* in 1943 through the next two and a half decades, or both. It was a time when theatre music filled the radio, production was plentiful, and, as Graciela Daniele, once a gypsy who caught the tail end of the era, says, "There was a new show for us to audition for every week." But whenever it was, most of the people in this book missed out on it. They are a talented group, and it is my contention that many of them would have been a lot better known by now were they not born too late.

What makes this particularly poignant is that our generation grew up when musicals were still in their heyday, eager to be part of that world—but when we got here, it no longer existed. As a group, we are engaged in a quest to get back the musical theatre we were first introduced to and fell hard for.

So please join me now on this journey through the small town of Broadway, through the wings and dressing rooms, the audition and rehearsal halls, the opening-night parties and award ceremonies, the joy and heartbreak of musical theatre.

As Margo Channing, perhaps our most beloved fictional Broadway leading lady, warned, "Fasten your seat belts. It's going to be a bumpy night."

MARTY BELL

Three people die and find themselves lined up at Heaven's Gate confronted by St. Peter.

"Before you enter, I have one question for each of you," St. Peter says. And he asks the first person in line, "How much money did you make last year?"

"About $400,000," the person says.

"Oh, a doctor," St. Peter says. "Please enter through that door there." St. Peter approaches the next person in line. "How much did you make last year?" he asks.

"About $250,000, give or take a little," the person says.

"Oh, a lawyer," St. Peter says. "That door right there." Then St. Peter turns to the third person. "And how much did you make last year?"

"$5,164," the person answers.

And St. Peter says, "Have I seen you in anything?"

THE FAVORITE JOKE OF ACTRESS COLLEEN DEWHURST

"No need reminding me that it all fell apart.
I need no lyric singing of stormy weather;
There's quite enough around me that's breaking my heart.
Sing happy!"

FRED EBB

VIRGINIA THEATRE

J A JUJAMCYN THEATRE

ROCCO LANDESMAN
PRESIDENT

JAMES H. BINGER
CHAIRMAN

Nick Vanoff   Roger Berlind

Jujamcyn Theaters Suntory International Corp. The Shubert Organization

present

James Naughton   Gregg Edelman

in

CITY OF ANGELS

Lyrics by
David Zippel ★

Music by
Cy Coleman

Book by
Larry Gelbart

with

Randy Graff   Dee Hoty   Kay McClelland

Scott Waara   Rachel York   Keith Perry   James Cahill   Jacquey Maltby
Herschel Sparber   Raymond Xifo   Doug Tompos   Alvin Lum
Tom Galantich   James Hindman   Evan Thompson   Eleanor Glockner
Peter Davis   Gary Kahn   Amy Jane London   Jackie Presti   Carolee Carmello

Shawn Elliott

and

Rene Auberjonois

Scenic Design by
Robin Wagner

Costume Designs by
Florence Klotz

Lighting Design by
Paul Gallo

Fight Staging by
B. H. Barry

Musical Direction by
Gordon Lowry Harrell

Vocal Arrangements by
Cy Coleman and
Yaron Gershovsky

Orchestrations by
Billy Byers

Sound Design by
Peter Fitzgerald
and **Bernard Fox**

Hair Styles by
Steve Atha

Production Stage Manager
Steven Zweigbaum

General Manager
Ralph Roseman

Casting by
Johnson-Liff & Zerman

Musical Numbers Staged by

Walter Painter

Directed by

Michael Blakemore

1

WRITING A SHOW

"This Job Is Not to Be Believed"

★

DAVID ZIPPEL *(Lyricist)* makes his Broadway musical-comedy debut with *City of Angels*. With Wally Harper he has written numerous songs for singer Barbara Cook, including "It's Better with a Band" from Miss Cook's live-at-Carnegie Hall album of the same name, and the original songs for her recent New York and West End concerts: "Barbara Cook: A Concert for the Theatre." Off-Broadway, Mr. Zippel has contributed lyrics to the revues *A . . . My Name Is Alice* and Hal Prince's *Diamonds;* and with composer Doug Katsaros, he wrote the musical comedy *Just So.* A revue of his songs, also titled *It's Better with a Band,* played off-Broadway and in London's West End. He wrote the original songs for *5, 6, 7, 8 . . . Dance!,* which starred Sandy Duncan at Radio City Music Hall. His songs have been performed by numerous theatre, cabaret, and recording artists, including Michael Feinstein, Gregory Hines, Lonette McKee, Debbie Shapiro, and Ann Reinking. With Jonathan Sheffer and Joe Leonardo, Mr. Zippel wrote *Going Hollywood,* a musical adaptation of Kaufman and Hart's *Once in a Lifetime.* A graduate of Harvard Law School, he is delighted not to practice law.

Every song has a story behind it," David Zippel tells the hundred or so people gathered in the upstairs cabaret at the Russian Tea Room in March of 1992 for an evening devoted to his lyrics. "This was the second song Cy Coleman and I wrote for *City of Angels*. I was kind of on probation at the time. Cy had called and invited me to work on this musical with him and Larry Gelbart, then called *Death Is for Suckers*. And I thought we were going to write a few songs and then he and Larry would meet and decide if I had the job."

When approached by Coleman, the then thirty-two-year-old Zippel was part of the pack of young New York musical-theatre writers whose opportunities had been limited by the steady decrease in activity in commercial theatre over the past two decades. This yielded a generation of frustrated and jealous Broadway wanna-bes. Zippel's career thus far consisted of supplying lyrics for an unsuccessful off-Broadway adaptation of Rudyard Kipling's *Just So Stories*; an adaptation of George Kaufman and Moss Hart's play *Once in a Lifetime* called *Going Hollywood*, which was never fully produced; and for scattered individual songs, including one for the Broadway flop *Marilyn*, a few for the off-Broadway flop *Diamonds*, and some for singer Barbara Cook's nightclub act.

Tonight, the thin, rather impish-looking Zippel, now thirty-seven, is wearing a suit. His delivery is off the cuff and informal. He's new to this celebrity-writer thing—and he doesn't pretend otherwise. A little embarrassed laugh sneaks into his repartee every once in a while. Most of his experience has consisted of trying to sell himself to people who don't want to be sold; now, following the nearly two-year run of his first Broadway show, he's suddenly faced with an audience of admirers who are already sold.

"Cy had written this melody that's very minor and haunting. He played it for me and I flipped," he says. "It had this strange shape that it would never have had if the lyrics were written first. That's sometimes an advantage of writing the music first. I found the title while he played the song. I said, How about 'With Every Breath I Take'? He loved the way it sounded with the music and was very enthusiastic. And then he went away for a week and left me with the music.

"I really wanted to please Cy. I wrote a draft of the lyric and I polished it and I liked it. But then I really got nervous. During the rest of that week I wrote twelve different drafts of the song, some of which had that title, some of which didn't. When he came back, I put the stack of twelve on the piano with my first draft on top. He sat down and played it straight through and sang the lyric and then said, 'It's beautiful. It's great.' As he continued to talk, I very innocently slipped the other twelve drafts off the piano and into my bag. That was a real great day because I said to myself, Oh, boy, this is going to be just fine."

Writers must sing at these evenings. Zippel chooses a tune he wrote with Alan Menken (composer for *The Little Mermaid* and *Beauty and the Beast*) for the baseball revue *Diamonds* called "In the Cards." It's about a boy whose attachment to the sport is limited to collecting. A few years back, this could have been Zippel's song about his own career in musical theatre. But not anymore. He's playing in the big leagues now. He's emerged from the pack.

David Zippel had prepared for his career in theatre by attending Harvard Law School. What he learned there was that he didn't want to be a lawyer. Upon graduation in 1979, while his classmates accepted associates' positions at prestigious law firms, Zippel moved into an apartment on Manhattan's Bleecker Street with some help from his parents (his father's a toy wholesaler) and pursued an interest that had begun when he'd started writing lyrics to 1960s rock-and-roll songs that made fun of his junior-high-school teachers.

If you come away from Harvard Law with nothing else, you're certain to have good contacts. One of Zippel's friends there, Russell DaSilva, was the son of lawyer Al DaSilva, who has an entertainment law practice. Among Al's clients was Cy Coleman, a very successful composer of both pop and Broadway tunes. Unlike most theatre composers, Coleman liked to work with a variety of lyricists. He had written *Sweet Charity* and *Seesaw* with Dorothy Fields; *Wildcat* and *Little Me* with Carolyn Leigh; *I Love My Wife* and *Barnum* with Michael Stewart; and *On the Twentieth Century* and later *The Will Rogers Follies* with Betty Comden and Adolph Green. DaSilva was eager to set up a meeting between his son's classmate and his client. But it wasn't until six years after graduation that Zippel received a call inviting him to meet with Coleman at his office.

"I went to the office on West Fifty-fourth Street, which is kind of legendary for its clutter," Zippel says, sitting at lunch a few weeks before the Tea Room affair. "Cy talked to me about writing a project that I really didn't take to, but I wasn't about to say no right away to working with Cy Coleman because I idolized him. We met a few more times and then finally I told him I remembered reading in what was then called the 'News of the Rialto' column in the *Times* that he and Larry Gelbart were collaborating on a detective story called *Death Is for Suckers* that was going to have a jazz score. I had a real affinity for jazz and I asked to be considered. He told me they were talking to a bunch of big shots, but he would think about it. About three months later, in the fall of 1986, he called and said, 'Let's go.' "

In Gelbart, Zippel found himself working with one of the funniest and most versatile writers in American pop culture; his clever work included "M*A*S*H" for television, *Tootsie* for film, and *A Funny Thing Happened On the Way to the Forum*—on which he shared book credit with director Bert Shevelove—for the musical theatre. Before Zippel joined this project, Gelbart had written an outline and a few scenes for a musical detective story. These inspired Coleman and Zippel to write "With Every Breath I Take," as well as a seduction song called "Lost and Found," which they brought out to Los Angeles for an initial creative meeting with the writer.

"Larry said that since we were doing something original by using jazz in the theatrical form," Zippel says, "he wanted to find a literary equivalent that he could have a good time with. He didn't just want to do a pastiche of a detective story. He asked for some time to think.

"About six months later, in the spring of 1987, he called us and said he had a concept, and Cy and I flew to Los Angeles to meet. Larry's concept was that there was going to be the detective story, and also the story of the writer creating that story, and the two were going to be interwoven. You would see a writer and his life, as well as the screenplay he was writing, come to life onstage.

"So that week we spent at Larry's house in Beverly Hills—a very good place to write a show about Hollywood—mostly by the pool, with a tape recorder, and together as a team we outlined the show scene by scene. It was the most exciting creative week I've ever had in my life."

As a relative novice getting his first shot at Broadway and working with an all-star team, Zippel was not so far removed from any of us who ever entertained any thoughts of writing a musical. The process of the year and a half of writing this show could have been the experience of any of us—provided, of course, we had Zippel's talent.

"Cy and Larry were very open and they treated me like I belonged there from the start, and that made me feel great," he says. "But I also knew what a great opportunity this was for me. I kept thinking, Wow! This is where I always wanted to be."

David Zippel is the son of a former basketball star at Lafayette College who went on to play semi-pro ball for Wilkes-Barre in the old Eastern League. Following in the footsteps of his father, Martin, Zippel joined the Pee Wee basketball league at the Jewish Community Center in his hometown, Easton, Pennsylvania. "The stage was in the gym," he says. "And I was never any good at basketball because I was more interested in what was going on on the stage." Zippel sat on the bench during a game one night, watching a rehearsal for a production of *Guys and Dolls*, in which his dad played Arvide and his mother was a Hot Box girl. Soon, while his friends were playing basketball, Zippel was playing FDR Jr. in the community center production of *Sunrise at Campobello* and a newsboy in *Gypsy*.

"When I got into junior high school," Zippel recalls, "I became interested in writing songs. I used to take whatever was popular on the radio and write sort of smart-ass songs to amuse my friends and myself. I remember writing a lyric to 'Winchester Cathedral' about our math teacher, Charlie Sandwick."

Zippel wrote his first musical while in high school, collaborating with his neighbor, Kevin Brau. Then, as a freshman at the University of Pennsylvania, he went to the 812 section of the stacks in the library and began paging through all the plays alphabetically in search of source material. When he got to George S. Kaufman and Moss Hart's 1937 comedy *Once in a Lifetime*, the search ended. He didn't bother inquiring about any rights. He and Kevin just set out to write the show.

In his senior year, Zippel grew fascinated with the work of a director across town at Temple University named Joe Leonardo. They became friends and later that year Leonardo called Zippel and said he was working on a new show called *Rotunda* at the L'Enfant Plaza Theatre in the basement of an office building in Washington, D.C. The lyricist had just walked out in a huff, so Leonardo needed help. Zippel collaborated with an undergraduate friend on five songs to complete the score—three of which were praised in *Washington Post* critic Richard Coe's otherwise negative review.

"That made me think, Hey, maybe I can really do this," Zippel says. "But I had also been accepted to Harvard Law School and decided I had better go."

Before entering Harvard, Zippel and Leonardo pledged to each other that they would collaborate on *Once in a Lifetime* when Zippel had the time. In his first year of law school, Zippel contributed lyrics to a student musical about Adam and Eve called *S.I.N. (Still in the Nude), the Original*. Then one night he went to a hotel nightclub in Boston to see singer Barbara Cook. He introduced himself to Cook's musical director, Wally Harper, and said how much he admired the songs Harper was writing with Paul Zakreski. Harper responded that he was not writing with Zakreski anymore. Zippel confessed he didn't really want to be a lawyer. That summer, Zippel came to New York to collaborate with Harper. Their first effort was a pop tune called "I Can't Remember Living Without Loving You," which a number of singers did in their club acts.

Then Zippel began collaborating with Harper on the score for *Once in a Lifetime*, renamed *Going Hollywood*, and with Leonardo on the book. But Harper had different ideas about the show, so the nascent team decided not to continue on that project.

After law school, Zippel moved to New York, lived in N.Y.U. student housing while he studied for the bar exam, and continued to work with Harper on songs for Barbara Cook. In 1981, Cook performed some of their tunes, including "It's Better with a Band," in a Carnegie Hall concert. Zippel made a little money writing for industrial shows, and composing jingles for the South Street Seaport, Uncle Ben's Converted Rice, and a Japanese brandy. A young composer named Jonathan Scheffer joined Zippel and Leonardo to write *Going Hollywood*.

Producer Michael Frazier, who had a big hit show with Lena Horne's concert at the Nederlander Theatre, optioned the property. In 1982, Frazier presented a staged reading/backers' audition of *Going Hollywood* to two packed houses at the Westside Arts Theatre. It featured an appealing and talented cast led by Harry Groener and Christine Ebersole, who had been enthusiastically reviewed as Will Parker and Ado Annie, respectively, in the 1980 revival of *Oklahoma!* at the Palace. The material was well performed and well received. Frazier smelled a hit.

With the backing of the Shubert Organization, Frazier produced a five-week rehearsal workshop that culminated in four performances in rehearsal dress presented in the basement theatre at City Center. The writers were convinced that the workshop was just that—a preparatory step for a Broadway production. But wholesale casting changes were made in all the important male roles, the direction was unwieldy, and somehow between the presentations the show lost its charm. Ten years later now, Zippel's pet project remains unproduced. The collapse of a show that seemed so close to a Broadway opening sent Zippel into an emotional tailspin. He wrote another show (*Just So*) and contributed songs to a couple of reviews, but the enthusiasm that had been the driving force behind *Going Hollywood* was zapped, and he talked often about abandoning theatre and concentrating on writing pop tunes.

Then in the fall of 1986, he received the unexpected phone call from Cy Coleman to join him and Gelbart on what became *City of Angels*.

"When we sat down to begin, Larry Gelbart led all the way," Zippel says. "But the atmosphere was such that anyone could say anything no matter how dumb it seemed at the time. The structure was very much Larry. There were times when we would feel a song right away as we went through the show. Then we went back and went through each act and placed the numbers more carefully. Cy has a very strong dramatic sense. He sees the emotional core of the music. I would go for the more detached, glib approach to a number, and Cy would push me more toward the emotional.

"We didn't want this show to be pretentious in any way. And whatever message you might have gotten, we wanted you to get it while you were enjoying yourself. We were having fun playing games and being clever— we thought we were clever! We wanted it to be a series of surprises that amused the audience a lot.

"By the time Cy and I left L.A. at the end of that week, we pretty much had—song for song, scene for scene—an outline of what opened on Broadway."

Over the next year, the show was written via a transcontinental collaboration facilitated by facsimile and FedEx.

"Larry would send us several pages, a scene or two at a time, every week or two," Zippel says. "And I really looked forward to getting those pages because he made everything we talked about so funny. He even makes the exposition funny. Larry said it was something he learned writing for television. There were such time constraints and he always found when the producers were cutting for time they cut some of his favorite jokes. So he put the jokes in the exposition since that never got cut."

The show they created did not open with a standard overture consisting of highlights from the songs you would hear the remainder of the evening, but with a musical theme as a mood-setter that underscores the screenplay section of the show like a movie theme.

"Because it was a film within a Broadway play," Zippel says, "we wanted to score it like a film, and Cy felt it was very important to have a movie-type theme. So Cy wrote this jazzy theme and I wrote a very dark, cynical lyric that kind of expressed the theme of the evening.

"But then, when Michael Blakemore came in to direct, he felt that Larry's opening words were so important to set up a complicated story that he didn't want people getting caught up in the lyrics that early. It probably had something to do with Michael not being of the musical theatre, but I think that turned out to be an asset here. So he cut the lyrics and we just went with the music and a scat [vocal sounds rather than words] overture."

So the first of David Zippel's lyrics heard at the Virginia Theatre were "Do-do-do-do-do-do-dah." The lyric he did write for what became known as the "City of Angels Theme" can be heard toward the end of the CBS Records original-cast album. In the show, which opened on December 11,

1989, this theme was played in front of a poster for the fictional motion picture *City of Angels*, and was soon joined by the voice-over narration of a cynical detective named Stone, played by James Naughton. The poster flew away to reveal Stone on a hospital gurney with a bullet in his shoulder. It then flashed back to the day, a week earlier, when a seductress all in white named Alaura Kingsley (Dee Hoty) showed up at the shamus's seedy office to hire him to find her missing stepdaughter. We are in the movie now and the design—sets and costumes—is all black and white. The scene is the standard detective-genre-story setup—with two exceptions: first, music interrupts the action for Stone, in a song called "Doubletalk," to take us inside his thoughts; second, a man at a typewriter named Stine (Gregg Edelman) appears across the stage, dressed in colors, and picks up the song to tell us he is adapting his novel into a screenplay (which is what we are seeing in black and white) and is excited by the opportunity.

"Larry wrote the opening scene first and then Cy and I had the idea that we should start with a jazz aria for both Stine and Stone," Zippel says. "Instead of a traditional opening number that tells you what the show's about, this set up the two characters, told you the style was jazz, and that we might not always be using music in a traditional sense. In the writer's part of the song, using music allowed us to say a lot of things you can't say in dialogue because it would be too simplistic. He tells us he's an eager beaver and a little naïve for Hollywood. It's pretty direct and you can get away with that in a song.

"The music is like a jazz riff. Cy wrote it and then I set the lyric. It's a very syncopated song using a lot of eighth- and sixteenth-notes that I had to wrap words around. I had to use interesting syllables and sounds that could curve with the music, which was challenging.

"And then when we cast Gregg Edelman as Stine, the writer—he has an enormous range, a great voice—we thought it would be a crime not to use it. So we added a cadenza at the end to give him the chance to really sing."

The show then moves to a scene between the writer and his wife, Gabby (Kay McClelland), a book editor who would rather see her husband concentrate on novels than write movies. Left alone on half the stage in her Technicolor bedroom, Gabby begins a number called "What You Don't Know About Women," in which she is soon joined by Oolie (Randy Graff), the detective's Gal Friday, who is on the other half of the stage in black and white.

"We came up with that song in the initial planning meetings," Zippel says. "We wanted to have a duet, half in reality and half in fiction. And two characters who didn't know they were singing together. We were excited about that image. And we wanted a song right here that underscored the similar approach to women shared by Stine and Stone. It set up the women as being a little smarter than the men in that they see where their men are coming from.

"I came up with the title and then I sketched out a few ideas. I think I wrote:

> *You are the type of man who*
> *Looks for understanding lovers.*
> *But never understands the girl*
> *Who lies beneath the covers.*

"And then when Cy took it home to set it, he came up with the idea of splitting the lines up so the two women were answering each other. He found a musical shape to the piece based on my notes and then I fit the lyrics to his tune. What we needed to accomplish here was to deepen the audience's understanding of these two women. But we also wanted to introduce the audience to the two worlds of fiction and reality and show they affected each other.

"When I came up with something funny, I couldn't wait to call Cy and Larry and make them laugh. And Larry would call me and read me a couple of lines that he liked. We all have a similar sense of humor and made one another laugh a lot."

After the women's number, the mystery resumes: Stone is in his bungalow, and on the radio is a 1940s pop-tune pastiche called "You Gotta Look Out for Yourself." The number foreshadows two hoods breaking in who don't want Stone on the case and beat him silly.

From there the show switches back to reality, to the office of Buddy Fiedler (Rene Auberjonois), the self-adoring producer of Stine's movie. In a waltz-tempo number called "The Buddy System," Fiedler lets the writer know, "The book may be yours, baby. Trust me, the movie is mine."

"We wanted to create a larger-than-life character with an ego even larger," Zippel says, "but, at the same time, show he was smart. I came up with the idea of 'The Buddy System' because I figured Buddy would refer to himself in the third person and think of himself constantly.

"Larry has Buddy saying all kinds of non sequiturs and malapropisms. Buddy doesn't hear himself, he just talks. This gave me an opportunity to indulge myself a little and be a little flashier. When we were working on the outline in L.A., I would go back to my hotel room at night and we were really cooking and I couldn't get the show out of my mind. So I would make lists of ideas for the songs. The day we came up with the Buddy number, I came up with the phrase 'I've been through De Mille.' But I didn't show it to the guys right away. I wanted to make it work in context.

"We wrote an original version of this song that we were very, very happy with," Zippel says. "And though Rene is just a wonderful actor, he wasn't comfortable with the difficult rhythms in that song. He was having a hard time and we felt like we were shooting him in the foot. The song just never got across the footlights in previews. So a week and a half before opening, we took the basic idea and rewrote the song with a simpler melody and a simpler line. But I managed to keep 'Let's face it, I've been through DeMille.' "

After establishing Buddy, the show moves back into the screenplay. We learn that Stone was once in love with a lounge singer named Bobbi, whom the writer is basing on his wife, Gabby, and, like her, is played by Kay McClelland. Onstage in a nightclub, she sings the ballad "With Every Breath I Take," which Zippel wrote early as part of his trial run with Coleman. "We knew all along that the song Bobbi would sing here would be more indicative of what Stone was feeling for her," Zippel says. "Many of the songs in the screenplay section, like this one, are commenting on the action, like movie underscoring, which was our intent."

Following this sequence, Stone visits Alaura at her mansion to complain about the beating he has taken. There Stone becomes aware of her much-older husband, encased in an iron lung. Stone's suspicions about Alaura build. But she tries to divert him and persuades him to remain on the case in a number full of double entendres called "The Tennis Song":

> STONE: *I may lack form and finesse, but I'll warm up in a jiff.*
> ALAURA: *It's not exciting unless the competition is stiff.*

"We wanted to create a musical scene that was like a Raymond Chandler–Howard Hawks film full of real obvious double entendres. Just like that scene in *The Big Sleep* where Lauren Bacall and Bogey are talking about horse racing but they're really talking about sex. I read all the Chandler novels and saw the film versions before we got started, and Larry gave me the collection of Chandler's letters written while he was in Hollywood. So we were steeped in that material.

"The number was a wink at the dialogue from the films of that period, and it accomplished two things for us: It established mutual sexual interest, and Alaura persuaded Stone to go on looking for her step-daughter, Mallory."

The next sequence is Stone's search for Mallory, which traditionally might have been staged as a dance number. But Blakemore and set designer Robin Wagner took a different approach—they filmed the streets Stone was walking through and created a sense of movement onstage by having actor Naughton walk in place as the projected scenes shifted behind him.

As it would be in a movie, the montage was underscored—by a scat-singing quartet in a number called "Everybody's Gotta Be Somewhere."

"Because of the style of the music, Cy knew from the beginning that he wanted to have a jazz quartet running through the piece," Zippel says. "And that device came in handy here. It gave us the chance to complement the visuals with words about Stone's feelings on the search."

With the search bungled, Stone returns home to his bungalow, where he finds what he's looking for—the precocious and seductive Mallory (Rachel York)—in his bed, and naked. The no-longer-missing stepdaughter attempts to seduce the detective in a song called "Lost and Found."

"This was the very first song Cy and I wrote when he invited me to give the show a shot," Zippel says. "We had Larry's outline for the detective story. All I knew was Stone comes back to his bungalow after bungling the search for the missing girl and finds her naked in his bed. Sing song! Cy had already written the music. I didn't have any sense of the characters yet. All I knew was I had to write a naked-girl-in-bed song. So I did. There are a few tricky little rhymes in the lyric. Like, 'If you're not celibate, we could raise hell a bit.' But whatever I did, they liked. It cemented my relationship with Cy. And it stayed in the show as it was."

Stone manages to resist Mallory's temptation. But a photographer breaks into Stone's bungalow and photographs the naked Mallory. Mallory then steals Stone's gun and disappears. When the photographer is found murdered with Stone's weapon nearby, Lieutenant Muñoz of the Los Angeles Police Department, a former partner and current rival of Stone's, arrests the dick with glee. Muñoz (Shawn Elliott) has had it in for Stone for some time and expresses it in a wiseguy number with a Latin beat called "All You Have to Do Is Wait."

This number is somewhat jarring: You're pedaling hard toward the end of a long first act here and the story is already very well populated. Then this character, who has not had much prominence and who you do not have much interest in, takes three minutes or so to do a number. Performing a song gives a character weight—which this character doesn't seem able to carry. Zippel and his collaborators disagree: "Abe Burrows said if you don't sing in a musical, you don't exist," Zippel says. "I think Muñoz's vendetta against Stone plays an important part in the detective story."

The act ends as the two stories—the real world and the reel world—come together. The initial optimism that Stine expressed in his first song has faded. His script is being tailored by the producer. His wife has lost respect for him and he has betrayed her. And now he and his alter ego turn on each other. In "You're Nothing Without Me," Stine tells Stone that he's a failed gumshoe, and Stone tells Stine he's just envious.

In this evening of strange duets, this one, between a writer and his alter ego, is a slick expression of the self-disgust that has set in over the course of the first act. "That's a moment that belongs to all of us and that we're very proud of," Zippel says. "We knew that the end of the act was going to find the writer and detective in competition. The song is a great tune, maybe the most memorable in the show. But the lyrics came first in this one. I took a first pass through and then handed it to Cy. Then he had a structural idea that caused me to reshape what I had written and we worked on it together. The song is rhymed within an inch of its life. I used triple rhymes here instead of double rhymes: 'Dumb gumshoe, some gumshoe.' 'Track record, hack record.' 'Eat, breathe, sleep fiction; knee-deep in cheap fiction.' But it's the music that's rousing and ends the act on the right note."

The second-act curtain of *City of Angels* rises on a recording studio where Jimmy Powers (Scott Waara), a Bing Crosby–like crooner, is recording a big-band, standard-type ballad called "Stay with Me," backed by the quartet.

"We knew from the beginning that Jimmy Powers was going to have a signature theme," Zippel says. "We wanted to write a pastiche of one of those classic songs from the forties that everyone just sighs over when they hear. 'Stay with Me' was a song that could have been Jimmy's theme on the radio. Because we had so many characters in the show, and almost all of them were playing double roles, a lot of songs were used to remind you who the important characters were, to give you a few moments to spend with them and focus on them."

Stone, the detective, is still in jail at this point, accused of the murder committed with his gun, and is visited and briefed by his Gal Friday, Oolie. Then Oolie, who has obvious affection for Stone, returns to her black-and-white bedroom, feeling like a fool about her relationships with men. She begins to sing a funny and self-deprecating song called "You Can Always Count on Me." After a couple of verses, the scene suddenly blacks out. In the time it takes to say, *What happened?*, the lights come up again. The bedroom is still there, but it's in color now. We are back in the real-life story. Actress Randy Graff has become her other character, Donna, Fiedler's Gal Friday, instead of Oolie. She picks up the same song she was singing as Oolie. It's strange-duet time again—this one sung by one actress as two characters.

"We knew we had to keep raising the stakes in the second act," Zippel says, "to keep surprising the audience. And so we came up with this idea to do a duet for one person. Oolie and Donna are at the same place emotionally, both being treated shabbily by men at this point, so it was right for the trick. We didn't know how this would be accomplished, but we just wrote it and left it to set designer Robin Wagner to figure it out.

"So Robin designed this bed that was gray, and the walls to the room were black and white. And Oolie was wearing black and white. But the bed was underdressed with a peach spread. The walls were panels with color paintings on the other side. And Randy had a peach nightgown under the black and white. So when we blacked out on the black and white, the gray bedspread was pulled up over Randy's head behind the bed, the panels turned, she ripped off her gray clothes, and in two seconds the whole scene went from black and white to color.

"For the song, I originally came up with the title 'It Goes Without Saying,' which I thought was kind of nice, and I wrote a draft with a lot of self-deprecating jokes based on the bad romantic experiences of a friend of mine who lives in L.A. But Cy thought it wasn't on the nose enough for this particular case. So we came up with 'You Can Always Count on Me,' and a lot of my same jokes worked with the new title.

"This was the one song in the show that was more in the Broadway idiom than jazz, but we thought that was what Oolie would sing. Nick Vanoff, who produced the show with Roger Berlind, was very nervous about this song. He said, 'This song sounds different from all the others in the show.' And we said, 'Yeah, we know. This is a sort of number.' He said, 'It's not going to work.' We said, 'Why don't you trust us and see what happens?' He said, 'Okay, but I know it won't work.' This went on for weeks during the writing. And then just before rehearsals began, we had dinner one night and I walked Nick back to his hotel and he said, 'Please, write another number. The music isn't as good as the other music. The lyrics aren't as funny as the other lyrics. Please.' The first night of previews, the show was a mess technically and we couldn't get the quick change right, but the number worked great anyway and Nick came over and said, 'Can we get that song into the first act?' "

The writer Stine's wife learns that in her absence he has had an affair with Donna, his producer's secretary. Stine flies to New York, meets Gabby at her hotel, and concocts an excuse for the tryst. Gabby responds in a song called "It Needs Work," perhaps the best song dramatically in the score—the lyrics are at once referring to Stine's alibi, his screenplay, and his marriage to Gabby.

"Gabby is the smartest character in the show," Zippel says. "She's the truth detector. To Stine, she represents everything that Hollywood isn't. She's a literary person, a book editor, and we thought this would be a chance for her to use her wit and her sense of humor.

"The title came to me in our first meeting in L.A. when we came to the moment. But the song evolved a bit. In the first pass at it, when she sings 'It needs work,' she was referring to a draft of a book that was going to be his next novel. But it was too complicated and it took the focus off the main story. So I rewrote the song so that she is singing about his screenplay, which she has just read. And then it switches to their relationship":

> *And come to think of it,*
> *Your writing always mirrors our relationship,*
> *With dangers cropping up*
> *And sweet young strangers popping up like weeds.*
> *So if you wish official pardoning*
> *You'd better do a little gardening;*
> *Ya know you needn't be so generous with your seeds.*
> *Your fertile lies don't fertilize.*
> *It needs work.*

As the screenplay reaches its conclusion, Stone discovers that Alaura killed a previous husband and plans to kill this one, as well as his children, to get at his fortune. The reason Alaura hired Stone to find Mallory at the outset was so that she could do away with the daughter and be the sole heiress. Stone confronts Alaura with this, the woman pulls a gun, they wrestle, shots go off. Alaura falls dead and Stone is seriously injured.

This gets us back to the opening scene of the movie and the show, where Stone is lying on a hospital gurney.

With the script finished, we return to real life, where Stine is depressed. His wife is gone. He finds out Donna has been rewriting his script. Alone at center stage, he sings a big jazz waltz called "Funny," but there are no jokes in it, just irony. His life is a joke—and he can't laugh anymore.

"I started out to write something more about ideas here," Zippel says. "It was a song about writing again. It was too inside. It wasn't right. And Cy pushed me to write what Stine was really feeling about his life now, how much he hurt. And that was right. Stine's angry at himself now, and everyone else, and he had to sing that."

As the song ends, Stine turns his back to the audience, and the backdrop irises to reveal the soundstage on which Stine's screenplay is being filmed. On the set, Stine discovers that Buddy has shared screenplay credit and he's hired the dull crooner Jimmy Powers to play the gritty Stone. Stine explodes, gets fired, and is about to be beaten up when Stone runs to the typewriter and taps out a Hollywood ending in which the writer beats up the goons and his wife returns to his side. Together Stine and Stone reprise "You're Nothing Without Me"—except this time it's "I'm Nothing Without You."

"This was one of those good things that was not planned," Zippel says. "It was the perfect ending for us to reverse this song and it probably seems obvious, which is good. But it wasn't obvious to us until well into the writing process."

And so the fifteen songs and two reprises listed in the *Playbill* for the first-ever performance of *City of Angels* were the same fifteen songs and two reprises listed in the opening-night program five weeks later. The only significant rewrite during the preview period was a makeover of "The Buddy System." In fact, during the entire three-year period between the first creative session beside Gelbart's pool in L.A. and opening night at the Virginia Theatre, no new musical moments were inserted into the original structural outline, and only a few lyric ideas were slightly altered. There are no trunk songs from this show to be pulled out for nightclub acts or fund-raising tributes. The show won highly favorable reviews and the Tony Award for Best Musical. This flies smack in the *punim* of everything we've come to believe about the process of creating a musical. Usually, musicals are not written—they're rewritten. Was it genius? Luck? Stubbornness? Or was this a show so dominated by its structure and jokes and stagecraft that the score went along for the ride?

"Cy, Larry, and I were a very cohesive group and we had a very strong common vision of what we wanted this show to be," Zippel says as an explanation. "And that group expanded to include Michael Blakemore, our director. A lot of songs are thrown out of shows not because they don't work, but because someone in the group doesn't like them, or doesn't know how to make them work, or doesn't like them enough to try to make them work. A director or a choreographer has a lot of power in this, and if they say, I don't know how to do this, what choice do you have except to write something else?

" 'It Needs Work' could've been thrown out when we didn't nail it the first time. In another show, it might've been. But we reshaped it. And 'You Can Always Count on Me' could've gone because the producer didn't like it. But he gave us a chance and the audience responded.

"This show just had a very cohesive team that liked sitting in a room for hours and talking everything through together. We loved to outline and we weren't in a hurry to write before we really thought through every moment. Even during previews when the show was three hours and word on us was not good and we couldn't get the technical part of the show right and the audience was confused by the same actors playing dual roles, and some of the producers got very nervous, we stuck together as a team to try to finish our shared vision. And it worked."

JOHN GOLDEN THEATRE

Ⓢ A Shubert Organization Theatre

Gerald Schoenfeld, *Chairman*

Bernard B. Jacobs, *President*

BARRY AND FRAN WEISSLER

present

MICHAEL RUPERT   STEPHEN BOGARDUS⭐   CHIP ZIEN

in

FALSETTOS

music and lyrics by
WILLIAM FINN

book by
WILLIAM FINN and JAMES LAPINE

starring
BARBARA WALSH
HEATHER MAC RAE   CAROLEE CARMELLO
JONATHAN KAPLAN   ANDREW HARRISON LEEDS

sound design
PETER FITZGERALD

lighting design
FRANCES ARONSON

set design
DOUGLAS STEIN

costume design
ANN HOULD-WARD

press representative
THE PETE SANDERS
GROUP

marketing consultant
DAN KLORES ASSOCS.
HAYLEY SUMNER

hair design
PHYLLIS
DELLA

WENDY
ETTINGER

STUART
HOWARD

AMY
SCHECTER

musical direction
SCOTT FRANKEL

musical contractor
JOHN MONACO

musical arrangements
MICHAEL STAROBIN

in association with

and

MASAKAZU SHIBAOKA
BROADWAY PACIFIC

JAMES AND MAUREEN
O'SULLIVAN CUSHING

technical supervisor
ARTHUR SICCARDI

production supervisor
CRAIG JACOBS

associate producer
ALECIA PARKER

general manager
BARBARA DARWALL

directed by
JAMES LAPINE

The Producers and Theatre Management are Members
of the League of American Theatres and Producers, Inc.
FALSETTOLAND was produced off-Broadway by
Maurice Rosenfield and Lois F. Rosenfield with Steven Suskin
The Producers wish to express their appreciation to Theatre Development Fund
for its support of this production.

The Theatre Management is a Member of The League of American Theatres and Producers, Inc.

2

DEVELOPMENTAL PRODUCTIONS

"Something Bad Is Happening"

STEPHEN BOGARDUS *(Whizzer)* has appeared in all three productions that comprise William Finn's *Marvin Trilogy*. He originated the role of Whizzer in *March of the Falsettos* at Playwrights Horizons. Nine years later he reprised the role for *Falsettoland* at Playwrights Horizon and the Lucille Lortel Theatre. Between these engagements he portrayed Marvin in a revival of Finn's *In Trousers* at the Promenade Theatre. Most recently, Mr. Bogardus costarred in the Los Angeles production of *City of Angels* with James Naughton. On Broadway he has appeared in *The Grapes of Wrath, Les Misérables,* and *West Side Story.* He played Freddie in the national tour of *Chess.* His off-Broadway work includes *Genesis, No Way to Treat a Lady, Feathertop,* and *The Umbrellas of Cherbourg.* He has performed regionally at the La Jolla Playhouse (*80 Days*) and the Long Wharf Theatre (*Progress*). Television appearances include guest roles on "Murder, She Wrote," "Tour of Duty," and "Cagney & Lacey." Mr. Bogardus is a graduate of Princeton University, where he was a member of the Triangle Club.

As the 1991–92 New York theatre season was cranking up in September, Stephen Bogardus was in Los Angeles starring as Stine the writer (not Stone the detective) in the national company of *City of Angels* (which must have been like reading from *All the President's Men* at a Nixon staff meeting). One evening, William Finn—composer and lyricist of a cycle of three short musicals that includes *In Trousers*, *March of the Falsettos*, and *Falsettoland*, in all of which Bogardus had performed—came to see the actor's show and went out with him afterward. At this same time, a production that consisted of *March of the Falsettos* as a first act and *Falsettoland* as a second act was in previews at the Hartford Stage Company in Connecticut under the direction of Graciela Daniele. Doing both hour-and-ten-minute pieces in tandem as a full evening had been a dream of Finn and Bogardus, as well as director James Lapine and actors Michael Rupert and Chip Zien, all of whom had worked together on the world premieres of each piece at Playwrights Horizons, an institutional theatre on Manhattan's West Forty-second Street Theatre Row, some nine years apart. In fact, in 1989, as *Falsettoland* was being finished and prepared for its first full production, they had performed both together as a workshop. But when *Falsettoland* opened at the theatre in June 1990, it did so without its companion piece. And despite advance rumors to the contrary, when *Falsettoland* later transferred to a commercial production at the Lucille Lortel Theatre in Greenwich Village that fall, it also traveled solo.

On that late-summer night in the city of angles, Finn reported to Bogardus that the double bill was receiving standing ovations nightly back in Hartford. Two weeks later, critic Frank Rich gave it a glowing review in *The New York Times*. Just two days after the review appeared, Bogardus heard from a friend-in-common with Finn that there was already a steady flow of commercial producers trekking up to northern Connecticut. It seemed like a forgone conclusion that this new production would achieve the dream that Bogardus and his colleagues never had—playing *Falsettos* on Broadway. That rumor started the phone lines burning among the *Falsettos* alumni association.

"We all sort of felt that if there's any justice in the world, we would be the people to go to Broadway with this," Bogardus says. "At the same time, I realized that it was that production that had gotten this wonderful review from Frank Rich, and why would a producer want to take a chance on the Lapine version when they had the review they needed from this production? I had this feeling that our cast was in trouble."

When you work on the first production of a new show, it is always *your* show. New shows are precious. Untested work is the most vulnerable and it makes the people involved that much more vulnerable. In a business that is always risky, you are taking the biggest risk. In a profession in which fear is rampant, premiering work is the most frightening. All this makes you devoted to the work, protective of it, possessive. Actors will talk of those who subsequently play roles they originate in terms equivalent to divorced people discussing their exes' subsequent spouses.

Few actors have as strong a claim on roles as Bogardus and his *Falsettos* costars, Michael Rupert and Chip Zien, have on these. "I don't know of any other musical," says Zien, "where the personalities of the individual performers so influenced how the characters were drawn."

The *Falsettos* chronology goes like this:

In 1979, Chip Zien played the pivotal role of Marvin at Playwrights Horizons in Finn's first piece, *In Trousers,* in which Marvin, a married man, discovers his feelings for Whizzer, another man, and leaves his wife and child.

In 1981, Michael Rupert played Marvin, Bogardus played Whizzer, and Zien played a new character, Mendel, in the first production of *March of the Falsettos,* also at Playwrights Horizons. *March* is the story of Marvin's attempt to establish a strong relationship with Whizzer and still maintain one with his wife and son. Mendel is the psychiatrist whom Marvin's wife, Trina, goes to for help and eventually marries, turning all the characters into an extended family. While Bogardus went on to do other work, Rupert and Zien moved with the piece to a commercial run at the off-Broadway Westside Arts Theatre.

The next year, Rupert, Bogardus, and Zien re-created their roles in a Los Angeles production of the show at the Doolittle Theatre.

In 1985, Bogardus played Whizzer and understudied and eventually played Marvin in an off-Broadway revival of *In Trousers* at the Promenade Theatre.

In 1988, Rupert, Bogardus, and Zien played their original *March of the Falsettos* characters in a series of readings to develop the continuation of the story, then called *Jason's Bar Mitzvah.* This culminated in 1989 in the workshop in which both pieces were performed, which was called *Marvin's Songs.*

In June 1990, Rupert, Bogardus, and Zien opened in the premiere of what was once *Jason's Bar Mitzvah* and was now called *Falsettoland* at Playwrights Horizons. While Zien went on to join *Grand Hotel* on Broadway, Rupert and Bogardus moved with the piece to the Lucille Lortel Theatre off-Broadway.

To this point, the entire history of Finn's minimusicals was confined to small, low-paying developmental and off-Broadway venues. Then in the fall of 1991, when rumor had it the show was headed for Broadway, where the pay and the recognition would be greater than in any of the previous productions, where the show would be eligible to be honored with Tony Awards, it appeared as if Rupert, Bogardus, and Zien would be left out. As if this were not upsetting enough, it was then reported in the New York newspapers that the likely destination for the Hartford *Falsettos* was Lincoln Center Theater, where André Bishop was about to become artistic director. Bishop had held the same job at Playwrights Horizons for the past decade and had worked closely with these actors to produce most of the previous *Falsettos*.

Bishop, a soft-spoken, sensitive man who has managed to sustain many long-term working relationships with fine artists in a business where loyalty is as lasting as soap bubbles, found himself caught in a maze of friendships. He had as much claim to the show as any of the actors or the director, and at Lincoln Center he would be in a position to provide Finn with a size of production and audiences he could not offer at Playwrights Horizons. But what about the original director and actors?

James Lapine called Bogardus in Los Angeles. "He asked me how I felt about the Hartford production going to Lincoln Center, and I said lousy," Bogardus says. "He said André hadn't called him about it and he had read everything in the papers. At which point he said, if Chip, Michael, and I were all interested in doing the show, he'd be willing to step in and pursue the matter with André and Billy. I told Lapine to count me in."

Bogardus called Lapine back a few days later and was told it was a done deal—the Hartford production would be going to Lincoln Center.

"I was never happier to be making a good salary and being on the West Coast," Bogardus says. "I didn't want to be in New York having this production staring me in the face."

On March 11, 1981, his twenty-seventh birthday, Steve Bogardus got a call from his agent telling him to get down to Playwrights Horizons for an audition. A piece called *March of the Falsettos* had been in rehearsal there for ten days and one of the actors, John Sloman, had been offered a Broadway job as a replacement in *A Day in Hollywood/A Night in the Ukraine*, which he accepted.

"There were like twenty guys walking into and out of the room," Bogardus says. "They were trying to find an immediate replacement. They wanted me to sing a rock-and-roll song. I didn't know any rock-and-roll. Up until then I had sung these weepy little ballads that showed your voice was pretty. But I had just done a workshop of *Battle of the Giants* for

Michael Bennett and to audition for that I had learned 'Pinball Wizard.' So I went in and sang 'Pinball Wizard' for James Lapine and Billy Finn.

"I sang and left, and an hour later I got a call telling me to go back there to start rehearsals," Bogardus says. Bogardus did not even get to read a script before accepting. The job paid only $92 a week. But it was important to him to be hired, whatever the results, because finding work the past year and a half had been difficult for him.

After graduating from Princeton in 1976, the son of a well-to-do insurance executive and former Ice Capades star from Old Greenwich, Connecticut, he had done summer stock, sold hats at Lord & Taylor, waited tables at Beefsteak Charlie's and Café Chiera, made his New York debut in *The Umbrellas of Cherbourg* off-Broadway at the Public, and sung songs from *West Side Story* in "A Celebration of Leonard Bernstein's Sixtieth Birthday" at Wolftrap in Virginia. That last gig led to a job as the understudy for Ken Marshall, who played Tony in the 1979 revival of *West Side Story* at the Minskoff Theatre. This was a great opportunity for Bogardus—his first Broadway show and his first Broadway paycheck. Until then he had been living on about $400 a month and splitting his $212.50 rent with his girlfriend Michele Sutter, also an actor, and depending on his parents to pay for acting and singing lessons. "It was peanut-butter-and-jelly sandwiches and Campbell's soup and never, ever taking a cab, no matter how late at night it was," he says.

It was a time in theatre when cocaine and Quaaludes were very visible backstage. Bogardus became involved in a drug-related incident that led to his dismissal from the company of his first Broadway show.

"It was a very painful event, and a pivotal point for me," Bogardus says. "It made me reexamine the way I conducted myself. It stopped the momentum of my career cold. At the same time, it brought me closer to my family because of the way they supported me. Eventually I was able to leave it behind me. The one lasting effect was that the casting people on that show did not use me for five years.

"I didn't work for eight months until Michael Bennett hired me for the workshop he was producing of *Battle of the Giants*. And then I got cast in *March of the Falsettos*.

"When I got to rehearsal we had three weeks left before we started performing. The whole show was only sixty-five minutes, but they had only about half the material. None of the actors had a clue what was going on. Lapine had these three-by-five cards, and the name of a song was written on each one, and he had a chart and he kept moving the cards around trying to structure the show, trying to find some way to give it a through-line. When he had two blank spaces between cards, it would mean he needed two songs

there to get to the next place. We just kept shuffling the cards. And the actors would go to Lapine and ask, What does all this mean? Where are we going? We don't understand anything about what we're doing.

"Lapine would say, Don't despair. He would tell Bill to go home and write this song and Bill would, and some of it might be good and some of it might be bad. We would do it up on its feet and try to make the song work in the context of the show. If it didn't work, Lapine would sometimes say, This is what we're trying to say, so let's try the music with some dummy lyrics. We would make up the lyrics to see if it helped the through-line and then Bill would go home and find his own way to make it work. It seemed totally trial and error. I've never been part of an experience like that, where I had no idea what it was I was doing in the show.

"I knew I was playing a gay character, and I knew I was a little uptight about playing a gay character. I was twenty-seven and it was a different time, and back then it seemed to mean more how you were perceived. I was uncomfortable about the physical aspects. Do Marvin and Whizzer embrace? Do they kiss? It was a maturing process for me. I mean, I had a lot of gay friends and I was aware of the life-style of the time. It was a period when people were sleeping around a lot. But I had never dated a lot of women. I had always been in a monogamous relationship. So Whizzer's promiscuous nature was something I didn't easily relate to. But Whizzer and Marvin were two people in a passionate relationship and I could relate to that.

"Sometimes we would run up to Billy's house to try out new material. And his house is like a cyclone hit it. You'd walk in and you'd have to weed your way through all the clothes that were everywhere, and he would be at the piano and sort of wail something out and ask you to decipher what he'd just sung. He couldn't play the piano well, and he'd try things out on people and then he'd say, Okay, go away. Then he'd continue to write some more. Billy can play chords, he can plunk out notes, but he can't do it together. And it was Michael Starobin, his orchestrator, who would say, Okay, this is what I'm hearing. Is this what you want? And Billy would say, Yeah, yeah, yeah, that's it. Billy would hand Starobin a piece of paper with a long list of chords side by side, and Starobin was responsible for writing it down as music. About a quarter of the material came in in the last ten days before our first public performance.

"We were allowed to invite some friends. I asked my scene partner from acting class, Suzanna Fraser, to come. I said, I have no idea what you're going to see. I just need you to come and see this show. Afterward, she said, You've got a really good show here, some real interesting stuff. There are seventy-five people in that room a night, all of them less than fifteen feet away from you, and you get an immediate sense whether you're in a good show or not. And I think we knew pretty quickly that we had developed something that was pretty different and on the cutting edge. About two and a half weeks into the run, Frank Rich came and christened it, saying Bill Finn was the next great voice in the musical theatre."

When Ted Tally's play *Coming Attractions* vacated the larger theatre downstairs at Playwrights Horizons, *March of the Falsettos* moved there and the actors' salaries went up to $250 per week. During the preview period of *March*, Bogardus was called by Michael Bennett, who offered him the one white principal role in a new musical he was developing in workshop called *Big Dreams*. It was the story of the rise of a group like the Supremes. Bogardus did the workshop and made a deal to join the Broadway company for its Boston tryout. But when *March* became a hit, Bogardus called Bennett and said, "This off-Broadway show, I'm not making any money in it, but it's going to have a much more important impact on my career, and I can't leave it."

Tom Eyen, who wrote the book and lyrics for the show that became known as *Dreamgirls,* told Bogardus that Bennett came to him and asked if he could write a song for the character. Eyen said no. When the show arrived at the Imperial Theatre to begin New York previews, Bennett made another appeal to Bogardus to join his company.

"I told some of my friends that Michael Bennett had asked me twice to do his show and I turned him down unless they wrote some additional material for the character," Bogardus says. "And they all said the same thing: 'You said no to Michael Bennett?' If I'd said yes, it would've been for three times as much as I was making. But there was talk at the time that when the new season started at Playwrights Horizons, *March of the Falsettos* was going to move to a small Broadway house. When we moved across the street to the Westside Arts, which was no bigger than where we were performing, it was a disappointment."

Bogardus left *March* to be in the tenth-anniversary production of Bernstein's *Mass* at the Kennedy Center. At the same time, he was cast in a workshop production at the Public Theatre of a new musical called *Gallery*, written by Ed Kleban, the lyricist of *A Chorus Line,* and directed by Richard Maltby, who had won a Tony for directing *Ain't Misbehavin'*. The *Mass* was a limited run, and *Gallery* closed without opening. Then Bogardus went to Paris to play Tony in *West Side Story* with nearly the same company he had been with on Broadway, which he described as a surreal and satisfying experience.

Soon Bogardus was Whizzer again, joining Rupert and Zien in a Los Angeles commercial production of *March of the Falsettos* at the 1,100-seat Doolittle Theatre in Hollywood. Because off-Broadway shows have extremely limited advertising budgets, there is usually very little awareness of them outside New York. Even with relatively strong reviews, the West Coast production of *March of the Falsettos* attracted only 250 to 350 people a night. It closed after just a week and a half.

After working regularly for the next two years, Bogardus hit an actor's dry spell in the winter of 1984. The following February, a new production of the first Marvin story, *In Trousers,* which had won the Los Angeles Drama Critics Award as Best Musical, went into rehearsals for a New York run at the Promenade Theatre on Broadway and Seventy-sixth Street. The same casting directors who had done *West Side Story* were on the show. Tony Cummings, the son of actor Robert Cummings, was hired to play Marvin. Bogardus was not asked to audition. In need of work, Bogardus bumped into Finn on the street. Finn said he had been told Bogardus was not available. A few weeks later, the show was still lacking an understudy for Marvin and someone to play Whizzer. In this production, Whizzer was seen only as a silhouette and a pair of legs under a blanket. Finn called Bogardus and asked him to do him a favor and take the role. Bogardus agreed, but only if he received no billing anywhere for the Whizzer role.

The production opened to generally negative reviews, though Rich, while not liking the production, again praised Bill Finn's score. In one scene, Cummings, playing Marvin as a child, crawled around the stage floor. Over the two weeks of previews and first two weeks of performances, he developed an infection in his knee.

"I remember looking at that knee and saying, Tony, you better see a doctor. I'm not ready to go on. I don't want to go on," Bogardus says. The infection caused a high fever. On a Saturday afternoon, Bogardus arrived home from seeing a matinee of *Joe Egg* to find a dozen messages on his answering machine that he was going on as Marvin that night.

"There were changes in the show all through previews and you can only assimilate so much as an understudy," Bogardus says. "I got on my bicycle at Eighty-eighth Street and rode down to the theatre and I cried the whole way. I said over and over again, God, you can't do this to me. I was petrified. As a child, the first time I ever performed publicly was when I sang 'Where Is Love?' from *Oliver* at the old community center in Old Greenwich. And halfway into the bridge, I completely forgot the lyric in front of all those people and I was traumatized by the incident. As I went to the theatre, all those bad feelings came back to me. I walked into the theatre and I started screaming, You can't do this to me! You can't do this to me! I'm gonna die!"

But Bogardus was onstage when the lights came up on the earlier of two Saturday-evening performances, and his energy and humor brought the whole production to life. Suddenly it was a different show. By Monday morning, the phones were ringing with calls from people in the business who had not liked the production, but had heard about Bogardus's performance, and wanted to see him during the show's last week.

"That I became focused enough to get through that, to come up with the lyrics, to this day amazes me," Bogardus says. "I stunned myself. It was a crazed moment, but ultimately an extremely fulfilling one."

During that production, Finn mentioned that he was planning a sequel to *March of the Falsettos*. It was going to be set around the bar mitzvah of Marvin's son, Jason, and the notion was that Marvin, too, was getting bar mitzvahed and thus finally growing up and learning to live with himself.

Over the next few years, Bogardus mixed work in developmental productions of new musicals at regional theatres (*No Way to Treat a Lady* at the Hudson Guild; *80 Days*, with a score by Ray Davies of The Kinks, at La Jolla Playhouse) with replacements parts in Broadway musicals (*Les Misérables*) and leads in national touring companies (*Chess*). He also went through a divorce from Michele and began dating dancer Dana Moore, whom he met in a workshop of a Tom Eyen/Alan Menken musical called *Kicks*, and whom he would marry in 1989 on her day off from *Dangerous Games* when the show was playing in San Francisco.

By June 1988, Bill Finn either had or hadn't written enough of *Jason's Bar Mitzvah* to persuade Playwrights Horizons to finance a two-week workshop. Bogardus, Rupert, and Zien were back as Whizzer, Marvin, and Mendel, respectively.

"It was a real mishmash," Bogardus says. "We had heard for a year that Bill had been writing it. But when we got there we were just helping Bill slosh through these kind of half-baked numbers that he had written. It was just a reading where we sat on stools and sang the material. Lapine was hardly there at all until the last few days. Then we learned that they didn't have a slot in the season for us at Playwrights Horizons anyway. It seemed we were really just there to help Bill finish his writing."

Life had changed since *March of the Falsettos* premiered in 1981, and with it Finn's story had changed. The turning point in Marvin's life was no longer simply Jason's bar mitzvah; it was Whizzer's contracting AIDS. The story climaxed with a powerful scene in which the extended family gathers for the boy's bar mitzvah in Whizzer's hospital room.

In December 1988, while waiting for the next go at the Marvin pieces, the story Bill Finn was working on caught up with Bogardus. "Edward Stone, a close friend and director for whom I had worked, went into the hospital to have some work done on his inner ear and then everything started to fall apart," Bogardus says. "At the time I was doing a musical called *Genesis* at the Public Theatre. During my lunch breaks I would go over to Cabrini Hospital to visit Eddie. He wasn't someone who was living in denial that he had AIDS, but he didn't want his friends to know. I knew, because someone who thought Ed had told me mentioned it inadvertently. He was in the AIDS ward and he would tell me they had him there as a precaution because he was gay and they didn't know exactly what was wrong with him. Like so many people in the theatre, he was afraid that no one would hire him if they knew he had AIDS.

"I was in the hospital, if not every day, then at least three times a week, and over a six-week period I saw him wither away to nothing. I saw him running such a high fever that they put on one of those cold blankets to chill the body down because he would've exploded if they didn't. I saw him die slowly, and it was just an overwhelming experience to see this really vibrant and passionate person who was always the life of the party have liquid food dropped in his body to keep him alive.

"When we got together in April for the next workshop, I had something to draw on. Something awful, but something.

"The rehearsal process was difficult. That's when I did a lot of my grieving. I had very emotional moments, but they were more of a private nature than something I shared with the company. When we rehearsed the scenes in the hospital, people were watching from the sides crying. The material was so emotional it made you ache. Many people in this business have watched someone go through what I watched Eddie go through. I based Whizzer's physical condition on Eddie—being wasted and having no energy. And I felt, if it's gonna be me, I'm gonna go out with some dignity, which is what I saw Eddie striving to maintain. These are the cards that have been dealt to him and he's just got to play with them. You may be bitter but you don't have a lot of time for self-pity. There are times when you may break down, but you don't see that in this particular character. That moment hasn't been written about. When I distanced myself, took myself outside the character and looked at what he was saying, I would become real emotional about it. And you could see by the way the others were reacting to the character that Bill Finn had tapped into something very real and honest.

"They decided we would do the two shows together this time. It was now called *Marvin's Songs*. And on the day we did it, both parts twice, afternoon and evening, we were all looking at one another and saying, How the fuck are we ever going to do this show? From a strictly physiological standpoint, you're singing all this demanding material. All of us were just totally played out emotionally and physically after we finished the second run-through, shaking our heads and saying, I just don't know if it's possible to do these two together."

After the workshop, Bogardus joined the national tour of *Chess* as Freddy Trumper, the ugly American. And then in June 1990, he began rehearsals for the next stage in the Marvin saga—a production at Playwrights Horizons of just the *Jason's Bar Mitzvah* half of the story, which eventually was retitled *Falsettoland*.

"I remember Lapine saying," Bogardus recalls, " 'Look, we're going to go and do this new show. We're not going to do the two together. The bottom line is, let's just go and have a good time. We're all coming back nine years later, let's enjoy ourselves, and if we end up having a product that's good, everything will take care of itself.'

"Once we got into rehearsals, Michael, Chip, and I were much more demanding of Billy and James. We kept demanding that they tell us where we were going, why we were going there, who we were, what the focus was. But it still wasn't clear in their minds. Neither of these guys worked in a way that you came into rehearsal and it was all laid out for you. We were prepared to go in and say, Okay, create the piece on us. That was one of the attractions. But we got into some of these rehearsals and I remember us turning to one another and saying, This AIDS thing and this bar mitzvah? How are we going to piece this together? I don't know why my character made this leap. I don't know why I got back with Marvin after we broke up. What is going on here?

"There's no doubt we all felt this is important, this has to be good. We didn't want to continue this story and have it just be mediocre. Michael, Chip, and I were all much more comfortable in our careers, we had attained a place in the business where our work was respected, where we knew we could work, where we weren't scrambling for jobs. We had careers in the theatre nine years later. That made us all more mellow. But it also added more pressure.

"When we got into previews, we still did not have the final ending of the show. And we didn't have the very beginning. But this time around we had something that could be very good, and the question was: Just how good?

"When the show did open to significantly wonderful reviews—although it still did have its detractors—I think all of us breathed a huge sigh of relief in one instant and were then incredibly exhilarated the next.

"Now Lapine wanted to find someone who would move both shows together to Broadway, and he wanted it to go to the Edison Theatre. Maurice and Lois Rosenfeld, wealthy people from Chicago who had produced *Singin' in the Rain*, were interested. But other producers were really scared of it. For all the laudatory things written about the piece, you wouldn't know it from the number of producers who stepped forward.

"We thought, This is it, if it's going to happen, if we're going to get to Broadway with this show, this is where it's going to happen right now. And then it didn't happen. The Rosenfelds were the only ones who wanted to do it, and they wanted to do only *Falsettoland*, at the Lucille Lortel

Theatre, which was not much bigger than Playwrights Horizons. Once again we were disappointed."

There was a gap of time between the two productions. Bogardus filled it by going into the cast of *The Grapes of Wrath*, which had won the Tony Award for Best Play. Then he joined Michael Rupert and most of the rest of the cast at the Lortel. Zien, who has a family to support, opted to replace Michael Jeter in *Grand Hotel*, where he could earn more than three times what he might make off-Broadway.

"We thought that the Lortel was a good place for the show," Bogardus says, "that being on Christopher Street would guarantee the gay audience. And when the show reopened down there to more good reviews, I thought we would play for a while. We had two or three months of sold-out audiences, and then it just evaporated. The recession caught up with us, the Gulf War kicked in."

Falsettoland closed in early February after just a four-and-a-half-month run.

"At that point, I think we all felt that that was it," Bogardus says. "It was the end of the line."

In January 1991, Bogardus was in Houston with the *City of Angels* tour, getting paid more than he had ever made before. After a few difficult months, including some restless nights and bad dreams, he became resigned to the fact that *Falsettos* would open at Lincoln Center without him. Then, on a Thursday night, he received a phone call from James Lapine informing him that *The New York Times* was going to report the next morning that the Lincoln Center production had fallen through. Instead, *Falsettos* would be opening on Broadway in a Shubert theatre in April, produced by Barry and Fran Weissler and directed by Lapine. Michael Rupert, Chip Zien, and Stephen Bogardus would be reunited in the leads.

Confused loyalty to artists, which had so complicated the Lincoln Center Theater staff's decision to present the Hartford version of *Falsettos*, now got in the way of that theatre's doing any version of Finn's work. Playwright John Guare, who had given Lincoln Center a big profitable hit two seasons back with *Six Degrees of Separation*, was in rehearsal there at the Vivian Beaumont Theatre with his next play, *Four Baboons Facing the Sun*. Bernard Gersten, the producing director at Lincoln Center Theater, knew he owed it to Guare to permit his play to run for as long as possible. Therefore, he and his new artistic director, André Bishop, could not guarantee Bill Finn that the space would be available for *Falsettos* by the April 30 Tony Awards qualification deadline. They offered to present *Falsettos* downstairs in the smaller Mitzi Newhouse Theatre. But the show had already played off-Broadway, and Finn was seeking a larger audience. In one of those oddities of the peculiar industry in which Finn works, the Newhouse is not a Tony-eligible theatre, while the larger Beaumont at the same address is. Were *Falsettos* to open at the Newhouse, Finn would be giving up every writer's dream of winning a Tony for his writing. In a season unexpectedly rich in critically acclaimed musicals (*The Most Happy Fella, Guys and Dolls, Crazy for You,* and *Jelly's Last Jam*), all of the other successful shows but *Jelly* had scores that had been previously heard on Broadway and were therefore ineligible. The odds were too irresistible for Finn. And Graciela Daniele, who had staged her Hartford production on a thrust stage similar to those at Lincoln Center, was not interested in restaging it for a proscenium on Broadway and competing with everyone's memory of Lapine's original.

So, in less than a week's time in January, Lincoln Center was no longer producing Daniele's *Falsettos,* and the husband-and-wife producing team of Fran and Barry Weissler were producing Lapine's. The Weisslers were successful producers of touring productions who had brought some revivals of classic musicals with big stars, most notably the Tyne Daly *Gypsy,* to New York. But their passion was for new work, and they had been in search of a show for a few years. Among their efforts in development was a musical called *Washington, D.C.,* with a book by Jerry Sterner (who wrote *Other People's Money*) and on which Bill Finn had worked on lyrics for a while. Aware of Finn's reputation for being slow to deliver, the Weisslers had put him up in a house in Stockbridge, Massachusetts, for a summer. They did not get a score, but they developed a lasting relationship. And now that Finn's masterwork was available, they got behind him again. *Falsettos* might not have been new, but it was new to Broadway. It would be a gutsy and respected producing effort, bringing this small musical about homosexuality and AIDS into the marketplace that writer-director George C. Wolfe likes to call "the brothel." And it might even win a Tony or two.

"Lapine called me at home while I was having dinner and said the item would be in the *Times* tomorrow," Chip Zien says. "I hung up and I was stunned and I said, 'This is unbelievable.'

"And my younger daughter said, 'Is this good news or bad news, Daddy?'

"Then all of a sudden it was very scary. We seemed to have nothing to gain and everything to lose."

On March 11, 1992, the *Falsettos* gang was back together, in rehearsal, joined by Barbara Walsh, who had played Trina for Daniele, and headed for the Golden Theatre on Broadway.

"Most of the work we did this time around was on the first act, *March of the Falsettos*," Bogardus says. "There were very minor changes in *Falsettoland*. *March* was written in 1981 and was very hard-edged and manic and sort of childish in its humor, everyone bickering and whatnot. And we were worried about the juxtaposition of that piece with the more mature, heartfelt, emotional piece that was *Falsettoland*. So we worked to meld the first into the second.

"The biggest change was in making Trina less of a caricature and more of a woman with all her defenses swirling around her, more of a real person.

"And all of us were now playing it as men in our late thirties rather than our late twenties. There was also a difference in all of our sensibilities. In 1981, we didn't know what AIDS was. I don't know if what we now knew about AIDS compromised my performance in the first act. But it was hard to be callous about love and sex now.

"We rehearsed for four weeks. A lot of it was integrating Barbara Walsh into our production, although she knew it better than we did since she had just done it in Hartford. Lapine was asking us to re-create what we had done ten years ago. And we would all be there racking our brains about what we did then.

"One thing we spent a lot of time on was finding an ending. I'm told the Hartford production used a pin spot, and during the show it picked up lines or lyrics from the show on the walls. Then at the end, as Whizzer was going off, it hit a spot that said 'Whizzer,' and when it widened we were looking at Whizzer's panel on the AIDS Memorial Quilt, and the whole stage was filled with the quilt. It was very effective, and Billy Finn felt that if we didn't have something similar in our show, we were going to suffer by comparison. Grazie gave us permission to use her ending. But Lapine didn't want to do it the same way. So we tried to do it vocally instead of visually. We would start saying people's names and there would be this layer of names and then you would hear, 'Whizzer.' It had an eerie effect but seemed somewhat gratuitous. After many tries we finally said, What the hell are we doing? Why are we trying to make ourselves something we're not? We finally used our ending, with everyone coming together in a circle.

"We started previews and on the first night when we finished the piece people leaped to their feet. And we said, Okay, it's just the first night. There are a lot of friends here. But it happened the next night, and the next night, and after a while, Chip and I looked at each other and said, You know, these people don't have to stand every night. Something is happening here.

"We were sensitive to the fact that there were two camps in the theatre community. There was the camp that said Lapine, Rupert, Zien, and

Bogardus deserve the chance to do this on Broadway. And then there was the camp that said, Not them again. The Hartford production should have come. That this production was just a ploy to get Tony Awards. But somehow when we started performing, Billy's message cut right through all that. It didn't matter anymore to anyone. Time had caught up with this piece. It was bigger and more meaningful than it ever was. AIDS was part of all of our lives and there was a bigger audience for this than ever before. More people were open to what the show is about.

"On the night the critics came to see the show, Lapine assembled the cast backstage and ritualistically sprinkled some fairy dust in each of our hands. And then he got very solemn and said that we should remember and dedicate this performance to all of our friends who have died from AIDS, at which point he became choked up and we all joined in an embrace. And then we went out there and did a great show.

"On opening night, we got to the party at Tavern on the Green and it wasn't like people came up to us and said perfunctorily it was great or it was marvelous. The responses were much more personal. Director Jerry Zaks, whom I don't know very well, said to me, 'You don't know how good this is and how it hits people.' I could feel that I was just part of something really important. And I knew I was never going to go through an experience like this again, a show that had this history, that I was a part of for so long, and that made such an impact on people.

"One night, I had six of my parents' friends from Connecticut come to see the show. We were standing in the alley behind the theatre talking after the show and this man came up to me and he said, 'I saw the show tonight and I can't leave. I can't leave these environs. I can't move yet and I need to talk.'

"So I said to him, 'Did you like the show?'

"And he said, 'I had trouble with the first act. I had trouble with the relationship between you and Marvin.'

"And I said, 'Because it's confrontational?'

"And he said, 'In the second act, when there's all that love—that's what I wanted to see.'

"So I reminded him that the first act was written in 1981, when relationships were much less monogamous.

"But he still wanted to tell me something. And then he said, 'My seventeen-year-old son saw the show two weeks ago and he called and said, "Dad, you have to go see this show. It's our life." So I came. And now I can't leave.'

"It took us eleven years to get the show to Broadway. But I think when we finally got here, it was the right time."

LINCOLN CENTER THEATER
AT THE VIVIAN BEAUMONT

UNDER THE DIRECTION OF
ANDRÉ BISHOP AND BERNARD GERSTEN

PRESENTS

MY FAVORITE YEAR

A NEW MUSICAL

BASED ON THE MOTION PICTURE "MY FAVORITE YEAR" COURTESY OF TURNER ENTERTAINMENT COMPANY
SCREENPLAY BY NORMAN STEINBERG & DENNIS PALUMBO, STORY BY DENNIS PALUMBO

LYRICS
LYNN AHRENS

MUSIC
STEPHEN FLAHERTY

BOOK
JOSEPH DOUGHERTY

THE COMPANY (IN ALPHABETICAL ORDER)

**ROBERT ASHFORD
LESLIE BELL
MARIA CALABRESE
KEVIN CHAMBERLIN
TIM CURRY
COLLEEN DUNN
KATIE FINNERAN
JAMES GERTH
MICHAEL GRUBER
THOMAS IKEDA**

**LAINIE KAZAN
DAVID LIPMAN
ROXIE LUCAS
NORA MAE LYNG
TOM MARDIROSIAN
ANDREA MARTIN
MICHAEL McGRATH
JOSH MOSTEL
ALAN MURAOKA
EVAN PAPPAS**

**ETHAN PHILLIPS
JAY POINDEXTER
RUSSELL RICARD
LANNYL STEPHENS
PAUL STOLARSKY
MARY STOUT
THOMAS TITONE
AMIEE TURNER
BRUCE WINANT
CHRISTINA YOUNGMAN**

COSTUMES
PATRICIA ZIPPRODT

LIGHTING
JULES FISHER

SOUND
SCOTT LEHRER

FIGHT DIRECTOR
B.H. BARRY

SETS
THOMAS LYNCH

ORCHESTRATIONS
MICHAEL STAROBIN

DANCE MUSIC ARRANGEMENTS
WALLY HARPER

HAIR
ANGELA GARI

MUSICAL DIRECTOR
TED SPERLING

POSTER ART
PAUL ROGERS

CASTING
DANIEL SWEE

GENERAL PRESS AGENT
MERLE DEBUSKEY

DIRECTOR OF MUSICAL THEATER
IRA WEITZMAN

PRODUCTION MANAGER
JEFF HAMLIN

GENERAL MANAGER
STEVEN C. CALLAHAN

CHOREOGRAPHED BY
THOMMIE WALSH

DIRECTED BY
RON LAGOMARSINO

PRESENTED IN ASSOCIATION WITH AT&T: ONSTAGE

LINCOLN CENTER THEATER THANKS
THE HAROLD AND MIMI STEINBERG CHARITABLE TRUST
FOR ITS VISIONARY SUPPORT OF OUR FALL 1992 PRODUCTIONS OF NEW AMERICAN PLAYS.

MY FAVORITE YEAR IS ALSO MADE POSSIBLE BY GENEROUS GRANTS FROM
THE ELEANOR NAYLOR DANA CHARITABLE TRUST, THE NATIONAL ENDOWMENT FOR THE ARTS,
AND BARCLAYS BANK'S SUPPORT FOR LCT'S MUSIC THEATER PROGRAM.

SPECIAL THANKS TO THE ALLIANCE FOR NEW AMERICAN MUSICALS FOR
UNDERWRITING THE WORKSHOP OF MY FAVORITE YEAR AT LINCOLN CENTER THEATER.

3

WORKSHOPS

"You Hold Your Breath, You Pray for Death, and Then You Do the Show"

★

STEPHEN FLAHERTY (*Musician*) and LYNN AHRENS (*Lyricist*). Broadway: *Once on This Island* (10 Best Plays, 1990, Burns Mantle Theatre Yearbook; eight 1991 Tony nominations, including Best Musical, Book, and Score; originally produced by Playwrights Horizons). Off-Broadway: *Lucky Stiff* (Playwrights Horizons; 1988 Richard Rodgers Award; 1990 Helen Hayes Award, Best Resident Musical, Washington, D.C.). Members, Dramatists Guild, B.M.I. Musical Theatre Workshop. Currently developing an animated movie musical for Walt Disney Company with John Weidman. Ms. Ahrens's TV: "H.E.L.P." (Emmy Award); created four Emmy-nominated shows; songs for ABC's "Schoolhouse Rock." Mr. Flaherty is a graduate of the Cincinnati College Conservatory of Music (Composition); N.Y.U. graduate work (musical theatre).

I t's summer in New York, and though this city may never sleep, it certainly vacations. It's that time when everyone has his or her favorite excuse for procrastination: Let's get to it right after Labor Day. But there's another theatre season 'round the bend and people who want to put on shows. Here, deep in the basement of the Lincoln Center Theater complex, three floors removed from where the July sun is shining, there's no sign of a respite. In a large white rehearsal room, lyricist Lynn Ahrens and composer Stephen Flaherty stand by eagerly as seventy-five invited guests sitting on folding chairs on risers take a first look at a bare-bones workshop production of their newest work, a musical based on the motion picture *My Favorite Year*. The team has been working on this piece with book writer Joseph Dougherty and director Ron Lagomarsino for close to four years now. In that time they've done readings among themselves and with a cast of actors, but this is the gym-floor test, their last look at the material stripped down to a cast wearing street clothes, with a few chairs and tables and a piano. Come November, there will be lots of scenery, lots of costumes, lots of musicians, lots of money on the line, and lots of pressure when a full production is presented at the Vivian Beaumont upstairs. But today there's no pressure. This is a stage of research and development.

Most everyone involved with musical theatre will tell you that the old way of getting a show ready for Broadway—an out-of-town tryout in a first-class theatre with full production values—is still the best way. It's a system that worked for the first seventy-five years of American musicals, and is now pretty much financially out of reach. Of the 1991–92 season's entries, only *Crazy for You*, which had the backing of Roger Horchow, the former owner of the Horchow Collection mail-order catalog, was able to afford this.

We've all been searching for the most helpful process to replace the luxury of New Haven, Boston, and Washington; or, in earlier days, Atlantic City, Jersey City, and Brighton Beach.

For Ahrens and Flaherty, the developmental process has always taken place in empty rehearsal rooms or in classrooms filled with fellow writers. "We're the original workshop kids," says Lynn Ahrens. "We've done them all. We used to go to the B.M.I. workshop [for musical-theatre writers] every single week (that's where we met), ASCAP, the Dramatists Guild. We've done readings or workshops of everything we've written and we've had input that would fill my apartment." Ahrens and Flaherty are part of the first generation of musical-theatre creators forced to do all their developmental work without the first-class out-of-town tryout. This room in the basement of Lincoln Center is their New Haven.

Ira Weitzman, the director of musical theatre at Lincoln Center, welcomes the small audience with the customary curtain speech for these unembellished presentations: We've been here for only four weeks. We've been making changes every day. We've made a lot of progress. Please use your imagination.

Then the cast enters informally, and in rehearsal dress, through a doorway draped with black velour. They stand on the side of the playing area as the piano player begins.

And then we're into the opening number, "Twenty Million People." As you may remember from the motion picture, *My Favorite Year* is set around a 1950s television variety show called "The King Kaiser Comedy Cavalcade," based on Sid Caesar's "Your Show of Shows." To a 1990s audience accustomed to videotape and cable, the most startling thing about the show is that it was presented *live*. And this is the point of the number. What we are seeing now is "the show before the show," as Benjy Stone, played by Evan Pappas, tells us—the last five frantic minutes of a frantic week as a very nervous cast and crew make last-minute adjustments until there aren't any minutes left, until "you hold your breath, you pray for death, and then you do the show."

"The thing that is great about doing this workshop," Stephen Flaherty says, "is that our show is about slapping a show together in seven days out of sheer will and energy, and the workshop has been exactly that. We had three pianists. So there would be our musical director working with the director on musical scenes, another pianist working with the choreographer doing dance numbers, a third working with the singers. Joe Dougherty was in a dressing room upstairs writing new scenes on his computer. Lynn was in the dressing room next to him working on lyrics. I was stuck in the dressing room Stockard Channing used for *Four Baboons Facing the Sun* [the previous show at the Beaumont] with a little electric keyboard pounding away at the keys, trying to keep ahead of what they were rehearsing. All these different departments were working simultaneously at a fast pace downstairs, and I was trying to keep pace with that so we'd have a new song by the time they finished working on the previous sequence.

"We really didn't know what was going on in the other rooms. At lunchtime we'd meet in Ron Lagomarsino's office, and it was like, So what did you do at school today?"

During the first week of rehearsal, Ahrens and Flaherty wrote a new mid–first-act number overnight. In a rehearsal sequence for the television show, there had been a group number called "It's Only Rehearsal." But Lagomarsino felt there weren't enough surprises, that it was "a poor cousin to 'Twenty Million People,'" Ahrens says. "He asked if we could think of something else there.

"We thought about it, and in the course of rewriting the show since a reading we did last year, the superstitious nature of King Kaiser became more of a theme. We thought, This is a perfect opportunity to just do a crazy song, a song to introduce Alan Swann, the show's guest star, to the world of television via King's personality."

"Then Lynn said, 'You know I have an idea for a number.'" Flaherty says, "'The Gospel According to King when you're rehearsing a show.' That's what we had to go on. Lynn started writing the lyrics for the first section, and then we did the rest of it in a room together over one night."

"One long night," Ahrens adds.

The next week, they found they needed a second-act song for the Alan Swann character, a dashing matinee idol based on Errol Flynn and played by Peter O'Toole in the motion picture. Swann was to be played here by Victor Garber, who missed the first week of rehearsal due to a previous commitment. He was coming in Monday, and Ahrens and Flaherty wanted to have the song ready for him, but they didn't know what the idea of the song would be. Late Friday, they came up with an idea about the character's pre–movie star identity, Clarence Duffy. Then Ahrens went home to her downtown loft, slept on the idea, and awoke at six in the morning to write the lyric. She faxed it to Flaherty, who wrote the tune in his head in a taxi on the way to rehearsal and played it for Ahrens as soon as he arrived at Lincoln Center. On Sunday, they played it for Lagomarsino and it was ready for Garber to learn when he arrived Monday morning. (Ultimately, this song would be rewritten, cut, and replaced by another, new song.)

"It's hilarious," Flaherty says, "because when you see those corny scenes in the movies in which the songwriter's at the piano saying, No, that's not the right note, and then the song comes out fully fleshed, then you say, Of course. This was not far from that. And it was a thrilling period. It was like floating."

The day before the first audience was due to see the workshop performance, the cast did a run-through and the writers realized they had to make a major structural shift in the first act.

"Looking at the show on its feet," Flaherty says, "we realized that they announce Alan Swann is going to be the guest star and he's on his way. . . ."

"Any minute now, any minute now," Ahrens says.

"We had it so that there was the opening number, a crossover about everyone arriving to work Monday morning, a scene where you meet the writers with a song for Benjy, then a scene in the commissary and a commissary crossover song. Then Benjy's mother sang her song. Then the writers wrote the sketch for Swann and then Alan Swann makes his entrance. It was a huge amount of stuff before he arrives."

The Monday crossover and the commissary scene and song were cut, and the number for Benjy's mother was moved back in the show after Swann's arrival, forcing a substantial rewrite of the scene in which the song was placed. The changes were all accomplished in two days, but that required canceling the workshop's first scheduled performance.

"I loved it all," Flaherty says. "It had to be my favorite writing period."

"They had all these assistants running around," Ahrens says. "And it was, Here, put these pages in. It was kinetic. And after the workshop a couple of the cast members wrote a parody of 'Twenty Million People' that went: 'Twenty million pages,/no, twenty million plus,/twenty million oak and maple trees/died for us.'"

The songwriting team of Lynn Ahrens and Stephen Flaherty was introduced to writer Joseph Dougherty in May 1988 to collaborate on a show for a new theatre company called New Musicals. Ahrens and Flaherty's first-produced show, *Lucky Stiff,* had just closed at Playwrights Horizons. Ahrens had written the book as well as the lyrics for that show, but was now interested in collaborating with a book writer. Dougherty, who had had one play called *Digby* produced at Manhattan Theatre Club, was writing on the staff of the television series "thirtysomething" in Los Angeles. They all made one another laugh and decided to try to find an idea for a musical.

After a week of batting around a lot of ideas, they decided to tackle *My Favorite Year.* It took months for the underlying rights to be obtained from Turner Entertainment (which owned the picture) and the original screenwriter. Then they went to work. "We all looked at the movie and we knew everyone loved it. We tried to figure out why, because it's not a perfect movie," Ahrens says. "We thought that what people loved was the relationship between the two characters, Benjy and Alan Swann. It worked because actors Mark-Linn Baker and Peter O'Toole were just adorable, it was a great buddy movie, but their relationship was never really explained. There was potential for emotion that was never explored in the movie; that's what we thought we could bring to the musical. One day Joe said, 'I know why this kid loves this movie star. It's because his father walked out on him and this guy is his surrogate father.' This movie star had a horrible relationship with his own child. That all became the springboard, emotionally, for the whole show. It enabled us to make it more a coming-of-age story for Benjy. He comes to terms with his father walking out on him and accepts his Filipino stepfather, who embarrasses him. It enables Swann to come to terms with his past and his relationship with his daughter and his failings, and to redeem himself. All of these elements were not really in the movie."

"We felt that every time the movie got to a song moment, to an emotional explosion of a character, it would cut," Flaherty says. "It seemed to us that it cried out, Make me a musical!"

"When Joe came to New York, which was periodically," Ahrens says, "we would sit in a room and discuss structure. Then he would go back to L.A. and write the scenes we discussed and send them to us. Because Joe had never written a musical, he would send us pages and pages of long scenes filled with monologues; it didn't have any shape or form to it. We would sit with it for a few days and tear our hair out and say, What are we going to do? Then we would find this little gem that was a song moment and we would reshape the scene around the song. Joe was very open to the process."

" 'Twenty Million People' was a distillation of around forty pages of scenes," Flaherty says. "There is a complete scene with Benjy's mother on the telephone to him as the television show's about to begin. There's a scene to introduce and get to know each of the comedy writers. There's a scene to get to know K.C., Benjy's love interest. We took all those scenes and worked them into one musical number."

The show had been announced as part of the New Musicals season at SUNY/Purchase for Christmas 1990. When the venture failed, the show was orphaned. The rights were then transferred to Playwrights Horizons, where Ahrens and Flaherty had done their first show, *Lucky Stiff*, and were now in development on their second, *Once on This Island*. In October 1990, Dougherty came to New York and the writers read their first draft to one another in Ahrens's living room.

"The first act was an hour and forty-five minutes, and the second act was about seventeen minutes," Ahrens says.

The show was rewritten. In June 1990 a cast was pulled together for a one-day reading at Playwrights Horizons. The actors did the lines and the composer and lyricist performed the score. It was followed closely by a two-week reading with a cast that included Evan Pappas as Benjy and Jim Dale as Alan Swann.

The writers had created a new character for the show that was not in the movie and was based on Sid Caesar's sidekick Imogene Coca. They named her Iphey Hopper; in the first reading she was played by Deborah Rush. But they realized that Iphey was too similar to another character—

the only woman on the television show's writing staff, Alice Miller, who was based on Lucille Kallen and played here by Faith Prince. In the two weeks between the two readings, the two characters were combined into one, a woman writer who used to perform with King Kaiser in the Catskills but wouldn't perform with him anymore because he was selfish and always hogged the stage.

"We thought it was important to have some sort of production number that suggested the type of musical entertainment that they did on the television shows in the fifties," Flaherty says. "And we wrote this number for King and Iphey called 'Professional Show Business Comedy.' Every time Ron Lagomarsino would read the script, he'd get to the number and just turn four pages to the next scene, which I took as a compliment. I figured, This is a great number and he doesn't need to spend time reading it. Instead he said, No, I'm skipping the pages because there's nothing dramatically happening in the number and I feel it needs a dramatic context. When we dropped Iphey, we made it Alice's number. In the workshop the idea came to us that they had had a romance, and this was Alice's getting even with King for the things he had done to her."

The script originally included a sequence in the Stork Club that was a great comic moment in the movie. In it, Benjy comes to the aid of Swann as the actor tries to seduce a woman; it cements the two men's relationship. For the sequence, Ahrens and Flaherty wrote two different numbers, one Latin and another called "Malaria," about a jungle temptress named after the disease. "It was deadly," Ahrens says. By the time the workshop at Lincoln Center was performed, not only were both songs gone, but the scene was cut.

After the two-week reading at Playwrights Horizons, the writers felt there was a sameness of rhythm to the show. "It seemed like there were big scenes that each ended with a little song," Flaherty says. "What we needed was more of a musical flow. So we started writing more musical crossover material to link the scenes. It is a standard device in fifties musicals that's rarely used anymore—a sort of musical wallpaper—to keep the show singing. We also shortened the scenes and started to get more rhythm and pace."

Around the time of the two-week reading, André Bishop was lured away from Playwrights Horizons to become artistic director of the Lincoln Center Theater. *My Favorite Year* was too big a production for Playwrights to mount or afford.

"The funny thing is," Flaherty says, "they kept telling us, This reading is just for you. It's just for you to see where you are. Then the audience came in and the Lincoln Center board is there."

After the reading, Bishop, who is usually restrained in his reactions, approached the writers and said, This has the potential to be a terrific show and I want to bring it over to Lincoln Center with me. But Bishop was not making the change until January 1992, and he would not be able to produce it there until the following September, which was more than a year away. Ira Weitzman, with whom the team had worked on all three of their shows now, was making the move with André. The writers decided it was best to wait and stay with the same group of supportive people.

"You want everything to happen now, now, now," Ahrens says. "But shows always take more work than you think they need, and postponement and more time usually help. The one thing you have to watch out for is, if you're away too long, you lose the impetus and you have to regain it. That's what this workshop at Lincoln Center was good for. The excitement is back. The fire is lit again."

In 1982, upon graduating from the Cincinnati College Conservatory of Music, twenty-two-year-old Stephen Flaherty came to New York to write musicals and faced the blues. Prior to arriving, he had rented an apartment in Brooklyn Heights with a friend of his who was a comedienne. Soon his prospective roommate informed him that her sister and her dog would be sharing the small apartment with them. Then the comedienne got a job with Second City in Chicago and Flaherty ended up moving into an apartment with a woman and a dog he didn't know. Flaherty, who had grown up in Pittsburgh, decided to cope with the situation since he was thrilled to be in New York and had been accepted to the N.Y.U. graduate program in musical-theatre writing. Then he was informed that the program was being restructured and postponed for a year and a half. When Flaherty had been a sophomore at the conservatory, Lehman Engel, the Broadway conductor, had visited, heard Flaherty's music, and suggested the student drop out of school immediately and come join the B.M.I. workshop in New York.

With N.Y.U. on hold, Flaherty decided to head to B.M.I. Then one day he picked up a copy of *Newsweek* magazine and read that Engel had died. Flaherty now had to audition for the program and was accepted. He went to the B.M.I. offices on West Fifty-seventh Street, walked into the classroom, and sat in an empty seat beside a woman named Lynn Ahrens.

Unlike the recent college grad determined to spend his life in musical theatre, Ahrens, thirty-four at the time, had already had four careers and been successful at all of them. After graduating from Syracuse University, she went to work as a secretary in an advertising agency and in seven years worked her way up to senior vice-president. A week after receiving that promotion, she quit to free-lance and wrote for both the "Schoolhouse

Rock" and "Captain Kangaroo" television programs. She became a partner in her own television production company and then later became affiliated with Smythe and Company, a successful commercial-jingle house, where she wrote both music and lyrics and also performed.

"Although I always loved the theatre, I never thought about writing for it until I heard about the B.M.I. workshop," Ahrens says. "Then I thought, I've written lyrics for everything else, maybe this would be fun. That workshop changed my life in a big way."

Flaherty was writing both music and lyrics at the time, so he and Ahrens didn't write together for most of the first year at B.M.I., during which time the students are given writing assignments to do situational songs. The last assignment of the year was to write a number for two people in two different places. As they were both leaving the building, Flaherty screamed up the street to Ahrens, "Hey, want to work on a song together?"

She said, "Okay."

"I was very flattered," Ahrens says, "because he was this shy little guy who didn't collaborate with anybody the whole year, but I really admired his talent. I guess he just got tired of working alone."

They wrote a song about two people, each of whom places a personal ad in the *Village Voice*. The theme of the song was how the two strangers' lives dovetailed.

"It was a bad song," Ahrens says, "but it was fun. I had written a very rough little bit of the lyric and he just sat right down at the keys and started setting it, and I just had this great feeling that this was it."

Making impetuous decisions was not foreign to Ahrens. She stayed with the first boy she ever dated at Syracuse for the whole four years there. Then, as soon as school ended, she married someone else. The marriage lasted only ten months. When she separated, she immediately began to date a man named Neil Costa, who worked at the same ad agency as she did. They were together for nineteen years before Neil finally got her to marry him by inviting a local judge to show up at their country home on Christmas morning in 1989 without telling Lynn in advance.

But her quick decision to work with Flaherty turned out to be as serendipitous as that about Costa, even though their backgrounds made them seem like unlikely collaborators.

Ahrens was born in New York, the oldest of three children of Diana and Carroll Siskind. Her father was a professional photographer. "My parents were bohemians," she says. "They had a circle of friends who were writers and sculptors and painters. And Weegee, the famous tabloid photographer, used to baby-sit for me.

"My mother read to me out loud constantly, and she would do all these different voices. Not too long ago she gave me this wonderful present—she wanted to read a story out loud to me and then give it to me as an adult. When I was about four or five, she made this tape on an old reel-to-reel tape recorder and I'm on the tape singing 'Frosty the Snowman' but setting my own lyrics to it. Then she reads *Winnie the Pooh and the Honey Pot*, doing the voices of all the characters. It's really a treasure.

"When I was nine we moved to Neptune, New Jersey. I remember when I was about thirteen, my mother took me to the city to visit her friend Eva. We went to a coffeehouse down in Greenwich Village and Eva's friend who was a poet came up and started banging on the table and reciting poetry. I thought it was the greatest thing I had ever seen in my life. I knew then that I wanted to live in the Village someday, and right after my divorce I moved there."

Stephen Flaherty was born in Pittsburgh in 1960, the son of Bill Flaherty, a draftsman, and the former Mildred Brady, a nursing professor at the University of Pittsburgh. Flaherty's family was originally from Ireland, but his parents were the third generation to live in Pittsburgh. Bill was an amateur trumpet player, but Steve believes his first interest in music came from hearing his mother sing him to sleep every night. His parents started him taking piano lessons at eight. But there was no piano in the Flaherty house, so Stephen had to go next door to the neighbors to practice. He played by ear from the beginning.

When Flaherty was eleven—at the same time that Ahrens was getting divorced and moving to Manhattan—he started taking the bus across town each week to the library in the Oakland section of town and coming home with scripts and scores for musicals. "I never saw the shows," Flaherty says. "But I studied the scores and staged the shows in my head."

At fourteen, Flaherty wrote his first musical, a satirical look at Pittsburgh in which the two main characters were Siamese twins and the subplot was about faith healing.

He entered the Cincinnati College Conservatory of Music in 1978. "There was no program in the country for writing theatre music," he says, "so I went into the classical composition program. The other people were all writing avant-garde and art music and I really felt out of place there. I hung out with the people in the musical theatre acting program."

In the summer of 1983, after writing their first song together, the daughter of Bohemia and the Catholic-school whiz kid decided to collaborate on a musical for the second year of the B.M.I. workshop. Ahrens taped the

Stanley Donen film *Bedazzled*, a whacked-out version of the Faust legend starring Peter Cook and Dudley Moore, from her television set and spent a couple of weeks transcribing the screenplay from the tape.

The night they presented *Bedazzled* at the ASCAP workshop, Ira Weitzman was there and invited them to write something for Playwrights Horizons. They had no underlying rights for *Bedazzled* and were unable to obtain them. So Weitzman helped them secure an N.E.A. Producer's Grant to do a new work and introduced them to a young writer named George C. Wolfe. The threesome collaborated on a musical called *Antler*, based on a story Ahrens had read in the newspaper.

"It was about a town in one of the Dakotas where the population had shrunk to about forty and the school system was about to close," Ahrens says. "To keep the town from dying, this farmer went on television and offered to give free land to anyone who would move there. I thought it was a great idea—all these different people coming to this town—but it was an idea in search of a story, and we never figured out how to structure it properly. George went on to write *The Colored Museum* after that."

With no work produced, and therefore no clout to obtain rights to well-known properties, Ahrens would comb the Village bookstores and the library for little-known novels. In 1985 she found one called *The Man Who Broke the Bank at Monte Carlo* that she was able to option; it became the team's first work produced off-Broadway, retitled *Lucky Stiff*. Frank Rich was complimentary to them in his *Times* review, comparing their style to that of Betty Comden and Adolph Green. The reviews were not good enough to get the show beyond Playwrights Horizons, so Ahrens went back to prowling the bookstores. On this search she grew intrigued with a novel called *My Love, My Love*, by Rosa Guy, which was a retelling of the fairy tale "The Little Mermaid," set on a Caribbean island. Flaherty, whose passions as a child included both show music and rhythm and blues, relished the opportunity to write in the Caribbean musical idiom. The work evolved into *Once on This Island*. As they prepared that show for production at Playwrights Horizons, they began work on *My Favorite Year*.

A week after the summer workshop of *My Favorite Year* at Lincoln Center, Ahrens and Flaherty sit side by side on the couch in the living-room area of Lynn's loft, looking ahead to the work they must do to get the show ready for a November rehearsal.

"We're going to have to cut some stuff in Act One," Ahrens says.

"André said it's luscious, like a wonderful cake," Flaherty adds. "Just a plum pudding with two many raisins."

"I'm much more eager to cut things than Stephen is," Ahrens admits. "I love cutting. I love streamlining. It comes from my background in advertising. I'm never that attached to anything I've written until the show is done—and then I get very attached to everything. But I always reserve a part of my soul because I feel everything may go at some point. The most important thing, for my money, is the structure, the flow, and just making the show work."

"I'm the opposite," Flaherty declares. "I get more attached to what we write. But I go along with the cutting unless I feel strongly about something.

"What's interesting about this collaboration is that Lynn also writes music, and when I started I also wrote lyrics," Flaherty says. "So we both understand what the other one does."

"If I hear something in his music that's not as good as it should be or doesn't have the right emotional feeling, I tell him," Ahrens says. "But we're getting better at landing the moment. The longer you write, the less wheel-spinning you do. When we wrote *Lucky Stiff* we must've written seventy songs that didn't get into the show. I'm not exaggerating."

"We took so many wrong turns," confesses Flaherty.

"With *Once on This Island* we wrote less," Ahrens says.

"It's hard because I think we both approach our work very emotionally," Flaherty says. "When you're writing an emotional moment, you have to inhabit the place and the character and you have to get yourself emotionally to where the character is and say what that character would say. Then you have an emotional commitment to what you've written. Lynn is wonderful at being able to step back and look objectively at the piece, and either something is serving the piece or it's not. I can't see something not work and say, Gee, let's throw it out this afternoon. I have to hang on to it for maybe a day. Then the next day, I say, All right, I'm ready to do something."

"But we still have a lot of decisions to make on this show," Ahrens says.

"It's very hard to make the Swann through-line work," Flaherty says. "And we have to address that. I'm not sure if we have the right songs for him in the right places. And his first number, the production number 'Swann Is in New York,' is over six minutes—that's much too long." (The song was eventually cut and replaced.)

"We need a little time and distance from this workshop," Ahrens says. "We don't want to make any commitments to changes now. Joe's back in L.A., but he'll come back to town and we'll all sit down and talk it out.

"But I think this show has been workshopped enough already. I think it's ready to go up. I mean, what show hasn't had numbers put in during rehearsal? I think at some point before we start rehearsals, it would be nice to do a living-room get-together again and just read through it ourselves with the changes. I don't know if this process is better than going out of town. It works for me. I don't like traveling too much. I would do it if it was necessary. What do you think, Stephen?"

"It's hard to say," Flaherty responds. "We've never worked on a show that's ever had an out-of-town tryout, so I have nothing to compare it with. This is the only way we know."

OPENING NIGHT: APRIL 26, 1992

VIRGINIA THEATRE

A JUJAMCYN THEATRE

ROCCO LANDESMAN
PRESIDENT

JAMES H. BINGER
CHAIRMAN

PAUL LIBIN
PRODUCING DIRECTOR

JACK VIERTEL
CREATIVE DIRECTOR

★ Margo Lion and Pamela Koslow
in association with
PolyGram Diversified Entertainment,
126 Second Ave Corp./Hal Luftig, Rodger Hess,
Jujamcyn Theaters/TV Asahi
and Herb Alpert
present

GREGORY HINES
in

JELLY'S LAST JAM

Music by
Jelly Roll Morton

Lyrics by
Susan Birkenhead

Book by
George C. Wolfe

Musical Adaptation and
Additional Music Composed by
Luther Henderson

with
(in alphabetical order)

Savion Glover   Stanley Wayne Mathis   Tonya Pinkins

and

Mary Bond Davis   Mamie Duncan-Gibbs   Ann Duquesnay
Stephanie Pope   Ruben Santiago-Hudson   Allison Williams

Ken Ard   Adrian Bailey   Clare Bathé   Sherry D. Boone   Bill Brassea   Brenda Braxton
Ralph Deaton   Melissa Haizlip   Lawrence Hamilton   Cee-Cee Harshaw   Janice Lorraine Holt
Don Johanson   Ted L. Levy   Victoria Gabrielle Platt   Gil Pritchett III   Ken Roberson
Michelle M. Robinson   La-Rose Saxon   Jimmy W. Tate   Gordon Joseph Weiss

and
Keith David

Scenic Design
Robin Wagner

Costume Design
Toni-Leslie James

Lighting Design
Jules Fisher

Musical Supervision and Orchestrations
Luther Henderson

Musical Direction
Linda Twine

Musical Coordinator
John Miller

Sound Design
Otts Munderloh

Mask & Puppet Design
Barbara Pollitt

Production Stage Manager
Arturo E. Porazzi

Hair Design
Jeffrey Frank

Technical Supervisor
Francis A. Hauser

Press Representation
Richard Kornberg
& Associates

Executive Producer
David Strong Warner, Inc.

Casting
Hughes/Moss
& Stanley Soble

Associate Producers
Marilyn Hall   Dentsu Inc., New York

Peggy Hill Rosenkranz

Tap Choreography
Gregory Hines and Ted L. Levy

Choreography
Hope Clarke

Directed by
George C. Wolfe

Originally Produced by Center Theatre Group of Los Angeles at the Mark Taper Forum,
Gordon Davidson, Artistic Director, Charles Dillingham, Managing Director
with the support of the Theatre Development Fund.

The producers wish to acknowledge the support of the Theatre Development Fund.

The producers wish to thank the Theatre Development Fund for its support of this production.

4

PRODUCING

"That's the Way We Do Things in New Yawk"

★

MARGO LION (*Producer*) was a co-producing director, along with Lyn Austin, of The Music-Theatre Group, where two of her productions, *Poppie Nongena* and *Metamorphosis in Miniature,* received off-Broadway Obie Awards. Subsequently she was a producer of Amlin Gray's *How I Got That Story* (Obie Award), Martha Clarke's *The Garden of Earthly Delights* (Drama Desk Award), and Terrence McNally's *Frankie and Johnny in the Clair de Lune.* On Broadway, she was a producer of last season's *I Hate Hamlet* by Paul Rudnick and an associate producer of the current Tony Award–winning *The Secret Garden* by Marsha Norman and Lucy Simon. Ms. Lion is the recipient of a National Endowment for the Arts Producer's Grant for *Jelly's Last Jam.* She lives in New York with her son, Matthew.

Margo Lion appears calm. She can't really be. But sitting in her office six floors above Broadway, tortoiseshell reading glasses resting on the tip of her nose, legs crossed at the knees, she is still managing to put together coherent thoughts in complete sentences. It is 11 A.M. on Thursday, April 23, 1991, and this evening at eight, the New York theatre critics will view *Jelly's Last Jam*, the show for which Lion is the originating producer. Another producer friend once said to me that on the night the critics come, your life passes before your eyes. But Lion (one of those people whose personality seems to be affected by her surname) has a lot of life left in her. She's been fighting for eleven years to get this show on Broadway. And she's realistic enough to know the struggle goes on beyond opening night.

"We're in the position you never want to be in as a producer," Lion says. "We're dependent on the critics."

Lion's show is at the critics' mercy because it is out of money. It has been financed with a limited-partnership offering referred to as a "mini-maxi," in which the production must raise a minimum amount of money (in this case $5 million) and cannot raise more than a maximum amount (in this case $5.5 million).

"All shows are broke when they open now," says Rocco Landesman, the president of Jujamcyn Theaters, which operates five Broadway houses and is both a producer and the landlord for *Jelly*. "They all use a mini-maxi and end up with the mini." Of the $5 million, *Jelly* had a reserve fund of $1.1 million left when it began previews at the Virginia Theatre four weeks before the official opening. But prior to opening night and the accompanying press attention, shows have both their greatest weekly expenses and their toughest time attracting audiences. The additional expenses are in advertising—where you try to build an image as a hedge against the critics—and in overtime costs to the stage crew, musicians, and other union personnel working beyond their allotted workweek to finish the show. That reserve will be all but gone by Sunday night, April 26, when *Jelly* opens.

Lion's producing partners in this venture are not without resources. Aside from Jujamcyn, they include PolyGram Entertainment and TV Asahi of Japan. If there is hope for the show, they will support it. But if the critical reception is poor, Lion knows the well will be dry.

In the eleven years since Lion decided she wanted to produce a Broadway musical about Jelly Roll Morton—the man who either did or did not invent jazz, depending on whom you ask—she has been through hell trying to raise $5 million for an African-American show in George Bush's America. She now has most of her own savings on the line. Much of the art in her apartment has recently been appraised, and she is ready to sell it to cover any remaining units in the limited partnership. She says she might have to sell the apartment in order to send her seventeen-year-old son, Matthew, to college if the show does not succeed. This is not just another annual effort by a career producer—this show has become her *cause célèbre*. In a market where money is so tight, a show will get to Broadway only if it is dragged by an obsessive producer willing to put his or her head down and run through walls.

"Because of the nature of this show," Lion says, "we weren't able to do the things that would've prevented us from being in this position. We weren't able to go out of town to work out the glitches because we would have needed another million dollars. And I couldn't even get an out-of-town place to present *Jelly*, which I think is appalling. This show is about black culture in a way that no other show has ever been. The audience and critical response in Los Angeles were terrific. But nobody wanted to say, Look at this. Look at this. This is important."

What's important about the show is its frankness. The vast majority of African-American musicals that have landed on Broadway are of the Bojangles variety—happy song-and-dance entertainments, celebrations of joy. There are, as always, exceptions to this, such as *Raisin*, the 1973 musical version of Lorraine Hansberry's triumphant play *A Raisin in the Sun*, and even Michael Bennett's *Dreamgirls*, which beneath all the stunning Bennett showmanship took a tough look at blacks clawing their way to the top of the recording industry. But, in reviewing the limited number of black American musicals produced over the past thirty years, one cannot help but be embarrassed that the only acceptable black in a Broadway musical is a happy singing-and-dancing black who makes us feel that everything's hunky-dory. They are part of a musical-theatre tradition of shows that deny the difficulty and pain and ambiguity of our lives—that make life simpler and more comfortable than we know it is. These are the shows that add validity to those generalizations about the theatre audience that I find disparaging—"tired businessmen" and "tunnel trade" and "tourist show." The irony is that the shows that seem to be the most optimistic are actually the most cynical since they sell the audience short.

Even among the more serious musicals, there are few in which the undercurrent is good old-fashioned outrage at the way we live—which has a strong tradition in playwrighting. The only contemporary director of musicals who has been able to combine outrage with the show-biz know-how that attracts a large enough audience to fill a Broadway-size musical house is Harold Prince. And now into that territory comes writer-director George C. Wolfe, thirty-seven years old, African-American, with only three off-Broadway plays behind him, and a tough $5 million musical on his hands that has to play at capacity for a year to recoup its initial investment.

After working with other directors and writers in the developmental stage for some seven years, Lion turned over the reins of her show, both the book writing and directing, to Wolfe. It was the kind of bold producing move not often seen in the Broadway arena anymore. Hiring Wolfe assured Lion of two things: she was going to get a tough, serious, strong-headed show told from a probing and passionate point of view; and it was going to be almost impossible to finance. Even with a writer and director with a shelf full of Tony Awards at the helm, *Jelly's Last Jam* would have been a difficult show to finance in the current ultra-conservative Broadway investor climate. But Lion and Pam Koslow, her long-term producing partner on this effort, managed to pull together the money Wolfe needed to execute his vision and land it on Broadway.

Now Lion says, "I think it's amazing that we got it up. Amazing on everybody's part, and I'm very, very proud of it. I had a great conversation with George the other day and I said, Look, this is why I went into this business in 1977. This was my dream, to produce work that not merely entertained but addressed the realities—even the painful ones—of contemporary society. I've done the best I can. If it doesn't find a way to live on Broadway, then I shouldn't be producing on Broadway. And I mean that without any sour grapes. If what I care about passionately isn't something that has a place in this market, then it's not the market for me. So when I look at it rationally, I feel very calm. On the other hand, how can you not hope that your child is going to be accepted by the world? So it's a very contradictory and ambivalent time for me."

There's nothing for Lion to do now but wait. Of course, there are plans to make for the opening-night celebration. Friends arriving from out of town to attend to. But a lot of her time today will be devoted to handicapping the critics' responses with Jack Viertel, the creative director of Jujamcyn Theaters, who served as a dramaturge on the show, and Richard Kornberg, her press agent. Together, they write the leads of the major critics' notices in their heads, hoping to send off telekinetic signals.

The *Jelly* opening would be the next-to-last of the 1991–92 season, a year of impressive producing efforts for musicals. That's not something you read about often. In this era dominated by shows that originate in regional theatres or in London, the New York commercial producer is often maligned by those who write about the business. What one often hears is that there are no more producers. But that's much too general and simplistic to hold any validity.

The producer is the C.E.O. of a Broadway show. Her responsibilities lie in both the creative and financial areas. In the creative sector, those tasks can include finding an idea for a show; acquiring rights to needed copyrighted material; hiring a writing team; serving as an editor during the writing process; hiring a director; assembling the rest of the creative team along with the writers and the director; setting up a developmental process for the creative team to realize the work; participating in the casting; and continuing as an editor and lending the essential extra, fresher pair of eyes during the rehearsal and preview period. On the business side, the responsibilities include raising the front money to fund the early creative stages; working with attorneys to create the legal framework under which the show can pursue financing; assembling the management and marketing teams; negotiating deals for everyone and everything from actors to a theatre contract; raising the funding; overseeing the cash flow; creating an image and audience for the show through advertising, marketing, and public relations; servicing the investors, including throwing an opening-night party; and then, once the show has opened, making the day-to-day creative and financial decisions that contribute to the venture's continuing health.

The ideal producer would have the artistic sensibility of Stephen Sondheim, the financial acumen of Felix Rohatyn, the negotiating skill of Mike Ovitz, the marketing savvy of Sam Walton, the cheerleading charisma of Bill Clinton, the showmanship of David Merrick, the nurturing sense of Mother Teresa, and the patience of Job.

Cy Feuer, the producer of the original 1951 production of *Guys and Dolls*, once told me, "Producing is too complicated for any one person. No one can do everything. You have to be honest about what you can do and hire the best people to do the other things."

As the cost of producing musicals has escalated far into the millions, the unenviable task of fund-raising has become increasingly difficult and demanding. In the glory days when David Merrick and Harold Prince each had many shows playing simultaneously, Broadway productions were financed with a lot of people, each one putting in a little money. In the early fifties, musicals would cost an average of $150,000 to $200,000, which a producer would raise from 100 to 200 investors. People would invest $1,000 or $2,000 each to be involved in the show, and if it did not succeed, it wasn't the end of the world and they'd invest another $1,000 or $2,000 the next time. At today's costs, the investment units for musicals are usually $100,000 per person or more. There are not a lot of people around who can invest that kind of money. Finding them takes a lot of time, and closing a deal with them takes a lot more.

Physical production has become technically tricky and expensive and is a sub-specialty. Musical presentation has become more complicated. The union rule books grow thicker every time there is an infraction, and having a handle on all of that has become comparable to studying for the bar exam. Every aspect of producing has become increasingly complex.

When you hear there are no producers, what you are hearing is the opinion that the real producing is no longer being done in the commercial sector, but by those people who run institutional theatres, where so many Broadway shows originate. The staffs of institutional theatres today are comparable to the staffs of the commercial producers' offices of twenty-five years ago. In the fifties and sixties, the active Broadway producing offices—those of David Merrick, Harold Prince, Alexander Cohen, Robert Whitehead, and Kermit Bloomgarden—employed a general manager, a casting director, a press agent, a dramaturge and production assistants, all of whom worked in-house. To support staff that size you had to produce a few shows a season. But the cost of mounting productions got too expensive for anyone to be able to keep that up. No one could raise enough money to do multiple shows in one season anymore. So the regional theatres sprang up and filled the void, and Broadway became a showcase for the best from those institutions as well as the big shows too costly for the not-for-profits to mount. What's happening in theatre has not changed: Lots of different shows of different sizes are being produced. Just the structure of how they are produced has been altered.

Today, the producing job is often shared by the institutions, which mount early productions of new work, and commercial managements, which transfer the shows to the Broadway arena, and market and operate them. The task of picking up a show that has already earned its pedigree at an institution—what I sometimes refer to in my more arrogant moments as the Seven Santini Brothers school of producing—may seem like a "gimme." But it's not. Financing a show and running it well are not efforts to belittle.

Despite all these demands, the 1991–92 season would turn out to be one of outstanding producing efforts in the musical theatre: Dodger Productions chose to approach *Guys and Dolls* as if it were a brand-new show, raised $5 million, and created a ticket as hot as that for any of the never-before-seen British megahits; Elizabeth Williams, at the urging of, and with support from, partner Roger Horchow, creator of the Horchow Collection mail-order catalog, began with the idea of reviving *Girl Crazy* and assembled the team to turn it into something fresh and contemporary and better than the original, newly titled *Crazy for You*; Barry and Fran Weissler had the courage and found the means to put *Falsettos*, a musical dealing with homosexual love and AIDS, into the Broadway arena and nursed it to financial success; Michael Price and his staff at the Goodspeed Opera House developed a smaller, rethought version of Frank Loesser's *The Most Happy Fella* for their home theatre, then guided it on a journey to widespread critical success on Broadway.

Of all these efforts, none was as comprehensive or as impressive as what Margo Lion did with *Jelly's Last Jam*. Lion was eventually supported and complemented by a large team of producers, most notably Koslow. It was she, however, who was there from the beginning and who had to tackle every single item on the producing agenda.

In 1981, Margo Lion was on the beach at Shelter Island discussing jazz with her cousin Martha Clarke, a choreographer, and Martha's boyfriend, the artist Robert Andrew Parker. Lion said she admired the recent Broadway musical *Ain't Misbehavin'*, the revue of Fats Waller's songs that had won the 1979 Tony Award for Best Musical. Her pet idea was to produce a musical that told the story of the jazz culture. Parker, who moonlighted as a jazz musician, suggested Lion read the Alan Lomax biography of Jelly Roll Morton entitled *Mr. Jelly Roll*.

When Lion arrived home in New York, she not only read the book, but also Lomax's original Library of Congress interviews. She steeped herself in all Morton's records. After working on the staff of Senator Robert F. Kennedy and teaching at the Town School in Manhattan, Lion was now working as co-producing director with Lyn Austin at The Music-Theatre Group, an adventurous not-for-profit company devoted to developing new works it performed in Manhattan and Lenox, Massachusetts. Divorced and the mother of a six-year-old son, Lion supported herself by way of the inheritance left to her when her father, Albert, a manufacturer of emblems, and mother, Gloria, were killed in a plane crash when she was eighteen.

Clarke, a former dancer with Pilobolus whose direction and choreography were being supported by Austin, introduced her cousin to her mentor. Lion took on a position at The Music-Theatre Group to learn the ropes from Austin, the founder and driving force of the company. On behalf of the company, Austin and Lion applied for and received a New Works development grant from the National Endowment for the Arts to commission a musical about Jelly Roll Morton.

At about the same time, Lion made an investment and became a co-producer of the transfer of Amlin Gray's Vietnam play *How I Got That Story* from an institutional theatre called the Second Stage to a commercial run off-Broadway. On that project, she met Pamela Koslow, who was working as an assistant to one of Lion's co-producers and was married to Gregory Hines, then enjoying great success starring in *Sophisticated Ladies* on Broadway. Lion described the Morton project to Koslow and asked if it might be something for Hines to star in. Koslow said that what Hines was interested in was directing. Lion explained that The Music-Theatre Group had given performer Tommy Tune his first chance to direct (*The Club*) and was now giving dancer Martha Clarke her first chance to direct (*Metamorphosis in Miniature*), and it could do the same for Hines.

For a short while, all the pieces seemed in place for an exciting project. Then Lion decided it was time to strike out on her own, so she left The Music-Theatre Group in the fall of 1982, taking the Morton idea with her. And Hines decided he didn't really want to direct, but wished to play Jelly Roll. Very quickly Lion was left without a director or a theatre.

Lion then planned to turn her attentions to commercial producing. She thought she needed a black writer for Morton's story and interviewed Richard Wesley and Oyamo and many other playwrights. But most of them were unsympathetic toward Morton, a Creole man from New Orleans who celebrated his light skin and was prejudiced toward darker-skinned blacks. His racist attitude left the writers cold. At the same time, Lion's son, Matthew, was suffering from his mother's absence, so Lion decided to take a hiatus and devote herself to the child.

During this period, Lion became romantically involved with Ken Cavander, a producer at WNET television and writer with theatre experience. Lion turned to Cavander, who agreed to adapt the material into a book for the musical. Lion and Koslow had formed a partnership to produce the show, which they "envisioned as a piece that pushed the boundary of musical theatre," says Lion.

They hired Tim Mayer, a director with an avant-garde background who had directed at The Music-Theatre Group; choreographer Talley Beatty; and they asked Luther Henderson, who had adapted the Waller songs for *Ain't Misbehavin'*, to help adapt Morton's music. They drafted papers for a limited partnership and held backers' auditions at Lion's apartment to raise the $190,000 they needed to do a workshop production.

"The script wasn't done at this point," Lion says. "All we really had was the songs. We had four singers and a piano and a bass. We showed a videotape of Gregory performing on the Academy Awards and at the Kennedy Center Honors. We served great bowls of shrimp, and champagne. I don't how we did it, it was nuts, but we raised the money."

A limited-partnership agreement is divided into two parts: the general partners (usually the producers), and the limited partners (the investors).

Historically in theatre, after the initial investment in the production is recouped, the profits are generally divided 50 percent to each part (though the investor share has grown as shows have gotten more expensive). This workshop was financed as a one-for-one rollover—which means that for each share of the limited-partner interest an investor purchased, he or she would also be given one share from the general partners' side. In other words, for putting up seed money—the riskiest investment in a show—these early investors were getting two shares for purchasing one share.

Thirty-two investors put up the initial $190,000, mostly in increments of $2,500 to $5,000.

"I had no idea how to raise money," Lion says. "I would make a phone call and my tension level was so high that I would just hang up and scream because I just couldn't stand it. I had put up most of my share for *How I Got That Story* because I felt so uncomfortable asking other people for money."

The workshop was scheduled to begin six weeks of rehearsals in late May. In the beginning of the month, both director Tim Mayer and choreographer Talley Beatty dropped out. Lion and Koslow had assembled a strong cast; in addition to Hines, it included Lonette McKee, Leilani Jones, and Ben Harney. But the ship had no captain. Someone recommended a director named Stan Lathan, who did not have experience with stage musicals but had directed some theatre, and episodes of *Roots* for television. Lathan wanted to do it, so Lion and Koslow grabbed him. He was joined by a choreographer named Ottis Sallid, who had no Broadway experience.

Since the book was not completed, they decided to present selections of scenes and numbers from the show they intended to do. The highlights from the show—then called *Mr. Jelly Lord* were presented for an invited audience at three performances the second week of July. It lacked a point of view and it was difficult to decipher who any of the characters were. But something exciting was going on there: Wonderful performers were singing and dancing to this exciting music, and a charismatic star was at the center of it all. The story wasn't there—but the explosion of energy was. It wasn't a project that could be easily dismissed.

James Nederlander, landlord for nine Broadway theatres, along with producers Marty Richards and Jonathan Farkas, met with Lion and Koslow to express interest in becoming partners and presenting *Mr. Jelly Lord* on Broadway in the upcoming 1985–86 season.

"But the show wasn't yet what I wanted," Lion says. "Instinctively I knew it wasn't the right team. It would just be another black musical. It was all surface. It was what George Wolfe would later call 'cultural strip-mining.' So I didn't pursue it. I knew we had to go in a different direction.

"The difficult thing was that I realized the material needed the sensibility of an African-American writer. This created a painful personal and professional dilemma for me. Ken reacted in a thoroughly professional way, but I can't deny that it dealt a serious blow to our relationship.

"And then we had to let Stan Lathan go. And I'll never forget that conversation. I called him up from my office and I said, I think we need to go in another direction. After all, his experience wasn't in the musical theatre. And he said, You cannot imagine what you've done to my life. I'll never forget it. I was so despondent, I thought I was going to be sick when I hung up the phone."

Lion and Koslow wrote to their investors, informing them that although the workshop had been very successful, they felt they had to go in a different direction. Then, in the fall of 1985, they approached probably the two hottest creators in the theatre to collaborate on Jelly's story: playwright August Wilson and director Jerry Zaks. What a coup it must have felt like when the producers corraled this team. An August Wilson–Jerry Zaks musical starring Gregory Hines was a thrilling prospect. Lion and Koslow paid Wilson $10,000 out of their own pockets to write a first draft of the script.

"August seemed to write musically," Lion says, referring to the dazzling prose arias his deeply felt characters drifted into in his two plays that had reached Broadway thus far, *Ma Rainey's Black Bottom* and *Fences*. "He had an interesting take on the material. He saw Jelly Roll as a cowboy coming into a town and challenging the town. I mean, he structured it like an August Wilson play. August had seen only one musical in his life— *Zorba*, with Anthony Quinn. There would be pages of dialogue and then six Jelly Roll Morton songs. It just wasn't a form he was at home with."

While Wilson was writing, Lion and Koslow formed the Jelly Roll II limited partnership to raise money for a workshop of the new version. They raised an additional $185,000 on the same one-for-one rollover formula. All the investors, with one exception, were repeaters from the first offering.

In this period, Lion also produced Martha Clarke's dance-theatre piece *Garden of Earthly Delights*, which had been developed at The Musical-Theatre Group, off-Broadway at the Minetta Lane Theatre.

Wilson's script was delivered in the summer of 1986. Neither Zaks nor the producers were happy with it. Under Zaks's guidance, Wilson spent some time making changes. But the revised version still did not work and Wilson bowed out amicably.

Disappointed with the show's progress, Lion went off on a summer vacation to Italy. Earlier in the year she had decided that a good way to earn money to support her producing work would be to sell off a piece of land she owned and invest the proceeds in the American premiere of *Les Misérables*, which was already a hit in London. But she could not find her way into the heavily subscribed show.

One day in Florence, she went to a church to hear a lecture by Joseph Forte, an art-history professor from Sarah Lawrence College. On the way out, she was accosted in the piazza by a band of Gypsies who stole her purse. Forte came out and chased the thieves, to no avail. To calm Lion, he took her out for coffee. There they got to know each other. Lion told Forte she was a theatre producer and, in passing, mentioned her *Les Misérables* plan. Forte told her his wife, Elizabeth Williams, and her partner, Karen Goodwin, raised money for the show's producer, Cameron Mackintosh, and, as luck would have it, a unit in *Les Misérables* had become available that very day. They placed a call to Elizabeth in New York; Lion had experienced a most profitable mugging.

When Lion returned home, she and Zaks began an extensive search for a new book writer. They met with a young black playwright named George C. Wolfe, who had attracted attention with productions of his play *The Colored Museum* at the Mark Taper Forum in Los Angeles and the Public Theatre in New York. Wolfe had put in some time at the N.Y.U. graduate program in musical-theatre writing. And he had collaborated with lyricist Lynn Ahrens and composer Steve Flaherty on an unproduced musical called *Antler* for Playwrights Horizons. In January 1987, Wolfe was hired to write *Mr. Jelly Lord*.

Wolfe delivered his first draft as scheduled in February 1988. Later in the year, Lion and Koslow began to hear some complaints from their investors in the 1986 offering that the producers were sitting on their money. Zaks was director-in-residence at Lincoln Center Theater at this point and the plan was for him to direct a production of *Mr. Jelly Lord* there in the spring of 1989. Given this plan, the workshop did not seem necessary, so the producers returned the $185,000 to the investors.

Then in May 1988, Lion heard through the grapevine that Zaks had agreed to direct *Miss Saigon*, a new musical that Cameron Mackintosh was developing with Alain Boublil and Claude-Michel Schonberg, who had written *Les Misérables*. "I called Jerry," Lion says, "and I confronted him and he said it was true, he had accepted *Miss Saigon*. I said, I'll tell you what, Jerry. I am so angry that you didn't tell me, that I had to find this out, I feel so intensely about this that I can't discuss it with you now. A few months later we sat down and talked it out and we are now good friends."

Zaks would not be available for a year and a half. And he had grown uncomfortable with the idea of directing the material. Now *Mr. Jelly Lord* was without a director and without a theatre. At Wolfe's suggestion, Susan Birkenhead, with whom he had collaborated on a rewrite of the Duke Ellington musical *Queenie Pie,* was brought in to write new lyrics to make the Jelly Roll Morton songs work in the new script. Lion and Koslow went searching for a new director.

In the midst of this change, Lion had developed a business relationship with Rocco Landesman, the president of Jujamcyn Theaters. Landesman had been hired by James Binger, the former C.E.O. of Honeywell and owner of the Jujamcyn chain, in 1987. Just about to reach his fortieth birthday at the time, the blond, bearded Landesman, whose father had once been a nightclub operator in their hometown of St. Louis, had produced just one Broadway show—*Big River*, at Jim Binger's O'Neill Theatre—and was about to produce another—*Into the Woods*, at Binger's Martin Beck Theatre.

Landesman held a doctorate from the Yale Drama School, where his focus was theatre criticism. While at Yale, he had struck up a friendship with Robert Brustein, then the dean of the school and director of the Yale Rep. Landesman had commissioned playwright William Hauptman and pop songwriter Roger Miller to write *Big River*, an adaptation of Mark Twain's *Huckleberry Finn*. He had developed the show with productions at the American Repertory Theatre at Harvard, where Brustein had moved, and at the La Jolla Playhouse before coming to Broadway and winning the 1985 Tony Award for Best Musical. This was the first instance in which a commercial producer had teamed with regional theatres to develop a musical. He used the same successful process with *Into the Woods* following a workshop at Playwrights Horizons with a production at the Old Globe Theatre in San Diego.

In 1985, Landesman had attended the series of meetings of the Producers Group, the disgruntled commercial producers, mostly in their thirties, who were upset about the increases in production costs and the decrease in the size of the Broadway audience, and felt their voices were not heard at the League of American Theatres and Producers, the trade association and labor negotiating group dominated by the Broadway landlords. Though the ad hoc Producers Group was not well received by much of the Broadway establishment, Jim Binger's interest was piqued and he began to attend the meetings. He was interested in the ideas of the younger producers, most particularly in the emphasis on developing new work for the commercial theatre in partnership with not-for-profit theatre. Those meetings, as well as his growing friendship with and respect for Landesman, persuaded Binger that his organization needed to take advantage of these fresh ideas. He had also spent time with Landesman at the race track (both men owned horses) and was convinced the young man had luck on his side.

In June 1987, Binger hired Landesman as president of his organization. Landesman was a good twenty years younger than anyone of authority at any of the three theatre-owning and producing chains on Broadway, and his sensibilities reflected this. He was attracted to more adventurous work, nonlinear storytelling, and rock and roll.

The week after Landesman was appointed, Lion saw and fell in love with Terrence McNally's play *Frankie and Johnny in the Clair de Lune* at the Manhattan Theatre Club. "I knew there was a commercial producing establishment I needed to be part of to be effective," she says. "I knew how to do non-profit shows, but I didn't know enough about producing in the commercial world. I heard Rocco had the rights to do *Frankie and Johnny* commercially and I wanted to be part of it. The big turning point in my career that led me down the road to legitimacy came when I met with Rocco and said I wanted to do *Frankie and Johnny*. He was open to everybody, which is the way he is, and one of the reasons he's so successful. So he convinced Tom Viertel, Steve Baruch, and Richard Frankel, his partners in that show, to take me in. He really supported me and encouraged me."

Jack Viertel, Landesman's creative director and Tom's brother, read Wolfe's version of *Mr. Jelly Lord* and initially passed on it. But after Viertel saw Wolfe's next play, *Spunk*, he called Lion and said, "Let's talk about *Jelly*." Then Gordon Davidson, the artistic director of the Mark Taper Forum in Los Angeles, offered to develop the piece through a series of workshops leading to a production there. Wolfe's *The Colored Museum* had set house records at the Taper, and Davidson was committed to the writer. The first stage in the work process, a staged reading of Act I, was scheduled for December. But the show still had no director.

On a very hot afternoon in September, there was a reading of Wolfe's script at Lion's apartment, which Davidson attended. "It was a terrible, sweltering day," Lion says. "There was no air conditioning and it was so hot no one could concentrate. The reading was terrible. And right after it, the man I was seeing called and canceled a weekend we had planned for a long time. Between the call and the reading, I felt like I wanted to just jump out the window.

"Then George started talking about the show. He said he could make it work. He could direct it and write it. His passion was so great and his ideas were so clear that for the first time I felt this show could be wonderful. That was the turning point.

"That night I realized this was no longer my show. It was now George Wolfe's show. My job was to support his vision. A few days later, when George and Susan Birkenhead and I were driving up to Hartford to see *Peer Gynt*, I told this to George. I told him he was now the director of the show."

As Wolfe rewrote the Jelly Roll story, Lion sought to continue to expand her financial base as she had with her successful investment in *Les Misérables*. Trying to bet on the favorites, she put some money into a London production of the 1982 Broadway success *Sugar Babies*, a burlesque review starring Mickey Rooney and Ann Miller. She signed on to join the large producing team of the Broadway-bound musical *Annie 2*, a long-planned sequel to the 1978 hit *Annie*. Both shows failed and lost their entire investment. *Annie 2* never made it out of Washington. What the show lacked was an idea. It had lots of plot and lots of songs and more than lots of scenery—but there was no reason for it to exist. It wasn't about anything—except plot and songs and scenery and the fact that *Annie* had made so much money. It was certainly among the most calculating producing efforts ever attempted.

What a relief it must have been for Lion to return now to the deliberate process of developing a Jelly Roll Morton musical and to George Wolfe, a field of energy always on the verge of an explosion of ideas. His show was about a Creole man who considered himself superior to others of his race, and by denying and running from his blackness, he lost anyone who meant anything to him and destroyed himself. It was a show about an outsider's self-hate. Though steeped in the sounds and style of African-American culture, its idea transcended race and spoke to anyone who felt outside the larger whole and wanted in. This was the biggest truth at the core of Jelly Roll Morton's life, and the story Wolfe and Lion believed had to be told. Definitely not one's idea of basic popular Broadway fare. But Lion had already gone fishing in those waters and nearly drowned.

Wolfe's expansive vision would need editing and fine-tuning. Here Gordon Davidson and his staff at the Taper came to the rescue. They provided the money and the time and the space for Wolfe to sort out the trickle of a good story from his waterfall of dazzling dialogue and staging ideas. There was a rehearsed reading of Wolfe's first act as part of the Taper Lab developmental program in December 1989. Another reading of the second act took place in June 1990. Then came a workshop production of Act II in August and September of that year. Davidson next scheduled the work as a main-stage full production beginning in February 1991.

Gregory Hines did not participate in any of the readings or the workshop or the mainstage production. He was not happy when Wolfe was made director of the show, expressing a preference for someone with experience in large Broadway musicals. He also didn't feel that the Jelly Roll character Wolfe had created was one he wanted to play. He decided to take a wait-and-see attitude.

This came at a time when the Lion-Koslow partnership was obligated to raise $350,000 to contribute to the Taper as enhancement money. Since original musicals come with expenses, such as orchestrations and extra rehearsal time, which are beyond the budgets of not-for-profit theatres, it is not unusual for a commercial entity with an interest in the future of the show to supplement the theatre's budget like this. With the support of Jujamcyn, Lion was able to raise $225,000. She and Koslow would be responsible for the rest. However, Koslow's belief in the material was shaken by her husband's doubts, necessitating that Lion take out a home equity loan on her apartment to come up with the last $125,000. This situation created tension between the partners.

The production at the Taper was very well received by the Los Angeles drama critics and would go on to set the Taper's house record for attendance for a production. But there is a history of musicals that become sensations in Los Angeles, only to meet derisive reviews and a short life when they arrive in New York. Most recently, a production of William Finn's *In Trousers* and of a musical called *Mail* had dominated the annual L.A. theatre awards, only to come to New York and disappear within two weeks' time.

The reception for this show, now named *Jelly's Last Jam*, was better than what was on the stage. The piece overflowed with tough ideas and it was apparent that Wolfe had an original eye for the stage. But though the show was about jazz, one was never persuaded that Jelly played music. Although it was about a man obsessed with ladies, it was lacking in sexuality. And Obba Babatunde, a fine performer in lesser roles in other works, did not have the charisma to call one's attention to Jelly Roll Morton amid all the excitement Wolfe staged around him.

Landesman did not really like the show he saw at the Taper. But Jack Viertel detected something original there. They were both impressed by Wolfe's talent. And Landesman identified with Lion's long struggle, having gone through something similar with *Big River*. He felt he had to support her to try to help her realize her dream. He committed $1 million to an eventual Broadway production, $100,000 of which could be used for another workshop of a rewrite based on what the creators had learned from the Taper production. He also committed a Jujamcyn theatre. Lion would have to raise another $60,000 for the New York workshop and nearly another $4 million to produce the show.

Hines came to see the show at the Taper and was impressed enough with what he saw that he wanted to meet with Wolfe when he returned to New York and discuss the project's future.

On the night of the last performance at the Taper, there was a cast party at a local pizza joint called the Itchy Foot. In attendance were many of Jelly Roll Morton's relatives. "It was the most love-filled evening," Lion says. "We had been tremendously successful. The whole run of the show had been about the work. And I said to George, 'You know, it's never going to be this way again.'

"And George said, 'That's right. This time it was about the art.' "

Back in New York after the Taper production closed, Lion met with Wolfe and told him she would love to have Gregory Hines in the show. But she wanted it to be very clear that the star was not the factor that would determine if the show was to be produced. What Lion was committed to now was putting George Wolfe's vision on Broadway. It would be Wolfe's choice whether or not to go with Hines.

During the summer, Hines and Wolfe spent time together discussing the piece. Hines wanted to explore dimensions of Morton's personality that were not yet probed in the script. Wolfe felt that he and Hines were headed in the same direction, and Hines signed on.

In November 1991, the next workshop production of *Jelly's Last Jam* was staged at 890 Broadway, with Gregory Hines as Jelly Roll Morton and Savion Glover, the teenage tap-dancing sensation, as young Jelly. It had a much-improved first act. But only selected scenes from the second act were presented.

What was performed was encouraging enough that Lion, Koslow, and Landesman decided the show was on a Broadway track. Both *Grand Hotel* and *City of Angels* were winding down at Jujamcyn theatres, and Landesman doubted they would make it through the annual January theatre slump. He would have a theatre available for the spring.

The Dodgers had come on as general managers now and budgeted the Broadway production at $5 million—including the money spent on all the developmental phases. In order to have six weeks of rehearsal, a month of previews, and open in time for the Tony Awards deadline, the show had to begin rehearsals in mid-February. To make that schedule, design work on the physical production elements and work on the music had to begin immediately. With the $1 million from Jujamcyn and about $825,000 already spent in the various developmental phases, Lion and Koslow had to raise an additional $3.175 million to $3.675 million—and they had just three months to do it.

The first month was lost because the investment documents were held up by the attorney general's office. While the workshop was playing, Alex Witchel had written in her Friday theatre gossip column in *The New York Times* that investors were parading down to 890 Broadway to see the show. The producers had invited the usual members of the theatre community who are invited to workshops, but since they were awaiting approval of their papers, investment was not yet legal or offered. Still, Witchel's damaging item caught the eye of the attorney general's staff that polices theatrical investment. Lion was forced to jump through some hoops until the office finally approved the *Jelly* offering on December 14, leaving just two months to reach the minimum financing level of $5 million before rehearsals were to begin.

In order to stay on schedule, contracts would have to be negotiated with actors and design work started. Since Lion was unable to touch the show's financing until it was complete, she had to tap into her own limited and shrinking resources to guarantee up-front costs.

Many of the major money players in the New York theatre community had come to the November workshop, but few of them were willing to bet on this frank, black show. Lion received a $750,000 commitment from Hal Luftig at the 126 Second Avenue Corporation, with whom she had worked previously. TV Asahi, the Japanese media corporation that had an ongoing relationship with Jujamcyn in which Lion had been a middle person, came in for $500,000 in exchange for the theatrical and television rights in Japan. Producer Rodger Hess came aboard as a co-producer with $250,000.

Then Koslow believed she had found a godfather in Chicago, a man who said he was going to invest $1 million. Lion flew out there to meet him. "He was a guy who had made a lot of money in real estate," Lion says. "He was coming to New York and I got him tickets to *Phantom*, made all these arrangements for him, and set up a meeting for him to meet Rocco at the Russian Tea Room. Rocco, Pam, and I got there and waited an hour and a half and the guy never showed up and we never heard anything from him. Rocco was great about it. He said every producer on every show has one of these."

Later, Roy Somlyo, a theatrical general manager, called Lion and said he had a Japanese company that was interested in putting $4 million in the show. Lion spent two weeks trying to win over the company. But its money went instead to producer Manny Azenberg for his upcoming production of *The Goodbye Girl*.

By mid-January Lion was still more than $1 million short. Then Hank Goldstein, a lawyer with Grubman, Indursky, and Schindler who had orchestrated the Jujamcyn-Asahi deal, attracted interest from PolyGram, the entertainment conglomerate. PolyGram was considering putting in a $1 million investment if it could obtain the rights to do the record album and a pay-per-view cable television broadcast of a live performance. The deal would put the production within striking distance. As negotiations began, PolyGram asked John Breglio at Paul, Weiss, Rifkind, Wharton, and Garrison to negotiate for them.

"The first thing John Breglio did was tell me this was going to be the hardest six weeks of the whole eleven years," Lion says. "And he was right. He did his own spreadsheet on the show and what he said was PolyGram had to get their million dollars back if we played at eighty-five percent of capacity for a year; otherwise they would not invest. That meant we had to recoup in a year at eighty-five percent of capacity, which no large musical does today. Breglio, on behalf of his clients, was determined in his attempt to reduce running costs. I had to persuade the authors' agents to accept reduced royalties. I had to sit in a meeting and watch Rocco, who made my career, hear that he could not take any income for his theatre except expenses, no rent at all, or there would be no show. Rocco agreed to it, because we had no choice. And then he called me up and said, 'I want you to know I'm miserable about this, I'm furious about this.' I've never been through stress like that in my life. Everything I had was on the line; everyone in the show was dependent on me and I had no negotiating position.

"Just as I thought the deal was done, PolyGram became furious because they hadn't realized that though Gregory had a one-year contract, he could, as is standard, take a few months off to do a movie, then come back. They insisted Gregory stay in the show for a year or there would be no deal. They made me agree that if Gregory left the show at all before a year, the $175,000 seed money Pam and I personally had in the show would not be paid back. I knew that money was gone. I was selling everything I had. I thought, I can't believe I'm doing this, but I have to. I just have to. I can't let go.

"Then PolyGram insisted that on the pay-per-view telecast they weren't going to pay George a fee for directing. George was insulted and wouldn't agree to it. The day I heard this, I was at a meeting of the Non-Traditional Casting Project, and Joanna Merlin announced the project was going to have a fund-raiser at *Jelly's Last Jam*, to which Bernie Jacobs, the president of the Shubert Organization, said, 'Why don't you choose a show that people want to see?' I left that meeting furious and went downstairs to a car I had hired. It had a phone in it and I put in a call to Breglio. He started in on me about how PolyGram was not going to do the deal because of George's fee. And I just lost it on the car phone. I screamed, 'What are you doing to me?' I had so much of my money in the show. I was desperate. I was exhausted. I was getting it from all ends and I was very frightened financially."

Lion persisted and eventually PolyGram withdrew the demands on Hines's commitment and Wolfe's fee and joined on as a co-producer, putting the total investment at $4.7 million. Lion put up a Matisse sculpture, Koslow put up her shares in her co-op apartment, and with their partner, Rodger Hess, they guaranteed the last $300,000 so the show could begin rehearsals as scheduled on February 13.

At this point, Lion was due for a gimme. And she got one. Hank Goldstein ran into Marilyn Hall, the wife of Monty Hall and mother of actress Joanna Gleason, at a party and told her about *Jelly's Last Jam*. Hall then ran into musician Herb Alpert at another party and told him. Alpert and his associate Kip Cohen obtained the Los Angeles reviews. Attracted by the provocativeness of the work, they invested the last $300,000. Subsequently an additional $350,000 came in. At that point, Landesman called Lion to his office and said, We can close at $5 million. I'm going to take back $250,000 to make up for the rent I'm losing because of PolyGram's demands, and, given your exposure, you should take back $100,000.

Eleven years after it was conceived, the show was finally financed. And, as the two shyster record producers sing in *Jelly's Last Jam*, "That's the way we do things in New Yawk."

Jelly's Last Jam played its first preview at the Virginia Theatre on Monday, February 23. The curtain came down at 11:20 P.M.

"We had a very difficult dress rehearsal," Lion says, "and a miraculous first preview. That's the first time that you see everything you've been working and slaving on at rehearsal at its best. It's the first time it has that sheen of performance level. That night we knew we had a brilliant first act. Long, but brilliant. And a flawed second act. But it was a real high for all of us."

As Landesman left the first preview, he said to Lion, If doing a show like this isn't what we're in the theatre for, we shouldn't be in the theatre.

To avoid overwhelming the director with too many opinions, Lion had informed the producers as each came on board that none of them would be sharing their thoughts directly with George C. Wolfe. Jack Viertel, who had come to Jujamcyn after serving as theatre critic for the *Los Angeles Herald Examiner* and dramaturge for Gordon Davidson at the Taper, had developed a good reputation working with writers and directors. Lion and Koslow decided early on that Viertel would work closely with Wolfe and that all comments would filter through him. Even Landesman would funnel all his reactions through Viertel.

Lion and Viertel met with Wolfe at his apartment the morning after the first preview. Viertel did the talking for the producers. The message to the director was that they didn't want him to concentrate on Act I, except for minor cuts. They wanted him to focus on solving the problems of Act II.

But Wolfe did not address the Act II problems for a week and a half. Perhaps he did not yet have a handle on what he wanted to do there. Instead, he made adjustments in Act I, dropping a scene and two numbers.

"The best way to work with George is not to give him specific suggestions," Lion says. "The best way to work with him is to say the moment isn't working. And he knows it. He's sitting in the audience and he can see it.

"George was having this ongoing, very dynamic—how shall I characterize it? not struggle—dialogue with Gregory. Gregory was fighting very hard to change moments that he knew were not working. George was trying to be self-controlled and responsive to Gregory's arguments without losing his own vision.

"Greg's instincts were good. He knew where the problems were. But he needed George to come up with the right solutions. That's why it was such a strong collaboration.

"I have a troubled relationship with Gregory. That's unfortunate. I feel badly about it. Gregory was an absolutely indispensable force in this project. And I am deeply, deeply grateful: for his talent, for his instinct, for his passion to push for what he needs. I really feel that the collaboration between him and George, the tension, was the best possible dynamic for the show.

"The way I was often heard was by working through other people on the creative team—Susan Birkenhead, Jack Viertel, set designer Robin Wagner—who could talk to George and Gregory. I don't have an ego thing about that. I think part of being successful is having an accurate estimate of how the world sees you and trying not to think of yourself in some other capacity. I said to Rocco, I feel like I'm more of a Medici, spotting and nurturing talent, than a Mackintosh."

During these first two weeks of performances, word of mouth on the street was not good. "We were working so hard," Lion says, "that I didn't realize the distance we still had to travel. Jack [Viertel] didn't tell me until the day before the opening that word of mouth was so mixed. And I wasn't even aware of it.

"My attitude toward money during previews was, Don't even think about how much money we're losing. This is your only chance to make it good. Work every hour you can work, cancel everything you can cancel, and just make it work.

"There were times during those first two weeks of previews that I wanted to go commit hara-kiri because it was all falling apart. As the show is being pulled apart and changed on a daily basis, the cast can lose confidence because they have to deal with new material. It's bumpy. The rhythms are off. And you start to wonder, Why in the world did I ever do this show?

Wolfe cut a whole first-act section of the show about Jelly's Mama. He cut a tough, confrontational number called "Coons" that ended the act. By the end of the second week, the show was half an hour shorter than when previews began. Then Wolfe turned his attention to the second act. By the time the show opened two weeks later, only one scene in the act that was seen in the first week of previews would remain. He cut a whole section including two songs about a woman Jelly Roll became involved with in New York. He brought back Savion Glover, playing Jelly as a kid, whom he felt the audience missed in Act II, adding a kind of mirror-dance number for him and Hines. He rewrote a scene in a Harlem nightclub in which the crowd tells Jelly it's too late for him and he's been passed by, because Hines was uncomfortable with the treatment of his character there. As the opening approached, Hines became more demanding. He wasn't happy with a song called "Creole Boy," and then he was happy with it. Wolfe didn't come up with a closing for the show he was content with—a New Orleans funeral parade for Jelly—until the night before the critics were to come.

As she sat in her office the next morning, Lion said, "I said to Jack last night I guess this will have to be a hit because after all these years I'm tired, I don't want to go to opening night, people aren't talking to each other, the feelings are strained. All the fun that there was in L.A.? There's none now. And George articulated that so well for me the other night. He said at the Taper because it was about the art, people's personal agendas were sublimated. We're on Broadway now. Everybody's personal agenda is on the table. Every one of those actors wants to look great, wants the review to be about them, and understandably so."

If you didn't know who the producer of *Jelly's Last Jam* was when you arrived at the Virginia Theatre on opening night, Sunday, April 26, you would as soon as you saw Margo Lion's dress. The top was form-fitting, shoulderless, beaded—but it was the bottom, the flowing blue-satin hoop skirt, that was the eye-catcher.

Lion had gone shopping for a dress at Saks Fifth Avenue with Toni-Leslie James, the show's costume designer. When she saw the dress, Lion said, "I don't want that. It looks like I'm being made queen of England."

To which James said, "After what's been going on for eleven years, you buy that dress!"

The show's costume department altered the dress, dyed Lion's shoes, and went out and found earrings for her.

The day of the opening started out as a celebration. Lion had brunch with eight of her friends who had come in from all over the country for the occasion. Rocco Landesman called and said, "I don't know why you should be nervous because it will either make your career or you'll have no career." She had her hair done at her house, dressed, and then went down to the theatre. At 5:30 she went backstage and wished everyone luck. Then she went to the back of the orchestra to stand and watch the show.

"I kept pinching myself," she says. "It's *opening night*, I thought. George didn't die. I didn't die. It's really happening. Then, during the last musical number, I went up to the balcony where all my friends were sitting and I just stared at Matthew. And I thought, He was six when I started to do this show, now look, he's a teenager. I thought how rich my life was."

After the final curtain, Lion walked next door to Roseland for the party. She got caught in the crowd of well-wishers at the entrance to the ballroom. Before she could see any of her friends or her cast, Richard Kornberg, her press agent, grabbed her and said they had to go to Serino, Coyne, and Nappi, the advertising agency office, to get the reviews. They took a cab and swung by the New York Times building on Forty-fourth Street and bought an early copy of the next morning's paper.

"As I read Frank Rich's review, I was very upset," Lion says. "It's funny because everyone outside of the business thought it was a rave. But I thought he was going to write the review that ultimately John Heilpern wrote [in *The Observer*], and anything short of that was a letdown."

Heilpern's review was unqualified praise and recognition of *Jelly's Last Jam* as a major event. Rich's review was 80 percent praise, particularly for Wolfe and Hines, but with reservations about the second act and the ending, which he saved for his closing paragraphs.

At the Serino office, Lion and Kornberg joined Nancy Coyne and Rick Elice, their advertising agents, to wait for the other newspaper notices and watch the television critics. "In my predictions, I had written off the *Daily News* and the *Post*," Lion says. "I thought Barnes would be wishy-washy. But they were both good. *Newsday* I thought would be very good—it was not great. *New York* magazine I thought would be a complete bomb—it was good. *Time* I thought would be good—it was bad. Television I thought would be terrible, but it was all wonderful."

If Lion had spent the night at the track, she would've been busted. But on Broadway, she was having a big night. By the time she got back to the party after midnight, many of her friends had already left. "That was a big disappointment," she says. "I wanted to keep all the bad news out of the party and let everyone have fun and then I'd come in with all the good news. But when I got there with all this good news, everyone had left." And so Lion stood with her dyed new shoes in her hand, talking with Landesman and Michael David, her general manager, about the work they had ahead of them—the task of taking the ammunition they had collected that night and using it to build an audience for the show.

The next morning at eleven, Lion was back in the conference room at Serino, sitting at the table with many of her co-producers—some of whom were meeting one another for the first time—for the morning-after advertising meeting. Each of the producers sat over a pile of Xeroxed reviews, combing the pages and pages of type in search of pearls that might help sell the show. The next week, *Variety* would report that this pile included fifteen positive reviews and just two negative ones.

"This is good," said one of the representatives from PolyGram. "I don't think I'm gonna get fired."

Rich's review ended with: "Anyone who cares about the future of the American musical must see it." Press agent Kornberg wanted to change it to read, "Anyone who cares about the future of the American musical must see *Jelly's Last Jam*." He wanted to call Rich at home to get permission. "If he likes the show, he'll give us permission," said Kornberg.

As Kornberg went off to make the call, Michael David, one of the best marketing minds in the producing community, came in to find the gaggle of producers huddled over the press clips.

"Can we not pick quotes here?" David said. "First let's determine what's the idea we want to express. What's the impression we want to make? The headline. Let's think about the competition and determine how to position ourselves. The headline doesn't have to be a quote. Make it up."

"The cover of *New York* magazine this week called *Guys and Dolls the* Broadway musical," someone said. "We need to quickly establish ourselves as something different."

"I love 'rollicking, excessive and overstuffed,'" Lion said.

"'Overstuffed' is not positive," said Jack Viertel.

"Linda Winer wrote, 'Somebody finally got it right,'" Lion said.

"But that's negative about everyone else—not positive about us," Viertel said.

Then Nancy Coyne entered with a large mock-up for a Sunday ad. The headline was "Jam-Packed." The borders around the artwork would then be jammed with quotes. "Words like *best* and *winner* get lost in the pack," Coyne said. " 'Jam-Packed' is all yours. No one else can use it."

Then Rocco Landesman walked into the brouhaha. He didn't ask what had transpired. He had his own take on the campaign.

"After the Tonys we'll sell this as a star vehicle," Landesman said. "Now we have to sell the show. Our whole campaign has to be to sell this as a breakthrough musical, as historically important. We have to win over the theatre community, convince them we're doing something bold and original."

Coyne left, then came back into the room and announced, "We got it from Frank [Rich]. We can say, 'Anyone who cares about the future of the American musical must see *Jelly's Last Jam*.' "

The room erupted in applause.

Then the conversation shifted to money. The plan was to aim for Tony voters for the moment, to go for the big prize—Best Musical. The Tony voters—about 650 of them, including the 300-plus members of the League of American Theatres and Producers, the theatre press, and the councils of the creative unions—read *The New York Times*. It was decided that was where the emphasis would be. A full-page ad the following Sunday. A double-truck (two facing pages) the Sunday after: pages that would cost $50,000-plus each. Lion was looking for $600,000 to get *Jelly* through the Tony campaign, hoping a good showing on the national Tony telecast would get the weekly receipts above weekly costs and set the show running on its own. The money would be loans to the production and would be paid back out of first operating profits ahead of the initial investment.

Landesman pledged $250,000 from Jujamcyn, the money he took back when the capitalization passed $5 million. He told the others, "We have to do this. Our choice is to put the money in or lose everything. We've got to go for it now."

Herb Alpert came in for $100,000. Luftig pledged $75,000 from his group. Koslow would raise an additional $50,000. Lion went on the line for another $50,000.

By the time Lion left the meeting, she had commitments from the group for more than $500,000. That week, the first after the reviews hit, the show grossed $266,000, still $34,000 below the usual weekly nut. Close to an additional $100,000 was spent that week on the Tony advertising push.

On Monday morning, May 4, a week after the ad meeting, the Tony nominating committee convened in the conference room of the League of

American Theatres and Producers in the Theatre Guild building on West Forty-seventh Street. As is traditional, a press conference was scheduled for noon at Sardi's, where the nominees would be announced.

Lion was in downtown Manhattan that morning. Never having been in this situation before, she wasn't sure if she should attend. She called her press agent, Richard Kornberg, and asked if she should go to Sardi's. He told her she should not, that it was mostly for the press. But she figured she might never have this opportunity again. She called Michael David and asked him. David said, Of course you should be there.

Lion hustled uptown. It was well past noon now and she assumed when she arrived it would be a done deal. But a few sticky issues kept the nominating committee in deliberations past 1 P.M. Lion walked into the third-floor room at Sardi's just as League president Cy Feuer began to read the list of nominations. Over the next twenty minutes, Lion heard that *Jelly's Last Jam* had been nominated for Best Costumes, Scenery, Lighting, Choreography, Book for a Musical, Musical Score, Director, Featured Actor, Featured Actress, Leading Actor, and Musical. Its eleven nominations were two more than those for its nearest competitor, *Crazy for You.*

That week, the box-office gross jumped to $356,000. On Sunday, instead of using Nancy Coyne's "Jam-Packed," quote-filled advertising idea, two nearly blank pages appeared in the Arts & Leisure section of the *Times*. In the center of one page was the logo for the show. In the center of the facing page it simply said that *Jelly's Last Jam* was the most nominated show of the year. The previous two pages was a double-truck ad for *Crazy for You*, with critics' quotes praising everyone in the show nominated for an award—the traditional pre-Tony advertisement. But the *Jelly* strategy here was to separate the show from the pack, to persuade Tony voters that *Jelly* was the important one.

By the next week, the third of the show's run, the gross was up over $400,000 and the show was paying for itself at the box office. Lion, Landesman, and Viertel and anyone else they could corral were on the phone constantly, campaigning with Tony voters, urging them to see the show and to support its effort. The message was, If you as a theatre artist have any interest in doing serious work, you must support this show since its success can create an opportunity for you.

The hitch here was that *Falsettos* was also nominated for Best Musical and was also a serious work. By nature of its subject matter, it would seem to have the support of the large gay segment of the theatre community. *Jelly* might have the emotional support of the African-American theatre professionals, but few of them were on the Tony voter list. *Falsettos* also appeared to have the support of the *Times*, which ran feature stories on the show's writer, William Finn, and on Jonathan Rosenblum, the child in the show who received a Best Featured Actor nomination, during the voting period, but postponed all story ideas suggested by Lion's press agent until after the Tonys.

The time that wasn't spent campaigning was spent handicapping the races. Landesman's sense was that *Falsettos* had the most support for Best Musical. Lion asked my opinion and I told her I thought her show and *Falsettos* were going to split the vote of the people who preferred serious-themed musicals, and *Crazy for You*, the cotton-candy show, would sneak in and win.

On the weekend before the Tonys, George Wolfe received a letter from Arthur Laurents thanking him for his work and for proving that someone could be both the writer and director of a successful show. Then in a post-script, Laurents wrote that the year he wrote *West Side Story*, he didn't win, the show didn't win, and Leonard Bernstein didn't win. And the year he wrote *Gypsy*, he didn't win, the show didn't win, and Ethel Merman didn't win. The message turned out to be prescient.

On the night of the Tonys, Sunday, May 30, Lion sat on the side of the orchestra of the Gershwin Theatre, anticipating three or four awards for her show. While she hoped for a pleasant surprise, she was realistic enough to admit to herself that she had opened her show in a season in which there were five highly praised musicals (*Crazy for You*, *The Most Happy Fella*, *Falsettos*, *Guys and Dolls*, and *Jelly's Last Jam*). If the awards were to reflect the season, they would be apportioned among them all. That turned out to be the case.

Early in the evening, the stunning Tonya Pinkins won the award for Best Featured Actress in a Musical for her portrayal of Anita, the female obsession of Jelly Roll's life. A short time later, Jules Fisher was honored for his lighting design for the show. In his acceptance speech, the gracious Fisher said, "And I would like to welcome George Wolfe to Broadway."

"The response to that was very tentative, very polite," Lion said. "At that point I became frightened that George was not going to be recognized."

Sure enough, Wolfe lost to Jerry Zaks of *Guys and Dolls* for Best Direction of a Musical, which was not unexpected; and to Finn and James Lapine of *Falsettos* for Best Book, which was.

The evening held more disappointment for Lion. *Crazy for You* beat out her show for the big prize—Best Musical. In accepting the award as Best Actor in a Musical, Hines thanked his wife, Pam Koslow, for creating the show for him, told her he loved her, and failed even to mention Margo Lion.

On the street outside the theatre entrance immediately following the show, I ran into Rocco Landesman and asked if he'd seen Lion. "I wouldn't be surprised if she's dead by now," Landesman said. "She worked so hard and got no recognition at all. This is a very hard night."

But a few minutes later, Lion showed up at the Tony Ball in the ball-room of the Marriott Marquis hotel, a big smile on her face, and said, "We projected four and we got three. The only disappointment for me is that George was not recognized. And he will be. It's hard to win your first time out. You're not part of the club yet. But George and I will do another show together.

"This is a complete success for me. I don't think there are too many things in life you can say that about. I feel very fulfilled about my career. I think, God knows, there are a dozen producers who could've produced this show and produced it well. But I don't think there is anyone else who would've done it at this time.

"And this has really helped me clear up in my mind how I see my own future. I never want to work on anything I can't feel as good about as I feel about this one. The point is, you're going to lose some of the time. A lot of the time. Yet, it would not have been a loss to me since I got to work with this incredible team with George Wolfe at the helm."

Lion left the ball, stopped at the *Jelly* cast party at the Renaissance Plaza hotel, then headed for the Stage Deli with half a dozen friends. When she hit Seventh Avenue, she removed her shoes and walked up the city street in her Mary McFadden dress and her stockinged feet. She could rest easy now. But only for as much time as it takes to eat a corned beef sand-wich. First thing tomorrow morning she'd be back in her office starting the next campaign—working on turning *Jelly*'s good showing on the Tony telecast into ticket sales. She might have cleared enough hurdles and dodged enough bullets to get *Jelly* to Broadway and establish it as an important, award-winning effort. But the fight ain't over yet: Now her focus must be on giving the show legs, keeping it healthy enough, long enough, to earn back its $5 million investment.

J MARTIN BECK THEATRE

A JUJAMCYN THEATRE

JAMES H. BINGER
CHAIRMAN

PAUL LIBIN
PRODUCING DIRECTOR

ROCCO LANDESMAN
PRESIDENT

JACK VIERTEL
CREATIVE DIRECTOR

Dodger Productions, Roger Berlind,
Jujamcyn Theaters/TV ASAHI, Kardana Productions,
The John F. Kennedy Center for the Performing Arts
present

Peter Gallagher Nathan Lane Carolyn Mignini Faith Prince

in

GUYS AND DOLLS

A Musical Fable of Broadway
Based on a story and characters by Damon Runyon

Music and Lyrics by
Frank Loesser

Book by
Jo Swerling and Abe Burrows

with
(in alphabetical order)

Walter Bobbie John Carpenter Steve Ryan Ernie Sabella
J.K. Simmons Herschel Sparber Ruth Williamson

and

Robert Michael Baker Larry Cahn Gary Chryst Victoria Clark Lloyd Culbreath
R.F. Daley Randy Andre Davis Tina Marie DeLeone Cory English Mark Esposito
Denise Faye Leslie Feagan Eleanor Glockner Michael Gaz JoAnn M. Hunter
Kenneth Kantor Nancy Lemenager John MacInnis Greta Martin Susan Misner
Stan Page Timothy Shew Steven Sofia Pascale Faye-Williams Scott Wise

Settings by
Tony Walton

Costumes by
William Ivey Long

Lighting by
Paul Gallo

Musical Supervision by
Edward Strauss

Dance Music by
Mark Hummel

Sound by
Tony Meola

Orchestrations by
George Bassman, Ted Royal and Michael Starobin

Production Stage Manager
Steven Beckler

Assistant Choreographer
Linda Haberman

Musical Coordinator
Seymour Red Press

Hair by
David H. Lawrence

Production Manager
Peter Fulbright

Press Representation
Boneau/Bryan-Brown

Executive Producer
David Strong Warner, Inc.

Casting
Johnson-Liff & Zerman

Associate Producers
Playhouse Square Center David B. Brode

Choreographed by
Christopher Chadman

Directed by
Jerry Zaks ★

The Producer and Theatre Management are Members
of The League of American Theatres and Producers, Inc.

5

DIRECTING

"All Right, Already, I'm Just a No-Goodnik"

JERRY ZAKS (*Director*) served from 1986 to 1990 as resident director of Lincoln Center Theater, where he directed *Six Degrees of Separation* and *The House of Blue Leaves* by John Guare; *Anything Goes*; and *The Front Page*. His original New York productions include *Assassins*, by Stephen Sondheim and John Weidman; *Square One*, by Steve Tesich; *Lend Me a Tenor*, by Ken Ludwig; *Wenceslas Square* and *The Foreigner*, by Larry Shue; and *The Marriage of Bette and Boo, Baby with the Bathwater, Sister Mary Ignatius . . .* , and *Beyond Therapy*, by Christopher Durang. National tours include *Tintypes* and *The Tap Dance Kid*. He appeared on Broadway in *Grease* and created the role of the Immigrant in *Tintypes*. For directing he has received three Tonys, three Drama Desks, two Outer Critics Circle Awards, an Obie, a Drama-Logue, and an NAACP Image Award nomination. He's directed at Playwrights Horizons, Second Stage, New York Shakespeare Festival, and Ensemble Studio Theatre, where he is a founding member. He's lectured at the Yale School of Drama, N.Y.U., and Columbia. A graduate of Dartmouth with an M.F.A. from Smith, he's married to actress Jill P. Rose. They have two daughters, Emma and Hannah. Mr. Zaks is affiliated with Jujamcyn Theaters.

It's 11 A.M. on Monday, January 27, 1992, and there are seventy-five people eating bagels and drinking coffee in Studio 4-3, the largest rehearsal hall at 890 Broadway. When you see a crowd of people having bagels and coffee on Monday morning in this building, it's safe to assume it's the first day of rehearsal for a new show. Everyone who will perform any function on the production usually comes to this celebration for a nosh, a peek at a model of the set, and a first read-through of the script. The next time they will all come together will be a very nervous time for all—opening night. But today they get to share a joyous hour since there is nothing yet in the way of hope.

This morning's gathering is particularly giddy since what this collection of actors, creative staff, producers, and production staff is about to tackle is perhaps the most beloved American musical of all time, *Guys and Dolls*. My hunch is that if I took a survey of this room, I'd find that almost everyone here has done this show at some other point in his or her life—at camp, at school, at church, at shul, at some theatre somewhere. But it's a safe bet none of them has ever done it in the way they're about to—as an in-your-face, ultra-$5 million–plus Broadway extravaganza. We all feel uneasy about the cost of doing Broadway musicals and the resultant high ticket prices, but it does permit a quality of production that simply cannot be found anywhere else.

One thing these folks know they don't have to worry about is getting the script right: the Abe Burrows–Jo Swerling libretto and Frank Loesser score are about as right as they come. This is comforting. It will save a lot of time (and thus, a lot of money) in rehearsal, which, for a new show, is often devoted to working on moments, scenes, and songs that end up cut from the finished piece that eventually opens. On the other hand, it puts an additional pressure on this production. A new show can be "just good enough" and be successful. But to do a *great* show well is a disappointment. A great show must be done great to really be a success. To that end, Dodger Productions, the producing office consisting of Michael David, Sherman Warner, and Ed Strong, which took the lead on this production, has approached it as if it is a fresh, new show rather than a shopworn revival. Most revivals of the classic musicals that come to New York (often after being out on the road for a while) are produced with the attitude that the popularity of the material will carry the evening and you can skimp on the production elements. Most of those shows—with the exception of those with a big-name star like Yul Brynner, Anthony Quinn, or, most recently, Tyne Daly—do not recoup their initial investments. But there will be no skimping this time out—even though the $5.5 million investment target has still not been fully reached as of today. Yet, money that can afford the highest quality does not always produce it.

When all those here cluster in front of the windows for a group photograph, the four actors whose names will appear above the show's title— Faith Prince, Nathan Lane, Peter Gallagher, and Carolyn Mignini—sit in the center of the first row, but leave a middle chair vacant. That seat is soon taken by the man who will ultimately be responsible for the fate of this production: director Jerry Zaks. Most of the pressure is on him. Even if it wasn't, he'd take it upon himself. Zaks, with his wire-rimmed glasses and toothsome omnipresent smile, is funny, fast-talking, enthusiastic, open in the way that people who have been through years of therapy tend to be, and is generally known as a great guy. But he will tell you, "The 'Mr. Nice Guy' thing makes me laugh. People have no idea how ruthless I am in pursuit of making a show work."

With the deaths of Gower Champion, Michael Bennett, and Bob Fosse in the 1980s, and with Harold Prince continuing to pursue the kind of adventurous work that is only sometimes commercially successful, Zaks has come to share a reputation with Tommy Tune as the only dependable hitmakers in town. Part of this is certainly due to Zaks's and Tune's talents. And part of it is due to the nature of the material they are drawn to— material that fits what they do best.

Zaks will rarely attend a reading or a presentation; he prefers to consider shows submitted in script form. He claims he will do a comedy only if it makes him laugh out loud while he is reading it. "The only funny plays are the ones that make you laugh out loud," he says. "The other ones— that are supposed to be comedies, but don't make you laugh out loud—are not funny. People will find reasons why they are going to be funny when they're produced. But they won't be. If you don't laugh out loud when you read it, no one ever will—*ever*—no matter who the director is."

Zaks has reason to be confident his sense of humor is shared with a large audience, given his commercial success with his productions of John Guare's *The House of Blue Leaves* and *Six Degrees of Separation*, Ken Ludwig's *Lend Me a Tenor*, Chris Durang's *Sister Mary Ignatius Explains It All for You*, Larry Shue's *The Foreigner*, and his reworking of the 1934 musical *Anything Goes*. If a script is funny, he's the first director to whom any producer in town will show it. If any of us were to play the parlor game at a dinner party of matching any director with any show we wanted to see mounted, it is likely that Jerry Zaks and *Guys and Dolls* would have been on everyone's list. There may be seventy-five people in this room—but this is clearly Jerry Zaks's *Guys and Dolls*. It will be his triumph—or his failure.

"Why don't we get started," Zaks says, following the photo opportunity. "I can't believe I am actually saying that." He is standing in the middle of the room now, in a charcoal gray sweater and red plaid shirt, with his hands in the pockets of his baggy black slacks. The cast sits in a semicircle of folding chairs on one side of him, and everyone else is in a semicircle on the other side.

"I've been looking forward to this day for a long time," Zaks tells his company. "And now that I'm here I want to get to work. I'm not going to bore you with how much I love this show and how precious it is and how much responsibility we all share to do it well. I don't want to scare us to death. I just want to do it."

Then the charming and soft-spoken scenic designer Tony Walton, with whom Zaks collaborates frequently, holds up his one-inch-to-a-foot scale models of the set, scene by scene. His approach is a homage to Jo Mielziner's designs for the original 1950 production that opened at the Forty-sixth Street Theatre on Broadway. It is a fantasy Times Square, largely painted on drops, using Walton's own palette of bright pastels. The only suggestion of the scenery now in the rehearsal hall is two wood, ceiling-high spiral towers that will be necessary for choreographer Chris Chadman to stage the famous crap game in the sewer.

"This show is a great play with great music," Zaks says. "And there's something about Tony's scheme that will let the play part play.

"Enough yak-yak-yak. The show that really knocked me out way back when was *Wonderful Town*. All I remember is the light and color and music exploding out of the proscenium. That's what this is going to be. This set is our world. This set is where our magic is going to take place. It's the vessel that will allow all this to happen. Now I'll stop yakking and let's read it."

The cast sits with scripts in hand and reads through the show's dialogue. When a song cue arrives, musical director Eddie Strauss plunks out a few bars of the songs everyone knows on the upright piano almost as a tease. The role of Arvide Abernathy, the elderly bass drum player in the Save a Soul Mission band, has not been cast yet. It's been offered to comic actor Eddie Bracken, but no deal has been made. So Zaks reads that role. His enthusiasm is infectious. His laughter leads the way. He loves funny. And there's not much funnier than this.

After the read-through, the cast takes a break and Zaks sends all but the actors and production team away. He's content with what he's heard.

"There are no surprises except seeing how far along some people are," he says. "They understand the music of the words."

And he's happy with the collection of character actors he's assembled. "This is the perfect New York show," he says. "It grows out of the fabric of the city. You don't want a lot of white-bread beauty. You need characters. The problem with the movie of this was that those actors weren't these characters, they were pretending to be. But onstage, you just have to find these people."

Directing is about making choices and having the ability to articulate those choices clearly so your collaborators can execute them. In several meetings between the first day of rehearsal and the week after the opening of *Guys and Dolls*, Jerry Zaks sat in his office above the St. James Theatre at the Jujamcyn organization's headquarters and discussed his job, and the decisions he was faced with—big and small—that went into the show. The very first decision a director must make, of course, is whether or not to do a specific show.

"The first time I ever heard of *Guys and Dolls* was when a friend of mine spoke about an all-male production he did at the Riverdale Country School," Zaks says. "I have a vague memory that somewhere way, way back I might have seen an amateurish summer stock production, but that might be a dream as much as a memory."

The possibility of directing *Guys and Dolls* was first brought up in 1989 when Zaks was director-in-residence at Lincoln Center.

"That's when I first really read it and listened to it," he says. "I laughed out loud. I liked it a lot. And I was also very aware of how it was perceived as either the greatest musical of all time or everyone's favorite musical, whether or not they'd seen it. But that was not intimidating enough to prevent me from saying, Okay, yeah, I want to do this.

"But before we really got it rolling, I read John Guare's *Six Degrees of Separation*, and I had to do that. It preempted everything else in my life at that point. That's how I react to reading something that good. Stop! Now I have to do this."

After five successful years and four successful shows at Lincoln Center Theater, Zaks left in 1990 because the works he wanted to select were subject to the approval of the artistic director, Gregory Mosher. When that approval was withheld on Barbara Lebow's play *A Shayna Maidel* and the Stephen Sondheim–John Weidman musical *Assassins*, Zaks realized it was not a condition he wanted to live with. Zaks directed *Assassins* at Playwrights Horizons, and a Steve Tesich play called *Square One* at the Second Stage. Then he entered into an agreement with Rocco Landesman at Jujamcyn under which Zaks would be given a comfortable salary, office space, and support staff in exchange for a right of first refusal to house commercial productions of his work in the organization's five theatres. It was the kind of housekeeping deal that is popular in the film industry, but is unprecedented in New York commercial theatre; it represented an innovative and savvy wager by Landesman, whose affinity for gambling has served him well on Broadway. If rumors at the time were true, and Zaks was indeed interested in *Guys and Dolls*, that alone was enough to secure Jujamcyn's investment.

But Zaks had drifted away from the thought of doing the show. "It's not a show that makes you laugh, laugh, laugh, laugh, and then cry," Zaks says. "It's not designed that way. It's designed to be an unapologetically happy evening in the theatre. It's been a long time, I think, since someone's done that full out. So I had a natural sort of suspicion about doing a show that ends with 'They get married and everyone sings.' I wondered if it needed to be more real. Did it somehow need a poignant twist somewhere that it didn't have? Yet, the stories are three-dimensional and have texture. It's not just fortissimo all the time."

While Zaks was having his doubts, his agent, Bill Craver, called and informed him that Lincoln Center's rights had expired, a number of commercial producers were competing for the rights, and whoever got them was going to offer the show to Zaks. Zaks discussed it with his wife, Jill, with his psychiatrist, and with writer John Weidman, his friend and sometime collaborator.

"The basic impulse from most of the people who know me is to nudge me in the direction of committing to do it," he says. "Because once the committing's over—whew!—now we've got to do it, which has its own bunch of terrors. And finally I said, Stop resisting, do the show, schmuck, do it."

So Zaks committed to the material, but not to any of the competing producers. When the rights holders, Jo Loesser and Ann Burrows, selected Michael David and the Dodgers as their producers, Zaks signed on. Landesman was a founding member of the Dodgers and had worked regularly with them since joining Jujamcyn, which made it a perfect fit for Zaks.

Zaks began work on the show during the summer of 1991, six months before rehearsals were to commence.

"The first consideration for me was," Zaks says, "what was the set going to look like and how was it going to work? The solution was inspired by a visit I made to Tony Walton's home in Sag Harbor about six years ago. There he showed me a book of plays by Oscar Wilde—or it could have been Shaw—and Tony had done the illustrations. They were extraordinary. And I thought, Wouldn't it be something if we did a show and that whole show was Tony's paintings, his palette! Wouldn't that impose an extraordinary design unity!

"As I studied the play, I knew it would have to be of a mythic size that takes the realism out of New York and leaves us with romantic myth. The show is subtitled *A Musical Fable of Broadway*. It's not a cartoon, because cartoons suggest the unreal, the phony. It's a myth grounded in reality.

"It seemed to me that the play would contain and allow for the expression of as much joy as possible. Joy to me was the word, and then under it you have comedy, music, lights, life, dancing. Watching Willie Mays play baseball, right? Joy.

"I kept reading the play over and over and asking myself, Was there any way to do this other than alternating between in-one and full-stage scene? That was the way it was originally designed. Is there a way to do this as a wraparound design? How are we going to be different? I called Cy Feuer, who produced the original, and asked if he had ever tried it with revolves, turntables. He said he did in L.A. and it didn't work. I couldn't come up with the answer.

"All the alternatives Tony or I thought of seemed to endanger the tempo that had to be maintained. The transitions would take too much time. Finally we came up with the right solution—to do it just the way they wrote it, just the way they did it, alternating between scenes in which the actors are very close to the audience, and then a stage full of energy and lots of people. So Tony and I committed to doing it that way, but not to hold back with the paintbrush, to use the boldest, brightest colors."

With Walton working on preliminary sketches, Zaks then turned his attention to finding a choreographer

"I didn't know who to go to," Zaks says. "This person would have to be as good at what they do, to put it bluntly, as I am at what I do. It had to be someone whose work made me feel that, if I were a choreographer, that's what I would've done. How do you find that out? I decided to have some choreographers do presentations for me.

"I felt a little guilty about this. It's a difficult question whether directors should be permitted to do this. But I found it to be an extraordinarily valuable tool for making a decision."

Zaks admits he did not think much about the politics of such a presentation, which he regrets. Aside from those auditioning, he was putting dancers in the awkward position of having to accept the invitation to help out even if they did not want to, in fear of having the choreographers blackball them from show jobs if they refused to cooperate. Conversely, those who did cooperate would be expecting jobs if the choreographer got hired. It was another case of extreme awkwardness created by the fact that there is a whole generation of people who have not had the opportunity to demonstrate their work as previous generations had.

Zaks prefers not to discuss the six choreographers (some, including Jerry Mitchell, D. J. Giagni, Joey McNeeley, and Tony Stevens, accepted; others, including Wayne Cilento, declined) who were invited to make presentations and were not selected. The seventh, and the first to present, was Christopher Chadman, once a favorite dancer of Bob Fosse's, and Fosse's assistant on his last show, *Big Deal*. Most of Chadman's choreographic work had been done in regional theatres. But he wrote Zaks a letter and was invited to meet with him.

"I told him I wanted it to be Broadway dance," Zaks says, "athletic, vital, sexy—Jack Cole–Bob Fosse dancing. Some cross between jazz and modern with show biz thrown in. He said, That's what I do."

Zaks asked Chadman and each of the others to get together a group of as many dancers as they needed and to stage three pieces: "Runyanland," the show's opening sequence, to demonstrate storytelling ability; "Take Back Your Mink," a nightclub number, to show how he would work with the girls; and the crapshooters' ballet, to demonstrate athletic dancing. The producers would cover expenses for the dancers and the space and give the choreographers a small stipend.

"Chadman's seven-and-a-half minute 'Runyonland' was terrific, funny, lively," Zaks says. "In 'Take Back Your Mink,' the girls were very attractive, very sexy. I had some notes about it, but it was very good. But when his crapshooters' ballet was over I just went, 'Wow!' It wasn't finished, but it was exciting. The best parts of it were there. And if it did that to me, I figured it would do it to the audience. In the bank.

"Not only was I knocked out by what Chris did, but when it was over, his company had a celebration. He broke out bagels and stuff and it was clear dancers loved dancing for him. He was a good leader. And I thought, The dancing was good, but this is good, too."

By the end of the summer, Zaks had his designer and his choreographer working. He asked costume designer William Ivey Long and lighting designer Paul Gallo, both of whom worked together with him and Walton often, to join the team. Additionally, Eddie Strauss came aboard; he had been the musical director of *Anything Goes* and did some planning on *Guys and Dolls* when Zaks was thinking of it for Lincoln Center. Zaks and Strauss invited orchestrator Michael Starobin, who had worked with them on *Assassins*, to listen to the score with them. Together they decided they wanted a bigger sound and quicker tempos in many places, so Starobin went to work reorchestrating in a style that would fit with what was kept from George Bassman's and Ted Royal's work on the original production.

With his team in place and working, Zaks turned to casting. Zaks is laboring and meticulous in his casting efforts, and the process for this show went on for five months on two coasts. With a billboard of the show's logo hanging over Times Square by September and very little other musical theatre promised for the season, the press so eagerly anticipated who would be selected for the four famous lead roles that rumors-presented-as-fact kept showing up in gossip columns. This creates audience interest in the show. But it also results in having to put out a lot of fires with embarrassed phone calls to actors' agents to explain that their clients are not being offered jobs.

Rumors had Kevin Kline, Mandy Patinkin, and James Naughton offered Sky Masterson, Judith Ivey offered Adelaide, Bernadette Peters offered Adelaide and/or Sarah. Actually, all of these people were offered these roles—but not for this production. About five years earlier, producer Manny Azenberg had the rights, hired Michael Kidd, the original show's choreographer, to direct and choreograph this time out, and had conducted a lengthy and comprehensive search for well-known stars. Azenberg, the astute producer of most of Neil Simon's works, was well aware of the history of Broadway revivals without ticket-selling names above the title. Finally, Azenberg was ready to go with Ron Silver as Nathan Detroit, Patti Cohenour as Sarah, and Judith Ivey as Adelaide—as long as he could corral a star to play Sky. Azenberg thought he had one when Tom Selleck sang—and apparently sang well—for Michael Kidd. When Selleck's film career got in the way, however, the effort fell apart.

"When I began casting I was torn between wanting to do my own version and the fact that they got it right the first time," Zaks says. "How affected would I be by what they had done? How willing was I to go beyond that? And if I were to go beyond that, why? You've got to have a good reason to put actors on roller skates if they didn't do that originally. And Nicely Nicely is the perfect example of what I'm talking about."

Nicely Nicely Johnson, a pal and messenger of floating-crap-game entrepreneur Nathan Detroit, who gets to sing the 11 o'clock show-stopper "Sit Down, You're Rockin' the Boat," is a role that for over forty years has been associated with just one actor—Stubby Kaye. Kaye played it in the original show in 1950, he played it in the movie in 1955, he's been playing it in stock productions ever since. When Azenberg and company were planning their revival, only one name was discussed for the role—Stubby Kaye. Stubby Kaye has two distinguishing characteristics—he has a big, lovely tenor voice; and he is very fat.

"When I started to look for Nicely, I had an idea," Zaks says. "The idea was that he should be a big fat guy. Why shouldn't I do it that way? So in come all the big fat guys, but they don't turn me on. They weren't funny, they weren't lively, and they had inadequate voices. You need a big voice in that role, and a sense of joy, and must be larger than life. I saw a lot of gross overactors. And a lot of effeminate guys. They were all fat, but none of them was large, in the mythic sense. There are large actors, and then there are large actors.

"After a month, I was really desperate and I had Walter Bobbie come in. I had worked with him a number of times, and he had this big, strong kind of tenor voice that embraced you. It was shot out of a gun and put a big grin on your face. But he's not big and fat. Walter projected skill and joy. So now I torment. I have him come in a couple of more times. I wonder if by casting him I'm abusing some essential something in the show that I'm not in touch with. I'm doing the show a disservice. I'm in tumult. I want to go with Walter. No, I'm not. I can't. Why can't I? I want a big fat guy to walk in the door and do exactly what Walter did. Then I remember, this is exactly what happened to him when they were casting the original Broadway company of *Grease*. He auditioned great but they wanted a big, heavy guy. Finally they went with him and he knocked them out. So I hired him."

As is the case with almost every musical, casting began with contacting a lot of Hollywood stars who reportedly can sing. After the West Coast contingent has been run through, to no avail, comes the Broadway-musical A-list—people who want to do both movies and theatre, but if they do theatre they don't want to do a revival.

"I didn't like what I felt like trying to entice someone to do the show," Zaks says. "Certainly the most serious mistakes I've made in my whole professional life have occurred when trying to convince anyone to do anything. Then the prevailing wisdom was actually articulated, that no revival had succeeded without stars. For me that's like hearing that no show ever worked on the Lincoln Center stage. That's a motivator. So I abandoned the idea of doing it with stars. It took the joy out of it for me, pursuing them and being rejected."

In a phone conversation I had with Zaks early on in the casting process, the only thing he would say to me was, "Nathan Lane's going to end up in there someplace."

Zaks now says, "Nathan Lane comes in, and you know he's one of the funniest guys in the world. And you think, Nathan's Nathan Detroit. Then you start talking yourself into and out of things. Maybe he's too young. He's supposed to be older. Maybe I should cast so-and-so because he's a little more Jewish. Then you hear fifty to a hundred people read Nathan Detroit, and Nathan Lane comes in again and you laugh so hard your stomach hurts. You gotta have him. Then he's done and you ask yourself, I laughed, but will an audience laugh? Am I laughing because I love Nathan Lane so much, or because he's good as Nathan Detroit? Does it matter? I'm laughing. And something extraordinary happened when he was in the room. So he's hired.

"I knew of Faith Prince though I didn't see her in *Jerome Robbins' Broadway*. A lot of people who auditioned for Adelaide had different things to recommend them. Then there were a lot who acted stupid, though Adelaide is smart. But for the total package, nobody came close to Faith. She knocked me out in her first audition and I wanted her. The funny voice, the funny look, but they were totally incidental to her reading of the lines. She was absolutely believable. And she had the voice to hit those notes at the end of 'Lament' ["... bad, bad cold"]. If you can't rock the people with that note, you can't get it done. I didn't give her the job at the first audition. Even though I wanted her, you have them come back, watch what happens when you give them some notes, some adjustments. See if they finish your sentences, or if they listen. Then I saw her in *Nick and Nora* and it helped because it impressed me that she was a wonderful performer. And it reminded me that she had to lose weight. She had to be credible as a show girl. I told her and she said what anybody who really wanted to do a show would say: 'Lose weight? Really? Watch me!' By the first day of rehearsal, it was clear she had taken me seriously.

"Sky Masterson was the only role for which there was a dead heat. Peter Gallagher came in and knocked me out. Again, he was a little on the young side. And Jimmy Naughton was a real consideration. I quickly discarded the idea that somehow his having done *City of Angels* so recently should be a reason we shouldn't consider him. His presence onstage is strong and somehow reassuring. I feel very good when he's onstage. But it comes down to a feeling; the sound of one voice as opposed to another. I don't know how to explain it. I went with Peter."

The most difficult of the four leads for Zaks to cast was the character of Sarah Brown. It would seem that if you made a list of working Broadway actors who were right for each of the four leads, the Sarah Brown list would be the longest. But Zaks told me before casting even began that he had an untraditional take on the role. He felt that the relationship between Sky and Sarah was the most difficult part of the show to make work. So he thought he might cast Sarah older than usual, have her be more of an experienced woman who had a lot of life and intelligence. "I didn't want

Sky to have to fall for a beautiful bimbo," he says. Everyone who would be on your list did audition, including some of the actresses whose stories are in this book.

Then, when he was going to audition in Los Angeles, Zaks received a phone call from his friend Carolyn Mignini, with whom he had appeared on Broadway in *Tintypes*. Carolyn had been living out west with her husband, actor Steve Vinovich, and their two kids, and working in television for the past five years. Zaks said he was thinking of someone a little younger, but that Carolyn should read the show again and, if she wanted, come in and audition.

"She came in and sang 'If I Were a Bell,' " Zaks said. "She's always been to my mind a good actress, and she is very witty and has character and a lovely voice. I found her audition thrilling. But I wondered, Why? Did I just see an old friend give a great audition, or did I just find my Sarah Brown?" Zaks's decision came down to Josie de Guzman, Patty Ben-Petersen, and Carolyn. "Ultimately, I decided Carolyn would work best for the relationship with Sky," he says. "At least, that's what I thought. Maybe I was casting with my heart."

Jerry Zaks discovered musical theatre on a blind date. He was a sophomore at Dartmouth College, it was Winter Carnival, and he was somewhat awkward socially at the time. He was fixed up and didn't know what to do with the girl except take her to the school play. The production was the Betty Comden–Adolph Green–Leonard Bernstein musical *Wonderful Town*. Zaks fell in love that night. But not with the girl. "It started with lots of people on the stage. Beatniks. And millions of people. And it was this music and color and light. And life. All that life. I had never seen a musical before and I just couldn't believe what I was seeing."

The arts did not play an integral role in Zaks's childhood. What joy existed in the family was tempered by a sense of the outside world as a hostile, life-threatening place. His parents, Sy and Lily, grew up and married in the little town of Bendzin, Poland. When World War II broke out, Lily Zaks was captured by the Nazis and spent a year in Auschwitz. Sy changed his name to Jan Byezek and masqueraded as a Gentile.

Later in life, Sy Zaks would tell his son the story of when he was Jan Byezek and working on a farm during the war and one day he was walking with another employee who said to him, "You know, it's funny, you look familiar to me. You look just like a guy I played football with in Bendzin. But you couldn't be him because he was Jewish."

Sy managed to ignore the remark, but the next week he went up to the guy and said, "Remember you thought I was so-and-so, but I couldn't be?

Well, I am. And I am working for the Polish resistance now. And I'm telling you because if anything happens to me, nothing will happen to you, but you will watch your wife and children die in front of you. So you decide what you want to do."

After the war, Sy went to work for Mercedes-Benz in Stuttgart. He found Lily working there at the Red Cross center. "There was a very loaded reunion," Jerry Zaks says. " 'Does he love me?' 'What has he been doing?' 'What has she been doing?' And somehow they got past that."

Once Lily had regained her health, she and Sy had a child they named Jerry. When he was twenty months old, the family moved to Omaha, Nebraska, where Sy Zaks broke a Clorox bottle over the head of a man who made an anti-Semitic remark. Then he promptly moved his family, first to the Bronx, then to Paterson, New Jersey, where he opened a butcher shop called Sy's Kosher Meat Market.

"He hated it," Zaks says. "He was not a good butcher, but he was a good schmoozer. He loved to *tummel*. He would make the women feel important. And on the weekend he would get dressed in the most immaculate suit and go to shul and tell people he was an M.D., which stood for meat dealer.

"No one in my house was interested in theatre. There wasn't any music in my house, any political discussion. It was two people from a very different world who were happy to have friends around from their part of Poland and spent all their time with them. My mother had a tremendous fear of something bad happening. Like all firstborns of concentration camp survivors who are treated as miracle children, I was protected within an inch of my life. And your ability to be self-reliant is undercut because you are so protected.

"My greatest role in life was to make people like me because I was terrified of not being liked. I was a good singer, and, even though I was fat and spongy, I could dance pretty well. After I finished my homework, I would go down in our knotty-pine basement and put an Everly Brothers record on, or the Drifters or Sam Cooke, or Marvin Gaye. I had a white-label promotional copy of Marvin Gaye songs before anyone knew who Marvin Gaye was. I perfected my impersonations to the point that I could convince my friends that I recorded the record and had changed my name to Marvin Gaye.

"My mother's reaction to this was an incredulous, 'Jerry, you're a singer?' That was not considered important in any way. In order for me to have fun I had to go down in the basement and make myself a soul singer.

"Then it came time to apply to college. Who knew anything about it? Where was I going to go? And I distinctly remember the day when I asked my friend Richie, Where are you applying? And he said Dartmouth. Dartmouth! It sounded so strong and different. So I sent away for the catalog, and when I saw that mist and those trees, I had to go there. So I applied and I got in. I didn't know how my father was doing in his butcher shop. We never discussed it. To my mind we were always on the brink of disaster. But it seemed important to go to school there. I didn't know why. But I remember calling this banker in New Jersey who was the head of the local alumni association and saying I just got accepted, and, before I could finish the sentence, he said, If you've been accepted, you're going. We'll make sure of that one way or the other.

"In retrospect, it was the most important decision in my life. And to my parents it was the saddest day in their lives because it meant absolute separation from them. Once I went away, I saw them in a whole different way, and only periodically.

"Dartmouth was terrifying at first. Buying my own pair of shoes was a traumatic experience. I remember the first day I needed a dime for a phone call and I only had a nickel and a quarter. I asked a kid if he had change of a quarter and he said, No, but here's a nickel. No stranger had ever been that generous to me. And I thought, I'm going to be very happy here. There was a whole world outside of the one I grew up in . . . and, in fact, it wasn't hostile."

Zaks entered Dartmouth as a pre-med student. Then he saw *Wonderful Town*. At the end of that year, he was told that the show was going to be produced again for reunion season. "So I auditioned and I got cast in the chorus," Zaks says. "I played seven or eight different parts: a beatnik, a Brazilian admiral, an Irish cop. I remember seeing my costumes on the rack and thinking, They're all for me!

"So much of my childhood was about getting good grades—literally and metaphorically. What kind of joy can there possibly be in that? None! Tremendously conflicted feelings about the war, what happened to my parents. And then there was *Wonderful Town*. It was what shul was supposed to be. What was happening in the theatre was what happened in synagogue at its best—but only momentarily. Joy in the music and the act of people singing together—that's what I loved. And there was laughter, too, which there never was in synagogue—except if you were fucking around with someone sitting next to you or unraveling your prayer shawl. Yes, it was joy that I had discovered. I didn't want to admit it. I didn't want to commit to it. But it was the first time. Yes. Yes. Joy."

When junior year began, Zaks switched his major to English and auditioned for every possible show. He even got his Actors' Equity card playing bit parts in the Dartmouth summer theatre company. At the same time, he studied for and took the law boards and applied to law school. He was still hedging. Then late in his senior year, he decided he had to pursue theatre and applied for an assistantship at Smith College.

"I spent two years at Dartmouth falling in love with the theatre," he says, "and two years at Smith preparing to take it seriously."

At Smith he was cast in a production of *The Crucible* that was directed by a visitor from the New York theatre, Curt Dempster. "This was the first time we were with someone for whom theatre was more than an academic pursuit or an extracurricular activity," Zaks says. "Here's a guy who could actually work at it eight, ten hours a day, and expected us to work at it the same way."

Inspired to pursue acting, Zaks lost forty pounds in his first few months at Smith, which he never put back on. "When I came home for Thanksgiving my mother opened the door," he says, "and she said, You're sick. They didn't understand what I was doing. Acting? It was the same way they reacted when I told them I was buying a motorcycle. They didn't know what to do. They thought I was crazy. It was in the realm of marrying a shiksa—which didn't happen until later."

Dempster told the students he was going to teach acting in New York; after receiving his master's degree at Smith, Zaks came to New York to study with him. With his Equity card in tow, he began to buy *Backstage* and to audition for anything and everything, including the role of Young Tom Edison for a musical to be produced by the PART Foundation, the children's theatre company today known as TheatreWorks USA. "I was in my mother's kitchen in Fair Lawn and the phone rings and it was Charlie Hull from PART to tell me I got the role," Zaks says. "And I turned to my mother, who was washing dishes, and I said, I got it. I got Tom Edison. And she said, That's nice. She had no idea what this meant."

When rehearsals began, Zaks moved into a $75-a-month apartment with two other actors on One Hundred First Street and Amsterdam Avenue, in Manhattan.

"I had no real sense of the future then," he says. "I was just acting. The present was so enjoyable, so enjoyable, that when relatives, always relatives, always family, would talk to me, it was as if they felt sorry for me. To them an actor was like Joey Bishop, or someone who made up good limericks. I'd want to take them by the lapels and say, Don't you understand? I have nobody to answer to, I'm doing what I love doing, and I'm getting paid."

"The first read-through, it's like the first day of school," Jerry Zaks says. "We have bagels and lox and everyone smacks each other on the back.

We're going to have a great show. This is what the set's going to look like. Here's a bit of the music. Oh, it's wonderful. See ya. Good-bye.

"From that point on, no one is allowed in the rehearsal room until I'm ready to use them. Then I'm left alone with the actors and the stage manager and I tell them the rules. Basically what I say is, We're going to work very hard, we're going to have a lot of fun. And before it's over you're all going to be speaking in one voice. Each of you will be pursuing what you need in the piece as if your life depends on it. See, what we're embarking on is the process of making every moment as much a life-and-death decision as possible.

"The rules? Very simple. There are twenty people in the room, right? You're an actor, you have a great idea about something you want to happen in the scene. You cannot tell me that idea in front of twenty people. I will not be able to hear it properly. I want to hear your idea. But you must tell me in private.

"Actors are not permitted to discuss or comment on the work of any other actor. I can't legislate that people fall in love with each other. But I can legislate what I consider will be the kind of behavior that will maximize the possibility of people growing to respect and to want to work with each other.

"I also will not criticize in front of other actors. Oh, I can say to move six inches left. It's more powerful over there. If you're going to get that close to him, you're not going to have space. And you need space. If you get too close you become vulnerable. But with the big things, I say, Come talk to me. The first person I do that to feels like he's being punished. And pretty soon everyone realizes I do it with everyone. That's the process. And they realize the reason I'm doing it and they're grateful. Because then I can tell them anything and they're not going to feel stupid. They can disagree without me feeling my authority is being threatened.

"Actors in rehearsal are very vulnerable. When I first started directing, because I hadn't done anything that was successful, the need for actors to please me and their fear of what would happen if I wasn't pleased was not significant. In those days, it was, Okay, let's go out and play. But I realize now I have to be much more careful. I can wreak havoc with just a wrong look and inhibit the actors—and that's the last thing I want to do."

Zaks hates feeling that he does not have control and claims he embraces structure to a fault. He arrives at rehearsal with something specific for the actors to try, rather than letting it evolve. He has key moments completely choreographed and hands out the movements. His scripts for the shows he has directed look like scorecards for extra-inning baseball games in which there have been a lot of substitutions. There is writing everywhere. Each scene is broken down into its important beats and even half-beats. Blocking (the movement of actors through the scene) is sketched in the margins.

"With some actors it works fine," he says. "Other actors feel a little inhibited. I'll suggest that you enter from there." He points to the door. "That way you don't have to worry about it. Why? Well, I'll give you four reasons if you need them, but hopefully you're a good enough actor not to ask me that and you've done that part of your homework. So you come in from there. Then I'll sit back and see what happens. When nothing begins to happen, which happens shortly after—because with actors there's a tremendous amount of uncertainty—I'll continue to impose my first draft.

"I give them entrances, I give them points to cross, points to pursue. Sometimes it's right, sometimes it's not. It's all based on my playing the parts myself and saying, Well, why do I cross here? There's got to be a reason. To either get away from this person or to get to this person. Now, who is pursuing whom in this scene? And how do they best pursue them? Do I best pursue you by walking away from you to force you to have to come to me? The possibilities are infinite. There's no right one. There's only one that seems best, and you keep searching for it.

"I love this stuff."

Zaks felt he began rehearsals for *Guys and Dolls* with a sound battle plan. It had either grown out of the discussions with Tony Walton about the style of the scenery or subconsciously informed those talks. After agreeing with Walton that the designer would be aggressive in his use of bright color, he encouraged William Ivey Long to be as uninhibited in designing the costumes. Now he needed a show that was big enough in performance to fill that space and those clothes. What Zaks was doing was getting away from the reality of New York City outside the theatre's doors and into a heightened, romantic version of the place. He would be attempting to make a large part of his audience reimagine their hometown.

"To me, a successful show is like having a wonderful dream," he says. "Not a nightmare, but a wonderful dream where strangely improbable things happen, but you never question for a second the logic of it in your dream. It always makes sense. It always makes sense.

"I had allowed myself to believe," he says, "that on some level, because it was a great show, a classic musical, somehow I wouldn't have to work as hard to find the answers—that the answers were in there."

But about three weeks into rehearsal, Zaks recalls, he found himself "uncharacteristically discouraged and almost transparently depressed."

"It was around the time that *Crazy for You* opened and received great reviews," he says. "And *The Most Happy Fella* had already opened to a good critical response. I was aware that the gosh-darn relationship between Sky and Sarah [Peter Gallagher and Carolyn Mignini] was not really happening. I was concerned that Walter [Bobbie] seemed self-conscious in rehearsals and maybe he was not as exciting a choice as I had felt during the audition."

At a full run-through late in the third week of rehearsals, Zaks's concerns were apparent. On the positive side, Faith Prince was already giving a memorable performance as Adelaide. The acting style of the show was very big, and Nathan Lane was bigger than everyone else, but very funny. The ensemble, particularly the collection of gamblers, was appealing and zany, and Chris Chadman's choreography took advantage of their personalities. The show was also filled with the kind of sharp comic business that is one of Zaks's trademarks—such as Prince and Lane getting stuck together on a note during their counterpoint in "Sue Me" and playing chicken to see who would quit first; and all the gamblers in the sewer popping up in the air when the very big Big Julie follows his toss of the dice with a Rumpelstiltskin-like jump.

But on the negative side, there was very little connection between Gallagher and Mignini. Her Sarah seemed too worldly, just too plain smart to fall for Sky Masterson's suave routine. Her performance was of a different size than the overall style of the show. And Bobbie had not found a style for Nicely and seemed to be self-consciously searching. He had the timidity that results from insecurity, which badly affected both the popular title tune and "Sit Down, You're Rockin' the Boat."

"I realized that I had somehow nudged Carolyn in the wrong direction," Zaks says. "It was a sterner and more businesslike approach to Sky and to the world than was right. We were trying to make the point that she was more tight-assed to begin with and that by virtue of getting to know him she lets her hair down. That is true to a certain extent in the dynamics of the way the relationship is written. But I pushed her so much the wrong way that you wondered, What could Sky possibly find appealing about her? So I pointed it out and both she and Peter worked very hard to make it work, and I wanted to believe that it was honestly on its way to working.

"Nicely was written for a fat guy, but it wasn't being performed by a fat guy. It kept me from being as happy about what Walter was doing as I wanted to be at the time. Walter could sense that and he was not happy with what he was doing, so he kept trying to force things. I didn't feel that what he was doing was of our world, but I couldn't put my finger on it. Maybe it was too big in a false kind of way.

"So Walter and I went through an extraordinary process together of finding out who this character was. He kept trying to find the right size of performance. Sometimes it would be too much and he seemed brain-damaged, like Crazy Guggenheim. He would experiment in a way that was either self-serving or indulgent—and I wasn't very understanding. There was one scene where Nicely came on eating. It was the only indication that he had to be fat, but it was there. He would bring in an apple and a milk-shake and a bag of groceries, keep trying to fix it with props. Then one night he came in and showed me this big carrot. And I laughed and said, No, no, no, I don't think so. But I miscommunicated and he didn't realize I really didn't want to see the carrot. When I saw that carrot, I got so mad, I said to myself, Okay, I'll cut the fucking scene. And I did. And now there was no reference to Nicely being fat. And the role started to work. He began to recapture the joy he had had during auditions—out of my anger.

"My impulse was frustration at how to make it work. The script was so sacred I never considered that it was an extraneous moment. But Walter's problems with the moment forced me to have to consider it. When things wouldn't work it would enrage me. Rage forced me to consider whether the scene was necessary, and it absolved Walter of having to do something that was not right for him.

"With the exception of Laurie Steinberg, my assistant, no one sees this side, but it's part of the things you go through. It's not like war, nobody's dying, but somehow it feels that way.

"I think all the time I was subject to the pressure of this being a long-awaited event. And I think that was what kept me acting in rehearsals in a way I don't usually do. I would tend to sulk. It didn't take much to trigger adolescent behavior in me.

"You have to understand, this is all about the fear of not being good."

Zaks began to get back his confidence in technical rehearsals at the Martin Beck Theatre during the week before previews began. All the design elements looked great and Chadman's dancing filled the theatre space and Zaks looked forward to getting an audience in.

On Monday night, March 16, *Guys and Dolls* played its first preview before a full house. Zaks stood in the back of the house and saw "bad entrances, bad exits, bad scenes, a bad scene before 'Sit Down, You're Rockin' the Boat' that hurt the number, slow pacing, self-indulgence, a lot of work that was not finished.

"People I knew came out of the theatre and avoided making eye contact with me," Zaks says. "I was not seeing any of the enthusiasm for something I've worked on that I usually see. And I realized, It's not special; we haven't made it special enough."

Jerry Zaks spent the 1970s as a working actor, mostly in New York. His home base was the Ensemble Studio Theatre that Curt Dempster had started. But he made it to Broadway in the 1976 production of Kaufman and Hart's *Once in a Lifetime* at Circle in the Square. Later he spent a year on the road and then another one on Broadway as Kenickie in *Grease*. In that production, Zaks met and fell in love with an actress named Jill P. Rose, who soon became his wife.

"I was not a great actor—I was a good actor," Zaks says. "Watching myself always kept me from really, really being as good an actor as I would have liked to have been. The director in me was always working a little bit."

In 1980, while Zaks was appearing at the Golden Theatre in *Tintypes*, a musical revue about the immigrant experience at the turn of the century, an actor friend from Smith College named Bill Cwikowski gave him the script of a play called *The Soft Touch*, by Neil Cuthbert. Cwikowski wanted to act in it and he suggested that Zaks direct it. Zaks read it and laughed out loud. So he gathered eight fellow members of the Ensemble Studio and, with no set, no budget, and no pay, they put on a bare-stage production for two evenings.

"I found myself loving going back to my room with this script and drawing little diagrams and being able to create little stage pictures of what this was about and who's pursuing who," Zaks says. "It was good. The place was filled with laughter and I liked that. But Neil had made a commitment to a professor of his at Rutgers to direct an official production of the show, so that was it for me.

"Right from the beginning I was developing a way with actors that encouraged them to become part of something larger than themselves. Without knowing it, I understood that if actors could get the attention off themselves and on to the other guy, on to whatever it was they were pursuing, they made themselves bigger than if they were aware of themselves. I was also aware of how delicate and short the rehearsal journey was, and that we had to operate in a place where no one ran the risk of being bruised.

"I kept it funny and fast and furious because I was deathly afraid of boring the audience. That's the ultimate sin. Because it's somehow more painful to be bored in the theatre than anywhere else.

"I've gotten better since *The Soft Touch*, but the process is the same. It all stems from the tremendous joy of making it seem natural and just the way it would be happening if it were a good dream you were having."

In 1981, Zaks directed Chris Durang's play *Sister Mary Ignatius Explains It All for You* in the annual one-act-play marathon at the Ensemble Studio Theatre, then with a companion piece, *An Actor's Nightmare*, at Playwrights Horizons. The production transferred to a successful commercial run off-Broadway. Zaks and Durang were a good fit—the irreverent, outrageous playwright and the director who could find the reality in the outrageousness.

With the success of *Sister Mary*, Zaks began to get more offers to direct than to act. "I discovered that once you have credibility as a director," he says, "you don't have to be six-foot-one and Greek, you don't have to be thin, and you don't have to audition."

Zaks then turned his attention to Durang's next play, *Beyond Therapy*, which he directed for the Phoenix Theatre Company in a production starring Stephen Collins and Sigourney Weaver. Based on that production, the play was optioned by Claire Nichtern, who was producing in association with Warner Bros., for a Broadway production. To direct that version, Nichtern hired director John Madden, not Jerry Zaks. "He was British. He had an accent," Zaks says bitterly. "In this business, you never forget the people who pay attention to you, and you never forget the people who don't pay attention to you. I wanted to shake her lapels and say, Don't you know that no one is better for this than I am? You don't know what something like this does to me, because it's out of my control. The experience only motivated me more. You're talking to a neurotic here. In my mind, this kind of thing is a personal affront."

Zaks continued to work with Durang, directing *Baby with the Bathwater* at Playwrights Horizons, and *The Marriage of Bette and Boo* at the Public Theatre. He directed two plays by Larry Shue, *The Foreigner* and *Wenceslas Square*. In order to have a chance to work on a larger scale, he directed the national touring company of the musical *The Tap Dance Kid*.

While working on that show, Zaks got a phone call from Gregory Mosher, the former artistic director of the Goodman Theatre in Chicago, who had just been hired along with Bernard Gersten to try to resuscitate the dormant Lincoln Center Theater. Zaks went to lunch with Mosher and playwright John Guare, at which time he was offered the chance to initiate the new administration's tenure with a production of Guare's *The House of Blue Leaves*. Zaks had already directed a production of the play at Dartmouth one summer—he still had his script broken down into beats—and relished the opportunity. The show was very well reviewed and transferred to Broadway. Zaks won his first Tony Award for Outstanding Director of a Play and formed an official alliance with Lincoln Center, where he went on to direct *The Front Page, Anything Goes*, and the world premiere of Guare's *Six Degrees of Separation*.

During his tenure at Lincoln Center, Zaks was also announced as director of, and put in time working on, two new musicals, *Mr. Jelly Lord* (which became *Jelly's Last Jam*) and *Miss Saigon*.

"The idea of *Jelly* excited me," Zaks says. "I think a lot of it had to do with the fact that Gregory Hines was going to be doing it. This may sound crazy, but I began to feel that I'm white and I don't in my *kishkes* know this world. I can certainly relate to self-hatred. But somehow I kept feeling someone black should be doing this. When *Miss Saigon* came along and I had such an overwhelming response to the material, by that point I felt my response to the Jelly Roll material was forced and labored, and that I would do no one a favor by doing it.

"I began the process on *Miss Saigon*, meeting with the designers in London and working with the actors. And then I began to grow tremendously anxious. All the traveling. To London. To the Philippines to cast. Being away from my family. And working with Cameron Mackintosh's production team, where it was not my control. People don't appreciate how much I need that control because I don't suggest it in any manner.

"I had a friend who died in Vietnam and I imagined how hard it was going to be opening night facing his parents with this celebration of Ho Chi Minh's victory parade that I directed on the stage.

"So I met with the writers, Claude-Michel Schonberg and Alain Boublil, to resign. It was a terrible thing for me to do. I was explaining and apologizing when Alain said to me, No, no, no. We understand. You—we—are Jews. We are Jews who are still living out of our suitcases. And you want to stop living out of your suitcase."

"There is only so much you can do in a rehearsal room," Jerry Zaks says. "Then you need the audience to tell you what's ka-ka and what's good.

"I took certain things for granted and was just a little cavalier until we started getting people in. I came to this having heard, Oh, *Guys and Dolls*, it's a natural, you were made to direct this. And I started to believe it.

"I worked harder on this show than I've worked on anything in my life, particularly from the time we got into previews. That's when I did major surgery, because the audience told me they needed it—and they don't lie. Until then, it's all theoretical. It doesn't mean shit. Now you really go to work."

There are five producers listed above the title in the *Playbill* for *Guys and Dolls*, four of which are producing organizations with a few principals. There are also two associate producers. The agreement between Zaks and Michael David, the lead producer, was that all producers would speak to David, and only he would relay their thoughts to Zaks. One of the unusual things about this production is that Zaks does not feel that agreement was ever violated.

David's first comment to Zaks was that the "Runyonland" sequence, Chadman's seven-and-a-half-minute opening ballet, was falling flat. "I had felt that before," Zaks says. "But hearing him say it, it automatically became something I had to deal with. I had hoped it would work better. You know these things stay in in proportion to how long you want to hope they will get better by themselves. They usually don't."

"The number was killing us, because you're asking the audience to follow a story in dance about characters we never see again, who are not important. When I told Chris Chadman we had to compress it, he said, No, let's throw it out and think of something else. It's not working. And that's why I can't wait to do another show with Chris."

In the second week of the four-and-a-half-week preview period, "Runyonland" was excised from the show. The evening now began with a bleed through a scrim to a stage filled with New Yorkers (Zaks's homage to the color and light he remembered from *Wonderful Town* at Dartmouth), then cleared for the first song, "Fugue for Tinhorns."

This was the most difficult period as Zaks studied his show to focus on the faults. "I didn't know it at the time," he says, "but I think it took a full two weeks for the cast just to grow into the sets and costumes. It also takes at least a week or two for me to let go of things that I was convinced were working in the rehearsal hall. It's a tough two weeks to get through, but it's a critical part of the process."

All of this was transpiring while the usual poisonous gossip spread through the theatre community like a contagious rash. "We were going through a natural continuation of the process we started at 890," Zaks says. "But it felt like we were in a tailspin with a huge motherfucker of a plane with no sign of the engine restarting. I'm trying to get the show right and I'm worrying that Cameron Mackintosh is sitting in the house. And if not him, fill in the blank."

One of the things that surprised Zaks most was how poorly the audience was responding to Nathan Lane's performance as Nathan Detroit. "I was really enjoying him in rehearsals," Zaks says, "but when he got onstage, the audience didn't understand a thing he was saying for five minutes because he was so overwrought. They didn't get a chance to know him. It's the beginning of the play, things are going badly for the character, but you don't want to cut your throat yet! But Nathan's got great technique and understands what's happening. He needed to be encouraged to trust the material.

"He had this speech at the top, before Sky enters, and we laughed at it in the rehearsal hall. It was not funny. It was not funny to an audience. But we laughed because it was Nathan Lane and we all know him. We love him so we laughed because we didn't believe anyone could be so bold. But we didn't pay sixty bucks! Both Nathan and Faith Prince had played their roles before. They both had memories of that, which they let go of fairly easily, which is not always easy to do when you've gotten laughs. But I suspect that Nathan did that particular speech that way and it worked, and now he was forced to try something else. He made the adjustment to take himself a little more seriously and not be quite as much on the verge of hysteria. Now the moment when he really did get angry paid off because we, the audience, had gotten to know him."

Zaks made a lot of small adjustments within scenes—lines, entrances, positioning. "It's all about making the storytelling better and better until you get it right," he says.

He changed the first entrance of the Mission Band, which is the first time we get to meet Sarah Brown. Originally he filled the stage with people immediately following "Fugue for Tinhorns," then brought the band on through the crowd. But the band was getting lost. So Zaks reversed it, having the band come on immediately following the applause for the number, then having the rest of the people come on and gather around them.

Though Walter Bobbie had made great progress as Nicely, his numbers were still not landing as well as Zaks had hoped for. So the director quickened the tempo on the title song and gave Bobbie a high note to hold at the end of "Sit Down, You're Rockin' the Boat." Now the audience responded more enthusiastically.

"In the first scene between Sky and Sarah," Zaks says, "she says, 'Mr. Masterson, why are you here?'

" 'I told you, I'm a sinner.'

" 'You're lying.'

"His next line is, 'Well, lying's a sin.'

"There's only one way to say that line to be funny. And Peter wasn't saying it that way. I listen to it over and over and then I get it. If it's anything but a simple throwaway, it doesn't pull the rug out from under Sarah and make us laugh. As much as the line is funny, it's her reaction that gets the laugh. You must say it in a way that will make her speechless.

"Then, at the end of 'I've Never Been in Love Before,' Sky and Sarah kiss and the Mission Band comes in and sees them. And Arvide [eventually cast with John Carpenter] says, 'Good morning, Brother Masterson,' and that gets sort of a chuckle. Now I'm home in the shower one night—why do these things always come in the shower?—and I go, He should hit the drum. He should hit the drum. What is he wearing the fucking thing around his neck for? Now we get two free laughs there. The applause ends, they're kissing, the band comes on and stands and stares at them. That's a laugh. Then Arvide hits the drum. Another laugh.

"Then there's the scene right before 'Sit Down, You're Rockin' the Boat.' Brannigan, a cop, comes in. Nathan puts his hat on his finger, says, 'We will now hear from brother Nicely Nicely Johnson.'

"Walter starts to stand up very slowly and says, 'It's like in a dream.' Song.

"One night I say to Jill, Why the hell does he sing 'Sit Down, You're Rockin' the Boat'?

"Then I'm in the shower again and it all comes to me. I see the whole scene. So I go in, call the company together, and say, Okay, there are two ways we can do it: this way, and I describe what we've been doing, or this way—Brannigan comes in and everybody screams. He's here to arrest you. Nathan jumps up and he's ad-libbing so you don't get arrested. Everyone ad-libs. Harry the Horse does his line. Then, 'We will now hear from Nicely.'. . . Walter jumps up and acts harder than he ever has before. His dream's an ad-lib, the song's an ad-lib. Everyone's falling all over themselves to keep from being arrested. Now it's funny.

"That simple adjustment made all the difference. It's all these little things. Looking for jokes. I love this stuff."

Zaks did not expect to make any more changes in the top of the show once the original "Runyonland" was cut. But about two weeks before opening night, Chadman came to him and said, "I got something else. I'll need everyone in a rehearsal hall at 890 in the morning."

The cast arrived at 11 A.M. and Chadman taught his new one-and-a-half-minute version of "Runyonland." Zaks came in at two o'clock to have a look and said, "That's it."

But with all the fixes, something was still gnawing away at Zaks—there was no romantic spark between Sky and Sarah. The audience did not find it credible that Sky would be knocked out by who she was. And since the whole last twenty minutes of the first act is about their relationship, if this didn't work, the audience would spend the intermission disappointed. Zaks resisted giving up on its working. He knew that, based on a one-year contract for the show, Mignini had rented out her house in Los Angeles, moved her family to New York, and put her kids in school here. But there was grumbling among the producers.

"Finally, having done as much as I could, I tried to look at the show as objectively as I could," Zaks says, "as if I had paid sixty bucks and was totally unaware of any of the personalities involved. And it was not right."

With eight days remaining until the critics were to see the show, Zaks felt that if he did not make a change now, there would not be enough time to prepare another actress to fill the role by opening night. He called Mignini at home first thing in the morning and told her that Josie de Guzman, her understudy, would be going on that night.

"I don't know how much of it was my responsibility and how much of it is just who Carolyn is chemically," Zaks says, "and how much of it was triggered by my own anxiety that it wasn't working, which I'm sure she picked up on."

De Guzman, who had herself been fired earlier in the season from *Nick & Nora*, was told she was a temporary replacement. But Zaks liked what he saw from the get-go.

"Finally, it was about five days before the critics came," Zaks says, "and I stood in the back of the house watching and I went, This is good now. I stood there *kvelling* rather than wanting to kill. I don't know how to tell you. The rage I experience when it's not right is really considerable. The joy that I feel when it is right is great."

A golf bag leaned against the wall in Jerry Zaks's office. He eyed it like Adelaide eyeing a wedding veil. It was two and a half weeks since *Guys and Dolls* opened officially and the show appeared to have the makings of a theatre phenomenon. The day the critics' notices ran, the show set the one-day record for a daily box-office take, surpassing *The Phantom of the Opera*. That long-absent Broadway prize—a line at the ticket window—was a constant outside the Martin Beck Theatre. The show was about to have cover stories in *New York* and *Newsweek* magazines, and Faith Prince was getting the kind of star treatment from the media that hadn't been seen in town since Michael Crawford had opened as the Phantom.

"Why has there been such a response?" Zaks says. "I'm the wrong guy to explain it. On the one hand I want to say, So why not? If it's in proportion to how relentlessly we tried to make this universally recognized wonderful show as wonderful as people think they remember it, or as wonderful as it is on paper, then it seems to be just.

"But of course it's not that. I don't know how to explain it sociologically or historically or temperamentally. I don't know how it relates to the current work in New York or to people's need for a wonderful fairy tale or fable. I want to believe it's connected to people just wanting to see a really first-rate production of really first-rate material on Broadway. Words and relationships. Something spiritually uplifting—the way that synagogue was when people were standing and singing together. For me that was like, Wow! Electricity. We're talking about impulses and emotions and not anything cerebral. Electricity is not intellectual. But when it happens to the audience or the critics, they rush out and tell everyone else.

"Laughter is not the function of a cerebral reaction. It has to do with the natural human need for joy in life. Like the sunflower turns to the sun. We want to laugh. We want to experience it."

OPENING NIGHT: APRIL 8, 1992

EUGENE O'NEILL THEATRE

A JUJAMCYN THEATRE   ROCCO LANDESMAN
PRESIDENT

JAMES H. BINGER
CHAIRMAN

PAUL LIBIN
PRODUCING DIRECTOR

JACK VIERTEL
CREATIVE DIRECTOR

CAMERON MACKINTOSH

presents

A Musical by **CLARKE PETERS**
Featuring **LOUIS JORDAN**'s Greatest Hits

starring

JERRY DIXON
DOUG ESKEW
MILTON CRAIG NEALY
KEVIN RAMSEY
JEFFREY D. SAMS
GLENN TURNER

Musical Direction &
Musical Supervision
REGINALD ROYAL

Vocal Arrangements &
Musical Supervision
CHAPMAN ROBERTS

Orchestrations
NEIL McARTHUR

Sound by
TONY MEOLA/AUTOGRAPH

Designed by
TIM GOODCHILD

Lighting by
ANDREW BRIDGE

Costumes by
NOEL HOWARD

General
Management
ALAN WASSER

Casting by
JOHNSON-LIFF & ZERMAN

Executive Producer
RICHARD JAY-ALEXANDER

Directed and Choreographed by
CHARLES AUGINS

Originally Produced at The Theatre Royal, Stratford East

6

AUDITIONING

"Ain't Nobody Here but Us Chickens"

MILTON CRAIG NEALY *(Four-Eyed Moe)* comes directly to *Five Guys Named Moe* from last season's Broadway hit *Once on This Island*, in which he created the role of Agwe, which he also performed in the original Playwrights Horizons production. In 1990, Milton toured the country as Judas in the twentieth-anniversary production of *Jesus Christ Superstar*. He was featured in the original Broadway production of *Dreamgirls* and returned for the 1987 revival. Other Broadway credits include *Ain't Misbehavin'* and *Mail*. Milton toured the country with *Sing, Mahalia, Sing*, starring Jennifer Holliday, and toured Europe with *Ain't Misbehavin'*. He can be seen in the film *The Blues Brothers* and can be heard on various radio jingles. Milton gives all honor and praise to the Lord Jesus Christ.

It was like old home week in the hallway at 890 Studios," Milton Craig Nealy says. "They had flown in from Germany, from England, from L.A. Every black male singer-dancer in the world must've been there."

The occasion was the first cattle-call audition in July 1991 for the Broadway-bound musical *Five Guys Named Moe*. This one looked like the sweepstakes prize. The revue of the music of composer Louis Jordan was already a big fat hit in London. And it was the latest venture for producer Cameron Mackintosh, whose previous four shows in New York—*Cats*, *Les Misérables*, *The Phantom of the Opera*, and *Miss Saigon*—were the kinds of successes Bernard Jacobs, president of the Shubert Organization, spoke of with a smile when he talked of "putting a theatre away," or taking it off the market for years to come.

Though there had been scattered roles for black actors in *Cats* and *Miss Saigon*, this was the first show sponsored by the Mackintosh office that was truly a black musical, one that celebrated African-American culture and performers.

"We were told they wanted an up-tempo song and a ballad, and they also wanted a comical monologue," Nealy says. "They kept stressing they wanted lots and lots of personality.

"Now, I hate to go and get one of those books of monologues. They're not funny to me. They're just stuff that people know already. So I decided I had to make something up. I wrote something down before I got there, but once I got in the room I got away from what I wrote, and other things kept coming into my mind. The whole thing was about my beginnings in show business. I started talking as soon as I walked in the door, talking about how I used to work as a busboy in a shack in the woods down south somewhere owned by someone I think I called Lottie Lube or something, and the minister used to sneak in occasionally. Then one night his wife, Reverend Mama, comes in and catches him there. And there was a big ruckus and a big fight and Lottie Lube said, 'Someone do something!' So I had jumped on the bandstand and started singing, 'Let the Good Times Roll.' And then I sang it for the people behind the table at the casting call. They were all laughing and having a good time and didn't even ask me to sing my ballad.

"Then in August I got a callback. They wanted you to do the same thing again! I said, Oh, my God, how am I ever gonna do that monologue again! I didn't remember it. I guess that's why people use monologues from the books."

Whatever Milton Craig Nealy did at his second audition impressed director-choreographer Charles Augins, because the next day Milton was the first of the five New York Moes to be hired. A day later, Doug Eskew, with whom Milton shares an apartment outside Manhattan and also previously shared three other shows, was the second Moe hired.

When *Once on This Island*, in which Nealy had a featured role, closed in December 1991, the two Moes had a little time off and they spent New Year's Eve at the Lyric Theatre in London taking a look at what they were in for. "After every number we would look at each other, like, Oh, my God, what have we gotten ourselves into! It's so fast-paced," Nealy says. "And, Oh, my God, look, they're on their knees. After the show we just sat there and said, We better go into training. We came home four days later, went straight to the gym, joined, and started working out.

"We started rehearsal February 7, and it was like I hadn't even gone to the gym. Charles knew how hard this show was to do and that rehearsal was really training. We learned the whole show in seven days and then we kept doing it over and over and over again. Wham-bam! We jumped right in and people were pulling hamstrings and hurting their knees and their backs. I'd never been through anything like it.

"Now all the time, we were all trying to figure out who our characters are. I'm Four-Eyed Moe. I wear the glasses. But who is he? And Charles telephoned us at home one day and said, I can see it in your eyes, all of you are looking for this great Shakespeare type of thing. But it's none of that at all. It's fluff. It's just having a good time. Don't get into an actor's thing, don't even think about it, just do it—fast. The Moes are like your hands, they've been together for a long time, they come out of nowhere, nobody knows where they come from. He said, You can do for yourself how you got to be a Moe, but it doesn't matter to the audience."

Everything the director told his actors about their characters, or lack thereof, turned up in the reviews when the show opened on April 8—and framed with disapproval. What was treated as fun in London was thought to be silliness in New York. For the first time in nearly a decade, Mackintosh had a show in New York that would have to struggle to find an audience each night.

"Cameron came in the next day and said, 'Don't worry, don't worry at all. We're in this for the long haul,'" Nealy says. "He said, 'The critics and I have never been great friends.' And if this had not been Mackintosh, I don't think we would have been here very long."

The show managed to sneak in and get the fourth Tony nomination for Best Musical, along with *Jelly's Last Jam*, *Falsettos*, and *Crazy for You*. That gave the Moes a chance to perform on the Tony telecast, which boosted business for a while. Even when ticket sales fell off, Mackintosh, the wise marketer and manager, stuck behind his show and kept the Eugene O'Neill Theatre lit. The producer knew that even though the Broadway version was unlikely to recoup its initial investment, he was breathing life into the show's future by keeping it visible.

Here's the thing about *Five Guys Named Moe*: It's a show that you're always going to see being done somewhere after it leaves Broadway. Theatres that do seasons of musicals—and there are more than a hundred of them across the country—always need a smaller show to balance out the costs of doing larger shows. And *Moe*, with six actors and a minimal band, is both small enough in company size to be affordable to smaller theatres and big enough in performance size to fill the bigger theatres.

These institutional musical theatres throughout the country don't have the budgets to rehearse for six weeks, like Broadway shows do. Many of them rehearse as little as one or two weeks and then play. So they're always looking to give themselves a head start by casting actors who already know the show. What this means for Milton Craig Nealy is that, although this Broadway experience was somewhat of a disappointment, it is going to provide him with job opportunities for years to come. Nealy gets to add *Moe* to his working repertoire, which is plentiful since it already includes *Ain't Misbehavin'* and *Dreamgirls*. With these two shows on his résumé, Nealy has been able to work almost every day for the thirteen years since he first auditioned for theatre. Therein lies our tale.

The musical-theatre repertoire includes a roster of black American musicals. But there are not a lot of roles for black performers in the shows that are not on this roster. Work is hard to come by for everyone in the theatre, and much harder still for African-Americans.

This problem inspired the formation of the Non-Traditional Casting Project, sponsored by Actors' Equity and chaired by actress and casting director Joanna Merlin. The philosophy of the project is that theatre is not reality; it is poetry, it is metaphor. Everything is representational. In musical theatre, for example, characters can break out singing in the office or at breakfast. Given such a convention, it is not necessary to cast according to preconceived notions about race. The approach asks us all to be color-blind, and with strong justification.

With a few exceptions—most notably the late Joseph Papp and his New York Shakespeare Festival—producers and directors have not been willing or able to make this leap. They are nervous about putting across their material and look for the most realistic representation of it. They would argue that casting a black person as a member of an otherwise white family, for example, would be viewed as disorienting or incorrectly interpreted as some kind of strident political statement. The argument of the Project is that the only statement is, This is the best actor for the role.

Of course, the reverse of the Project's argument is practiced frequently. White actors not of the ethnicity specified in the script are cast to be something they're not, and the audience accepts it. This controversy came to a head with the casting of Englishman Jonathan Pryce as a Eurasian in *Miss Saigon*, which drew protests from Actors' Equity until producer Cameron Mackintosh threatened to cancel his New York production. Then, as is the way of commercial theatre, economics won out over social concerns and the protest dissipated.

All casting is subjective and critical, and actors, particularly less established ones, go through a lot of confusion about how to present themselves. Is it best to be a blank slate in auditions or to let your own peculiar shades shine through? Many people try to hide what they are in an attempt to widen the net of opportunity open to them. Hispanic actors Americanize their names and their résumés. Everyone lies about his or her age. Gay actors for the most part still prefer not to have their sexual orientation known, fearing it will eliminate them from consideration for roles that involve heterosexual romance. In general, the theatre community is extremely liberal; the only people in the closet recently have been Republicans—except in the matter of casting.

Most African-American and Asian-American people do not have the option of disguising what they are. And so their work opportunities are limited. Yet, when I met with Milton Craig Nealy, instead of finding an actor frustrated by the limitations imposed on him, I found a young man who is unaware of the limitations. For him, there has always been a job.

"If I wasn't doing this professionally, I'd be one of those people singing in the subway," Nealy says. "It would come out somewhere. Some people are just born to do something."

He was born in Wichita, Kansas, the son of Clarice and Clay Nealy, who moved to Chicago when the boy was two and divorced when he was nine. "We lived on the North Side, in a community called Cabrini Green," Nealy says. "It was the projects, housing authority, really, really bad. We had a bad time there in the sixties. I remember running home from school through the riots when Martin Luther King was killed, seeing the police crouched behind cars and shooting and having to dodge the gunfire. That whole project situation was a bad dream. Too many people living on top of each other with no jobs, not enough to pay the rent, thinking nobody cares about them, and, This is about the best I'm ever going to be in my life.

"I don't know how I escaped all that because there were no positive influences on me. But somehow I was always focused and didn't care a lot about peer pressure. Just about when I got into my teen years, when kids were joining tough gangs, my grandfather died and left my mother some money, and, with my stepfather, we moved out of there to a house on the South Side. We got out just as the really bad stuff was starting.

"I used to dance all the time. And I joined the gymnastics team in school because that was as close as I could get to dancing without dancing. And I was always performing. Even when I got up in front of the class to speak, I was performing.

"I went to Bowen High and it probably really changed my life because we had people of every race and nationality there. It was a shock to me, coming from Cooley High, where everyone was black. Here I heard black people speaking French. There were people from Armenia and Japan, Jewish kids and Italians. I was just in heaven. Before that I didn't know there was anything but black.

"In my junior year, I joined this thing called the All-City Theatrical Troupe and we did a production of *West Side Story*. I was a Jet. There were black Jets and Jewish Jets. The Sharks were all mixed up, too. Maria was black. Tony was white. Anita was black. Bernardo was Japanese. And one of the guys out of that company, Marshall Lindsay, started a dance troupe, which I joined when I graduated from school.

"I expected that as soon as I got out of Bowen High, I was going right to California to be in the movies and television. Then, when I was sixteen, I saw the touring company of *Hair* in Chicago, and that opened up a whole new area for me.

"I joined Lindsay and we did modern dance, interpretive dance, African dance. It wasn't full-time. So I worked selling shoes at Flagg Brothers in the Loop. Then I auditioned for a touring company of *Godspell* that was playing at the Marriott Lincolnshire Theatre. That's where I got my Equity card. Back to selling shoes, at Naturalizer in the Water Tower now. Then the movie *The Blues Brothers* shot in Chicago and they were looking for dancers to do the twist and mashed potato and stuff in a number with Ray Charles, and I got that. That made me think, I'm going to save my money and next year I'm going to California. So I moved in with my dad downtown. We hadn't spent a lot of time together. I was twenty-four at the time and we were like two bachelors sharing an apartment.

"That summer, I came to New York for the first time for a vacation. While I was here I auditioned for a show called *Black Light* that Billy Wilson was directing for a tour of Europe and Israel. Wilson eventually dropped out and the new director did his own casting. But now I felt, if I could come here on a vacation and get offered a job, I better move here soon.

"Then in 1980 I saw a notice in the Chicago Equity office that they were auditioning for a Chicago company of *Evita*. They were looking for a tall, good-looking Latin type. And I thought, Well, I'm not that, but I'm going anyway because I want to audition for these people. So I took off from work and went down to the Shubert Theatre and did this kind of stand-up comedy thing off the top of my head. I walked on the stage and said, I'm not a tall, good-looking Latin, but here in Chicago you kind of take what you get. I just kind of heard laughter beyond the lights and I had no idea Hal Prince was out there. I could tell they really liked me and I got a callback. That convinced me I could do this, so I better move to New York now.

"Soon as I move here, to Cambria Heights in Queens, I get another call-back, only it's in Chicago. So I called the office and I said, I'm black and I'm five-foot-seven. Do I really have a chance for this? I just got here and now I'll have to fly back to Chicago. The person on the phone told me to hold on, then came back and said, You have a really, really good chance; I would say you should come back and audition. I did, and I ended up getting offered the job. But I didn't take it because when I went back there, they were auditioning for replacements for the bus and truck of *Ain't Misbehavin'*, and I got that one, too—the Andre DeShields role. So I've been in my New York apartment all of two days and now I go out on the road for ten months.

"I had never been anyplace to this point, except New York. I joined the company in Portland, Oregon, and four days later we were in Hawaii. Then we went to San Francisco and Montreal and all over Canada.

"I had had no formal dance training. I could just look at certain things and say, I could do that. There wasn't anything I ever saw that I couldn't do. And the same thing with music—no formal training, and I couldn't read music. But if you could play it, I could sing it.

"When I got back to New York after the tour, I started taking dance and vocal classes. I got a job singing backup for a woman singer named Roz Burrows. Then I got a call from a casting agent telling me they were auditioning for covers and chorus for a show called *Big Dreams*. I didn't know anything about the show or about Michael Bennett, but I went to an audition and a couple of callbacks. Then I got a call telling me they wanted to offer me a contract as a swing dancer in *Dreamgirls*. I said, I think you have the wrong number, I didn't audition for anything called *Dreamgirls*. And he said, You auditioned for *Big Dreams*, but now it's called *Dreamgirls*. I went down and signed the contract. I was working out at the Jack LaLanne Health Club before rehearsals started, and the guys there were talking about the show. They said it was like the Motown story and supposedly based on Diana Ross and the Supremes. Now I started to get excited.

"The first day of rehearsals I got off the elevator on the seventh floor at 890 and walked toward the studio. It was something like I never saw in my life. They had all the sketches of all the costumes on the floor all around the studio. The room was filled with women who were just amazingly beautiful to me, all dolled up for the first day of rehearsal. Then they sat us down and showed us how this incredible set would work. Michael ran it all and he was witty and bright and there were a lot of things I didn't understand because I didn't know the language. He made some references to the critics and everyone laughed and I didn't get it because I didn't know who they were, but I laughed, too.

"There's a picture of Michael someone took that ended up in the program book, and in it you can see me sitting right beside him. That's where I stayed for the whole rehearsal. You see, when I signed they told me I was a swing dancer, but I really didn't know what that was. Then when I got there I found out I had to cover every single guy in the chorus, and I said, Oh, God, how am I gonna do this? So I decided I was just gonna go wherever Michael stood and see whatever he saw. I think from that they knew I didn't know how to do this, but no one ever said anything."

Dreamgirls was scheduled to preview in Boston for a month, but ended up staying longer, then arrived in New York Christmas week of 1982. "Once we got into the theatre in Boston, I went to all the rehearsals, whether I was needed or not. Covering everyone, I just wanted to be aware of everything. I was never on in Boston until the last two days, when one of the dancers hurt an ankle. But then I played it all through previews in New York and I was on opening night. That night I didn't have any thoughts of what are the critics going to say, are we going to run? I didn't think like that yet. I just thought it was the best show in the world and I didn't know what that meant, 'Are we going to run?' The thought never crossed my mind.

"Eventually I got to cover all the men in the show, except for C.C., Effie's brother. I never really had a relationship with Michael. I was just the swing and stayed away. Then one night Vondie Curtis-Hall was on vacation and I went on as Marty, and Michael comes into the dressing room and he says to me, You know, you have the potential to be anything you want in this business. I said, Excuse me? He wouldn't let the gaze go, he kept looking at me, and he hugged me and left. He never said 'I saw you' or 'You were good' or 'You were bad.' He just said that and left."

When Milton Craig Nealy left *Dreamgirls* in November 1984, he didn't know it at the time, but with that show and *Ain't Misbehavin'* on his résumé, there would almost always be work for him. And that's all he ever wanted.

"One of my friends from Chicago left the business and came to see me recently," he says. "And he said to me, How long you gonna wait around to get rich? But that's never been my objective. That's such a long shot. I have friends who got here before I did and they've got no shows and aren't in the union yet. And look at me. All I ever wanted to do was sing and dance forever. I'm just a kid. I never wanna grow up. I just wanna do shows."

From *Dreamgirls*, Nealy went on to play the Leading Player in a production of *Pippin* at the Lamb's Theatre, then into a workshop for a review of Johnny Mercer tunes called *Accentuate the Positive*. In 1985, he toured the country in *Sing, Mahalia, Sing*, the life of the gospel singer told through music, starring Jennifer Holliday. The producers deserted that show in midstream and it continued on for six months at the mercy of the local promoters. "We played gospel towns and large arenas," Nealy says. "We never knew when we were going to get paid."

Nealy returned to New York from nine months on the road on Labor Day. He was planning to go and feel out L.A. with Doug Eskew, whom he had met in *Ain't Misbehavin'* and had also done *Sing, Mahalia, Sing*. He was home just two days when he got a call from general manager Marvin Krauss's office, offering him the chance to join the national tour of *Dreamgirls*, playing a small role and covering for James "Thunder" Early. He spent the next two years in that tour, including trips to Japan and Paris, then came back with it to the Ambassador Theatre in New York City.

"Michael rehearsed the tour. Then all of a sudden he disappeared," Nealy says. "No one heard from him ever again and there were all kinds of rumors. Then finally we heard he was really ill. It was so hard for us to accept, we barely spoke about it. We would look at one another and you could tell what the other person was thinking, and then we'd go off alone somewhere and cry. It was a real quiet kind of sadness when we lost him."

After understudying in a short-lived new Broadway show called *Mail*, Nealy played Jimmy Early in a production of *Dreamgirls* at An Evening

Dinner Theatre in Elmsford, New York. From there he joined another company of the show at the Burt Reynolds Theatre in Jupiter, Florida. While Nealy was in Florida, a first-class revival of *Ain't Misbehavin'* opened at the Ambassador Theatre, where *Dreamgirls* had been, starring Nell Carter and Andre DeShields from the original Broadway company. When DeShields left that production, his understudy, Eric Riley, moved up and Nealy came in to understudy Riley. When that show closed, Nealy joined a new company of *Dreamgirls* at the Candlelight Dinner Theatre in Chicago, then joined another tour of the show at the Westbury Music Fair on Long Island. From there, he joined a tour of *Ain't Misbehavin'* in Europe, then came home to another production of *Dreamgirls* at the Forum Theatre in Metuchen, New Jersey.

Nealy finally broke the string of *Ain't Misbehavin'* and *Dreamgirls* in the fall of 1989, when Graciela Daniele cast him as Ague, the God of the Sea, in the workshop production of *Once on This Island* at Playwrights Horizons. In the months between the workshop and the full production of this show, Nealy joined a revue called *Do Wop Love* at a small theatre in Queens. During this run, he flew to Frankfurt to perform for one night in *Ain't Misbehavin'* in a festival.

Milton Craig Nealy has the star dressing room at the Eugene O'Neill Theatre, one flight up, stage right. There's no white light in the room, only red. His dressing table is not usable since it's covered with a portable stereo system and nose-high piles of cassettes. There's a photo on the wall of the company of *Once on This Island*, and another of the Five Moes. Nealy is considerably thinner in the Moe photo. He slips into the bright-colored zoot suit that is his costume for the show, pulls on the suspenders, then peeks over the tapes at what's left of the mirror to check out the curl in his hair. He's originated two roles in succession in new Broadway shows now after almost ten years of constant travel. But he doesn't have any expectations beyond the Moe show and would go back on the road in a second. "There you don't have to worry about anything," he says. "Your bed's made, you eat out, and you just send in your bills."

Nealy's an oddity in this business. He started with no formal training and even now has had very little. He's never signed with an agent, although he's free-lanced with a couple of different ones occasionally. He's gotten most of his jobs through the network of alumni from the two shows that have been the focal point of much of his career to date. And he's done more shows in the past thirteen years than anyone else in this book. He's the closest thing I've seen to a natural. He hasn't gotten caught up in the anxiety of having to stay in New York City to be available for the big break when it comes along. He doesn't seem to think about getting to the next level of fame or fortune. There's no crying need for self-advancement here. He'll go anywhere just to be able to sing and dance.

"When I look at where I came from and where I am now . . . whew!" he says, as he puts on his white-framed Four-Eyed Moe specs. He looks at himself in the mirror, likes what he sees, and smiles. "I'm exactly where I always wanted to be."

SAM S. SHUBERT THEATRE

A Shubert Organization Theatre

Gerald Schoenfeld, *Chairman*

Bernard B. Jacobs, *President*

ROGER HORCHOW and ELIZABETH WILLIAMS
present

HARRY GROENER · JODI BENSON
in

The new GERSHWIN musical comedy

CRAZY FOR YOU

book by
KEN LUDWIG

lyrics by
IRA GERSHWIN

music by
GEORGE GERSHWIN

co-conceived by
KEN LUDWIG and MIKE OCKRENT

inspired by material by
GUY BOLTON and JOHN McGOWAN

with

JOHN HILLNER · MICHELE PAWK
RONN CARROLL · JANE CONNELL · BETH LEAVEL
STEPHEN TEMPERLEY · AMELIA WHITE · STACEY LOGAN
THE MANHATTAN RHYTHM KINGS

and

BRUCE ADLER

scenic design by
ROBIN WAGNER

costume design by
WILLIAM IVEY LONG

lighting design by
PAUL GALLO

musical consultant
TOMMY KRASKER

sound design by
OTTS MUNDERLOH

dance & incidental music arranged by
PETER HOWARD

fight staging by
B.H. BARRY

hair by
ANGELA GARI

casting by
JULIE HUGHES & BARRY MOSS, CSA

production manager
PETER FULBRIGHT

general press representative
BILL EVANS & ASSOCIATES

general management
GATCHELL & NEUFELD, LTD.

associate director
STEVEN ZWEIGBAUM

associate producers
RICHARD GODWIN · VALERIE GORDON

orchestrations by
WILLIAM D. BROHN

musical direction by
PAUL GEMIGNANI

choreography by
SUSAN STROMAN

directed by
MIKE OCKRENT

7

CHOREOGRAPHY

"Up Among the Stars"

★

SUSAN STROMAN (*Choreographer*) co-conceived and choreographed the critically acclaimed off-Broadway show *And the World Goes 'Round*. She received the Outer Critics Circle Award for Outstanding Choreography for the 1991 season and was nominated for a Drama Desk Award. Ms. Stroman most recently worked with Liza Minnelli choreographing *Liza—Stepping Out at Radio City Music Hall*. She has choreographed for the New York City Opera, working with director Hal Prince on *Don Giovanni* and director Scott Ellis on *A Little Night Music*. In New York Ms. Stroman directed the comedy revue *Living Color* and *Broadway Babylon* and choreographed the successful off-Broadway show *Flora, the Red Menace*. For television she directed "An Evening with the Boston Pops—A Tribute to Leonard Bernstein," and choreographed *A Little Night Music* for "Live from Lincoln Center."

Now . . . 'I Got Rhythm,'" Susan Stroman says. "This is the first-act finale. I have a concept here based on the set and the characters."

Stroman—in white T-shirt, pink-nylon sweat pants with cotton skirt tied around the waist, black ankle warmers, and the blue eye makeup and dangling earrings the onetime show girl is never without—leans on an upright piano in Studio 4-1 of the Lawrence Wein Center at 890 Broadway. It's a Saturday morning in October, and two weeks from Monday rehearsals will begin for a musical now called *Crazy for You*, a rethinking of the 1930 hit *Girl Crazy*, which had a book by Guy Bolton and John McGowan, a score by George and Ira Gershwin, and which introduced Ethel Merman to Broadway audiences. British director Mike Ockrent, who had a hit in London and New York with a revival of *Me and My Girl*, and Ken Ludwig, the Washington lawyer turned playwright who wrote the farce *Lend Me a Tenor*, have created an entirely new story for this show, kept five songs from the original, and interpolated another dozen or so from the Gershwin catalog. The plan is for the show to play a pre-Broadway tryout at the National Theatre in Washington in November, then open at the Shubert Theatre in New York City on February 19, 1992.

Stro (which is the way she announces herself on the telephone and what all her friends call her) has worked her way up through the ranks from Broadway Gypsy to choreographer at summer stock and regional theatres to great success in New York recently, collaborating with director Scott Ellis on a matchbox production of *Flora, the Red Menace*, at the Vineyard Theatre off-Broadway; *And the World Goes 'Round*, for which she won the Outer Critics Circle Award for Outstanding Choreography, at the West Side Arts; and *A Little Night Music*, at New York City Opera. This past summer, she also had a triumph creating the dances for Liza Minnelli's show, which began at Radio City Music Hall and subsequently went on tour. A little bit on one side or the other of her fortieth birthday, this is Stro's first shot at choreographing for Broadway.

"The idea here," Stro tells her dance arranger, Peter Howard, seated at the piano, and Chris Peterson, her assistant, who stands beside her, "is that Bobby Childs, who has disguised himself as Bella Zangler, a legendary Broadway producer, has directed a show to try to save the lone theatre in the depleted mining town of Dead Rock, Nevada. But the train is four miles across the desert and no one shows up for the opening. He tells his cast that he has failed them. But Polly, whose father owns the theatre, tells him, You haven't failed. You've brought this whole town to life. And 'I Got Rhythm' is the metaphor for the joy he's brought to town.

"So we've got all the townspeople onstage in tap shoes and costumes because they thought they were going to do a show. The idea for this number grew out of Robin Wagner [the scenic designer] showing me what the town looks like. I saw he had a hardware store there and I thought we could use all the mining equipment in the store to instigate the rhythm. The props will give the actors the chance to dance in character. I asked Robin to put some tin on the roof of the store so we can dance up there, and then we got the idea of corrugated tin.

"So let's try every variation on 'I Got Rhythm' and take this old score and make it like no one ever heard it before."

Stro sits in a folding chair to put on her beat-up, high-heeled green tap shoes. "People like to use the same tap shoes for years," she says. "You change the taps, but the leather gets soft and molds to your feet."

"I keep my taps even if I change my shoes," Peterson says. "They're worn down and give you that thin sound you want. I don't like those heavy Capezio taps. The sound is so clunky."

Peterson goes to tape the corrugated tin to the floor and Howard begins to play variations of "I Got Rhythm" on the piano. He plays it as a cakewalk and Stro begins to tap along while sitting in her chair.

"How about a clocklike section?" she says. Howard plays it. "That's good," she says. "We can use temple blocks on mining hats like a xylophone effect."

"I want to use the mining pans like tambourines," she says.

"How about a minstrel sound?" Howard asks, and he plays it.

"That's good. We've got tin signs hanging on the hotel and the saloon," Stro says. "We can take a moment and do an attack on them."

"What about gasoline cans or industrial drums?" Howard asks. "For the number to soar, eventually you want everyone onstage banging on something."

"Brian Nalepka [one of the three Manhattan Rhythm Kings who has been cast in the show] is learning to play the saw," Stro says. "He calls my answering machine and there's no message. Just the saw. And Tripp Hansen wants to play the bicycle pump."

"That's like Le Petomain," Howard says. "You must've heard of him. He farted music. Seriously. They made a movie about him."

Stro shakes her head with a smile. "And at one point, everyone'll have a pickax," she says. "You'll just see a stage filled with those silver pickaxes picking up the light."

Howard plays the tune as a tango, as a rag, a little honky-tonk, a little Hungarian. Then in the style of "The 1812 Overture."

"Let's get a scenario," Howard says. He turns the script to the page containing the song. "I love scripts. It's all in here. See, you get to the dance and it says Dance Break. That tells you everything."

"Okay, from the top," Stro says. "Polly sings. . . ." Stro sings, "Days will be sunny, la, la, la, la." Then she says, "Then the song once through. Boys sing, girls sing, they all sing. Now, how do we get into this?"

"You know what might be interesting?" Howard says. "If people are actually working."

"Good," Stro says. "We'll have Lank [one of the characters] hammering on a sign. That's the first rhythm. Then we'll add seven more rhythms. A saw, sandpaper, banging a shovel."

"Here, everyone take a pen and let's try it," Howard says.

They tap pens on metal folding chairs. First one rhythm begins, then it is joined by another until there are eight.

"Then we're into the rag," Stro says. Howard starts plunking it out and Stro is up on her feet, holding the edge of her skirt in her hands and trying out steps in front of the mirror. "Good. Twenty-eight bars of that," she says. "And it'll be interrupted by the men dancing on the roof. Let's see what we can do with the roof."

Stro and Peterson do some tapping on the corrugated tin. Then they step off and pound their toes on it. Next they try running leaps, dragging one foot across the corrugation.

"The boys'll dance on the roof and then we'll have a challenge dance on the tin of the stage floor," Stro says. "Then we'll get into the xylophone section with Polly playing on the miners' hats. That takes us into the minstrel section. I want a whole stage filled with girls using the mining pans as tambourines."

Howard plays the minstrel version as Stro hits the mining pan on her elbow, her knee, her rear, spins it on her finger and her head, trying out every option.

"Good," she says. "Then we'll use the saw for a transition to get us into stop-time tap with everyone. And then the pickaxes. Full out."

"Let's see what we've got," Howard says.

Stro pops a tape into her boom box.

"This is a taste of 'I Got Rhythm,'" Howard says. And he plays through what they've selected, with Stro singing in the appropriate places, then trying out steps with Peterson in the rag and minstrel sections.

"Well?" Howard says when he's finished.

"It's a start," Stro says.

Six days later Stro is back at this old factory, which was converted into the most complete and popular rehearsal studio in town by Michael Bennett with his earnings from *A Chorus Line*. Though Bennett died from AIDS five years ago, many of the Gypsies still refer to it as "Michael's." Howard has a sketch of the dance arrangement now. As he plays it, Stro and Peterson make some choices on the steps for each section. When they get to the mining pans, Peterson puts his on the floor and starts to tap on it.

Stro's eyes open wide. She likes the sound of the metal taps on the metal pans. She starts tapping on her pan. "We gotta add this section . . . for the boys," she says.

So Howard tries some more variations on the theme—a bolero, a tango, a Mexican hat dance, a march. But they all slow down the pace.

They move on to the pickaxes. Stro takes an ax that the prop department has constructed from balsa wood so it will be light enough to dance with. "Now what can we do with the pickaxes?" she says. "We can rock on them. We can interlock them. We can twirl them. We can do leaps over them." She tries each.

"The pickaxes are a comedown from dancing on the pans," Howard says. "You're not topping yourself."

"We'll think of something to top it," Stro says.

Then actress Karen Ziémba shows up in the room unexpectedly in a pretty cotton dress and heels. Audition clothes. She's been upstairs singing for director Jerry Zaks for the role of Sarah Brown in the planned revival of *Guys and Dolls*. Last week, she says, she was there auditioning for Adelaide. "As usual, I'm a little bit of both," she says.

Stro tells Ziémba that this morning she and Scott Ellis were making a videotape for Music Theatre International, a company that licenses rights to stock and amateur groups, to help such groups do productions of *And the World Goes 'Round*, in which Ziémba is now starring at the Westside Arts Theatre. "I got to 'All That Jazz,'" Stro says. "And I say, 'She mounts the piano.' And they yell, 'Cut! You can't say *she mounts*.' They start the tape again and I say, 'She has a relationship with this piano player. They've had sex or done drugs.' And they yell, 'Cut! You can't say *sex* or *drugs*.' So how was I supposed to explain the number?"

It is fifty years now since Richard Rodgers and Oscar Hammerstein's *Oklahoma!* opened at New York's St. James Theatre on March 31, 1943. That event is generally recognized as the starting point of a new and more mature form of musical theatre in which the song and dance grew out of character and were used as elements of storytelling rather than just as diversions. The integration of song and story was not really a novelty and, in fact, had been well realized by Hammerstein, this show's librettist and lyricist, in *Showboat*, seventeen years earlier. But somehow *Oklahoma!*

seemed to have an effect on everyone else who was creating musicals at the time and looms large as the work that all but eliminated shows in which story was merely an excuse to present songs.

Among the influential storytelling techniques devised for that show was Agnes De Mille's choreography, particularly her "Out of My Dreams" ballet at the end of Act I in which Laurie sorts out her confused feelings about the two men, Curly and Jud, battling for her affections.

The next year, Jerome Robbins, who had become a star dancer with Ballet Theatre in De Mille's *Three Virgins and a Devil*, created a ballet for that company called *Fancy Free*, about three sailors on leave in Manhattan. Betty Comden and Adolph Green, a pair of twenty-nine-year-old performers with a Greenwich Village satirical group called the Revuers, saw the potential for something larger in the ballet, and teamed up with Leonard Bernstein, the twenty-six-year-old wunderkind of the classical-music world, to extend *Fancy Free* into the musical comedy *On the Town*. Less than a year after *Fancy Free* was first performed, *On the Town* opened at the Adelphi Theatre on December 28, 1944. It was directed by the dean of musical-theatre directors of the era, George Abbott, and choreographed by Robbins. For the show, Robbins created two additional storytelling ballets, "Miss Turnstyles" and "Gaby in the Playground of the Rich."

In April of that same season, Rodgers and Hammerstein's next show, *Carousel*, opened at the Majestic Theatre and the curtain rose on Agnes De Mille's nearly ten-minute ballet to Rodgers's "Carousel Waltz" (Has anyone ever written better waltzes than Rodgers?), in which the meeting, flirting, and attraction of the two protagonists, Billy Bigelow and Julie Jordan, that will serve as the basis of the entire story is established without a word of dialogue. Then in the second act of this show, Billy Bigelow stabs himself, arrives in heaven, and is given the chance to peek back down to earth at the daughter he did not live to meet. The ensuing ballet reveals to him, as well as the audience, that the child, Louise, is on a track to make the same mistakes that eventually cost him his life and love.

The confluence of these three hit shows on Broadway grounded theatre dance as an essential and exciting storytelling element of musical theatre.

In 1956, after having choreographed more shows for Abbott and other directors, Robbins assumed the roles of both director and choreographer for *Bells Are Ringing*. He teamed up again with Comden and Green, now writing with composer Jule Styne and for actress Judy Holliday (who had also been a member of the Revuers) on a charming and successful but traditional musical comedy. Then Robbins decided to create his own show in which dance would be an equal element with the words and music in the telling of the story. He had an idea for a contemporary version of Romeo and

Juliet, about Irish and Jewish families in New York City. In collaboration with Bernstein again, and joined by a twenty-seven-year-old lyricist named Stephen Sondheim and librettist Arthur Laurents, they pieced together a story about American and Puerto Rican gang warfare and called it *West Side Story*. The show that opened on September 26, 1957, at the Winter Garden was a thrilling, evening-long dance in which lyrics and dialogue served the dancing.

Over the next few years Robbins went on to direct and choreograph *Gypsy* and *Fiddler on the Roof*, and to restage and thus save *Funny Girl* in the few weeks before its opening. He then departed from theatre work to concentrate on ballet, and left behind the interrelated concepts of the director-choreographer and of dance as a storytelling element woven into a show from its inception.

During the next twenty years of musical theatre, there were four dominant directors—Gower Champion, Bob Fosse, Harold Prince, and Michael Bennett. Of them, only Prince was not also a choreographer. (He was and remains the most important booster of young artists' careers, and worked during this period with choreographers Ron Field [*Cabaret*], Michael Bennett [*Company* and *Follies*], Patricia Birch [*A Little Night Music*, *Pacific Overtures*, and *Candide*], and Larry Fuller [*On the Twentieth Century*, *Sweeney Todd*, and *Evita*].)

For a time in the late 1970s, the Gypsy community seemed to be distributed into teams of the Champion dancers, the Bennett dancers, and the Fosse dancers. Then Champion died of a heart attack on the opening day of his *42nd Street* in December 1980. Bennett died of AIDS in Tucson on July 2, 1987. Fosse died of a heart attack on the opening night of the *Sweet Charity* revival in Washington, D.C., on September 23 of the same year.

At the same time, the collaboration of Stephen Sondheim, the composer-lyricist, and Harold Prince, which had given us *Company*, *Follies*, and *A Little Night Music*, in which dancing was an essential element, created *Pacific Overtures* and *Sweeney Todd*, in which there was much less dancing. And then Sondheim drifted toward new collaborators and works (*Sunday in the Park with George*, *Into the Woods*, and *Assassins*) in which dance played even a smaller role.

With the exception of Gillian Lynne's work in *Cats*, the dancing in the British pop operas of Andrew Lloyd Webber or Alain Boublil and Claude-Michel Schonberg that producer Cameron Mackintosh presented on Broadway and around the world in the past decade was performed mostly by the scenery.

In the 1980s, the only star director-choreographer to emerge was Tommy Tune. As the decade ended, it seemed that he alone would have to keep Broadway dance vital.

Everyone who writes or directs or produces musicals has sat in a production meeting in which someone finally asks, "Who are we going to get to choreograph?" and the room falls silent. Heidi and Rocco Landesman and the Dodgers, the producers of the 1989 *Into the Woods*, even tried the novel strategy of inviting half a dozen choreographers to assemble a group of dancers and stage an audition of material from the planned show, a method the Dodgers used again for their revival of *Guys and Dolls*.

In a society where there are increasingly available forms of leisure-time entertainment, and in an economy where there are fewer and fewer dollars available for the arts, to attract a share of the audience each art form has to take advantage of what is unique about it. You rarely get dancing in the movies or on television, and it doesn't lend itself well to either medium. You don't find characters you have spent time getting to know expressing their emotions through dance in any other dance venue. It's not an accident that the initial use of dance as a storytelling element by De Mille and Robbins coincided with the beginning of American musical theatre's Golden Age.

And so, living in the theatre community in New York, you frequently hear expressed a frustration that dance is playing a diminishing role in the new musicals. You hear people ask time and again, Where are the new choreographers going to come from?

It's 2:35 on Thursday, October 30, and the cast of *Crazy for You*, in the second week of a six-week rehearsal period, strays back in from its lunch break. The stage managers are taping two large rectangles of corrugated aluminum to the floor.

Susan Stroman, in pink and purple with a sweater hanging off her left shoulder, and her green tap shoes, runs a few tap steps in front of the mirror. She stops, lets out a whistle to quiet the company scattered around the large room, and says, "Okay, we're going to start 'I Got Rhythm.' This dance has lots of parts and this is going to be tedious, so just bear with me. The thing I'll do first is teach a lot of the focal points. Then later I'll show you how we're going to put it all together."

"Okay, let's get the boys around the piano." She looks around and can't find something. She runs to the door. "Bonnani!" she yells. John Bonnani, a stage manager, sticks his head in. "I need the hammers and screwdrivers and nails and all the props in here."

As Peter Howard teaches the boys the eight rhythms with the various tools coming in one at a time, the chorus girls sit along the wall in their leotards and beige tap shoes reading *Premiere* and *Vanity Fair*, both with Warren Beatty on the cover. "Okay, let's put it together," Howard says.

The first rhythm, a hammer on a tin sign, begins, and the magazines drop. The other rhythms come in. When Howard cuts them off with the honky-tonk version of the tune, the room erupts in applause.

"Okay, I need the eight girls and Jodi now," Stro says.

Jodi Benson—in a pink-and-gray-patterned leotard, gray skirt, pink leg warmers, and hair piled up on her head—takes her place in a line with the eight chorus girls.

"Everyone learn this step," Stro says, "and then I'll feed you into the number accordingly."

Standing facing the mirror with the dancers behind her, Stro demonstrates the tap combination, slowly at first, then faster and faster as the girls pick it up until, without being cued, Howard pipes in on the piano.

The process of creating a music-theatre dance is not unlike cooking: You begin with your recipe and you prepare each of the ingredients individually, tasting to make sure it's to your liking, veering away from the recipe when necessary. When all the ingredients have been prepared, you add them together little by little, again tasting all the way and making adjustments.

Stro works fast. On some shows, the choreographer and dancers will come in a week before the director and the rest of the company and cook up the dance numbers so that they are ready to be placed in the show as it is blocked. But much of the storytelling in this production is in the dance, and the steps have been designed for the specific characters. So director Mike Ockrent and Stro decided to give the cast the numbers as they occur on the first journey through the script so that the actors will understand how the dances advance the story.

"I only know how to do dancing that grows out of character," Stro says. "I stage the emotion. The hardest thing for me to do is to put a combination of steps together for an audition. I don't have characters, so I don't know how to do it."

In half an hour, Stro has taught the nine girls the thirty-two-bar honky-tonk section. Now they run it, the nine dancers in a row in front of the mirror with Stro and Peterson dancing in front of them. The sound of the taps on the wood floor is loud and exciting in this room, and Stro breaks out in a big smile as she dances.

But the section is not finished. It has been designed as a kind of round, with three dancers beginning the combination and three others entering at a time. Stro breaks the nine girls up into threes and runs it again. The girls don't finish together. Stro looks at Peterson in a confused manner and says, "What's not right?" She walks to the piano and makes a few trims at the end, gives it to the girls, and runs it. This time they finish together. "Okay, to the roof," Stro says.

Peterson goes off to one side with the three boys who will tap on a tin roof. At the same time, Stro takes the three girls and three other boys who will dance on the corrugated tin on the floor. The girls who are not in this section continue to practice the honky-tonk section. The rehearsal pianist runs through the tin dance section. Suddenly, the room is like a three-ring circus, with different sounds and steps scattered about. When the five-minute break required by the Actors' Equity contract is called, the dancing pours out into the hall, with individual dancers lining the thin corridor practicing their own sections.

In all, Stro spends an hour teaching the two tin sections, then turns to the xylophone. In this break between the dancing sections, Benson will stand behind five men in miners' hats and tap on their hats with screwdrivers as the xylophone in the orchestra pit provides the sounds. There's a light on the front of each miners' hat that will be illuminated by pushing a button in the back as Benson strikes that hat.

Stro used lights inside top hats to create an eerie glow on the actors' faces in the "Money, Money, Money" number in *And the World Goes 'Round*. In that show she also had her cast dancing on roller skates and playing banjos. In the Liza Minnelli show, she gave the star a break while the chorus kicked and jumped on and pounded large Japanese *taiko* drums, a number she first created for a musical version of *Sayonara* at New Jersey's Paper Mill Playhouse.

There are voices in the theatre community—almost all nondancers—who criticize Stro's dependence on props. "I was in a Gower Champion show and a Michael Bennett show," Karen Ziémba says. "And Stro's got the best and most interesting steps of all. All the dancers will tell you that."

At 11 the next morning, Halloween, the *Crazy for You* company gathers again for one more day of work on "I Got Rhythm." To get everybody involved, Stro jumps ahead of herself and teaches the capper for the number, a tap section that includes everyone. Scattered around the stage, the members of the ensemble tap their way into a line and put their arms around the waists of the people next to them. Then they all tap their way to the front of the stage with a cross-step. The forward movement stops as the dancers remain in place in the line to tap and clap, then to alternate clapping of their own hands first and then one hand of each person on either side of them. As the company comes dancing toward the mirror, they're all smiles. They like what they see. They know Stro has given them one of those dance moments when the audience can't wait until the end of the number to applaud. Then Stro tops herself, adding a head bob to the left on the beat off the clap at the end.

Two weeks later the whole music department for the show gathers at the rehearsal hall. Howard is joined now by conductor Paul Gemignani and orchestrator Bill Brohn. There's a set of drums beside the piano.

"We need for you to go all the way through 'I Got Rhythm' for Bill Brohn, orchestrator extraordinaire," Stro announces to the company. "So just plow through it all-out and then we may go back to some sections. Make sure all your props are in place."

Brohn says to the drummer, "We'll double all the sound effects in the music parts." Then he switches on a tape recorder and the rehearsal pianist begins. Jodi Benson sings the song leading into the eight percussive rhythms and we're off. The number's like a Disneyland ride—you keep turning corners wondering what you'll see next. Each section tops the last one. She's managed to keep the attention focused on one section while the next one is clandestinely being set up. She's topped the mining-pan dance in the pickax section by creating a circle of girls standing on the axes held by the men and spinning in a Busby Berkeley montage.

Charlie Willard, a company manager on Broadway who taught the structure of musicals at Carnegie-Mellon in Pittsburgh, used to call musicals "energy machines." "The evening is devoted to building up to explosions of music and dance that energize the audience," he said. Stro is trying to create one of those explosions here. This number can't afford just polite applause or the audience will spend the intermission complacent. This is a high-adrenaline number.

As it progresses, the story shines through. Polly sings to Bobby, who is disguised as Zangler, that he's given the whole town rhythm. The boys in town and then the girls join her in dance to prove it. Bobby stands aside, taking it all in until he feels better and gets caught up in it and joins the tapping. When the tapping line forms, he and Polly come together at its center, arms around each other. Then at the end, as a kind of parade of rhythm begins to march in a circle, the real Zangler stumbles into town, having walked four miles through the desert with a large suitcase. He passes out in the center of the stage. Curtain! The audience leaves at intermission buzzing from the excitement of the number and wondering what Bobby will do now that the real Zangler's in town.

"It's terrific," orchestrator Brohn says to director Ockrent.

"I know," Ockrent says. "But how are we going to top it in Act Two?"

Susan Stroman grew up in Wilmington, Delaware, where her father, Charles Stroman, played honky-tonk piano in a downtown bar called Ye Olde Pub. The house Charles shared with his wife, Frances, and their three children was filled with music, usually the old standards. "My parents always made a big fuss over the old romantic movie musicals, especially the Fred Astaire movies," Stro says. "Hermes Pan [who choreographed for Astaire] had the biggest influence on me. He used chairs and hat racks, but his dancers always danced with emotion."

Susan, the Stromans' middle child, began taking dance classes at age five. She began choreographing as a student at John Dickinson High School, where she directed the band, baton twirlers, and kick line through the football halftime shows. "I did what every mother dreads," Stro says. "I developed the routines at home, and so there were all these marks in the ceiling and on the furniture from my tossing anything I could find in the air."

While attending the University of Delaware, Stroman cut her classes one day to go see the pre-Broadway tryout of *Seesaw* at the Wilmington Playhouse.

"I sat in the front row and that day changed my life," she says. "When I saw those girls dancing covered in balloons and then this giant Tommy Tune came out and danced in clogs, I said to myself, I gotta get out of here and do this for real."

Her first audition in New York was for the Goodspeed Opera House's 1974 production of *Hit the Deck*. She got the job and her Equity card. Then she was cast as a Hungarian murderess in the national company of *Chicago*, where she met John Kander and Fred Ebb and had the opportunity to work for Bob Fosse.

"From Fosse I learned that every step is motivated by thought," she says. "A step is a realistic action. It might not always be pretty, but it's an action."

After a year on the road with Gwen Verdon and Chita Rivera in *Chicago*, she was cast as a blond Indian in Goodspeed's revival of the 1928 musical *Whoopee*, originally a vehicle that Florenz Ziegfeld (the model for the character of Bella Zangler) created for Eddie Cantor.

"Though this was a revival," Stro says, "the hope was that it would go to Broadway, and choreographer Dan Siretta approached it like a new show. So I got to see how many departments were affected when the choreographer decided to make a change. The dance arranger; the orchestrator; the copyist; the lighting, scenic, and sound designers; the chorus; the stage manager—it took them all to make a single change."

Stro appeared in a production of *Sweet Charity* in Philadelphia and *Peter Pan* in Cincinnati. Then in 1980 she was hired by director-choreographer Rudy Tronto to appear in and assist him with a Broadway-bound musical called *Musical Chairs*, which was a show about the audience watching a musical. The show opened at the Rialto Theatre on Broadway and played only a week, but Stro met and became friendly with an actor in the company named Scott Ellis. Both she and Ellis were more interested in directing than performing. Stro decided to put performing aside and pursue choreography.

"I was concerned people wouldn't take me seriously," Stro says. "I mean, here I was with this blond-bombshell look and this body. I had to put my hair up, wear suits to cover up my figure, put pencils in my hair, look older and less attractive to be taken seriously."

She staged some industrial shows and some summer stock. Then she collaborated with Ellis for the first time on a production of *Grease*, starring Andrea McArdle, in Philadelphia.

Though she didn't audition for more shows, Stro continued to perform as part of a Fred-and-Ginger-type dance team with Jeff Veazey, whom she had met doing an industrial show and who became her best friend. They performed at nightclubs and were hired by MGM to open at video conventions, where they would burst through a movie screen to "Begin the Beguine."

"The greatest thing in the world to me has always been slow dancing," she says. "A man and a woman touching and moving with each other. It was my favorite thing when I was fourteen or fifteen, and it still is. The pas-de-deux love scene was my favorite moment in *And the World Goes 'Round*. And I get to do that again in 'Shall We Dance' in *Crazy for You*."

In 1989, Veazey died of AIDS. "When he died, I couldn't dance anymore," she says.

Meanwhile, Stro directed two off-Broadway shows, two reviews called *Living Color* and *Broadway Babylon*, and was then hired by Robert Johansen, artistic director at the Paper Mill Playhouse, to choreograph *Sayonara*. "That was the first time I had enough money to work with to really put my vision on the stage," she said. "And I liked it."

But from the 1,400-seat Paper Mill, she went on to collaborate with Scott Ellis and book writer David Thompson on a revival of *Flora, the Red Menace* at the 75-seat Vineyard Theatre on the ground floor of an apartment complex on Manhattan's East Twenty-fourth Street. "I was paid three hundred dollars and working in a hole in the wall and wondered who was going to come see this," she says. "I did it because I wanted to work with Scott. But everyone in town came to see it and it changed my life."

Among the people who came to see it was Harold Prince, who asked Stro to choreograph his production of *Don Giovanni* at the New York City Opera and also recommended Stroman and Ellis to Stephen Sondheim, who was to do *A Little Night Music* there. The collaboration on *Flora* was so enjoyable and successful that Stro, Ellis, and David Thompson suggested to Kander and Ebb that they work together again on a revue of songs from the composer's and lyricist's shows.

Kander and Ebb, two very modest people, wondered if anyone would be interested in such a show. But they gave their blessing to their young collaborators, whom they adored. *And the World Goes 'Round* opened at the Whole Theatre Company in Bloomfield, New Jersey, half an hour from Manhattan and promptly became required viewing for the commercial producers looking for material to bring to Manhattan. The day after Prince saw this show, he spent half an hour describing it number by number to the staff in his office. He soon asked Stro to choreograph a stage version of Manuel Puig's novel *Kiss of the Spider Woman* at a new developmental theatre called New Musicals, providing her with another opportunity to work with Kander and Ebb. When that show was reviewed prematurely by uninvited critics, everyone took it hard, Stro the hardest of all. She had been on a roll. Her career had been picking up steam. "Here I had the chance to work with my idols and it turned awful," she said. She seemed to take personal responsibility for the bad reviews. Driving Kander and Ebb up to the Westchester theatre in a rented car, she would have to pull over to the side of the road because she felt sick.

At the same time, she was having a rough go with her live-in boyfriend, Michael Maguire, who had won a Tony Award in 1987 playing the student leader in *Les Misérables* on Broadway. While Stroman was flitting from show to show, Maguire was having a difficult time finding satisfying work. He was spending a good deal of his time in Los Angeles, where work in general was more plentiful, but not for him.

Soon after the *Kiss* production closed, the relationship ended. Then Stro had to begin rehearsals for *A Little Night Music*, in which Maguire had been cast. "It was a year I plan to forget," Stro says. But at opening night of *Night Music*, as the audience at the New York State Theater stood and cheered, Sondheim, Ellis, and Stroman took a curtain call and Sondheim said to his young collaborators, "Don't ever forget this because it's not always like this."

To revive her spirits, Stro buried herself in her work. "It obsesses me," she says. "People sometimes ask me what music I listen to at home. The answer is none. When I hear music I immediately see pictures of sailors or girls dancing. Music is not relaxing for me. I'm in the gynecologist's office and there's music, and my brain just starts moving. It exhausts me."

She choreographed the Liza Minnelli show, which was directed by Fred Ebb; along with *World Goes 'Round* and *Night Music*, this gave her three pieces playing simultaneously in Manhattan. Mike Ockrent came to New York from London to begin work on *Crazy for You*, took the opportunity to see Stro's work, and hired her for her Broadway debut.

★ ★ ★

Stro stands at the back of the National Theater in Washington, D.C., at 7:41 on December 12 as the first audience that will ever see *Crazy for You* wanders in. She wears a red blazer and slacks and black-and-white heels and the tiny smile she sports when she's nervous.

Tonight's audience appears to consist largely of young people in suits (both the men and women) from the government offices that surround this theatre for blocks on all sides. There are no people from the New York theatre community here, except for those involved with the production. This will save the show from the vicious gossip that spreads like chicken pox in a kindergarten class when you preview in New York.

"I don't know what you're gonna see tonight," Stro says. "For the past two weeks since we've been down here all we've been concentrating on is the lights and scenery and sound and some rewriting of the second act. I just have to wait for my turn."

But the show gets off to a smooth start and has a certain professional confidence about it from the get-go. Then seven or eight minutes in, Harry Groener as Bobby Childs, a rich boy who wants to be a dancer, is bookended by the mother and fiancée who want him to be something he isn't. A chauffeured car pulls onto the stage, the three actors get in the back, and then Bobby reappears via an elevator on the roof of the car singing and dancing to "I Can't Be Bothered Now." He dances his way down the car, hears a knock, and opens the hood to find a chorus girl all in pink. She then opens the car door as a stream of seven more girls in pink appear in a takeoff on the old circus-clowns-in-the-Volkswagen routine, and he lives out his dancing fantasy in a number that sets the mood for the rest of the evening and energizes the audience. Now they know that the vernacular of this show is romantic fantasy. From the length of the number, they know that dancing will not get short shrift in this production.

A few scenes later, Bobby has arrived in Dead Rock, Nevada, to foreclose on the theatre whose mortgage is held by his family's bank. He has seen Polly (Jodi Benson) and fallen for her at first sight. (This is a 1990s look at a 1930s musical, after all.) Sitting in the town's saloon, Bobby offers himself to Polly and she cockily rejects him in "Could You Use Me?" Then, as the tempo of the music accelerates, she storms out of the bar through the swinging doors and he follows. In a thrilling theatrical moment that had to be conceived months ago, before the sets were designed, the saloon moves in the opposite direction from Groener, disappearing without losing a beat and leaving the couple on the street, where he seduces her in song and dance. The song is "Shall We Dance?," once performed by Fred Astaire and Ginger Rogers, and choreographed by Hermes Pan in the motion picture of the same name. This is Stro's tribute to her childhood inspiration, with Groener inviting Benson to "dance," meeting resistance at first, then pulling her into it and whirling her around the entire stage in a burst of budding romance until they go off into the sunset.

"This whole show has been my dream of a collaboration," Stro says. "Mike Ockrent's way of working is that no decisions are made unless we're all in the room—Mike, Ken Ludwig [the book writer], the three designers, and I. We all plan every aspect of the production together. Last week we all sat in a room discussing the rewrite of Act Two. It's this process that allows things like the transition from 'Could You Use Me?' to 'Shall We Dance?' to happen."

The act unfolds without mishap. There is one priceless physical comedy gag that Ockrent will cut tonight because of the show's length and that will never be seen again: Benson is cranking out handbills for the show on a hand-operated printing press with a mind of its own that refuses to stop printing. Groener tries to stop the machine, but the press keeps going faster until it starts lifting off the table and neighing like a horse. Groener finally must mount it like a bucking bronco and ride it until it stops.

Then the plot turns as Benson discovers that Groener has been sent here to foreclose on the theatre and walks out on him. To win her back, Groener disguises himself as Zangler and offers to put on a show, which brings us into "I Got Rhythm." Benson sings it, the rhythms start, and then the number takes off as the nine girls with Benson in front tap-dance the honky-tonk section. The number seems to lose its confidence a bit with the dancing on the tin, the xylophone section is flat, and when the Rhythm Kings play the saw and tire pump and plunger, they are blocked from the audience by the girls around them. The minstrel dance with the mining pans gets applause from the audience. Then the energy level dips with the Hungarian section and rises again with the men tapping on the pans. When the company taps its way into a line and taps forward with the cross-step, you can feel everyone around you in the audience coming forward in their seats. The applause starts even before they get to the head nod. When the song ends with one more chorus sung by the whole company, a touchdown cheer erupts from the audience as the first-act curtain falls.

"It's different looking at dances from above at the rehearsal hall and then from below in the theatre," Stro says at intermission. "A lot of the pictures don't work for me so I'll make adjustments."

The second act doesn't end until 11:15. In New York, this would give rise to rumors that the show was in trouble. Here in Washington, the audience gives the show a standing ovation.

At 1:45 in the morning, Ockrent, Ludwig, scenic designer Robin Wagner, costume designer William Ivey Long, lighting designer Paul Gallo, and Stro are still sitting at the bar of the Washington Marriott planning changes and fixes. The waitress informs them that the bar will be closing. Ockrent announces that they will resume in his hotel room at 8:30 the next morning.

Ten weeks later, Stro and Ken Ludwig stand in the corridor leading to the bathrooms on the upper floor of the Supper Club on West Forty-seventh Street in Manhattan. She's in a very short, body-hugging, pink-spangled dress. He's in a tuxedo. Guests heading for the bathroom at this party celebrating the opening night of *Crazy for You* in New York see Ludwig holding the next morning's *Times* and clamor for a peek over his shoulder. The huddle grows. When Stro emerges from it, her eye makeup is streaking down her face at the same time that she wears a big, pretty smile.

"It's unbelievable," she says. And she grabs on to me and hugs me with all her might and cries on my shoulder.

"When future historians try to find the exact moment at which Broadway finally rose up to grab the musical back from the British, they just may conclude that the revolution began last night," Frank Rich wrote in the *Times*. "The shot was fired at the Shubert Theatre, where a riotously entertaining show called *Crazy for You* uncorked the American musical's classic blend of music, laughter, dancing, sentiment and showmanship with a freshness and confidence rarely seen during the *Cats* decade."

He continued: "Ms. Stroman's dances do not comment on such apparent influences as Fred Astaire, Hermes Pan, and Busby Berkeley so much as reinvent them. Rather than piling on exhausting tap routines to steamroll the audience into enjoying itself, the choreographer uses the old forms in human proportions, to bring out specific feelings in the music and lyrics. . . .

"Short of George Balanchine's *Who Cares?* at the New York City Ballet, I have not seen a more imaginative choreographic response to Gershwin onstage."

In *Newsday*, Linda Winer wrote: "If this quasi-revival, inspired by the 1930 *Girl Crazy*, is remembered for nothing else—which is unlikely—it will be marked as the show that added a new name, Susan Stroman, to the shriveled roster of choreographers who can get Broadway moving again."

Broadway had finally found itself a new star choreographer.

MARTIN BECK THEATRE

A JUJAMCYN THEATER

ROCCO LANDESMAN
PRESIDENT

JAMES H. BINGER
CHAIRMAN

MARTIN RICHARDS

MARY LEA JOHNSON   SAM CROTHERS

SANDER JACOBS   KENNETH D. GREENBLATT

PARAMOUNT PICTURES

JUJAMCYN THEATERS

in association with PATTY GRUBMAN and MARVIN A. KRAUSS

present

Grand
HOTEL
THE MUSICAL

Songs by

ROBERT WRIGHT and GEORGE FORREST

Book by

LUTHER DAVIS

Based on VICKI BAUM'S "GRAND HOTEL"
by arrangement with TURNER ENTERTAINMENT CO.,
owner of the motion picture "GRAND HOTEL"

The Company
(in alphabetical order)

KAREN AKERS
JENNIFER LEE ANDREWS
DAVID CARROLL
KEITH CROWNINGSHIELD
GERRIT de BEER
PIERRE DULAINE
DAVID ELLEDGE
BEN GEORGE
HENRY GROSSMAN
REX D. HAYS

SUZANNE HENDERSON
DAVID JACKSON
MITCHELL JASON
KEN JENNINGS
J.J. JEPSON
TIMOTHY JEROME
MICHAEL JETER
JANE KRAKOWSKI
CHARLES MANDRACCHIA
YVONNE MARCEAU

MICHEL MOINOT
LILIANE MONTEVECCHI
KATHI MOSS
LYNNETTE PERRY
HAL ROBINSON
WILLIAM RYALL
BOB STILLMAN
DANNY STRAYHORN
WALTER WILLISON
JOHN WYLIE

Production Associate
KATHLEEN RAITT

General Manager
JOEY PARNES

Associate Producers
SANDRA GREENBLATT   MARTIN R. KAUFMAN   KIM POSTER

Casting
JULIE HUGHES and BARRY MOSS, CSA

Hair Design
WERNER SHERER

General Press
Representative
JUDY JACKSINA

Musical Coordinator
JOHN MONACO

Musical
and Vocal Direction
JACK LEE

Music Supervision
& Additional Music
WALLY HARPER

Associate Director
BRUCE LUMPKIN

Orchestrations
PETER MATZ

Costume Design
SANTO LOQUASTO

Lighting Design
JULES FISHER

Sound Design
OTTS MUNDERLOH

Setting Design
TONY WALTON

Directed and Choreographed by

TOMMY TUNE

PREVIEWS

"Time Is Running Out"

★

PETER STONE (*Book*) won a Tony Award, the Drama Critics Circle Award, and the Drama Desk Award for his musical *1776*; another Tony for the musical *Woman of the Year*; an Academy Award for his screenplay of *Father Goose*; an Emmy Award for an episode of "The Defenders"; and the Mystery Writers of America Award for his film *Charade*. His other Broadway credits include the musicals *My One and Only*, *Sugar*, *Two by Two*, *Kean*, and *Skyscraper*; and his adaptation of Erich Maria Remarque's *Full Circle*. Among his many films are *Sweet Charity*, *Mirage*, *Arabesque*, *The Taking of Pelham 1-2-3*, and *Who's Killing the Great Chefs of Europe?* He is currently president of the Dramatists Guild.

As the 1991–92 season began, there were two holdover shows from the previous two seasons—*Grand Hotel* and *The Will Rogers Follies*—that were often linked together in conversation among people on the street as "the Tommy Tune shows." Tune, both the tallest song-and-dance man in town and its only star director-choreographer at the moment, has such a powerful presence that following the 1990 Tony Awards, when he won both Best Director and Best Choreographer for *Grand Hotel*, the producers of that show chose to use his image in its print-advertising campaign, even though he was not on the stage when you got to the theatre. In addition to Tune's role as director-choreographer, what the two shows shared were a design team—Tony Walton (sets) and Jules Fisher (lights)—and a book writer, Peter Stone. You will find all their names and bios in the *Playbill* for *Will Rogers*, but you will not find any mention of Stone in the program for *Grand Hotel*.

When you are ill, you call a doctor. When a musical is sick, the producers do the same thing. The only difference is that in the theatre world doctors still make house calls. In the early fall of 1989, two weeks after *Grand Hotel* had opened to poor reviews at the Colonial Theatre in Boston, Tune realized he could not fix the show with the writing talent that originally created it, so he summoned Peter Stone. Tune had been in an identical situation in the same theatre six years earlier with *My One and Only*, in which he also starred. He had summoned Stone, and the result was a show that ran on Broadway for two years. This emergency call for *Grand Hotel* would end up producing the same result. Though the original book writer on the show, Luther Davis, maintained sole writing credit and received the Tony nomination that season in his category, he had no further input into the show for the final eight weeks between the time Stone came on board and the Broadway opening.

A few years ago there was that joke circulating about the dumb starlet who wanted to get ahead in Hollywood so she slept with the screenwriter. Were the joke told about Broadway, the object of her misplaced ambition would have been the musical's book writer. Book writing is the Rodney Dangerfield job on a musical. Shows are always identified as the possessions of the individual or team who wrote the score (Bock and Harnick's *Fiddler on the Roof*), or the director ("the Tommy Tune musical"), but never has a musical been described by linking its title and book writer. And yet, when musicals *don't* work, the most frequently heard reason is book problems.

Let's try to settle that one once and for all here, because it's just a lot of bunk. You see a show and the music's charming and the sets are pretty and the cast is talented and the dancing is fun, but the show doesn't work—so the problem has to be the book, right? Wrong! What good is a charming song or a pretty set that doesn't serve the book? The goal here is not to write hummable tunes or paint pretty pictures; it's to tell a story. Storytelling is not the task of the book writer alone—it's also the job of the composer, lyricist, director, designers, actors, and everyone else involved with the production. Every element is there to help tell the story. When a show fails, it is because the storytelling is not good enough. The book writer alone hasn't failed—the collaboration has failed.

Fallacious as it may be, this public wisdom makes the occupation of writing books for musicals an unappealing and underpopulated one. My kid has a lot of friends who want to be actors or musicians, but I've never heard one say he or she wants to be a book writer someday. Of course, all of us who put on shows receive a steady flow of unsolicited manuscripts in the mail, which indicates there are folks out there somewhere trying to do this, but they must be people so frustrated in their real jobs that even writing books for musicals seems appealing.

Peter Stone is a one-man army defending the importance and dignity of musical-theatre book writers—and defending it loudly, which is his style. He is also the only person in our country today who for the past fifteen years has made his living solely and continually by writing books for new musicals. That sounds like a gross exaggeration, but it happens to be true.

Stone had other options in his professional life that could have saved him from slumming in musical theatre. While in his twenties he won an Emmy Award for an episode of "The Defenders," and he hung out in Paris with Cary Grant and Audrey Hepburn as they filmed his first screenplay, *Charade*. But after shuttling among the various media for a while, he settled in the musical theatre because he found the process of creating a show the most exhilarating. The best way to explain the choice is to see him at work, both as a doctor and an original-book writer.

In 1958 a new musical called *At the Grand* opened at the Los Angeles Civic Light Opera as a pre-Broadway engagement. It was based on the classic 1932 MGM melodrama *Grand Hotel*, starring Greta Garbo, John Barrymore, Lionel Barrymore, Joan Crawford, and Wallace Beery, that had been adapted from Vicki Baum's melodramatic novel. The musical had a book by Luther Davis, and the first totally original score by Richard Forrest and Robert Wright, who had had previous success adapting classical music and adding lyrics to create a Broadway score (Borodin for *Kismet* and Grieg for *Song of Norway*). The raison d'être for the adaptation was the presence of movie star Paul Muni, who was making his musical-theatre debut as Kringelein, a man who comes to steep himself in the opulence of Berlin's Grand Hotel before he dies. Muni became seriously ill during the run and the show never made it beyond California.

Wright and Forrest's next original score was for a 1961 musical called *Kean*, about the life of actor Edmund Kean, and based on plays by Alexandre Dumas and Jean-Paul Sartre. The book writer on that show was a rookie at the craft named Peter Stone. The show, which played for seventy-seven performances at the Broadway Theatre, starred Alfred Drake, previously the star of *Oklahoma!*, *Kismet*, and *Kiss Me Kate*, and, like Mary Martin, John Raitt, and Ethel Merman, a box-office attraction strictly because of the work he had done on Broadway—a cultural phenomenon that no longer exists.

"I knew the old *At the Grand*," Stone says. "I never saw it, but I had the score played for me by Wright and Forrest, and I had read the book. But this was thirty years ago. Then I hear that Tommy is smitten with it and wants to do it. I can't believe it's the old *At the Grand* because I don't know what the hell Tommy is going to do with it in 1989. But it turns out it is, and I'm invited to a run-through at the Diplomat Hotel in Manhattan before the show heads for Boston. I didn't know what was going on. It was very hodge-podge. The book had become old-fashioned. I had to tell Tommy what I thought, and so I did: Tommy's concept was fighting the original show. Tommy was doing it the 1989 way, and the book and score were still a 1958 musical. They had written a traditional linear show with one scene following the other in very distinct settings. Tommy had a unit set with no moving pieces and all the actors sitting on chairs on the side throughout the evening, and the whole show was like a nonstop march through the hotel. I told him that whatever he was interested in wasn't really there in what he had. What Tommy really liked was the Vicki Baum novel, and he kept trying to force the show back to that book.

"It was odd because my stepfather had been Vicki Baum's agent and had sold it to MGM, and I had met Vicki Baum a couple of times.

"And so off they go to Boston and they get very bad reviews. Two weeks later I get a call asking if I'll come up and see it. It turns out that things had turned very awkward up there. Tommy had persuaded the three writers to sign a piece of paper that said they would not come to rehearsal. During that time Tommy was putting things into the show mostly from the original novel."

The essence of the Dramatists Guild contract is that writers own the copyright on their work and no changes can be made without their permis-

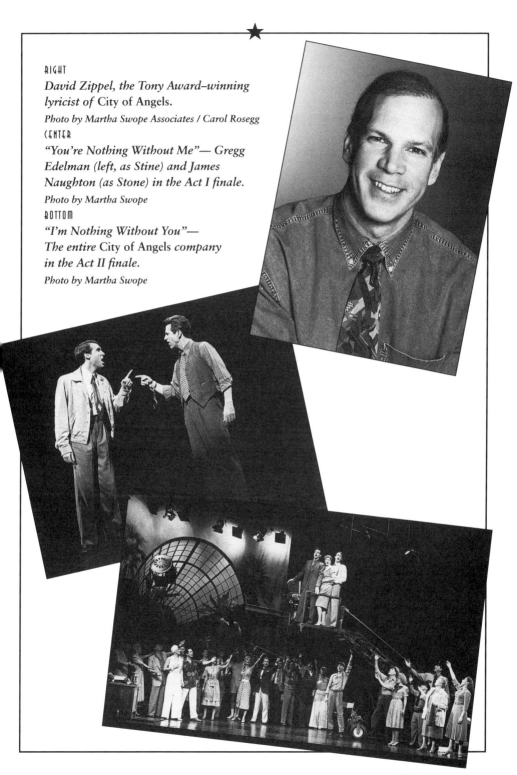

RIGHT
*David Zippel, the Tony Award–winning
lyricist of* City of Angels.
Photo by Martha Swope Associates / Carol Rosegg
CENTER
*"You're Nothing Without Me"— Gregg
Edelman (left, as Stine) and James
Naughton (as Stone) in the Act I finale.*
Photo by Martha Swope
BOTTOM
*"I'm Nothing Without You"—
The entire* City of Angels *company
in the Act II finale.*
Photo by Martha Swope

TOP
Stephen Bogardus as Whizzer in Falsettos *at Broadway's Golden Theatre.*
Photo by Martha Swope Associates / Carol Rosegg

CENTER
Michael Rupert (left, as Marvin), Bogardus, and the lesbians from next door (Heather MacRae and Carolee Carmello) sing "Four Unlikely Lovers."
Photo by Martha Swope Associates / Carol Rosegg

BOTTOM
Bogardus and Rupert, who worked together in Falsettos *for eleven years.*
Photo by Martha Swope Associates / Carol Rosegg

Composer Stephen Flaherty (right) and lyricist Lynn Ahrens (center) catch up with director Ron Lagomarsino during a break from rehearsing the workshop of My Favorite Year.

Photo by Joan Marcus

The finale of the production of My Favorite Year *at the Vivian Beaumont Theater at Lincoln Center.*

Photo by Joan Marcus

LEFT
Margo Lion, producer of Jelly's Last Jam.
Photo by Martha Swope
CENTER
George C. Wolfe (right) directs Gregory Hines in rehearsals for Jelly's Last Jam *at 890 Broadway.*
Photo by Martha Swope
BOTTOM
Gregory Hines (as Jelly Roll Morton) seduces Tonya Pinkins (as Anita) in a daring scene from Jelly's Last Jam *at the Virginia Theatre.*
Photo by Martha Swope

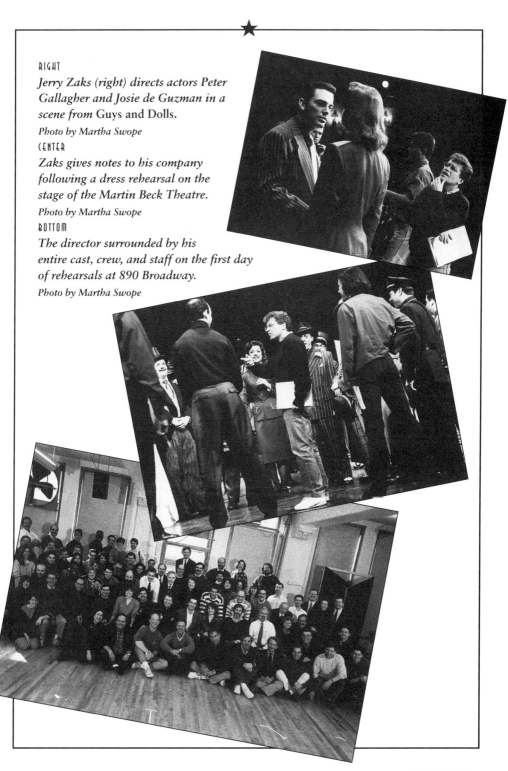

RIGHT
*Jerry Zaks (right) directs actors Peter
Gallagher and Josie de Guzman in a
scene from* Guys and Dolls.
Photo by Martha Swope
CENTER
*Zaks gives notes to his company
following a dress rehearsal on the
stage of the Martin Beck Theatre.*
Photo by Martha Swope
BOTTOM
*The director surrounded by his
entire cast, crew, and staff on the first day
of rehearsals at 890 Broadway.*
Photo by Martha Swope

Milton Craig Nealy (in glasses)
as Four-Eyed Moe, with the Other Moes
(front to back: Kevin Ramsey, Glenn Turner,
Jeffrey D. Sams, and Doug Eskew),
at the Eugene O'Neill Theatre.
Photo by Joan Marcus

RIGHT
Susan Stroman, Tony Award–winning choreographer of Crazy for You.

CENTER
Stroman and her dancing partner, Jeff Veazey.

BOTTOM
The national company of Crazy for You *taps and claps the Act I finale, "I've Got Rhythm."*
Photo by Joan Marcus

LEFT

Peter Stone, book writer and Broadway's most frequently called-upon show doctor.

CENTER

The "Time is running out" scene from the opening number of Grand Hotel *at the Martin Beck Theatre (left to right: Jane Krakowski, Timothy Jerome, Michael Jeter, Karen Akers, and David Carroll).*
Photo by Martha Swope

BOTTOM

Keith Carradine (on the rope), as Will Rogers, and the company perform the finale of The Will Rogers Follies.
Photo by Martha Swope

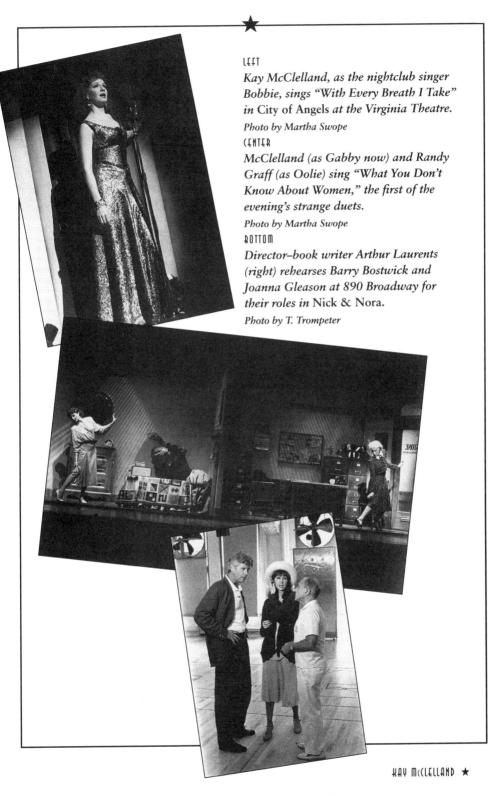

LEFT

Kay McClelland, as the nightclub singer Bobbie, sings "With Every Breath I Take" in City of Angels *at the Virginia Theatre.*

Photo by Martha Swope

CENTER

McClelland (as Gabby now) and Randy Graff (as Oolie) sing "What You Don't Know About Women," the first of the evening's strange duets.

Photo by Martha Swope

BOTTOM

Director–book writer Arthur Laurents (right) rehearses Barry Bostwick and Joanna Gleason at 890 Broadway for their roles in Nick & Nora.

Photo by T. Trompeter

KAY McCLELLAND ★

TOP

Graciela Daniele choreographs Dangerous Games.

Photo by Martha Swope

CENTER

"We Dance"—The Company of Once on This Island *performs the opening number onstage at Broadway's Booth Theatre.*

Photo by Martha Swope

RIGHT

"We Dance II"—Graciela Daniele at the opening-night party for the Broadway production of Once on This Island.

Photo by Martha Swope

RIGHT

*In the afternoon, Karen Ziémba (with
Bob Cuccioli) performs "Arthur in the
Afternoon" in* And the World Goes 'Round
at the Westside Theatre off-Broadway.
Photo by Joan Marcus

BOTTOM

*That evening, Ziémba (as Clio) joins Lara
Teeter (as Herman) as they strut their way
through "Dallas" in* The Most Happy
Fella *at the New York City Opera.*
Photo by Martha Swope Associates / Carol Rosegg

TOP

*Kevin Gray as the Phantom in
the national touring company of*
The Phantom of the Opera *at the
Kennedy Center in Washington.*

Photo by Joan Marcus

BOTTOM

*Gray, as Raoul, with Rebecca Luker,
in the Broadway production of*
Phantom *at the Majestic Theatre.*

Photo by Bob Marshak

TOP, BOTTOM
*Twelve-year-old Lydia Ooghe
as Mary Lennox in two scenes from
The Secret Garden.*
Photos by Martha Swope Associates / Carol Rosegg

TOP, BOTTOM

Metropolitan Opera star Spiro Malas in his Broadway debut as Tony in The Most Happy Fella *at the Booth Theatre.*

Photos by Martha Swope

TOP
*Actress Marlene Danielle, who has been in
the company of* Cats *since it opened at the
Winter Garden Theatre in 1982.*

BOTTOM
*Danielle (left) as Bombalurina performs
"McCavity, the Mystery Cat."*
Photo by Martha Swope

LEFT
*Faith Prince (as Miss Adelaide) performs
"A Bushel and a Peck" in* Guys and Dolls
at Broadway's Martin Beck Theatre.
Photo by Martha Swope
CENTER
*Prince and her costar, Nathan Lane, as
Nathan Detroit, to whom Adelaide has
been engaged for fourteen years.*
Photo by Martha Swope
BOTTOM
Prince and the company of Guys and
Dolls *perform the finale on
Tony Award–winning set designer Tony
Walton's fantasy of Broadway.*
Photo by Martha Swope

sion. In movies and television, the production company owns the copyright and can make changes in the material or replace the writers at whim. In the theatre, whatever the condition of a show, a producer cannot replace a writer or bring in outside help without the writer's consent. Stone has been the president of the Dramatists Guild for the past decade and an activist in protecting an author's rights. It is an awkward role to combine with being the most-often-called-upon show doctor of this era.

"The first thing I did was have lunch with Luther Davis," Stone says. "I said, Look, you know what's going on. You know the show is failing, and you know it's probably going to close unless they can effect some kind of changes. But you have the right not to have them effect any changes.

"Now this was a particularly complicated situation because the writers on this show had signed a substandard contract with the producers. The three of them could have been drummed out of the guild. So I said, The guild would be behind you whatever you choose to do, but you haven't got a guild contract here. You've got no real guild protection because you didn't sign a guild minimum contract."

At the same time Stone was asked to come in and work on the book, composer-lyricist Maury Yeston, who had written the score for *Nine*, which Tune had directed, was asked to help make improvements in the score. Stone had a meeting with Wright and Forrest, who agreed to step aside so that Yeston could do the work Tune needed. But Davis refused to agree to relinquish his role as book writer.

"He said, 'This is what I want,'" Stone recalls. "'I can't go to rehearsal. So you go to rehearsal and find out what Tommy wants, then you come report to me and I'll write it.' I said, 'I'm not doing anything unless you guys bring your contracts up to the standard. I'm not working on a substandard show.' And so a standard deal was subsequently signed.

"Then for the first couple of days what I did was go to rehearsal, and then go back to Luther's place to tell him what was going on. But no new writing was being done. I had to look at the show for a while anyway just to get a sense of what had to be done. One of the biggest problems to me was the love story, which was the core of the show. It had been cast with Liliane Montevecchi as the ballerina, and David Carroll, who is much younger, as the count who becomes her lover. But almost no reference was made to their ages. It wasn't mentioned in the script that she was old enough to be his mother. Completely unacknowledged. My theory has always been when you fix a show you start in the middle and you work out in both directions. And the love scene between them was the center of the show. So on the very last day in Boston, Maury and I met in the ladies' room of the Colonial, a wonderful lounge with murals and a piano, and in about forty minutes we wrote the love scene and the song to go with it. The whole concept of that scene was a very young man and an older, very experienced woman. That's what the scene had to be about.

"Then the show closed in Boston and went back into a very short rehearsal period in New York, followed by a longer period of previews. What I decided to do was to make no changes at all outside the theatre. Not a word was written anywhere else. Every idea came during rehearsal; it was discussed right there by Tommy and me right in front of the cast, and then we made the changes.

"The biggest change we made was in the structure of the show. As I said, the original script was very linear with scene following scene. What we did was intercut many of the scenes so that things were happening simultaneously. At times we had three different things running on the stage in three different places with the dialogue interspersed. Not a hard thing to do. You just have to sit down for a minute, put the scenes side by side, and find the places where they interrelate. This made it feel like a contemporary show and made the scenic concept of a single set work. It was the show Tommy had always had in his head.

"One of the specific changes was to take the doctor in the show and make him a much more important character. He straightened things out for the audience, set scenes a little bit. I used him to start the show with a very hard edge that set the tone. In the novel he was a drug addict. So I had the show open with him injecting himself with morphine.

"Second, we refocused the whole ending. In Boston, the ending was focused on the tragedy of the ballerina when the count, her young lover, dies. What I did was take the story that was more optimistic—the Kringelein story—and make that the final statement of the show.

"A lot of this was really just smoke and mirrors. We were hiding the parts of the show that didn't work and highlighting the parts that did. And focusing and simplifying.

"Maury wrote a whole new opening number, a title song for the show that introduced everyone. In the beginning of the show there were these five telephone conversations with each of the main characters that let you know they were in trouble. Tommy had put the five together, run them simultaneously. Now the conversations were placed in the middle of Maury's number, but there was no reason for them to be happening together, no theme for them. So I took the simple phrase 'Time is running out,' taking it from the idea that time was running out in Germany— you're about to get Hitler—time is running out on the twenties, time is running out on prosperity, time is running out on everything. In those phone conversations, the characters each have a reason to use that phrase.

Time was running out on the young girl Flaemmchen's chance to do anything about her pregnancy; time was running out on Kringelein's life; on the count's debts; on the ballerina's career; on the businessman's proxy vote to keep his company. Suddenly, because of that phrase, it was one scene. It's these little threads that can sometimes pull a disjointed musical together.

"Doing it this way, we had no time to make mistakes. And there was no protocol. Go tell the actors; go do that, go do this; stop him in the middle; wait, that's not working; stop, we have to change it. Everything very free and easy and there was a lot of give-and-take and no ego. There are a lot of directors who say you can't do this in front of the actors, you'll scare them. But Tommy didn't have that problem.

"Tommy and I had no problem with disagreeing in public. When something wasn't working for either of us, we would just stop the action and sit down together and talk it out. If we could come up with something, we put it in. If not, we left it to come back to.

"There was no writing at night because there was no night. We were working those eighteen-hour days in the theatre when you start early in the morning and work after the performance."

Peter Stone and Tommy Tune began a working relationship in 1981 when Tune was brought to Boston to fix some of Tony Charmoli's dances for *Woman of the Year*. Stone wrote that show in collaboration with John Kander and Fred Ebb as a vehicle for Lauren Bacall.

"Kander and Ebb and I had liked Tommy's work on *Seesaw* and *The Best Little Whorehouse in Texas*. He was in London at the time, and I called to see when he was returning. He showed up at the theatre on the midnight separating my birthday from his. That was the first time I had ever met him.

"And then two years later, Sam Cohn at ICM [International Creative Management] became my agent. The very first thing that he did, literally, was to send Mike Nichols and me to Boston to look at *My One and Only*. This was halfway through its run up there."

The show was a rethinking of the 1927 Gershwin musical *Funny Face*, using the score but nothing else. "Peter Sellars had been the director," Stone says. "During the week before performances started, he evidently had some kind of nervous block because he couldn't finish the technical rehearsals. He couldn't get through the show. Sellars was let go three days before the show opened.

"It was a disaster. Nothing was working. The concept, above all, was not working. It was very hard to describe because it was a neo-Brechtian, socioeconomic pageant using the trappings of an old Gershwin show. Tim Mayer had written the book and it was terribly disjointed. There was a narrator who was played by Miss Sweden. Very, very beautiful, but her part was awful.

"Before I arrived, Nichols had gone up there before the opening and in twenty-four hours had removed about a third of the show, cleaned it out: scenes, numbers, Miss Sweden—all gone. He was trying to get to the bare bones. It opened, it was a disaster, and Nichols went home thinking he had ruined something, feeling very despondent.

"Now Tommy Tune, who was starring in the show, took over and became the driving force. Every night at the curtain call, Tommy would speak for five or six minutes to the audience, apologizing for the condition of the show. Then Nichols and I went up together and an odd thing happened: We fell in love with certain elements of the show—Twiggy, specifically. Both Nichols and I felt she was truly captivating and talented and interesting. We loved Tommy, we loved some of the other characters. We loved the Gershwin score. We loved the idea of the all-black male chorus and the all-white female chorus. We loved Adrian Lobell's scenic design, which was very original in its concept.

"So Nichols and I sat and talked for days and days. Not about the show. About everything else on earth except the show. We talked about our lives, other people, Paris, Hollywood. We went to see the show every night, then went out and talked about everything except the show. We were getting to know each other. Finally we said, What are we going to do about this? Do we want to do it? And he said, I love him, I love her, I love the songs, I love the cast, I love the sets—what do we do? And I said, Well, why don't we write a complete new book using all of the things we've got and see what happens.

"So then we went to Paramount—Barry Diller was the main person—and asked what they intended to do as producers. They said they were closing it. Nichols and I said, We have an idea. We'll make you a deal. We'll work for free. We'll rewrite the book completely and you put the show back into rehearsal. At the end of ten days, you come back and look at what we've done. If you like it, you'll put up another million and a half bucks and we'll go forward, and if you don't, you close it then and there. We said, You already have three million bucks in the show and this way you have a chance of saving it. And they agreed.

"So we came back to New York and started this very strange process. I would work on new scenes all night, then bring them to Nichols, who was cutting his *Silkwood* picture, in the morning. We'd discuss the scene, make some changes, then deliver it to Tune at noon at the rehearsal studio, where he would put it in. A scene a day, and we never saw what we wrote because Nichols was cutting and I was writing.

"I always start with the center of the show, the core. And after talking with Nichols for a long time, we decided to make the core of the show, in terms of structure, the Honi Coles character.

"A musical is all structure. When the structure works, the show works; when the structure doesn't work, the show doesn't work. That's what book writing really is. It's not dialogue, it's structure. You could have the greatest score in the world, but if the structure doesn't work . . . *Follies* is a good example. Sondheim's score is about as good as you're ever gonna have. Hal Prince and Michael Bennett staged the shit out of it. But if the book isn't functional, I don't care how good the score is. Yet, you could do a show where the book works and the score doesn't, and you can still have a hit.

"Anyway, Honi Coles had been playing several parts in the show. He played some kind of dope runner, something Cuban, and a character where you only saw his feet—Mr. Red Shoes, he was called—and then in the second act he was the captain of a ship from some island. But we liked him and said, Let's make him into some kind of fable character. We named him Mr. Magix. There had been four barber chairs in the original show. It had opened with the four richest men in the world—Vanderbilt, Astor, Carnegie, and Rockefeller—in the barber chairs. So I said, Let me use the barber chairs. Let me make it a barber shop uptown where Mr. Magix remakes people. So we plant Mr. Magix in one of those barber chairs. When Tommy comes in to ask for advice on how to get the girl, we'll put him in the other barber chair. And for the whole first act, Honi Coles just sits there in the barber chair. Tommy said, Are you crazy? We have the best tap dancer in the world, and he's *sitting*? And I said, That's it! Then in the second act, Tommy comes back to see Mr. Magix again, to get more advice, and Honi asks to see Tommy dance. Finally, Mr. Magix says, No, no, no, no, and he looks at the audience and says, 'Oh, Lord, this boy's gonna make me get up out of this chair.' And the audience will go wild. They've been waiting for him to dance all night. Mr. Magix was the good fairy, he was Tinker Bell, and once we had that, we had the structure."

With the new concept of the show, the *Funny Face* score did not provide enough options to tell the story. So the creative team decided to go back to the Gershwin people and ask for more songs. Michael Feinstein was working at the time as the caretaker of the Gershwin catalog. So we gained access to hundreds of songs, and Feinstein was helpful in that he knew them all.

"Mike and I delivered the last scene on the last day of rehearsal, as the producers and the people Paramount and the agents were gathering in a room at the Minskoff Rehearsal Studios to have the new show done for them. We gave it to Tommy and he gave it to the cast and they just did it. Everyone was crazy about it all and Paramount said, Go. Two more weeks in rehearsal and then we started previewing.

"I didn't realize it at the time, but what I was first developing was this dislocation of space and time, people onstage who talk to the audience, who skip things that might traditionally be in a show that aren't necessary anymore in this age of the television remote control. We were writing a 1983 version of a 1927 show that included all the advantages—technically, scenically, and conceptually—of what we had learned in the past sixty years."

The show began six weeks of previews at the St. James Theatre. Tony Walton was brought in to doctor Adrian Lobell's sets, adding color and some curves to what had been only sharp angles. Audiences seemed to like the new show, but Tommy Tune was becoming increasingly frustrated that because he was in it he could not see it. He was particularly concerned when a musical number did not work because neither Nichols nor Stone could help him there.

Then about ten days before the opening, after a performance one night, Tune went to a birthday party for Michael Bennett. Tune and Bennett had been friends and had worked together on *A Joyful Noise* and *Seesaw*, but the relationship had turned into more of a rivalry—in Bennett's mind, anyway—when Tune's *Nine* beat out Bennett's *Dreamgirls* for the 1982 Tony for Best Musical. At the party, Tune complained to Bennett that the fact that he could not see his show was driving him crazy. Bennett said he'd come and look at it for him at the next day's matinee. Nichols's assistant, Sue McNair, had once been Bennett's secretary, and as Bennett entered the theatre he asked her to sit with him and take notes. Later that day, twenty-one pages of typewritten notes were delivered to Tune, who was dazzled by Bennett's perceptions.

"Sunday morning. Nine-thirty. Call from Michael Bennett," Stone recalls. "Of a pace and a frenzy and a wildness that are impossible to reproduce. 'Here's what we're going to do. Here's what we're going to do. I'm taking over the show. Here's what we're going to do. We're going to throw out the book entirely. The entire book goes. We're going to make the entire show two musical numbers, Act One and Act Two. Nobody's ever done this before. No book, no nothing. We're just going to do it with songs and movement and dancing. No scenes anymore, but you and me, kid— you and me together, kid—we're going to do it. And don't worry, kid, it's going to be you and me, and it's going to be great, and I'm taking over.'

"I called everybody immediately. This was all I had to hear at this point. We're sitting on what is clearly a giant hit and suddenly this madness is there. I call people, they don't believe me. Finally they persuade me I've misunderstood. I call Michael back at two in the afternoon. And he says, 'Hey, kid, it's going to be you and me, we're going to throw out the entire thing, the whole book will go, there will be two musical numbers of equal length, Act One and Act Two, and don't worry, kid, I'm taking over tonight!'

"I spent the rest of the day trying to convince someone this was trouble, but nobody took it seriously. We had scheduled a Sunday-night rehearsal, and I go in at seven and there's Michael. He's already started to work. I said to Tommy, 'What the hell is going on?' And he said, 'I don't know. He's taking over the show.' I call Nichols at home and now he knows about it and he says, 'It's fine. I have enough work to do. I'm staying in Connecticut.' The whole show is about to go up in smoke and then in walks Sam Cohn. And I say, 'Look, Sam, we've got to have Nichols drive in for a meeting after rehearsal tonight.' I said to Tommy, 'Let Michael work up some numbers, let's not do any scenes, let's not do any restructuring of the book, let him do numbers and we'll have a meeting.'

"Meanwhile, Michael's on the phone with Tony Walton telling him to start to build a giant wedding cake, and he's on the phone with Barry Diller asking for another six hundred grand. Then I ask Tommy, Why did you ask him to take over the show? And Tommy says, I didn't ask him. It turned out that no one had asked him, but everyone thought someone else had. There were those who thought that this was going to be Michael's great revenge on Tommy for losing the Tony the previous year—he was going to ruin the show, and then when it was a flop he was going to say, Well, I tried everything, but even I couldn't save it.

"So we had a meeting at Nichols's suite at the Carlyle with Tommy, Sam, and me. Sam said Bennett's out, Tommy said he's out, I said he's out. But Mike said, Let's not be hasty. Maybe he has some good ideas. So Bennett stayed.

"A few days later came the weirdest part. We're rehearsing Twiggy and Tommy and now we have three directors in the room directing only two people. And their styles are so completely different. Michael's style was to drag people around the set. He'd grab Twiggy by the arm and bring her over here, then he'd drag Tommy and tell him to go over there. Mike just sat by, not saying anything. I sat there watching this in amazement. At one point, when he grabbed Twiggy, she said, 'Watch that! If you touch me again I'm going to slug you.' Then a moment later, in the middle of rehearsing the scene, Bennett just got up and left. He never went near a scene again; he only got involved in the numbers.

"After every preview at about midnight, Bennett would take the entire chorus to his studio downtown and work until four or five in the morning.

Then, on a Thursday night, his first number went into the show, and it was a disaster. Tommy had given each of the girls a character, a specific thing to make each one different. One ate, one smoked; each of them had a gimmick. Michael came in and said, Get all that crap out of there and put them in identical wigs. Nobody's interested in the chorus, anyway.

"Then on Friday—a week before opening now—we had a meeting in Tommy's dressing room. There was this representative there from Paramount, Dan Sherkow, a surrogate for Diller, and we all said, Okay, who's going to fire him? And Sherkow said, I will, and he did and Bennett was never to be seen again. We put everything back the way it was, the show opened, and it was a hit.

"I loved coming in on both shows—*My One and Only* and *Grand Hotel*. It's a no-lose proposition. If it fails, it wasn't your fault. If it succeeds, you've done a miracle. So I love doing it. I love the pressure. I love the out-of-town, the rehearsal and the preview period. I like being in trouble and having to solve it. I just get very adrenalized by it. We turned both shows around and they both worked."

Peter Stone's father, John, grew up in grinding poverty on Manhattan's Lower East Side and taught a class of "incorrigibles" in a New York public high school for thirteen years. His students included Bugsy Siegel, who went on to build the Flamingo Hotel in Las Vegas before he was gunned down in Los Angeles, and Whitey Buchalter, who ran the S.S. *Rex*, a gambling boat offshore from Los Angeles, before he was gunned down in the streets of New York. When John Stone's father and sister both died of tuberculosis, the family was advised to leave the East Coast climate, and in 1919 they moved to Los Angeles.

John had a friend who was a script reader at Fox Studios, got his own job there, and within a few months he was writing the stories for Tom Mix's silent pictures. Mix was the best man at Stone's 1926 wedding to Hilda Hess, whose Bavarian family ran a general store in a mining town in central Mexico frequented by Pancho Villa. Stone worked his way up to the third-in-charge at the studio and was given his own unit, which produced Spanish-language features with Mexican actors. He survived Darryl F. Zanuck's takeover of the studio in the early 1930s, when it became 20th-Century Fox, and he produced several Shirley Temple films before taking over the B-movie unit that made second features for double bills, for which he created the Charlie Chan, Mr. Moto, and Cisco Kid series.

In 1933 he was producing Shirley Temple's first starring vehicle for Fox, *Baby Take a Bow*, and he brought his three-year-old son, Peter, to the star's birthday party.

"It wasn't a question of wanting to go, it was a question of *having* to go," Peter Stone says. "The party was on the Fox lot on Western Avenue, and my brother and I were picked up and brought to the studio. My father led us through an alley and into a soundstage and the darkness. We didn't know where we were going. And then a very crinkly man came over and my father introduced us both to Will Rogers, whose column my father read out loud to us every morning at breakfast. That was it. But it was a great thing. A few months later, Rogers died in a plane crash."

During the war, John Stone moved on to Columbia Pictures. "But he hated the grind," Peter says. "He hated the rat race, he hated the back-stabbing and the politics. So he quit and later went to work for this association of five major American Jewish organizations as a liaison between these groups and the picture business, to make sure there was no anti-Semitism in films. I was determined to be a film writer from the time I was ten years old. But somewhere around 1945, my interest switched to theatre. I don't know why, because there was practically none in Los Angeles. There were only two theatres in the whole town—the Biltmore and the Philharmonic Auditorium. Broadway road companies would come to town and I could get no one to go with me. But my parents would get me a ticket and I used to have to take the bus from West Los Angeles, where we lived, to downtown. It was an hour-and-a-half ride then, no freeways yet, and I would sit in the second balcony and see *Lady in the Dark*, *Mexican Hayride* with Bobby Clark, *Arsenic and Old Lace*, and so forth. The dynamics of theatre—with live actors—really appealed to me. Was it a revolt against film because my father hated the film business so? I don't know. Straight theatre was my interest back then, not musicals. I wanted to be a playwright."

Stone had never been east, but when it came time for him to go to college it was understood that he would leave California; he ended up at Bard College, about twenty miles north of Poughkeepsie, New York. As a freshman there he wrote his first play. As a senior he wrote and directed a play adapted from an obscure Dostoyevsky novel. Upon graduating, he entered the Yale Graduate School of Drama. "But I didn't like it much. Their play-writing program was a waste of my time," he says. "I spent all of my time going to the movies and auditing classes at the law school, which was much more interesting."

What Stone did like about being in New Haven was that so many Broadway-bound plays tried out there at the Shubert.

"While I was still at Bard," Stone says, "my parents got divorced [after twenty-three years of marriage] and my mother ran off to Paris with a Hungarian-American literary agent named George Marton, who had been quite influential in Central Europe before the war. His clients included Ferenc Molnár, Franz Werfel, Bertolt Brecht, Thomas Mann, and Vicki Baum. He sold plays from Europe to American theatre producers and, coming to Hollywood during the war, sold several books and plays by his clients to the studios. My mother and George moved to Paris after the war, and in 1949 I went there for the first time to visit. I adored it and I eventually ended up spending thirteen years there."

Stone worked for CBS Radio, doing news features ranging from covering Princess Grace's wedding in Monaco to the Cannes and Venice film festivals. Soon he began writing drama for television. He became involved with producer Herb Brodkin, for whom, among other things, he wrote a few episodes of "The Defenders" as well as a play for the dramatic series "Studio One." He maintained his residence in Paris, but also rented a $69.50-a-month apartment on East Thirty-fourth Street and traveled back and forth. While in Paris, he saw Jean-Paul Sartre's adaptation of the Alexandre Dumas play about actor Edmund Kean at the Sarah Bernhardt Theatre. Sartre's approach, of course, was existential. "It dealt with the nature of an actor's identity," Stone says. "He plays the great heroes, he plays royalty, he plays the great tragic figures, but who is he?"

On one visit to New York in 1961, Stone's agent, Robert Lantz, told him that another client, Alfred Drake, was interested in doing a musicalized version of *Kean*, and that he, Lantz, intended to produce it. Drake had had a success with Wright and Forrest on *Kismet*, and they were set to write the score. "Robby said to me, You saw it, you loved it, you can speak French, you can adapt it for a musical," Stone says.

Stone was friends with Frank Loesser, who at the time was writing *How to Succeed in Business Without Really Trying*. Stone went to him and said, "Tell me how to write a musical. I don't know the first thing about it. I never tried."

Stone recalls, "Frank was articulate and patient and very wise and really taught me everything. He taught me where a song goes. He told me, When you get to a certain point and your characters can't speak anymore, when suddenly the emotion rises and you want to say, Oh gosh, Wow, Gee, that's when you sing. That's why so many wonderful theatre songs begin with 'Oh'—'Oh, What a Beautiful Mornin' 'Oh, How I Hate to Get Up in the Morning'; and so on.

"He taught me how to lead into a song. What you had to do was pave the way for a change in literary style from prose to poetry by lifting up your language, making it more flowery, in order to ease your way in, but without giving away the idea of the song.

"He taught me that you have only an hour to tell two hours of play, so you have to learn how to write differently because the songs aren't really going to help your story. You may be lucky to get a few seconds of story out of an entire musical number.

"He told me dozens of anecdotes that were funny, but all had wisdom. Things George Kaufman would say. The foolishness and irresponsibility of going into rehearsal with a long script because you're just wasting precious rehearsal time."

One February day in 1961, Peter Stone married Mary O'Hanley, then they walked up Fifth Avenue and stopped at the office of Robby Lantz, where Stone signed a contract to write *Kean*.

"It was very hard to get the right director. We ended up with Jack Cole, a terrific choreographer, a very bright, interesting man, but with a very difficult temperament. We went out of town to Boston, where we were a gigantic hit. Six papers, six raves. But Alfred Drake got sick, and the night after the opening the understudy was on. We were out of town for six weeks—three in Boston, three in Philadelphia—but Alfred never played three consecutive performances. He couldn't rehearse and he couldn't play, which made rewriting impossible. But everybody was complacent and convinced we were a huge hit and we didn't have to do any work. We were wrong. The show was sick and we had a lot of problems to solve.

"One of the things I learned here was how to read reviews on the road. A rave review is of no help to you and neither is an out-of-town pan. What you want is a review that tells you you're promising but you haven't done this or haven't done that. You need critics who don't judge you as a finished show, but by your progress up to that point. Elliot Norton was very good about that in Boston, and Dick Coe in Washington.

"So we came to New York, played one preview before a theatre party of academics who loathed the show, then opened. Alfred wasn't strong enough, he didn't have enough rehearsal time, and his voice was weak. The reviews weren't good enough, and we lasted about ten weeks at the Broadway Theatre.

"But I had a great time. A wonderful time. I seemed to like the whole process. I liked being around the music, around the first orchestra reading, around the singing and dancing, around the whole company."

Before taking on this project and while still in Paris, Stone had written his first screenplay, a mystery called *Charade*. Stone sold it to director Stanley Donen, whose pictures he liked (*Singing in the Rain*, *Indiscreet*, *Funny Face*) and who had worked with Cary Grant and Audrey Hepburn, whom Stone had had in mind when he wrote it.

"Audrey said she would do it if Cary did, but Cary wouldn't commit. Then Cary changed his mind and said he would make it if he could talk to me and iron out some problems.

"I was still living in Paris, so I flew to New York and went to the Plaza, where I was to stay in Cary's suite in order to work with him. I rang the doorbell and he had just come out of the shower and he came to the door in a towel. He was magnificent. You couldn't take your eyes off him. Dyan Cannon, whom he had just met and would eventually marry, was there with him.

"His main concern was very interesting: In the script, the guy chases the girl, and he said, I'm about to turn sixty and I'm too old to chase the girl. It would be unseemly. The girl has to chase me or it's not going to work. I said, All right, and I stayed in the suite for three days and rewrote it until he was satisfied.

"In no time at all we made the picture, and it opened as the Christmas picture at Radio City Music Hall. That started a run of about six or seven of my pictures that were Christmas shows at the Music Hall."

Stone then signed a five-picture deal with Universal, moved back to the States, and purchased houses on both coasts. His pictures at Universal included *Father Goose*, for which he shared the Oscar for Best Original Screenplay. "I met the guy who wrote the original on the stage at the Oscars," Stone says. "If our names hadn't been called, I never would've known who he was."

In the mid-1960s, he wrote his second book for a musical, *Skyscraper*, which was scored by Sammy Cahn and Jimmy Van Heusen, produced by Cy Feuer and Ernie Martin, directed by Feuer, and starred Julie Harris, in the only musical of her career. "It's mysterious, there's performing and there's acting," Stone says. "Julie Harris was the best actress in America, an angel, a saint, the most pleasant and professional person I ever worked with, and she sang and danced charmingly, but somehow she didn't land as a performer in the numbers.

"But I learned a big lesson on how to rewrite musicals from Cy Feuer. We were in trouble in Detroit and Sammy and Jimmy were despairing. One day at a matinee, the whole show just falls apart in the first act and they're ready to explode. Cy was sitting in the fifth row taking notes, and he walks up the aisle and they are ready to pounce on him. Cy says, Just a minute. The ballad is a little slow. Let's pick up the tempo a little bit. At that, they just blew their stacks. The ballad is too slow! For God's sake, the show is dead and you're worried about the ballad. Then Sammy said, It's like manicuring the nails on a corpse. And Cy said, I'm going to tell you this just once: Tomorrow the ballad will be right.

"And that's the lesson. You can't fix it all at once. You fix just one thing at a time. That's why it's so hard to preview in New York. There are too many haters in New York, too many people of influence, and you don't want them to see a show in trouble so you tend to make cosmetic changes. On the road, frankly, you don't care that much about the audience so you dig much deeper.

"Later, when I did *1776* in Washington, we had a number late in the show that we never staged. It was delivered late and we didn't have time to get to it, so we left it unstaged. We knew we'd fix it, but we had to fix other things first. But you can't do that in New York."

Stone calls *1776*, the next show he did, the turning point in his career. The first few times he was called by producer Stuart Ostrow to listen to a score by a high-school history teacher from New Jersey for a show about the signing of the Declaration of Independence, he begged off. Finally, in February 1968, Stone agreed, in order to get Ostrow off his back as much as anything else, and went to the producer's office in the Paramount Building to meet Sherman Edwards.

"Sherman was a very gruff, undiplomatic guy who, it turned out, had also written his own book and was not happy that Ostrow wanted another book writer," Stone says. "He had the world's worst singing voice. But he had only to get sixteen bars into his opening number, 'Sit down, John, Sit down, John,' for me to recognize it was a wonderful idea. The entire fabric of the show was in that song—that they were calling John Adams 'John,' that they were complaining about the heat and the flies, that they were human beings instead of cardboard cutouts, and there was an irreverence but at the same time an affection. Then I realized an amazing thing: History was something I was interested in, I'd taken history courses all through school, and I didn't know anything about the American Revolution.

"It appealed to me because I'm very political. Most of what I do is political. However, I couldn't make a commitment. It seemed like a death wish. It appeared to be the most boring subject, the most boring title; I would mention it to someone and he or she would fall asleep somewhere between the *17* and the *76*. But I kept reading about the subject and finally I had to admit I was too fascinated to let it go.

"Now I was committed, but Sherman was still not willing to accept me. This apparently had been optioned umpteen times, but it always fell apart when the producer tried to bring in a book writer. But Stuart was smart. He scheduled it, gave it an opening night, got a theatre, and let Sherman get used to the fact that there was a planned production, so that Sherman himself would start spreading the news. Then he told Sherman he was going to cancel the whole thing unless he could bring me in. So Sherman agreed."

The show played a pre-Broadway engagement at the National Theatre in Washington, then came to the Forty-sixth Street Theatre—a play by two unknowns in a season (1968–69) that had works involving Harold Prince, Kander and Ebb (*Zorba*), Jerry Herman and Angela Lansbury (*Dear World*), the first rock musical (*Hair*), and the first and only musical by Burt Bacharach and Hal David (*Promises, Promises*, with a book by Neil Simon). But *1776* was the sleeper that got the rave reviews and won the Tony Award for Best Musical, as well as for Sherman Edwards for Best Score, and for Stone for Best Book.

"It was by far the happiest and best work I've ever done and probably ever will do," Stone says. "I've done a lot of very successful work since then—I've had six hits in a row and four that have run a thousand performances—but nothing I've done is as good, or even in the neighborhood. I was just inspired. Something happened, and it was a combination of my interest, my passion, my compulsion—and everything came out.

"Up until then, although my interest was musical theatre, I had been a success only in Hollywood. I couldn't live on what I was making from Broadway, maybe twenty thousand to thirty thousand dollars on a whole show—and that you had to spread over the two years of writing it and getting it on. But this show made me financially independent. I had my killing. In addition to Broadway and two road companies, there was the film sale and I wrote the screenplay and made amazing stock and amateur money. After we were closed a few years, there had been eighteen hundred productions across the country in summer stock and high schools and the like."

Two years later, Stone wrote the book for a musical called *Two by Two*, based on Clifford Odets's play about Noah and his family called *The Flowering Peach*. The score for the show was written by Martin Charnin, who conceived the project, and Richard Rodgers. It was directed by Joe Layton and starred Danny Kaye.

"The show didn't work because every one of us was working on a different show," Stone says. "Charnin and I were doing one show, which was the Odets concept of Noah's family being a lower-middle-class Jewish family from Queens. Rodgers wanted something less Jewish, less lower class, more lyrical, which was his experience. Layton wanted stage magic and brought in concepts that only hurt the show. And Danny Kaye was interested in being Danny Kaye, and why shouldn't he be? That's where his security was, right? He wanted up-front, downstage Danny Kaye numbers, so he never really played too well with the rest of the company." Despite mediocre reviews, Kaye was enough to keep the show running for a year, including a stint during which he had a broken leg and played the show in a wheelchair.

The next season, David Merrick asked Stone to come in to replace George Axelrod on the book for a musical based on the motion picture *Some Like It Hot*, which was scheduled to begin rehearsals a few weeks after the producer made the call. The production, then called *Nobody's Perfect* (which gave away the movie's and the show's last joke), had a score by Jule Styne and Bob Merrill and was directed by Gower Champion.

"I ran the Billy Wilder movie and I read the musical's script. Axelrod had written something very, very different from the successful original," Stone says. "I said I would do it under one condition—that we return to the story of the movie.

"I like George and I like his writing; it turned out he'd made the changes at Gower's instigation. As was always the case with Gower, he leads you someplace, he gets to a point where he hates it, and he turns on it. I came in and said, Why try to improve on what's already terrific?

"I think I came up with the title for the show, *Sugar*, and everything would have been all right except for two things: One was that Gower was never forthright with anybody. He was supporting you, only you found out later that he wasn't supporting you and would undermine you and you didn't know it. The other was that Merrick honestly believed that the only way to get good work out of people was to frighten them, to tyrannize them. He would threaten, he would bully. He wore this homburg hat, and when we were out of town, whenever we saw the homburg hanging on the hat tree, our blood ran cold.

"Under Gower's guidance, Jo Mielziner, a brilliant designer, had done this brown set for the show. You have to understand that Gower worked in utter secrecy and no one saw the drawings for the set. But the set goes up at the Kennedy Center, and it's terribly unattractive and drab. We all looked on in astonishment and said, How can you be funny on a brown set? How do you get light and happy on a brown set? Merrick came in and said, Those sets are out as of today. I'm hiring Robin Wagner to design an entirely new visual show from scratch, and you, Gower, are going to pay for it. As far as I know, Gower did. They had a very strange love-hate relationship.

"Up to now, I'm getting along very well with Merrick. We're really relating to each other. But the night before the opening in Washington he comes up behind me and says, 'The show's a disaster and I'm closing it.' We've got ten weeks on the road and we haven't opened yet. 'It's a disaster and I'm closing it.' He doesn't, it opens and gets good reviews, and the audience likes it. We have a lot of work to do, but the audience likes it.

"Then three days after the Washington opening, we're working well, we're all in an up mood, and I'm there with Styne and Merrill and I get told that Merrick's on the phone for me. I say, David, how are you? He says, 'You're fired. Get out of town.' Hangs up. Of course I wasn't fired—my contract didn't allow it. We came to New York and ran for over a year."

Perhaps it was the experience with Merrick and Champion that drove him away from the theatre, but Stone spent the rest of the decade writing for television and motion pictures again. And then came a phone call from producer Larry Kasha. "What do you think of Bacall as *The Woman of the Year*?" Thus began the creative alliance with Tommy Tune that brought Stone back to the theatre and so far has yielded *My One and Only, Grand Hotel,* and *The Will Rogers Follies*.

"Sam Cohn called and asked me to come to his office to meet with Pierre Cossette, who was primarily a producer of television specials at that point," Stone says, "and there Cossette told me that he owned the rights to the life story of Will Rogers and wanted to do it as a musical with a score by, and starring, John Denver. I said, How can you own the rights to a life? He said, Well, I made a deal with the family. And I said, I don't know. I don't like biography at all onstage. People's lives don't come ordered the way drama does. If you want to make it interesting you have to lie, or if you want to make it historically correct you have to face the fact that it's badly structured and boring. Frankly, I know Will Rogers's life, and there's nothing in it except his career and the things he said. The only troubles in his life were an infant who died of diphtheria, and when he first went to Hollywood he invested in three of his own pictures and went bust. The only really interesting thing about his life is the way he left it—in an airplane crash in Alaska. So I said no and I went home.

"Then I started to think. Will Rogers had been a presence in my life because I'd met him and my father read his columns to us every morning. Later in life I had gone to work for Will Junior when he ran for Congress. I handed out pamphlets. And then I got this really terrific idea that Will had been the star of the Ziegfeld Follies for about ten years, and what if this was not the story of Will Rogers but the story as Ziegfeld presented it? That was an idea I really liked. It fit with this new concept of mine that in a musical today you either have to write in shorthand or start dislocating time and space, the way a television clicker does it. People don't watch television anymore—they graze, they go around the dial. They watch as long as they're interested and then they zip along, then come back later if something grabs them. A few shows back I started writing like this, in shorthand instead of in full scenes. And I got this concept of doing it here, as a forum that allowed Will to talk to the audience constantly. So he'd say things like, 'Well, I'll skip the next few lines and get right to the good part.' The audience doesn't need those few lines anymore, not in a musical."

Stone met with Tommy Tune in California and told him the concept just this way. Tune said, I love it, I want to do it. Then he went to meet with John Denver. "Denver looked like Will Rogers and had a lot in common with him," Stone says. "They both had Indian ancestors, they both lived in the Southwest, they were both interested in airplanes, they both saw themselves as populists. John was going to write the score and I liked the idea.

"For a year we would meet and then John would fly off to China, then to Russia, then to South America. He was also training to go up in the space shuttle, plans that were canceled after the *Challenger* mishap. Finally we had this very drunken Mexican lunch where we drank margaritas till we were both blasted and he said, I feel so guilty. I'm not giving any time to this thing. I said, Look, John, maybe this is something you should star in but not write the score for. He said, You're right.

"A whole year had gone down the drain. But by this time Cossette saw what was coming and had already talked with Cy Coleman about writing the music. We asked Cy who he wanted to collaborate with, and he thought the right lyricists were Betty Comden and Adolph Green.

"In the meantime, Denver was suddenly getting very upset. Why was it taking so long? I reminded him he'd been responsible for a year-long delay. What I didn't know was that CBS had offered him a series. We played the first act for him and he started interfering. He wanted to change a lot of the lyrics and said, This is an old-fashioned show. We said, No, this is a new-fashioned idea that's never been tried before. What he was talking about, I think, was that the music was not rock. I sort of made a hard shove, because that seemed to be what he wanted, and he separated himself from it.

"We kept working and we started to have a lot of songs with content that Tommy didn't like. This was the beginning of my starting to feel a little silly, that paranoid feeling book writers get when they try to accommodate everyone else. The only way to get a song that Tommy didn't like out of the show without offending anyone was to cut the scene. Then there was no song anymore. But what if I liked the scene? It didn't matter, because we had to get rid of the song.

"Then we started to realize there was no producer on the show. Cossette was in California, he knew nothing about Broadway, it was all foreign to him, but he didn't behave like it was. We finished the show and began to do some backers' auditions. Cossette had originally said to us, 'I don't know how to produce a show, but I can raise the money in twenty minutes.' The first backers' audition was at 21, very expensive, a hundred people invited, and I don't think we raised a dollar and a half. Betty, Adolph, Cy, and I did the presentation. People didn't understand the concept; we'd done a bad job of presenting it. Another expensive audition at the Regency Hotel, same thing. Two more at the Dramatists Guild, another buck and a quarter.

"Finally Tommy gets back to town and I tell him what's been going on. I said, We've got to do something or we have no show.

"In the meantime we did some casting and Pierre's wife recommends Keith Carradine. I thought it was a terrible idea. He was too sexy; Will Rogers wasn't sexy. And I didn't know if he could play comedy. He was a leading man, while Will Rogers was a character part. But Keith wants to do it, he flies in at his own expense, and we go to get it over and done with, and out he walks on the stage, and he had gone to the trouble of getting a cowboy Stetson and boots and an outfit, and he'd even learned a couple of rope tricks. He came out as Will Rogers, and even when we were talking to him as Keith Carradine he was Will Rogers. Talked like Will, never dropped the dialect. He knocked us out. Tear up the list. It was a done deal."

Now that they had their star, Tune and Stone decided to use him to help finance the show. Stone wrote a new backers' audition piece for Carradine and an actress to be Rogers's wife. Coleman said he had a terrific girl in *City of Angels* and asked Dee Hoty to play the wife. (She would eventually get the role in the show.)

"Betty and Adolph were upset," Stone says. "They wanted to do their own songs. I went to them quite honestly and said, Look, one of our problems is that you're Comden and Green, you're performing artists, and when you get up to sing they're seeing you as Comden and Green, not as the characters in the play."

According to Stone, Cossette had very little to do with this new audition. The creators invited potential backers they knew and the entire capitalization was raised.

"At the same time," Stone says, "we went to Pierre and said, We can't let you produce this show alone. You don't have the experience, you don't know how. He fought it and fought it but finally agreed to let Marty Richards come in. And we brought in Marvin Krauss as the general manager.

"Then Pierre got very cold feet; he kept postponing, then agreeing to go ahead, then canceling. It's too expensive, it's impossible—this, that, and the other thing. Finally it was Tommy who laid down the law. He had signed to go on the road on tour in *Bye Bye, Birdie* on May 3. He said, You either do it now so we can make the Tony deadline, or you'll have to wait a year. Pierre said, We'll wait a year. Tommy said, I don't think I'll be interested in a year.

"Shows just don't happen that way. When you've got this much together, this much energy, they don't wait. They disappear. So we told Pierre, We have to start in three days or we won't make our dates. He said we'd go, then got cold feet again, but we started the workshop on time and got rolling.

"During the rehearsal period, we did a lot of rewriting, much of it for Will. A lot of Will's material was lovely but gentle. Tommy said if you can't land a big laugh, the material is weak and therefore cut it out. Then I found I could write Will Rogers–like jokes—jokes the way he would've done them.

"We had a hard time solving the second act musically. We had to write in some new numbers to adjust to what the actors could and could not do. The Ziegfeld's Favorite character—the leading chorus person who delivered newspapers and ropes to Will, or showed up with telegrams (there was always one of those in a Ziegfeld show)—became more important.

"But what was there from the beginning was the structure. I am far from the best writer in the theatre, but I see myself as a first-rate structuralist. Without structure nothing will work—not the songs, not the dialogue, not the characters. You can fix all those in rehearsal in no time at all. But if you don't have the structure right, whatever fixing you do on the other things, the musical simply is not going to work."

MARQUIS THEATRE

Under the direction of
James M. Nederlander, Terry Allen Kramer and Harry J. Nederlander
in association with Marvin I. Danto and Jesse Philips

Terry Allen Kramer, Charlene & James M. Nederlander,
Daryl Roth & Elizabeth Ireland McCann
present

Barry Bostwick in Joanna Gleason

NICK & NORA

with

Christine Baranski

Remak Ramsay
Faith Prince
Michael Lombard
Debra Monk
Yvette Lawrence
Kip Niven
Jeff Brooks
Thom Sesma

and

Chris Sarandon

Music by
Book by   Charles Strouse   Lyrics by
Arthur Laurents   Richard Maltby, Jr.

Scenic Design by   Costume Design by   Lighting Design by   Sound Design by
Douglas W. Schmidt   Theoni V. Aldredge   Jules Fisher   Peter Fitzgerald

Dance & Incidental Music by   Dance & Incidental Music Arranged by
Charles Strouse   Gordon Lowry Harrell

Orchestrations by   Musical and Vocal Direction by   General Press Representative
Jonathan Tunick   Jack Lee   Jeffrey Richards Associates

Production Supervisor   Technical Supervisor
Janet Beroza   Jeremiah J. Harris

Hair and Makeup Design by   General Manager   Animals by
Robert DiNiro   Ralph Roseman   William Berloni Theatrical Animals, Inc.

Production Stage Manager
Robert Bennett

Casting   Choreography by
Stuart Howard / Amy Schecter   Tina Paul

Directed by

Arthur Laurents

Based on the characters created by Dashiell Hammett & on "The Thin Man" motion pictures owned by Turner Entertainment Co.

IN ASSOCIATION WITH JAMES PENTECOST & CHARLES SUISMAN

FLOP

"Let's Go Home"

KAY McCLELLAND (*Understudy*) last appeared on Broadway as Gabby/Bobbi in *City of Angels*. Before that she played the Baker's Wife, after creating the role of Florinda in *Into the Woods*. Prior to that, she played the Soubrette in *Sugar Babies* (national tour with Mickey Rooney and Ann Miller) and Sarah in *No Way to Treat a Lady* at The Hudson Guild. Regional credits include Petra in *A Little Night Music*, and Polly in *Threepenny Opera*. Film and television credits include Neil Simon's *The Slugger's Wife* and "Guiding Light," respectively. Ms. McClelland began her career with The Wits End Players in Atlanta, her hometown.

his has been a truly unforgettable evening. And just the shot in the arm Broadway needed. A few hours ago, the new American musical *Nick & Nora* opened to unanimous rave reviews at the Marquis Theatre. Eager theatre-goers have begun to set up cots and folding chairs on the cold street outside, awaiting the opening of the box office the following morning. The show is already a phenomenon, and it's not just because of the orgasmic xenophobic eruption of the morning critics ("Take that, Webber, Boublil, and Schonberg," writes Rich. "Now, when theatre-goers hear Mackintosh, they'll think only of apples or computers," writes Kissell), but also because of the fairy-tale nature of the event: As if right out of such fables as *Cinderella* and *42nd Street*, just a minute or two into the performance, star Joanna Gleason, whose portrayal of the elegant Nora Charles has been eagerly anticipated by the waggiest of theatre wags, slipped on a banana peel tossed onstage at the matinee, tearing her Achilles' tendon. Kay McClelland, who arrived at the stage door at half-hour as merely an understudy, rushed onstage to the rescue and left three hours later a genuine Broadway star. What made the event even more remarkable is that due to the abundance of rewriting that occurred during the production's troublesome preview period (and right up to the opening-night curtain), Ms. McClelland never had the chance to learn writer Arthur Laurents's words—so she made up her own as she went along!

Well, when you set out to write about an understudy, that's the scenario you hope for.

Actually, it's a couple of hours past midnight on the morning of December 9, 1991, and I'm here at Joe Allen's, the theatre-district restaurant, with Kay McClelland and her date, Mark. This is the third place we've been to, and everyone has drunk too much and smoked too much and feels like crap. But no one wants to leave because they know when they wake up in the morning, in addition to having a terrible headache, they'll have to face what has occurred tonight. Barry Bostwick, who's had a lot of success in Hollywood recently and who hoped to make this show his triumphant return to Broadway fifteen years after he'd won a Tony Award for *The Robber Bridegroom*, sits with a friend at another table, looking as if he just ate bad clams. Behind him is the eatery's famous wall of posters from flops, and Bostwick knows if he ever gets up and leaves, his name is going to be up there.

It's more than four hours now since we got a look at the morning papers' reviews for *Nick & Nora*, the first new musical of the 1991–92 season, and they are the kind of notices that make you feel that every time you overhear someone laughing on the streets or in restaurants, they're laughing at you. We were at Sardi's at the time, at an opening-night party pulled together by the producers at the last minute. This has been one of those shows rumored to be fraught with backstage back-stabbing, some of it reported by, and some of it concocted by, the press. One of the rumors was that the producers were so disgusted with their creative team that there wasn't going to be a party. But there was—until at about 10 P.M., when producer Terry Allen Kramer, director Arthur Laurents, and press agent Jeffrey Richards stood huddled over *The New York Times* in the little downstairs bar, and just the looks on their faces started a steady but rather rapid exodus.

From Sardi's, the cast drifted uptown to the bar at Gallagher's on West Fifty-second Street. This fine group of actors, with such good reputations that the producers saw fit to prominently bill twelve of them in much of the show's advertising, was now sharing in the humiliation.

There, sitting on a bar stool nursing a martini, McClelland, in a lacy black bustier, with her long silvery-blond hair piled on top of her head, said to Richard Muenz, the understudy for Bostwick, "Well, we kept asking each other, Do we want this thing to run or not? If it did, we'd get a weekly paycheck, but we'd be stuck here. So how do we feel now?"

"Terrible," Muenz said.

"Bet your ass," McClelland said.

Kay McClelland had been playing one of the four female leads in *City of Angels*—the 1990 Tony Award winner for Best Musical—for the fifteen months since that show opened when she was called in to audition for *Nick & Nora* in the summer of 1991. She had come to *City of Angels* directly from *Into the Woods*, her first Broadway show, in which she and Lauren Mitchell were hilarious as Cinderella's bitchy-funny stepsisters. She stayed with that show for its entire twenty-two-month run, serving double duty as Joanna Gleason's understudy for the Baker's Wife's role, and eventually playing that central character from mid-May until Labor Day weekend of 1989, when the show closed.

When the creative team of *Nick & Nora*—director-librettist Arthur Laurents, composer Charles Strouse, and lyricist Richard Maltby, Jr.— needed a talented actress of some stature to stand by for both Gleason and their second female lead, Christine Baranski, they decided to take a shot at lassoing McClelland. It may seem a bit nutty for a performer to go from a visible role in one show to being a standby in another (and take a salary cut of 50 percent), but McClelland was ready to try something different.

"I was never completely happy in *City of Angels*," McClelland says. "There was something I needed in the show that I wasn't getting. As Gabby, the writer's wife, I was on in the second scene and then came back once in the second act, and that was it. There was a big hole in the relationship between her and Stine. There was never a tender moment between them. And this was the real part of the show, the part the audience was supposed to care about. Since they didn't have that, they didn't care, and I could feel it because I wasn't getting enough back from the audience. My reviews weren't that good either. All Frank Rich wrote in his rave of the show was '. . . decently played by Kay McClelland,' which killed me. John Simon wrote that I wasn't pretty enough to turn one man's head, much less two—which got me started fast on a heavy workout regimen.

"Despite this, it was great in the beginning because I fell in love with so many people in the original company. I grew really emotionally attached to them. During rehearsals, we'd spend fifteen hours together in the theatre, and then go out, a whole group of us, and spend whatever was left of the day and night together. We couldn't get enough of one another.

"I had lunch with Dee Hoty the other day," McClelland says of her co-star in *City of Angels* who went on to play opposite Keith Carradine in *The Will Rogers Follies*. "She was saying, 'My whole life is the show. That's all I have. I go to work. That's all I do.' And I thought, Yeah, that's right. Wait till you see how much you miss that when it's gone."

When the original company started leaving the show, the things that bothered McClelland became more significant.

"I gave some of those replacements a helluva time," she says. Especially Tom Wopat, the former star of television's "Dukes of Hazzard" who replaced Tony winner James Naughton as Stone. "One night I said to him, 'You're upstaging me.' He said, 'I'm *what*?' 'You're upstaging me.' 'What does that mean?' he asked. 'You don't know what *upstaging* means?' 'No,' he said. 'Give me a break here. I don't know what *upstaging* means.' '*Upstaging* means you're standing upstage of me, so I have to turn to look at you.' 'Oh, I won't do that anymore,' he said. But he kept doing it. Finally, I said, Hell! I'm just going to stay downstage and say my lines alone and play the scene with him behind me.

"Then one night he kissed me during a scene and put his tongue in my mouth. So I went into his dressing room and closed the door and read him the riot act. 'What did I do?' he said. 'You know what you did, and don't you ever do it again,' I said. 'I'm sorry. I lost my head,' he said. 'Do it again and you're going to lose something else,' I said. After that we were cool."

One day that summer, McClelland was in the shower in her apartment in the theatre district with her cellular phone on the sink when her agent, Cindy Alexander, called. Alexander said the *Nick & Nora* gang had called because Kay had already covered Joanna Gleason, who had to miss a weekend of performances next January, and they needed someone competent to step in. "And one more thing," Alexander said. "They want you to audition."

"They want me to audition for an understudy?" McClelland shrieked. "Who the hell are they?

"But Arthur Laurents had never seen me," McClelland now says. "And this was my chance." Laurents is probably best known as the librettist for *Gypsy*, which is often cited as the best book ever written for a musical, and *West Side Story*. But he also had had great success directing the original Broadway production of *La Cage aux Folles* in 1983, and both the Angela Lansbury and Tyne Daly revivals of *Gypsy*. "He's one of the reasons any of us is in this business," McClelland says.

She showed up for her audition in a studio at 890 Broadway in high-waisted pants and heels—"a kind of Katharine Hepburn look"—stood with her hands in her pockets, and sang "It's Almost Like Being in Love" from *Brigadoon*.

"I have a tendency to hide my vocal ability, sliding around and adorning it with tricks," she says. "I have a quirky voice—two different voices, actually. And an area I slide over.

"So Arthur Laurents came up to me and put his face right up close to mine and said, 'First of all, I think you're terrific. But let's do this . . . Can you just sing it straight? No style. Just the notes.' "

McClelland sang, then returned home. An hour later Cindy Alexander called and said, "They want to use you. Let's talk about this."

"I looked at this opportunity as a training session," McClelland says. "Applause is great, but there's something to be said for being behind the scenes sometimes. I knew I'd be sitting on my butt most of the time. But it was a chance to see Arthur work. And I'd learn so much watching Joanna Gleason."

McClelland read the *Nick & Nora* script. "I thought it was very confusing," she says. "But I assumed they'd figure it out."

She had left *City of Angels* on June 30, 1991, needed a rest, and was granted permission to miss the first three weeks of rehearsal. She went on vacation until Labor Day, then joined the rehearsal process. During this time, the understudy's primary job is to observe the actor playing her role, or, in this instance, roles.

"When I told my father I was going to understudy," McClelland says, "knowing that I need to keep my mind occupied, he said, 'Now, don't bring your knitting in there. Just sit and concentrate.' "

McClelland sat in a corner of the rehearsal studio at 890 Broadway six days a week, usually beside Muenz, watching Laurents build the details of a performance with Gleason and Christine Baranski.

"They were still going through the show moment to moment when I got there," she says. "They were doing structural scene work and talking a lot about through-lines. I knew I had a ton of work ahead of me. I looked at these two women and what they had accomplished in three weeks' time and I thought, Oh, dear God, I'm in over my head. There's no way I can do this."

In *Nick & Nora*, we join the San Francisco couple Nick and Nora Charles in Los Angeles, where they have come for a wedding. Nick is retired from detective work now, happy to live off Nora's family money. But Tracy Gardner (Baranski), a fading movie star and old school chum of Nora's, shows up at their Garden of Allah hotel suite and announces that the director of the musical she is starring in has been arrested and charged with the murder of his bookkeeper, a blond floozy named Lorraine (played by Faith Prince). This picture is important to Tracy's career, the director swears he is innocent, and Tracy needs her best friend's spouse, Nick, to take the case and clear the director so the film can be completed. When Nick claims he is no longer in the business, Nora decides she will do the detection. But Nick, of course, cannot sit idly by while his wife does his life's work, so they end up competing to identify the murderer. This provokes questions on both their parts about their feelings for each other and the strength of their marriage.

"I think what Arthur wanted it to be about was two people finding themselves in a different relationship than they started out with," McClelland says. "How to stay with that, how not to throw it away. Certainly the murder mystery was important, but the real story was Nick and Nora, what they meant to each other, and whether or not they could have the perfect marriage, perfect communication, and the kind of unqualified love we all strive for."

The task for the creators was to examine this marriage, while at the same time constructing a credible murder mystery, one with lots of suspects whom the audience had to have the time to get to know so there would be some "whodunit" guessing. Mysteries are generally considered poor source material for musicals. Historically the musical is, as writer Peter Stone says, an optimistic form; crime genre stories are not. Since the evening must contain an hour or so of music, there is only another hour of book in which to develop the plot. But for a writer as talented as Laurents, these negatives are the attraction to the material. They pose the challenge that inspires.

Laurents's approach to the material was one of high comedy. He advised his cast not to watch any Frank Capra films or anything with Clark Gable. He wanted them to see Preston Sturges's *The Lady Eve* and Billy Wilder's film version of James M. Cain's novel *Double Indemnity*. "Arthur told us that even though we were dealing with some serious issues—marriage, drug abuse, sleeping with people to get to the top, and murder—we had to keep it light," McClelland says. "He wanted everything quick and tightened because the material itself could be dark.

"He is not a director who works with actors on details of performance. That came from the actors. He is most concerned with clarity and the truth of the moment. There were a few times when he would say things like, React more strongly. Or if someone completely failed to deliver a line the way he wanted it, he would say, I'm going to give you a line reading here, so don't freak out. And everyone was very, very open to what he wanted to do."

During an early week of rehearsals, a newspaper interview with Laurents and his choreographer, Tina Paul, appeared in which they claimed an important image of this show was dance (apparently representing sex); the evening would glide across the stage from beginning to end. But the show had been cast with actors-who-sing rather than dancers (including Gleason and Bostwick), and before the show moved from the rehearsal hall into the Marquis Theatre, most of the dancing was cut.

During their three weeks of rehearsals, McClelland and Richard Muenz had but one forty-five-minute session with the piano player to run through their songs. They spent only one morning going over the blocking of some scenes with the stage manager. Occasionally they would go off alone together and run the scenes without supervision. But that was the entire extent of their preparation.

"But when you get a little of it under your belt," McClelland says, "you start to realize that they knew what they were doing when they hired you—that you can do it. Then you start to want to get up and do it."

During this period of observation, McClelland did not discuss the script or the creation of the characters she would play with either Gleason or Baranski.

"I never felt it was my place to do that," she says. "My approach was that it was my job to do as much as I could to be the other actress. When I went on as Nora, it was not going to be the performance I built, but the performance Joanna built. Nora is all over the stage and involved with all the other characters, and I'm not going to be my own Nora and throw new energy out there that confuses everyone else. For me, it isn't about going out and proving myself, it's just about carrying the ball."

As the company moved into the theatre to begin technical rehearsals with the physical production elements, they were extremely confident. "The general feeling was that we had a hit," McClelland says. "I saw a lot of work that had to be done, but I was never afraid it wouldn't get done. I had never worked with Arthur before, but he had a great track record. I had worked with Joanna and knew that she wasn't going to let anything fly by her. The whole company was totally engrossed with Arthur and had absolute faith in his ability."

The six weeks generally allotted to rehearse a new musical are barely enough time to get a show on its feet. Usually the first four of those weeks are spent in the rehearsal hall, blocking and choreographing and teaching the music, and the focus is on traffic direction rather than performance. Then the action moves onto the stage for the next two weeks of tech. With the ever-increasing complexity of the scenic movement and the lights, the primary concern is keeping the actors from getting killed by sets traveling in the darkness. During these last two weeks, you devote very little time to moments and you lose whatever little performing you had coming out of the rehearsal hall.

"Before we got to the theatre," McClelland says, "Arthur told us, Take a breather. You're not going to have what you had at 890. It's not going to be that comfort of a small room and the cast out there watching you and feeding back, so don't fight it."

On Monday night, October 6, the company performed a dress rehearsal, and reports from those associated with the effort were very encouraging. No production is easy to mount these days, and this one had had its own set of difficulties and delays, including original producers who could not raise the necessary funds and were pushed aside, and conflict among the three writers about the direction of the story. But as the show headed into previews, the mood around it was good.

Then on Tuesday night, the cast of *Nick & Nora* faced its first paying audience. In an act of generosity that turned out to be foolhardy, the producers had sold all the tickets at half price to the industry's three AIDS service organizations—the Actors Fund, Equity Fights AIDS, and Broadway Cares—to use for fund-raising. This provided a full house, but what it was full of were people who work in the theatre. Arthur Laurents greeted the audience from the stage and said the company was honored to present this preview to benefit an important cause. What he and his colleagues hoped for was that their generosity would be returned.

It was not. The show did not work at all. You could feel the strain in the audience. With the exception of a number called "Men," sung by Faith Prince, the show was greeted throughout by only polite applause. Everyone in this business will happily tell you (and anyone else who'll listen) how to fix your show. And they're almost always wrong. What was clear was that the piece was not eliciting any of the excitement from the audience that would result in people telling their friends to go see it. The plot was confusing, the musical numbers never lifted the show to a high entertainment level, and in trying to contrast the genuine love between Nick and Nora with the mercenary attitudes of the Hollywood types they encountered, Laurents had surrounded his hero and heroine with a bunch of unusually unappealing characters. Underlying all this were doubts about the basic premise: The appeal of the Nick and Nora Charles of Hammett's books and the films was that they tolerated all of each other's habits and quirks and remained admiring of each other. Did we want to see a story in which they separate, or was that destroying the unique fabric of Nick and Nora and making them as commonplace as, say, Donald and Ivana?

Going into this evening, the public's image of this show was neutral. If anything, people who worked in the industry were rooting for it since it was the only completely new American musical with an original score that was slated for the entire season. But with just one performance, that all changed. Perhaps the most embarrassing aspect of being associated with this business is the delight we seem to take in ripping apart one another's shows. By Wednesday morning, everyone in the business had heard that *Nick & Nora* was in trouble. The fact that the production was the only new game in town would have worked to its advantage if those who saw it liked it. But they didn't, and so this exclusivity became a curse.

Jimmy Nederlander, the owner of the Marquis Theatre and a producer of the venture, reportedly told the writers the next morning that in thirty-five years in the theatre, he had never been so disappointed in a show. (After making that comment the morning after the very first performance, Mr. Nederlander might as well have packed up and gone to Tortola until opening night; nothing else he said would be heard by the writers.)

"The morning after," McClelland says, "we all felt like frightened rabbits coming to the theatre. Because we just didn't know what we had anymore."

Kay McClelland never had the fire in her belly like most of the whipper-snappers who head to New York determined to become stars. She came here at age twenty-seven—ancient for an aspiring actress—and on a spur-of-the-moment decision. She had been living with her boyfriend, Rudy, whom she met at the Atlanta Costume Company, where they both worked days, performing at night with a comedy troupe called The Wits End Players in the basement of the Peachtree Plaza Hotel. She was very much in love with Rudy, expected to marry him, but when she realized that was not in the cards, she broke up with him. After a performance one midnight, Kay and another Wits End Player packed up his car and headed to New York.

"I didn't know how I was going to get through the breakup," she says. "Something inside me said to go to New York. What the hell do you have to lose?"

It wasn't until she arrived here that she got to see her first Broadway show, *Sunday in the Park with George*. Within a few months she was cast as the Soubrette in the national touring company of *Sugar Babies*, with Mickey Rooney and Ann Miller.

"The night before my first audition for that show," she says, "Rudy was in New York and we spent the night together. It was a very emotional time and I was still very sad. I was told to walk into this audition in a leotard and tights and sing a love song. I woke up and I looked like hell. I put ice on my eyes. Then I put on a three-piece suit and sunglasses and went to the office of the agent who was nice enough to be sending me out, and I said, There's no way in hell I can sing, and there's no way on God's green earth I can get through a love song. Please reschedule me. But he said, No. Go do it. And I hated him. He said, You're already dressed wrong. You're supposed to be wearing a body-conscious outfit and you've got this man-tailored suit on. So I said, I don't care about this audition. I don't care. But I went in and my ballad was 'Autumn,' a horrible song to sing when your heart is breaking. I sang the first half with my sunglasses on and then, when I started to cry, I thought, Shit, I don't care anymore. And I took off my glasses and finished. Ernie Flatt, the director, said to me, Come back in two days and wear a leotard.

"So I came back in a leotard cut up to my hips and down to my belly button, mile-high shoes, nude-colored tights, and I sang 'Autumn' again and read. The room was filled with a slew of tall, blond, big-breasted, long-legged women who could sing the glass out of windows. And they hired me. They said they liked my sense of humor."

McClelland had grown up in the northeast section of Atlanta, the youngest of four children of a Scottish "country doctor who lived in the city," she says, and his Irish wife, originally from North Carolina. "I think I was a mistake, and Mom and Dad were pretty much over raising kids when I came along," she says. "By the time I was eleven, I was pretty much left alone."

Her best friends in her youth were her animals. She thought she'd grow up to be a veterinarian until she realized how much schooling it would take. Then at twelve, Kay saw Barbra Streisand in the motion picture *Funny Lady*. "I didn't know anyone who spoke like that," she says. "I didn't know anyone from Brooklyn or New York or that whole idea of getting onstage and fighting for it. That's when it first entered my mind."

As a sophomore she was elected to represent the junior varsity cheerleading squad in the Miss Ridgefield High School Pageant. She sat on a piano in a dress she borrowed from her sister and sang "Second-Hand Rose," "à la Streisand," she says. "People came up to me and said, You were wonderful. Where have you been keeping that voice? And I thought, Me? I'm wonderful to watch? Hmm."

The next year the chorus voted for her to represent them in the pageant, in which she sang a medley of "Sing a Song" and "Happy Days Are Here Again" right off another Streisand album and won first runner-up. "And I loved it," she says. "All I wanted was a microphone, a little pink light, and a dance floor where people could come in and dance."

After graduation, she went off to Mercer College, two hours south of Atlanta, in Macon.

"I wasn't thinking of theatre as a career at the time, but I auditioned for all the plays and got roles," she says. "At that point, I wasn't enthralled with the mainstream musicals like *West Side Story* and *Gypsy*. They were too square, too middle-of-the-road for me. I wanted something a little strange. I liked torch songs and Brecht. I liked the chance to emote in some strange way.

"Then I was dating a guy in sophomore year who said to me, What are you doing here? This is a little town in Georgia. If this is something you want to do, you'd better start thinking about your future."

She dropped out of Mercer, intending to pursue a career in theatre. But her father, with whom she had a strained relationship, told her acting was not a serious profession. In anger, she entered the business school of the University of Georgia, Atlanta branch, as an accounting major. After one quarter, she switched to the drama department.

"All I expected out of life was that I'd get married someday," she says. "But the people I was attracted to were theatre people, and they were crazy and their passion was their work, so that's what I got into." After graduation, she was hired by The Wits End Players and worked days at Atlanta Costume.

"I never had an ounce of ambition," she says. "I never had huge goals—I just wanted to be in a club and sing. I didn't want to make a ton of money, I didn't want to be a star, I just wanted to do what I wanted to do, and everybody else leave me alone. And then the thing with Rudy happened and here I was in New York."

Rehearsal is a period abundant with esprit de corps. People have chosen to work on this show because they believe in it. They are all in one room together all the time, forty or fifty of them, and everyone has a stake in the success of the piece, so the hall is filled with encouragement and approval. There are no outsiders there to burst the balloon.

Then you move into a theatre and open the doors and it all changes. The transformation is not so pronounced when you're out of town; there at least the company usually lives in close proximity to one another and no one's hometown friends are around to come see the show and fill their heads with criticism and doubts. But New York can be a destructive work environment. Opening a show here cold is as safe as walking down the hotel corridor at a U.S. Navy convention—everyone seems to want to get a piece of you.

The audience response during the rest of the first week of previews of *Nick & Nora* was no better than it had been the first night. The panic that inevitably sets in when word of mouth is bad brought to the surface the tension among the creative team. Throughout the writing process, Laurents had been content with his book and sent his songwriting team off time and again to compose new pieces. Maltby and Strouse had written between fifty and sixty songs by the time previews began with fifteen of them. They could not help but feel that every time there was a problem, Laurents traced it to the score. He was clearly the muscle on this production. It was his vision and the others were there to execute it.

But the company of a show is not always privy to the discord permeating the pre- and post-rehearsal work sessions. "Arthur said to us, I know you're all hearing a lot of opinions from a lot of your friends. God knows I am," McClelland recounts. "He said, I have faith in our work, however, and they don't know what we're doing, so screw them. Let's do what we do and keep going.

"The changes during the first few weeks were not major. There were note sessions after the show each night, often until past midnight, and rehearsals each day began at twelve-thirty. Mostly we were trying to make what was there work better.

"Now I know this may keep me from ever working for the man again, but Arthur is very confrontational in his notes. He knows exactly what he wants and, without much regard for what it sounds like when it comes out of his mouth, he says it. His notes are personal—not personal about the character you are playing, but personal about your own character. As an example, he might say something like, 'You can't do this moment because you don't think you're attractive enough and you don't believe what's coming out of your own mouth.' And to me, that's stepping over the line. You don't know how I feel about myself and that's not your job. Don't psychoanalyze me. Direct. You hired me because I'm a good actor. Now use me.

"He was equally brutal with everybody, and I give the company a lot of credit for being strong enough and confident enough to take what he was saying and swallow it and work with it."

There was concern even among the production team that Laurents, being both director and writer, was prevented from seeing the problems in his own work, so he harped on other things that may not have been as problematical. He had received some of the best reviews of his directing career for his production of *Gypsy*, starring Tyne Daly, in 1989. His colleagues feared he believed the audience was not sophisticated enough to recognize the quality of his work, but the critics appreciated him and would tell the audience what to like.

"I kept thinking, Why the hell isn't he moving faster?" McClelland says. "Why isn't it happening now? Things aren't working and you never want to perform them again. But then I started to think, Well, he knows exactly what he's doing. He's letting the dust settle. Instead of diving in and changing everything furiously, he'd change one little thing, see if it worked, then maybe change it again, then even go back to what he originally had and change something else."

During the third week of rehearsals, some of the company became aware that Yvette Lawrence, an understudy, was being rehearsed in the role of Maria Valdez, a Latin-fireball saloon singer, which was being performed by Josie de Guzman. The character was forced to play one of the worst moments in the show, a late-second-act number called "Boom Chicka Boom," in which she sang a lyric about her shaking her maracas that seemed a curious choice for the socially sensitive Maltby. Late in the week, de Guzman was fired.

"We all said, Oh, yeah, that's what's wrong with the show. Everything'll be fine now that Josie's gone," McClelland says with heavy sarcasm. "It threw us all. With all our problems, was that the solution? But Josie called everyone and said she was fine, and if her performance wasn't working, she didn't want to be in the show anyway."

The original opening had been scheduled for Sunday, November 15, in which case the show would have gone through a four-week preview period in New York, fairly standard for those shows that do not have out-of-town tryouts. But in early November the opening was postponed, first to December 2, then, when the producers claimed critics complained about cutting short their Thanksgiving Day weekend, to December 8. But now the presenters of *Nick & Nora* found themselves flirting with one of the more heated controversies of the time between New York producers and critics: How long should a show be permitted to preview?

Producers who are responsible for millions of investment dollars—in this case, reportedly $4.3 million—must do whatever is necessary to get their show right. You have only one shot to establish a show, and either it makes it and goes on to a life in the repertoire or it disappears. If finishing your creative work requires additional time, you must provide it. This is not work that can be done in a rehearsal hall. You have no gauge of your progress without an audience in the room. So, if you determine you need more time to work, that time must be in the form of previews.

Critics, of course, have always taken the position that they are the protectors of the consumers. On a few very rare occasions, the producers of Broadway shows have postponed their openings because business in previews was satisfactory and they feared the critics could only hurt this, which seems to have created suspicion among some critics about all producers who elect to postpone. Some critics also object to the fact that most Broadway producers charge the same price for tickets during the preview period as after opening and do not state in their advertising that the show is still previewing. They feel that this is duping the public to pay top dollar for unfinished work. (What we have here is another problem caused by the runaway economics of the business. The costs of running a show are no less during previews than after opening; in fact, with the cost of extra rehearsal time and changes in physical production and music, they are substantially greater.) Some critics claim they receive complaints from consumers about extended preview periods with full-priced tickets—though the complaints are extremely minimal relative to the size of the audience. Producers claim that the New York audience is savvy enough to know when shows are in previews and what previews signify.

Refusing to identify previews in advertising was one of a number of ticket-selling practices that are off-putting to the audience and yet had become standard operating procedure among producers of Broadway shows as costs escalated and the community grew more frantic. (In addition, discount tickets are available via twofers or at the TKTS booth on Duffy Square on the day of performance, so people paying full price can be sitting beside someone paying half price. The service charge for tickets purchased by telephone can run from $3.50 to more than $6 on top of the full ticket price.) All of these practices tended to make consumers feel uneasy. They created bad public relations for a consumer-oriented business. As a group, theatre producers had not attempted to lessen the confusion with, for example, a well-thought-out public-relations campaign to explain the various methods of obtaining tickets; if anything, they appeared to be attempting to conceal them. Again, there had been no research compiled to measure the audience's attitude toward these ticket-selling practices. But no one likes to feel confused or conned. One must suspect that this uneasiness was at least partially responsible for the 25 percent decrease in Broadway theatre attendance from 1980 to 1990. And it gave those who wrote about the theatre something to get angry about.

The *Nick & Nora* postponement attracted the wrath of Linda Winer of *Newsday* and Greg Evans of *Variety*, who brought up the old arguments about duping the public. This was not a controversy needed by a show that was trying to work its way out of trouble and bad word of mouth. It prompted New York City Consumer Affairs Commissioner Mark Green to require that all shows in previews must now be labeled accordingly.

Then, on Friday, November 15, Alex Witchel wrote in her theatre gossip column in the Weekend section of *The New York Times*: ". . . the original opening date for the long-awaited Broadway musical *Nick & Nora* has come and gone, so the unofficial statute of limitations has run out on holding back the dish. . . ."

"From the very beginning, company grumbles have centered on Mr. Laurents, a man of no small ego, having written *Gypsy*, acknowledged by musical-theatre historians as one of the greatest book musicals. The specific gripe among company members is that Mr. Laurents has an inherent conflict in being both the director and book writer. He doesn't like hearing when the book needs changing, and instead of keeping an objective perspective, as a director should, about how well the book works with the songs, he protects his writing turf and, early on, alienated composer Charles Strouse."

"Arthur came to rehearsal in a rage that day," McClelland says. "He stood in front of us and said something like, Someone here has betrayed me and I'm going to stand here until they admit it. Finally, Joanna said to him, Look, Arthur, no one here said any of that. You know it. We all know it. So let's not let that kind of stuff get in here. Let's go to work.

"But I think the article did a lot for us. Obviously that Witchel woman sat at the bar at Sam's and heard some scuttlebutt and wrote it like it was fact. And we thought that sucked. We all thought she was a mean, hateful woman for doing it. But we understood that we were the only game in town, and people were champing at the bit to see us fail. But the article pumped us all up. Our attitude became, Hey, girl, watch this. We'll show you. It probably gave us the lift we needed."

What finally seemed to get Laurents cracking were visits to the show by Stephen Sondheim and playwright Peter Shaffer, two writers who had the director's respect and knew the genre in which he was working. What they emphasized to Laurents was clarity.

"Now the changes became fast and furious," McClelland says. "Arthur rewrote constantly. It scared the hell out of me. Any night someone could call in sick and I would have to go on. It's hard to do that even when you rehearse the changes. But I didn't have that opportunity.

"What I did love watching, though, was Joanna and Barry falling in love on the stage. During the first previews, one of the things I would hear was that there was no chemistry between them. Well, there was at 890. But once they got onstage, there were so many things going on. There was a little dance, and pour this drink over here, and then someone comes in and interrupts them, and the scenery moves around them. It was all so busy, it pulled them apart. I don't know how they did it, but somehow over time they managed to recapture the feeling that even though they were in deep shit in their relationship, they still loved each other.

"With the Tracy character, there were these lines she would say in the last scene—when it was revealed that she was married to the man who pretended to be her houseboy and he was really devoted to her—that would make us all cry at 890. But when we got onstage it was sappy and made the audience laugh. How Christine kept it together and got through the performance, I don't know. I know a little bit about what it's like to feel humiliated on the stage.

"What I was hearing from my friends was that everything was horrible and everything was fine. Some told me it was charming the way Nick and Nora danced through the show. Charming, charming. I heard 'charming' a million times. Others said it should be called *Nora* because there's no Nick in it. But I never heard that it was fabulous and it was a smash. Frankly, that's the kind of show I prefer to be in. I don't want to be in a show everybody loves, because that's just corn. Other musicals on Broadway have lasted for years and have bored the hell out of me. I'd rather be in something controversial—that half the people like and half the people hate.

"As we got closer to the opening, somehow I went from wishing I was up there to thanking God I wasn't. There's something wonderful about being a standby. You want it to be a smash, but you don't have anything at stake except a paycheck."

On the day before the critics were to start coming, Kay McClelland said that she did not expect the show to get rave reviews, but she thought they would be good enough so that the production would run awhile. She felt that a lot of good work had been done and that the Nick-Nora relationship was unusually well developed for a musical.

The next day, Laurents called the company in at three, did a little clean-up rehearsing, then said, "That's all."

To which Christine Baranski said, "Arthur, we have no place to go. We have no other lives now. You're just going to have to rehearse us."

On opening night, McClelland sat in Row O of the orchestra and watched. By the following weekend, the producers decided the critical reception and box-office response were so poor that it wasn't worth trying to run through Christmas—the busiest week in the New York theatre. The show closed on Sunday, December 15, after seventy-one previews and nine performances.

Kay McClelland never got to go on.

A few nights after the show closed, McClelland went to a movie with Barry Bostwick. Afterward, they went back to his apartment, drank some wine, and talked. "But it was very awkward," she says. "The pain was too great and we just reminded each other of it."

During the holiday week, Joanna Gleason invited the cast to her apartment to celebrate the season. "But that was awkward, too," McClelland says. "I went to make sure everyone was all right. But once I saw that, all I felt was sad.

"And that's what's so strange—you spend the whole time working on a show supporting one another and making one another feel good. You get very close and fall in love with one another. Then, when the show fails, you try hard to leave the disappointment behind you, but seeing one another just makes you feel bad."

NEDERLANDER THEATRE

Jules Fisher   James M. Nederlander
Arthur Rubin

In association with Mary Kantor
present

DANGEROUS GAMES

Music
Astor Piazzolla

Lyrics
William Finn

Book
Jim Lewis & Graciela Daniele ⭐

The Company
Richard Amaro   Ken Ard   René Ceballos   John Mineo
Adrienne Hurd-Sharlein   Philip Jerry   Diana Laurenson   Tina Paul
Gregory Mitchell   Dana Moore   Elizabeth Mozer   Danyelle Weaver
Luis Perez   Malinda Shaffer   Marc Villa

The Musicians
Rodolfo Alchourron   Jorge Alfano   Miguel Arrabal
Adrian Brito   Jon Kass   James Kowal

Scenic Design
Tony Straiges

Costume Design
Patricia Zipprodt

Lighting Design
Peggy Eisenhauer

Sound Design
Otts Munderloh

Musical Direction & Arrangements
James Kowal

Musical Consultant & Arrangements
Rodolfo Alchourron

Fight Direction-Tango
B.H. Barry

Fight Direction-Orfeo
Luis Perez

Production Stage Manager
Robert Mark Kalfin

Music Coordinator
John Monaco

General Management
Marvin A. Krauss & Joey Parnes

General Press Representative
Shirley Herz Associates

Casting
Brian Chavanne & Julie Mossberg

Co-Choreographed by
Tina Paul

Conceived, Choreographed and Directed by
Graciela Daniele ⭐

Originally produced by The American Music Theater Festival, Philadelphia;
Spoleto Festival USA, Charleston and La Jolla Playhouse, San Diego.

THE BOOTH THEATRE

nfeld, Chairman   Ⓢ A Shubert Organization Theatre   Bernard B. Jacobs

The Shubert Organization, Capital Cities/ABC Inc.,
Suntory International Corp.
and James Walsh,
in association with Playwrights Horizons
present

ONCE ON THIS ISLAND

a new musical

Book and Lyrics by
_YNN AHRENS

Music by
HEN FLAHERTY

novel "My Love, My Love" by Rosa Guy

Cast
(in alphabetical order)

_KINOLA   RUFUS BONDS, JR.   JERRY DIXON
_ILA GIBBS   VANITA HARBOUR   KECIA LEWIS-EVANS
GERRY McINTYRE   ROZZ MOREHEAD
NIKKI RENE   ERIC RILEY   ELLIS E. WILLIAMS

Set Design by
LOY ARCENAS

Costume Design by
JUDY DEARING

Lighting Design by
ALLEN LEE HUGHES

Sound Design by
SCOTT LEHRER

Orchestrations by
MICHAEL STAROBIN

Musical Direction by
STEVE MARZULLO

Casting by
ALAN FILDERMAN & DANIEL SWEE

Associate Choreographer
WILLIE ROSARIO

Production Stage Manager
LESLIE LOEB

Directed and Choreographed by
GRACIELA DANIELE ⭐

Original Cast Recording available on RCA VICTOR

10

THE CRITICS' EFFECT

"We Dance"

★

GRACIELA DANIELE (*Director-Choreographer*). Broadway: *Dangerous Games* (San Diego Critics' Circle Award), *The Mystery of Edwin Drood* (Tony nomination), *The Rink* (Tony nomination), *The Pirates of Penzance* (Tony and Drama Desk nominations, L.A. Drama Critics' Circle Award), *Zorba*, *The Most Happy Fella*, and *History of the American Film*. Her New York Shakespeare Festival credits include *The Knife*, *The Mystery of Edwin Drood*, *A Midsummer Night's Dream*, *Alice in Concert*, and *The Pirates of Penzance*. She has worked at numerous other institutions, including Brooklyn Academy of Music; New York City Opera and Boston Opera Co.; The Great Lakes Theater Festival, where she co-directed *Blood Wedding* with Gerald Freedman; the Second Stage, where she directed *In a Pig's Valise*; and Intar, where she co-adapted, choreographed, and directed *Tango Apasionado*. She worked on the movie version of *The Pirates of Penzance*, as well as other films.

There are no chandeliers on the stage. And no barricades. No cars, no staircases, no flats, no drops, not even a stool. The three stage walls are painted like a threatening sky and some swaying palms. The painting style is primitive. The colors are primary, bright. It looks like the kind of shoebox set we made as children. All that fills the box are ten black men and women and one child. They are the actors and they are the scenery and they are the special effects. They dance the trees and they dance the breeze. They dance frogs and rain and a car and a car crash. They even dance the calendar.

It is the first day of December 1991, and this is the 457th and last Broadway performance of a musical called *Once on This Island*. As at all final performances, the audience at the Booth Theatre this Sunday afternoon consists largely of friends of the company and fans of the piece who know the show well. They both welcome and say good-bye to each number with wild applause and hoots and whistles. The mood at a last performance is always somewhat sad. At the same time, it is closer to the mood at a ball game than at any other performance of a show. What sports has that theatre doesn't is the tension of immediacy—you must see this game today because it will never be played again. So it is with last performances.

When the intermissionless ninety minutes of singing and dancing ends, the eleven cast members stand in a line across the stage, holding hands and crying. Lynn Ahrens and Stephen Flaherty, who wrote the show, their first to play on Broadway, are crying. André Bishop, artistic director at Playwrights Horizons, that fine little institutional theatre on Forty-second Street's Theatre Row where this show was developed, is crying. But Graciela Daniele is not. For the smallish, athletically built director-choreographer, with her short dark hair, olive skin, and sparkling smile, there is a national company to begin staging in just a couple of months. But there must also be a sense of strength and even triumph kindled by this particular show.

On Sunday, October 22, 1989, just the day before rehearsals were to begin for a workshop of *Once on This Island* at Playwrights Horizons, Daniele had a lengthy four-way phone conversation with Ahrens and Flaherty and Bishop in which she offered to withdraw as director-choreographer. Three nights earlier her production of *Dangerous Games*, two sexually and politically charged theatre dance pieces set in her native

Argentina, had opened to scathing reviews. Frank Rich of *The New York Times* used the opportunity to attack Daniele's entire fifteen-year career of work in the New York theatre:

"The production was conceived, co-written, directed, and choreographed by Graciela Daniele," Rich wrote, "an artisan of show-biz perkiness who has folded simulated Bob Fosse struts into entertainments like *Drood* and *The Pirates of Penzance*. Since Jerome Robbins, there have been no Broadway choreographers, Fosse included, with the imagination and varied dance vocabulary necessary to sustain a full theatrical evening of dancing. Ms. Daniele would seem an unlikely candidate even to make the attempt—her previous musicals have been neither dominated nor distinguished by their choreography. And yet, presumably inspired by serious dance-theatre experimenters like Pina Bausch and Martha Clarke, she has slammed together two hours of mediocre Broadway routines padded by repetition and crushed by pretense."

Dangerous Games closed Saturday night after four official performances. On Sunday, Daniele called her next collaborators.

"I never read any reviews," Daniele says, "because I believe you know anyway. By the way people talk to you, the things they say to you. What I find is that the power of the printed word to me is very harmful. I have this photographic mind and what I read stays with me and affects me a lot. So I decided a long time ago, I didn't want to be affected by either the good things or the bad things. I will know what is good and bad from the audience response.

"I knew how bad this was by how supportive and angry friends were when they called. So I said to Lynn and Stephen, This is just your second musical. Are you sure you want to give it to someone who has just been run out of town by a major critic? It is a tough thing for new writers who are trying to break into the business, and I absolutely understand that you might not want to give your baby to someone who just had such a flop. And they said, We don't care what anybody says. We think you're the right person and we want you."

The next morning, Daniele showed up at the upstairs rehearsal room above the theatre on Forty-second Street to go to work.

"I was a mess. I was exhausted," she says. "I didn't know if I had the energy to start the show because I was so down. But I believe in something that Martha Graham once said in a wonderful conversation with Agnes De Mille: It's not up to you to decide if you're good or bad—it's up to you to keep the channel open.

"The worst moment for me in choreographing or directing is those first five minutes. You see all those people looking at you and expecting something. I've done research up the wazoo—but I'm still not sure exactly what I'm going to do. So I have learned that the best thing to do is just to get up and do something, even if it's the wrong thing. I start right in with acting, not talking; action—that's what acting is. So for the first five or ten minutes everyone is doing something and then the channel opens and we start to find things. Then it is about finding things, and whatever bad feelings you came in with are gone."

The workshop was promising enough that, six months later, rehearsals commenced for a full production of *Once on This Island*. It was a gutsy production in the current marketplace that only could have been done in an institutional theatre. It went against the grain of the overproduced spectaculars filling the Broadway houses. It would be one of the few recent musicals in which the dancing was performed by people instead of by the scenery. The show opened on the small main stage at Playwrights Horizons's 146-seat auditorium on May 6. In the next morning's *Times*, Rich wrote a lengthy review of unqualified praise for all involved, including the following:

"The musical's director and choreographer is Graciela Daniele, who opened this theatre season with the short-lived *Dangerous Games* on Broadway and now ends it, show-biz fairy-tale fashion, with the most effervescent achievement of her career. *Once on This Island* is wall-to-wall dancing, movement, and mime. From the mood-setting first number, titled 'We Dance,' and reminiscent in spirit of Bob Fosse's 'Magic to Do' in *Pippin*, the audience is drawn into the evening's once-upon-a-time storytelling style and fantastical atmosphere. Yet to come are high-stepping, swivel-hipped calypso routines, ecstatic ritual dances to demanding gods, a rollicking Caribbean counterpart to 'Follow the Yellow Brick Road,' and even a delicate European waltz in the elegant hotel. . . ."

On October 18, a year to the day from the opening of *Dangerous Games* at the Nederlander, *Once on This Island* moved to new digs at the Booth Theatre on Broadway.

There are so many movie critics and television critics and book reviewers assessing each new work in the United States that no matter how good or how bad a work might be, it will probably receive the full critical spectrum of opinions. These opinions tend to cancel one another out and leave it to the audience to determine the work's success.

But theatre is not so fortunate.

Unlike the other media, which can unveil a new work all over the country at one time, a show can only be launched in one city. And though the growing influence of the institutional theatre movement over the past thirty years has changed this somewhat, particularly for plays, the going wisdom among those who put on shows is that a work needs a New York imprimatur to have a widespread life elsewhere.

Because theatre is so much more costly to attend than the other art or media forms, the audience is less willing to take a chance on the unknown and more dependent on a consumer guide—which is to say the critics. So the success of a show is generally much more dependent upon critical opinion than is the case with any other art or media form.

In New York, the success of shows is largely dependent on that person who happens to hold the critic's job at *The New York Times*. Many people in the business will tell you that this is the only opinion that matters. Theatre is a business peculiarly shy of consumer research in this era of numbers in which we live, and there are no statistics, no smart research, that quantifies this—only experience that indicates to us all that those people who are most likely to come see your show early on and start the word of mouth that builds a following are readers of the *Times*.

While institutional theatre gives an extended life to work via subscription audiences, commercial or Broadway theatre productions can have no audience without critical approval. Of course, there are marketing strategies designed to overcome this; in some instances they are effective, and in all instances they are expensive. Generally, though, there is a feeling among those working in commercial theatre that all the time and all the money and all the effort up to opening night are all about pleasing one person. (And if you don't please him, all your money is going to be spent to overcome him—most of it spent on advertising in the *Times*.)

This is the New York theatre predicament. It casts a pallor over the entire profession. The joy of creation gives way to the dread of execution. What you have is a community of people living in constant fear of failure, and more often than not behavior is shaped by this fear.

Different people handle the predicament in a variety of ways. Many decide they want no part of it. Go to Orso in Los Angeles any night of the week and you'll run into lots of your favorite New York actors whose first love is theatre but who refuse to come back here and risk being humiliated. I once overheard Glenn Close saying just this to Gerald Schoenfeld, chairman of the Shubert Organization, in a very loud voice and with very harsh words, following her treatment when she opened in the Ariel Dorfman play *Death and the Maiden*.

The nasty critical reception for their 1986 musical *Smile* drove both composer Marvin Hamlisch and writer-lyricist-director Howard Ashman to run from the theatre. Hamlisch is only now coming back, seven years later, with *The Goodbye Girl*. Ashman, who went on to be instrumental in the creation of *The Little Mermaid* and *Beauty and the Beast* for Disney, died of AIDS in 1991. In 1988 and 1989, I had three meetings with Ashman, attempting to persuade him to direct one project and write and direct another, both of which he was attracted to. He left those meetings committed to the projects, then called a few days later to say he could not work again in New York and expose himself to the *Times*.

People who worked at the Public Theatre tell you that Joseph Papp's method of coping with the predicament was that he always looked to hire artists who had been favorably reviewed in the *Times*.

Hal Prince handles the predicament by always scheduling a creative meeting for his next show at eleven A.M. the morning after an opening night. That's why he's been successfully plying his trade for thirty-eight years.

The predicament is on everyone's mind all the time. It affects the projects many people choose to work on and what shows get financed. Producers walk out of readings and say, It's not a *Times* show. And those who don't say it aloud nevertheless think it.

The artists who manage to have active and sustained careers are those whose work is guided by a personal artistic philosophy, those who have a vision of what they are trying to accomplish, and use this— rather than other people's judgments—as their compass.

Graciela Daniele's vision was shaped by an exotic youth spent on three continents. It was that experience that went into both her flop—*Dangerous Games*—and her hit—*Once on This Island*.

"What I'm always trying to do," Daniele says, "is to use dance as another language to express ideas and emotions as opposed to just for entertainment value. I want the dance to stand equally with the words and the music in telling the story of a show."

Dance became a part of Daniele's life to solve a physical problem. She was born in Buenos Aires, Argentina, in 1939, the daughter of a Sicilian insurance salesman and an Argentine mother. Her parents divorced when she was seven, "which was scandalous in Argentina," she says, and she was raised in a house with her mother, her grandmother, and her aunt, "a world of all women in which I was the little princess."

The young Grazie had no arch in her foot. A muscle was atrophied. Rather than give her corrective shoes, the doctor told her mother to put the child in the ballet.

"I went to audition for the Theatre Colón in this huge studio with four hundred kids, and this barre that was too high for me," she says. "This teacher comes over and looks at my foot and I could tell something's wrong. But she must have seen something in my eyes because she said, Send this one in.

"It was like a convent. For seven years we studied from seven in the morning until noon. Then I went to my real school, and then I came back at night for rehearsal for performances. Since I was seven, eight years old, I was on the stage holding candles in Wagnerian operas or while Maria Callas was singing."

At fourteen, Daniele was offered a contract with a new company that a ballerina named Nina Verchinina was forming in Brazil, and Grazie and her mother left Argentina. Daniele would not return to her homeland for thirty-five years. The company traveled in South America, and while in Colombia at age seventeen, Grazie was asked by a local television station to direct and choreograph a weekly show about the history of ballet.

"I didn't know how to put a dance together," she says. "I was so innocent and ignorant. I would just do anything at that point. I had that blissful ignorance that makes you go your own way without second thoughts. I look at actresses now and I say, Don't stop yourself. Go for it. Because when you're young and ignorant that's when great things happen, that's when you fly."

So Daniele replanted herself once again, in Bogotá, but not for long. "The center of the ballet world was Paris then," she says. "I wanted to go there very much. My mother had married a man in Bogotá. So she stayed, and at eighteen, I got on a plane by myself and flew thirty hours to Paris.

"Paris in the 1950s was a very romantic place to be. And being eighteen, I had my romantic adventures. I had a deep relationship that lasted for two years. And other great affairs. And I was in the ballet of the Opéra of Nice, and we were there for the season, where I had a wonderful relationship with a lawyer who had a villa in Cap d'Or. I would spend weekends there and see Ingrid Bergman and her husband. And Brigitte Bardot. And I walked and saw Picasso on the street. I went on tour in a revue that Josephine Baker did, the story of her life in musical numbers.

"And then I started to feel, Okay, I can do this; now what else is there? Frustration started to set in. I needed more. In 1961 or 1962, I saw *West Side Story* in Paris. It was all in English and they had French subtitles above the proscenium. I didn't speak any English, but after about three minutes I stopped reading the subtitles and never looked there again. It was all so clear to me what was happening. The language was dance, and that told you everything.

"I got out of that theatre and I just walked alone through the Paris streets until two or three in the morning. That night I made a decision: I just have to go to New York and learn how to do this."

In 1963, the twenty-four-year-old Daniele moved into a railroad flat on Ninth Avenue and Fifty-seventh Street in Manhattan, began taking classes at Ballet Theatre, and also took jazz classes with a teacher named Matt Mattox.

"I was in class for three or four weeks," she says, "and Matt called me and said, Grazie, I'm choreographing a Broadway show and I think you would be terrific for it. I didn't have an Equity card and I couldn't even speak English. I said, What is it? He said it was called *What Makes Sammy Run?* and Abe Burrows was the director. He said he had a little role, in this ten-minute ballet, for a missionary, and he needed a great dancer. So after just three months being here, I was on Broadway. And I remember for opening night Abe Burrows's telegram said: 'I hope the bogeymen like you as much as I do.'"

Daniele spent a couple of years as a dancer on television's "Bell Telephone Hour," then was cast in a new musical based on John Steinbeck's novel *East of Eden* called *Here's Where I Belong*, with a book by Terrence McNally and a score by Alfred Uhry and Robert Waldman. The choreographer was Hanya Holm, who had created the dances for the original productions of *Kiss Me Kate* and *My Fair Lady*. But when the show opened to poor notices in Philadelphia, Holm, the only member of the creative team with any significant experience in musical theatre, was replaced by Tony Mordente, the ex-husband of Chita Rivera. The show came to the Billy Rose Theatre in Manhattan to preview, and among the folks Mordente called in for advice was a young friend named Michael Bennett, who was choreographing "Hullabaloo," a weekly rock-and-roll show on NBC-TV. *Here's Where I Belong* opened and closed on March 3, 1968.

"At that time, there were shows auditioning every week," Daniele says. "I immediately went to audition for and got in *Love Match*," a first show by the young team of Richard Maltby and David Shire. "The next morning the phone rings and it's Michael Bennett, who I didn't know at all," Daniele says. "Michael said to me, I'm doing a show and I'd like you to be in it. I said, Well, I can't. I'm doing this. He said, I'll get you out of it. And I said, Why should I do that? And he said, Well, this is written by Neil Simon, and the music's by Burt Bacharach, and I think it would be better for you than *Love Match*. I thought, Who the hell does he think he is? But there was something about his chutzpah and his charm."

Daniele dropped out of *Love Match*, which never made it to Broadway, and signed on with Bennett for *Promises, Promises*, which opened at the Shubert Theatre in December 1968 and stayed there for more than three years. But Grazie stayed less than a year before Bennett took her with him to dance in his next show, *Coco*. When that closed, Bennett and Hal Prince cast her in their company of *Follies*.

"That—meeting, working with Michael—was the turning point of my life," she says. "It is the reason I am doing what I am doing now. It was the opening of the door to a greater way of creation.

"Michael's concentration was amazing. Every single moment of a show was important to him. Sometimes when you direct, you say, This piece is good, now I don't know how to solve this problem, but the next thing is going to be good so we can get by. But Michael never allowed that.

"He put months of research into everything before he started rehearsing. The laboratory that became so famous with *Chorus Line*—he was doing that all along. When he was going to do *Coco*, he knew that I had lived in France and I had friends who were models, even one who modeled for Chanel. One day he took me over to the old Manhattan Theatre Club and he said, Just pose. Like a model. And for hours he just had me posing and he watched.

"But the best thing about him was his sense of editing. It was almost like he had this timing machine inside that he knew exactly where something was too long, or not quick enough or not visually interesting enough.

"We were very close and spent a lot of time together for three or four years there. As a person he was kind of aloof, and passionate, but his work was so humanistic. He really knew how to get you emotionally.

"I just became a Michael Bennett girl. Bobby [Fosse] had his own, and Gower [Champion] had his own. It was just this nucleus of people that were almost constantly working with the same choreographer and director."

Daniele soon became Bennett's assistant choreographer on the annual Milliken Breakfast Show, the best known and most lavish of the corporately financed industrial shows that use the elements of musical theatre to introduce new products. She was tired of dancing on Broadway and now intended to focus on learning to choreograph. She had not danced in a show for three years when, in 1975, Bob Fosse offered her a role in the new musical he was working on with John Kander and Fred Ebb, called *Chicago*. She took the job as an opportunity to learn firsthand from Fosse.

"Bobby was totally different from Michael in that Bobby was a stylist," she says. "Michael was a genius but he was always working in different worlds—*Promises* was not the same world as *Coco*, and *Coco* was not the same world as *Follies*. But Bobby was the center of everything, and the world was always focused through him. Like you would say about Picasso—if Picasso paints a woman or a chair, it's Picasso, not the woman or the chair. That's how Bobby was.

"He had an extraordinary personality and he was a nurturing person. He respected and admired dancers, perhaps even more than Michael. His expectations and his standards were so high that somehow we all grew to meet them.

"On the first day of rehearsal for *Chicago*, he opened a new way of thinking for me. We were going to start right off with 'All That Jazz,' the opening number. He had this box of hats and canes and wigs and feathers, just a mishmash. He said to us, Grab anything you want. And we did. If we liked what we put on, our characters and even our costumes would be based on what we chose. And I said, Whew, I've got to pick up on this, this bringing the actor in as a strong collaborator, using the personality of the actor as opposed to saying to the dancer, Five, six, seven, eight, you do this and this."

After working as an assistant choreographer on the Milliken show for seven years, Daniele was offered the main choreographer's job. Her work attracted offers to choreograph productions of the old chestnuts at stock theatres around the country. She made her Broadway staging debut with Chris Durang's play with music *History of the American Film*, which had a brief run in 1979. She choreographed a new production of *The Most Happy Fella* for director Jack O'Brien, which appeared on public television. Then she joined director Wilford Leach in mounting a newly orchestrated and irreverent production of Gilbert and Sullivan's *The Pirates of Penzance* at the outdoor stage in Central Park for Joseph Papp's New York Shakespeare Festival in the summer of 1980; this production reopened at the Uris Theatre on Broadway the following January, and for her efforts Daniele received a Tony nomination for Best Choreography.

"In Wilford, I found one of my best friends in my whole life," she says. "We had a very unusual kind of relationship because our backgrounds were so different. He was this sweet Virginia gentleman, a professor at Sarah Lawrence, who had this great Buddha kind of wisdom; and here was I, this Latin American yelling and screaming. But we liked the same things. He was my best friend of all the people I worked with, and I think I talked less with him about anything I did. We were just of one mind.

"Wilford had this uncanny sense of casting, and I remember asking him how he knew whom to select. He said to me—this incredible intellectual, literate man—he said, Look at two small dogs who don't know each other. They come and they smell each other and either their hair goes up and they become enemies or they start playing with each other like puppies. He was so right. Because when the door opens in an audition and the actors walk in, they can be preceded by the greatest background in history and be an extraordinary talent, but if you don't smell that kind of unity and understanding of wanting to play together, what's the sense?

"Wilford's shows were all play. I would watch him and whenever anyone suggested anything he would say, Try it. Not, No, that won't work. Try it. It only takes a few minutes. That encouraged the actors to play. That's why he could bring these incredibly motley groups together. Kevin Kline and George Rose and Linda Ronstadt. People with their own styles who all got into the playfulness of it.

"For the first week, we would just sit around and watch and listen to the actors. So their personalities would come out. He would just sit back and smile and encourage them and let everything come up before homing in."

Her achievement on *The Pirates of Penzance* placed Daniele on the list of choreographers in demand. She went on to do *Drood* with Leach, *The Rink*, the revival of *Zorba* starring Anthony Quinn, and both directed and choreographed the first workshop of *Smile*.

Then, within a short time, both Bennett and Leach died of AIDS, and Fosse had a fatal heart attack. "The people I called late at night to help me were all gone," she says. "I had no one to call anymore. No one to discuss my work with. I was all on my own."

Perhaps surprisingly, the loss of her support network inspired Daniele not to play it safe, but to take new risks. "I became more frustrated by dance on Broadway," she says. "There isn't enough of it, and what little there is is a rational, conventional form of dance. It's not as intricate as I would like to see, as *West Side Story* was, because there it helped the show emotionally instead of being just an entertainment outside of the show. I knew that in the commercial theatre, expectations for dance, for choreographers, were not high—it was all so limiting. I didn't feel like I was doing enough. And to do it I had to get out of the commercial arena.

"As usually happens in life, when you are feeling a certain way, opportunity knocks at the door. Max Ferra at INTAR, a Hispanic theatre organization, asked me if I would like to develop something of my own. Someone was asking me for the first time in my life, Is there something *you* want to do? I realized I didn't really know what that was. All of a sudden everything is presented in front of you, and how do you choose?

"So I met with INTAR's dramaturge, James Lewis, and he asked me, Is there any Latin person alive—writer, composer, actor, anyone—who I wanted to work with? And I immediately said Astor Piazzolla. He was my favorite Argentine composer. He had taken the tango and raised it to a very contemporary, universal level.

"When I was a kid, my mother used to take me to this tea salon in Buenos Aires, and Astor was there playing the bandoneon. When I left Argentina, I was carrying the records of Mozart and Piazzolla.

"Three days later Jim had me on the phone with Astor in Paris. I told him I had an idea for a dance-theatre piece and he said sure. I almost died. It turned out he had written music for a film based on stories by Jorge Luis Borges. So I said, He's not very theatrical, but let's look for something."

Daniele and Lewis settled on two of Borges's short stories—"The Street Corner Man" and "The Intruder"—and a monologue entitled "Borges and Myself." The piece would be about a writer lost in the world of his own characters.

"So Astor came to meet me in New York," Daniele says, "and he says, Okay, what is the first beat? And I start to explain the story to him. He says, No, just tell me the first beat. So I said, Okay, this is a moment of sexuality and male dominance. He said, How many minutes? I said, I don't know yet. He said, Tell me how many minutes. So I guessed. And he wrote.

"In Argentina, where we all came from, the machismo is very strong. The tango is a great metaphor for it. In the tango, the man is always directing the woman. The woman never knows what the man is going to do. She is always responding to the man. I thought that is a wonderful metaphor for what I saw in Argentina.

"So we constructed this piece, using all dance to tell the story except when we needed to clarify something with words. We did a workshop. This was probably the best time of my life because I dared everything. There was nothing I thought of stopping. I never thought, I can't do that. I just went ahead and did it."

Representatives of AT&T On-Stage, an arts support program, saw the workshop and offered to finance a production. On November 9, 1987, *Tango Apasionado* opened in the large rehearsal space at Westbeth, an artists' housing development in Greenwich Village. The reviews were encouraging, and Mel Gussow, the second-string critic to Rich at the *Times*, was ecstatic:

"Graciela Daniele's *Tango Apasionado* is a brilliant musical adaptation of that Borges world—a labyrinthine world that is, at once, both erotic and bloodthirsty.

"As co-adaptor, director, and choreographer, Ms. Daniele has taken several Borges tales, extracted their essence, and merged them with the passionate rhythm of the tango (music by Astor Piazzolla, lyrics by William Finn). The result is a music-theatre dance piece of breathtaking intensity.

". . . Until now, she [Daniele] has been known primarily as a choreographer of Broadway musicals. With *Tango Apasionado*, she takes a striking tango step into the arena of innovative theatrical conceptualists."

In the current theatrical market, where many producers are in the business of transferring well-reviewed regional-theatre shows to commercial venues, Westbeth became the Mecca-of-the-month.

"We were the toast of New York," Daniele says. "We had everything offered to us on a silver tray. A transfer to Broadway. Tours—even in Europe and Canada. A movie. Everything. But we were only able to obtain the rights from the widow Borges for this workshop. Now we had to try to extend them.

"We had lunch and the widow told us she didn't want to extend. She hated the piece. She said her husband had never been touched by a whore and he was very badly portrayed. I begged her and finally we were presented with seventeen clauses that had to be changed. She said we should make the changes and then she would come back and look at it and decide if she would grant us the rights. At that moment, I could've taken my fork and killed her. I felt as if someone had killed my first baby. Until then, I had been sort of a midwife in my work. But this was my baby from beginning to end. I never thought I was able to hate so deeply. I never had before. What I was hating was the pain of my loss."

With this news, James Lewis and Daniele retreated to the basement living room of her apartment in Chelsea to get very drunk. There they turned their energy to a new piece. "I wanted to do something political about Argentina because I had been reading all these terrible things," Daniele says. "I know that this is very hard to do for American audiences, so we decided it had to be something mythical, a metaphor. So we focused on the Orpheus legend."

A year after the *Tango* production, *Orfeo* was presented as a workshop in the same Westbeth space. Jules Fisher, the talented lighting designer and sometime producer who lives with Daniele, then obtained an agreement from the La Jolla Playhouse in California and the Spoleto Festival in Charleston, South Carolina, to co-produce a production. But the work was only an hour in length. So Daniele decided to edit all the Borges out of *Tango Apasionado*, while keeping the theme of male sexual dominance as a first act to be paired with *Orfeo*. Together the two pieces, renamed *Dangerous Games*, would show that both sexual and political repression in a society devoted to machismo led to violence.

Dangerous Games opened at The American Music Theater Festival in Philadelphia, traveled to Spoleto, and then to La Jolla, while Daniele took a two-week break and went back to Argentina for the first time in thirty-five years to choreograph a film.

"I had left the country because of Perón," she says, "and now I went back to find it in ruins, financially and morally. I was horrified. I couldn't work. I cried for two weeks.

"As soon as I arrived, I was picked up at the airport and told that that day a state of siege had been declared. As a kid, I had lived from one state of siege to another. Then I assumed the rest of the world was like that. Going back now, I was not only shocked to be in it again, but it brought back terrible memories from when I was young.

"The banks had been closed for two weeks and I could not exchange any money. I couldn't go anywhere unless I was picked up. I could not pay for a cup of coffee. Finally, I had to exchange some dollars through the black market.

"I still carried an Argentine passport, which had been revalidated in New York. When I arrived at Immigration, the man picks up my passport and says, We're going to keep this. I said, What do you mean you're going to keep it? He said, It's not valid. I said, It's valid until '94. He said, You go to the federal police to renew your passport because this one is no good in Argentina. So I was in a state of siege in my own country, with no money and no passport. For someone who lived there, maybe it was no problem. For me, it was like a nightmare.

"So I went to the federal police and they said, Come back Monday to pick up your passport. So I went and they said they didn't have it ready, come back Wednesday. I went Wednesday and they said to come back Friday. I went Friday and they still didn't have it. Finally I paid someone to activate it, which is the way my country works. I went the next Friday, the day before I was supposed to leave, and they said to come back Saturday at seven in the morning. I came back Saturday at seven and the building was closed, so I had to postpone my trip back. I went back later in the day, and when no one would help me I started to cry. Then one man came up to me and said he would help. He took me to this building and it was like Kafka. I walked through the hallways and all the office doors were shut. I don't know, I felt scared, like there was torture going on there. Finally, I got my passport and flew to La Jolla and I called my lawyer and said I could not go back and finish the movie. It was the first time I had not finished a job in my life. But I just couldn't.

"I went back to work on *Orfeo* in La Jolla and I started to change it. I made the costumes more military. I changed choreography, I changed music, I changed the intention. I made it much angrier. We did very well in La Jolla. And then we moved to San Francisco. At the first preview, on a Wednesday afternoon, the piece starts and within three minutes people in the audience start screaming at one another, getting up walking around the theatre and shouting. They scream at the actors. Then the rest of the audience screams at them to shut up. It was like a riot. I've never seen anything like it before. It was like the times you hear about in the Irish theatre with Sean O'Casey. It was very controversial and the controversy got in all the papers. And we got the best reviews we had anywhere.

"Then Jules and Jimmy Nederlander told me they wanted to bring it to Broadway. I didn't want to. I knew somehow inside me that it was the wrong venue. I felt it could have a long life touring regional theatres and universities and in Europe. But I went along with them, and I was wrong. It's a good thing I did not read Mr. Rich's review, because if I had I would have quit. And Mr. Rich wouldn't have had *Once on This Island* to like and to take his children to two or three times."

Daniele was in rehearsal for the workshop of *Orfeo* when she received a call from Ira Weitzman, director of the musical-theatre program at Play-wrights Horizons, asking her to listen to a score for a new musical by the young team of Lynn Ahrens and Stephen Flaherty.

Daniele told the writers she would have to meet them on her lunch break and could hear only a few songs. So Daniele went to Ahrens's loft, where the composer and lyricist performed their work. After three songs Daniele called the theatre and said she would be late for rehearsal. "I had to hear more," Daniele says. "And I needed Kleenex because I was crying so much. It was the kind of thing where you just go, Yes, I understand these people. I know these people. I feel this show.

"The piece seemed to be about who I am. The first number they played for me was the opening, called 'We Dance.' It was about the connection between success and failure. What do you do after you have success or after you have failure? I know what I do, the same thing in both cases—I just get up and dance.

"I loved the naïve artistry of the story. It was almost childlike in its simplicity. I was very interested in that it was about blacks in a black culture. It was about racism in black culture, and it said we are all racists somehow, somewhere. I had turned down other black musicals, about the black American culture, because that is so specific, I thought it would be disrespectful for me to try to do it. But I didn't feel that with *Once on This Island*, perhaps because of the mythical aspect of it. Myths exist in every culture and in every race, so I felt close to it. It took place in the

Caribbean, and I am a Latin woman. I lived in Brazil, I lived in the Caribbean islands, I lived in Cuba for a while when I was young. So I felt very much a part of what this was about."

Early on, Daniele made the decision to tell the simple story of a poor, dark-skinned girl who saves the life of and falls in love with a rich, light-skinned boy, only to lose him and then her life on a bare stage filled only with movement. "It was right there in the words in the opening," she says. "We dance to celebrate life. And I've been on this island, and when people walk on the island they sway to a certain rhythm. There is music in their walk. So it was natural that this was a world in which people didn't talk—they sang—and in which people didn't walk—they danced.

"For the setting I thought of Rousseau, because his work is primitive, which is naïve like the storytelling here. Rousseau with the colors of Matisse.

"I never thought that the simple way we were doing it would make it a Broadway show. I don't think Broadway because I'm not from this culture. The kind of aura Broadway has for a lot of people was never mine. Since I was seven I have worked in a theatre. That's what I think about—being in a theatre.

"When we first started out on the show, the story was being told to the audience. It was presentational. I thought that wouldn't work; I felt that for sophisticated audiences, being told this common, direct story of love and death would make it seem too simplistic, too conventional. But I thought, We all have a child inside ourselves. If we can peer at the story through the eyes of a child, which we already had onstage, it would be all right to speak such simple language. So we decided to have the cast tell the story to the child. Then we needed a reason why they were telling her the story. We realized it was because there was a big storm and she was afraid of the storm. That's when I remember my grandmother and my mother telling me stories.

"Now we were out of the presentational trap, which is a thing I don't love in American musicals. You know: Love me, love me, and I can kick and I kick and I can do this and now you like me. It just drives me crazy. I came to this country because of *West Side Story*. It was a story lived by those people onstage. They didn't turn to us and tell us about it; they talked to one another. That's the kind of musical theatre I like doing."

The opening-night performance of *Once on This Island* in May 1990 was followed by a party in the lobby of Playwrights Horizons. Daniele was dancing to a calypso band with associate choreographer Willie Rosario when André Bishop called her aside and said, "I know you don't read reviews, but the *Times*'s is a rave."

"I hugged him and cried," Daniele says. "I was so relieved because of Lynn and Stephen. I couldn't go any lower than I was, but I could hurt them and I didn't want to because I adored them and I want to work with them again. So I cried with relief. Then I found Willie again and we continued to dance."

WESTSIDE THEATRE

R. TYLER GATCHELL, JR.   PETER NEUFELD   PATRICK J. PATEK   GENE R. KORF
IN ASSOCIATION WITH THE McCARTER THEATRE

PRESENT

AND THE
WORLD
GOES
'ROUND
THE SONGS OF KANDER & EBB

LYRICS BY
MUSIC BY
JOHN KANDER   FRED EBB

CONCEIVED BY   DAVID
SCOTT   SUSAN   THOMPSON
ELLIS   STROMAN

THE COMPANY   JIM   KAREN
BRENDA   WALTON   ZIEMBA ★
PRESSLEY

BOB   KAREN
CUCCIOLI   MASON

SCENERY   COSTUMES   LIGHTING   SOUND
BILL   LINDSAY W.   PHIL   GARY
HOFFMAN   DAVIS   MONAT   STOCKER

MUSICAL DIRECTION   ORCHESTRATIONS   CASTING   PRODUCTION STAGE MANAGER
VOCAL & DANCE ARRANGEMENTS   DAVID   JOSEPH   MICHAEL A.
DAVID   KRANE   ABALDO   CLARKE
LOUD

CHOREOGRAPHY BY
SUSAN STROMAN

DIRECTED BY
SCOTT ELLIS

THIS PRODUCTION IS MADE POSSIBLE BY GRANTS TO THE MCCARTER THEATRE BY
THE STEPHEN & MARY BIRCH FOUNDATION, INC. AND THE BLANCHE & IRVING LAURIE FOUNDATION, INC.

11

LEADING LADY

"Happiness Comes In on Tiptoe"

★

KAREN ZIÉMBA (*Cleo*) starred in the Outer Critics' Circle Award–winning off-Broadway production of *And the World Goes 'Round*, for which she won a Drama Desk Award as Best Featured Actress in a Musical. On Broadway, she debuted in *A Chorus Line*, then soon after starred as Peggy Sawyer in *42nd Street*. She also performed in *Stardust* at Washington's Kennedy Center, appeared as Alice Roosevelt in Broadway's *Teddy and Alice*, and portrayed five different roles in *Jerome Robbins' Broadway* during its Los Angeles run. Her regional credits include *The Foreigner*, Lanford Wilson's *Fifth of July*, the role of Alice Mitchell in *Dennis the Menace*, and the title role in *Annie, Get Your Gun*. She performed in the concert version of Cole Porter's 1929 musical *Fifty Million Frenchmen*, which she also recorded for New World Records. Ms. Ziémba made her New York City Opera debut as Gladys in *The Pajama Game* in 1989 and also appeared here in *Candide*, following in the footsteps of her grandmother, Winifred Heidt, who was a leading mezzo-soprano at NYCO from 1945 to 1950.

At 1:30 on a gray and misty September Saturday afternoon, Karen Ziémba strides across Forty-third Street west of Ninth Avenue, her neck-length brown hair bouncing along with her step. Clad in a white T-shirt, blue blazer, and blue jeans, Ziémba is indistinguishable from the casually dressed ticketholders beginning to gather outside the yellow-sandstone facade of the Westside Theatre—unless you look at her feet. The toes of her black cowboy boots are pointed to two o'clock and ten o'clock. These feet belong to a dancer.

In reviewing *And the World Goes 'Round*, the show in which Ziémba will perform in this theatre this afternoon, Frank Rich, drama critic of the *Times*, wrote: ". . . she manages to tread wittily on the turf once owned by Gwen Verdon and Chita Rivera without losing her own somewhat daffier profile." There's not a theatre dancer in town who wouldn't do splits on nails to have that quote among her press clippings.

Those words as well as the rest of Rich's enthusiastic opening-night notice stand blown up shoulder-high in the lobby of this structure, which was built as a church, converted to a disco in the sixties, then to a pair of theatres in the seventies. At 1:32, just past half-hour, the time designated for actors in all the shows around town to report to work, Ziémba breezes through the lobby and down a flight of stairs to the basement dressing room she shares with her two female costars and their two understudies. Terry Burrell, one of the costars, and Andrea Green, an understudy who will perform this afternoon, are already here sitting in front of the mirror that covers the long cinder-block wall in the bare rectangular room.

Ziémba is one of those people who always seems taller than you remember her to be. While the movie screen makes actors appear larger than they are, the stage, with its proscenium opening, tends to have the opposite effect. She hangs up her blazer and sits down on a folding chair in her little space before the mirror. Her area is delineated by photographs of her husband, Bill Tatum (also an actor), and her nieces and nephews; a Japanese postcard picturing Ziémba doing the Charleston in the international company of *Jerome Robbins' Broadway*; and an old black-and-white of a large, *zaftig* woman wearing a mantilla and holding a fan.

"That's my grandmother, Winifred Heidt, playing Carmen," Ziémba says, her mouth forming a little smile that is both fond and sad. "She played it hundreds of times all over the world, including at the City Center Opera." One of the thousands of people who were introduced to the beguiling Carmen by Winifred Heidt was John Kander, a twenty-one-year-old boy about to leave Kansas City to go off to war. He also wrote all the music that Ziémba will be onstage singing in twenty-five minutes.

Ziémba begins to apply her makeup in the same routine way that she has done six nights a week and on Wednesday and Saturday afternoons for the seven months since this show opened in March, and before that, for the month that the show was developed at the Whole Theatre Company, a not-for-profit theatre in Montclair, New Jersey, run by actress Olympia Dukakis.

But this is by no means a routine day for an actress. "I ran through *Most Happy Fella* in my mind as I was coming here," Ziémba says. "Now I'd better use this time to get back into this show. I play so many characters that you don't have much time to think about them. And you're so close to the audience in this theatre, it's very distracting—especially after you've been in a show for a long time."

This afternoon Ziémba will perform various songs and characters before an audience of three hundred in *And the World Goes 'Round*, a revue celebrating the theatre-music collaboration of composer John Kander and lyricist Fred Ebb, whose scores include those for *Cabaret*, *Chicago*, and the motion picture *New York, New York*. This evening at 8, while Andrea Green fills in for her here, Ziémba will be on the stage of the New York State Theater before 3,000 people when the curtain rises on the New York City Opera production of Frank Loesser's *The Most Happy Fella*. Playing Cleo, the second female lead, she's accumulated the best set of reviews in that large company. Most nights when her show comes up in the City Opera repertory, Ziémba is excused from a performance of *And the World Goes 'Round*. This is the one day when she will perform both shows.

The only similar feat I can recall was in the summer of 1984, when Cynthia Nixon was doing concurrent performances in David Hare's *HurlyBurly* at the Ethel Barrymore Theatre on Forty-seventh Street and Tom Stoppard's *The Real Thing* at the Plymouth Theatre on Forty-fifth Street. Nixon began the evening performing the first act of Rabe's play, then ran two blocks, changed costumes, and performed her scene in Stoppard's play, then ran back for her character's return in Rabe's final scene. At least Ziémba will get to take both her curtain calls.

To an observer, the day Ziémba has ahead of her appears to be a thrilling feat, a feast for any kid who grew up acting out musicals in her bedroom with the door closed, immortalized for us all by Gilda Radner's Judy Miller character on "Saturday Night Live." But Ziémba is no more giddy than a Kelly Girl about to start her workday. "All I can think about is getting through it all," she says.

★ ★ ★

At 2:04, stage manager Valerie Lau-Kee senses that the audience is settled and announces, "Ladies and gentlemen, places, please," on the backstage public-address system. Ziémba, costumed in a purple skirt and purple-and-blue blouse designed by Lindsay Davis, follows her costars up a black-steel spiral staircase to the small offstage area, stage left.

The lights dim to half and the audience buzz ceases beneath the bowed ceiling of the church steeple in this recently refurbished theatre.

The lights go to black, and a bluesy clarinet begins to wail. Then a spotlight picks up Terry Burrell in the center of the stage singing the revue's title song, originally written for Liza Minnelli to sing in the motion picture *New York, New York.*

The false proscenium framing Burrell is decorated with dictionary definitions of terms that describe the work of Kander and Ebb. The singer is bookended by "inner passion" and "emotion." At her feet, visible only to the performers, painted across the floor is "And that's show biz, kid."

Then the five-piece band—hidden for now high at the rear of the stage—picks up the tempo, gliding into "Yes," originally written for the 1971 musical *70, Girls, 70.* Two panels slide off and now we discover Ziémba, who blends with the rest of the cast in this group number. Onstage, her eyes are tiny and round, her mouth is a straight line, and all the rest of her is points: her nose, her chin, her elbows, her knees—arrows flying in different directions. She uses her sharp features for great comic effect, turning into a robot with her eyes spinning in the next number, "Coffee in a Cardboard Cup" (also from *70, Girls, 70*), in which the pace of the number accelerates from a walk to a gallop as the cast succumbs to mock caffeine intoxication. Her appearance seems custom-designed for a musical-comedy comedienne. You can imagine her in the roles played by Mary Martin or Judy Holliday, or in anything written by Betty Comden and Adolph Green. She's a throwback to another day of musical theatre when almost every show seemed to feature a funny woman who sang and danced, a role that's been lacking in this era dominated by the largely sung-through British musicals.

A short while later Ziémba is back onstage, dowdy now in a silly flowered hat, a red shoulder bag hanging at her side, wearing dainty white gloves. "I'm an insecure and neurotic housewife with a secret I have to tell," she says later. Soon the hat and the gloves are gone, and Ziémba is tossing her great gams around the neck and shoulders of a hunk in dark glasses as she performs "Arthur in the Afternoon" from *The Act.* The shy, quiet Midwestern girl suddenly has all this surprising sex and passion and humor spurting out of her. Plain Jane becomes one hot pistol. And she puts a funny and surprising twist on the number by pulling her American Express card out of her bodice. "I wasn't sure I wanted to do that," she says, "but Susan Stroman [the choreographer] made me, and she was right. It's a big laugh."

When we see her again she's in a spangled red-and-blue camisole worn over a crepe skirt, accompanied by a honky-tonk piano player on a stool, stage left, and having the audacity to turn "All That Jazz," the number Chita Rivera and a chorus of leggy Fosse girls (including Stroman in the national company) opened *Chicago* with, into a kind of one-woman production number. Instead of having a lot of girls on the stage, we get a lot of Ziémba—arms and legs and fingers and pelvis.

"In that number, I have to be totally in control of my body, the piano player, and the audience," Ziémba says. "It's a kind of striptease without taking off your clothes."

Midway through the second act, she enters hand in hand with actor Joel Blum. They sit on a bench and he asks her to "Marry Me," a song Kander and Ebb wrote for *The Rink*. She's happy and flattered and scared. Left alone for a few minutes, she expresses all this by singing "A Quiet Thing," a lovely ballad from *Flora, the Red Menace*. She expected this moment in her life to be an explosion. Instead, as Ebb writes, "Happiness comes in on tiptoe."

Then the boy returns, and Ziémba's on tiptoes in a romantic pas de deux that builds from freezing to boiling, from zero to sixty miles per hour, as the two lovers tap their joy in the kind of Fred Astaire–and–Ginger Rogers heart-melting duet of which choreographer Stroman seems to be the lone practitioner left in town.

It's a glitzy showcase for this thirtysomething performer, now reaching her prime. The Kander-and-Ebb songs are written for characters that tap facets of Ziémba's personality. And in this dancer Stroman has found a performing alter ego with the sensibility and athleticism to express her own take on romance and sensuality.

Yet, watching Ziémba's kaleidoscopic performance in these excerpts from so many musicals written over the thirty-year collaboration of Kander and Ebb, I wonder whether anything has been written in the past decade that would permit this musical-theatre actress to use all of her diverse talents. It's not that she's incapable of filling roles provided by Stephen Sondheim (particularly in *Into the Woods*) or Andrew Lloyd Webber (she could be lots of different *Cats*) or the team of Alain Boublil and Claude-Michel Schonberg. But Ziémba's performing in these people's shows would be akin to restricting Bobby Bonds to the role of designated hitter and robbing the audience of the thrill of seeing him catch and throw.

Sitting over a salad at a corner table at Joe Allen's restaurant between her two shows, Ziémba says, "In the old musicals I grew up on, there was always an ingenue and a wisecracking friend, and I was trained to play both of them. But now I go in to read and they see this girl who reads well, sings well, dances great—but she's a five-foot-seven, one-hundred-twenty-five pound brunette. I'm not your little fragile-type girl, and I guess I'm hard to cast."

Ziémba got the best set of reviews of all the cast members in *And the World Goes 'Round*, received a Drama Desk Award, and she's the only original cast member still in the show. You would expect that this kind of reception would attract a shower of offers. But it hasn't—partly because there simply is not a lot around to offer. She's upset about recently losing the leading role in the upcoming production of *Crazy for You* to Jodi Benson, best known until now as the voice of the title character in the animated film *The Little Mermaid*. "They're all big losses today," Ziémba says, "because it's a long time until another role like that comes along."

One would hate to believe that what Ziémba's performance in this revue proves is that she is an anachronism—that the era of her style of performer—the singer-dancer-comedienne—is over.

What is more likely true is that she is living in a strange era of musical theatre in which we are being robbed of the opportunity to see some of the kinds of performing that made us fans of the genre in the first place. The lack of roles for someone of Karen Ziémba's talents—call it the Ziémba Dilemma—is another example of the current sad state of the musical theatre caused by the economics of the business and the limited number of productions.

Theatre is a cyclical business. And it would be foolish to pronounce dead the fast-talking, wisecracking style of comedy that energized musical classics like *Guys and Dolls* and *Kiss Me Kate*, and that recently has shown its head only in Larry Gelbart's book and David Zippel's lyrics for *City of Angels*. But time is no ally for actors, particularly those who are athletic dancers as well. And someone like Karen Ziémba, who has gone through all the training and worked her way up through the ranks to become a headliner, and whose time is now, has to wonder if she was born too late.

Karen Ziémba is one of the few people in this town who really seems to have been born to be a performer.

To explain what may appear to be a glib remark, we need to go back a few generations to that "Carmen" whose photo sits on Ziémba's dressing table—her grandmother, Winifred Heidt.

In the early 1940s the then Winifred Huntoon, a mezzo-soprano-contralto, sang Sigmund Romberg and Victor Herbert on the NBC radio affiliate in Detroit. One evening, the sturdily built singer ("a Wagnerian woman," Ziémba says) was invited to entertain at a dinner for the Detroit Edison Company and caught the eye of one of the corporation's attorneys,

William Heidt, a very serious, very hard-nosed man ("a crotchety old German," according to Ziémba). They courted and married and soon had three children, the middle one being a daughter they named Barbara.

During the war, Winifred Heidt auditioned for the Metropolitan Opera of the Air in Detroit. She was so impressive that she was then asked to audition for the Metropolitan Opera in New York. She was offered a contract and decided to move to New York with her father, leaving her husband, William, home in Detroit with their three children. The separation riled and embarrassed the tradition-bound lawyer. He sued his wife for divorce, using the Metropolitan Opera, where she was studying, as his grounds. One can imagine the scandal provoked by this independent woman from middle America at midcentury. Were her life made into a film, she could have been played only by Bette Davis.

Winifred Heidt later sang for the City Center Opera, married the Metropolitan Opera tenor Eugene Conley, and settled on a farm in Flemington, New Jersey. Relations were strained with her ex-husband, and most of her contact with her children in Detroit was through the postcards and photos she sent them of her performing all over the world in *Aïda*, *Samson and Delilah*, *Cavalleria Rusticana*, and, most often, *Carmen*. In 1949, her daughter Barbara came for a rare visit to the farm. What the teenager remembered most about the trip was seeing Ezio Pinza perform in *South Pacific* at the Mark Hellinger Theatre on Broadway.

At home in Detroit, Barbara was studying singing and tap dancing. Her inspiration was her mother, and her idol was Eleanor Powell. The young Barbara had to take a number of connecting bus routes from her home to her lessons in downtown Detroit. One day she got lost. When she told this to her father, he proclaimed in anger, "You got lost? That's enough of that. No more lessons."

"Her mother was gone," Ziémba says. "Now everything her mother stood for was gone. And the thing she loved to do most was gone."

Barbara Heidt went on to attend Wayne State University, where she fell for one of the stars of the school's basketball team, Oscar Ziémba. Oscar's father had emigrated from Königsberg, Germany, was hired as a machinist by the Whirlpool Corporation in St. Joseph, Michigan, then returned to Germany to marry and bring back his sweetheart. Oscar, an only child, graduated from Wayne State, got a job as a securities salesman, and married his own college sweetheart. Oscar and Barbara Ziémba then settled in St. Joseph and had four children. When their second child, their only daughter, was born, Barbara Ziémba was determined to give the girl, Karen, the opportunity to perform that she herself had been denied because of William Heidt's anger at his ex-wife.

At age six, Karen began ballet lessons with a Russian woman who taught at the local Y in St. Joseph. "In recitals, everyone in my class wore a blue or pink tutu," Ziémba recalls. "But my mom said, 'I want you to be different.' And I had a yellow tutu."

She sang in her church choir, began tap lessons at age nine, and, taking a year of piano, learned how to read music.

"My idol at the time was Mary Martin," Ziémba says. "I mean, she was Peter Pan. I was in love with her because I thought if a boy could ever love me the way she loved Tinker Bell, that would be it. It was pretty confusing realizing she was really an older woman.

"My father would go to New York on business and bring me back all the original-cast albums. I remember looking at the *Sweet Charity* album and seeing this woman in a black dress—kind of turned around with a funny-looking purse on her shoulder—and thinking, Ooooh, what kind of show is that? I never realized that that's what I would become."

As Oscar Ziémba's business grew, the family moved to more upscale suburbs, first to Grosse Pointe, then to Farmington Hills, where Karen began taking ballet classes with a woman who believed it was necessary to bring the young girls to New York for them to see what it was like to be a professional. At fifteen, Karen came to Manhattan with her ballet class and spent two weeks at a hotel on Fifty-sixth Street and Sixth Avenue, "where our favorite activity was hanging out the windows and dropping Triskets on the call girls," Ziémba says. The following summer, Barbara Ziémba encouraged her daughter to spend a month in New York City, and she sublet an apartment for Karen and a friend.

Back home, Karen began performing with a local community ballet company for which her mother chaired the board of directors and sewed the costumes. At dinner, Barbara Ziémba would tell her three sons, "We're spending more money and time on Karen because she has to do this now if she's ever going to pursue it."

Karen went to dance class three nights a week, performed with the ballet company on weekends, sang at school and in the church choir, and at North Farmington High School she played Maria in *West Side Story* and Aldonza in *Man of La Mancha*.

"I missed all the football and basketball games the kids went to," she says. "I dated the older brothers of the girls I met in dance class. I was quite a prude. The sexuality in my life was in the roles I played in the musicals, and that was great. I acted it like I saw it in the movies."

Ziémba went to college because she wasn't yet prepared to venture out professionally. She chose the University of Akron because the Ohio Ballet, a professional company, was in residence there. She danced in the corps during her sophomore year, which included performing at the first Spoleto Festival in Charleston, South Carolina. "But I was never really suited for a ballet company," she says. "I'm not a skinny little waif. I wasn't into technique and into the corps—I wanted to perform." She was not retained by the company as a junior; but she decided to go ahead and finish college.

In the summer of her junior year, Ziémba auditioned for the Akron-area company of the Kenley Players, the venerable summer-stock outfit. Since her liberation from ballet, Ziémba had developed an affinity for beer, and she was rejected from the company because she was too chubby. The budding actress was, however, hired to sell programs.

"One night I was watching John Raitt in *Man of La Mancha*," she recalls, "and this man I had never met came up to me and asked me if I sang. I said I did. He said he was a conductor and would like to hear me. He invited me to come to his house in Cleveland and sing for him. I was so young and eager that I drove there from Akron and sung on tape.

"Being a ballet dancer, I grew up with tunnel vision. I still had the maturity of a seventeen-year-old. I was very trusting and eager. I didn't stop to think what an older man might have on his mind."

In her senior year, Ziémba performed the role Gwen Verdon had originated in a production of *Can-Can* at the Goodyear Theatre, a community-theatre company that staged productions in a large, old vaudeville house in Akron. Upon graduation, she returned home to Michigan, where, one night, the aforementioned conductor called and spoke with Karen's father. The conductor said Karen had the talent to succeed in New York. He invited her to go there and rent a spare room in his apartment. Oscar and Barbara Ziémba thought it was a good opportunity for their daughter. So, right out of college, Karen moved to New York.

"I was not in the union," she says. "I didn't know much about how the business worked. He kept telling me how little I knew. I would stand beside the piano and sing for him and he would yell at me and I would cry.

"In the evenings, I would do anything I could to get out of that apartment. I was so uncomfortable there."

During this period, Ziémba supported herself waitressing at Cronie's on Second Avenue and Eighty-eighth Street and ushering at the Beacon Theatre. Then the conductor was hired as musical director of a production of *My Fair Lady* at the North Shore Music Theatre in Beverly, Massachusetts. There were parts for four dancers in the production. The conductor got Ziémba her first professional work and, as a result, her Actors' Equity membership card. She earned enough money from this job to get her own place when she returned to New York.

★ ★ ★

At 7 P.M., Ziémba enters her dressing room in the cavernous underworld of the New York State Theater. Here she has the room to herself. She puts on her makeup, then pulls on a sweatshirt, sweatpants, and booties to get herself warm. Warmth will help her to meet the vocal requirements of performing Cleo in *The Most Happy Fella*.

This production is part of the repertory season of the New York City Opera. The City Center Opera, for which Winifred Heidt performed for so many years, became the New York City Opera when it moved Lincoln Center in 1963. "When my grandmother was too old for the operas," Ziémba says, "she did musicals for the City Center. I have a framed caricature of her that appeared in the *Brooklyn Sun*, from when she played Mrs. Mullin in *Carousel* with Barbara Cook and Jo Sullivan. Now that I've worked here, I guess it completes the family circle."

Ziémba first performed for the New York City Opera in its production of *The Pajama Game*, in the summer of 1991. She played the role of Gladys, for which Carol Haney won the Tony Award for Best Supporting Actress in the 1953–54 Broadway season. One of the showiest of the funny-girl sidekick roles, it features both the humor of composers Richard Adler and Jerry Ross's "Hernando's Hideaway" and the slinky dancing for their "Steam Heat"—numbers that attracted widespread attention for Bob Fosse choreographing his first Broadway show.

The role proved to be both unexpected and fateful for Ziémba. She was not originally cast in the role—Leonora Nemetz was. Ziémba was her standby. But Nemetz became ill and director Ted Pappas then asked Ziémba to replace her that night. There was no rehearsal time. Ziémba had watched Nemetz perform the role a few times over a two-week period, then went on.

A few months later, Scott Ellis and Susan Stroman were having a hard time casting their production of *And the World Goes 'Round* for its run in New Jersey. They could not find a woman who could both land Kander and Ebb's character-driven songs and perform the showy choreography that Stroman had designed for some of the numbers. Ellis and musical director David Loud called everyone they knew, including Pappas, for recommendations. Pappas raved about Ziémba, who got the job.

Nemetz was also originally cast as Cleo in this production of *The Most Happy Fella*. The City Opera uses alternate casts for some performances, and Ziémba was invited to audition for the second cast. She appeared at the audition hall in the basement of the State Theater in a pretty red dress and sang Irving Berlin's "I Got the Sun in the Morning and the Moon at Night" from *Annie Get Your Gun*. But Joanna Glushak got the job. Ziémba felt she had dressed in a manner that was too dignified for the creative team to recognize the character.

Meanwhile, out in Seattle, Ann Reinking chose not to continue playing opposite Tommy Tune in the national touring company of *Bye Bye Birdie*. The role was offered to Leonora Nemetz, who grabbed it. Ziémba was called in to audition for the role of Cleo again. This time she dressed down in a plain white top and a blue skirt. She sang Richard Maltby and David Shire's "Starting Here, Starting Now" and also Cleo's opening number, "Ooh, My Feet." She got the first-cast job, replacing Nemetz.

At 8:04, the curtain rises on the basketball court–size stage occupied by a 1950s-style diner done all in pink with turquoise trim, occupied now only by Karen Ziémba in a pink waitress's dress with a white hat and apron. One woman alone onstage in front of 3,000 people filling six balconies seven stories high. The orchestra vamps and Ziémba opens her mouth and out comes "Ooh, my feet. My poor, poor feet" in a big voice completely different from any voice heard by the 300 people at the Westside Theatre this afternoon. It's not just that it's loud—with amplification anyone can be loud. But it's a rich, deep roar of a voice. To the legendary performers whose roles Ziémba can play, add Merman. She does the scene with her waitress friend Amy (Elizabeth Walsh), who will soon be invited to come and marry an aging Italian immigrant vintner named Tony, whom she has never met, in the Napa Valley. Amy does receive a photo sent by Tony—but, afraid she will not come if she sees what he looks like, he sends a photo of his foreman, the young and handsome Joe, instead.

Then Ziémba is offstage for the rest of the act as Amy goes to meet Tony, who drives his car off the road and injures himself on the way to meet her, realizes the scam operating here, and in her loneliness succumbs to the temptation of Joe.

"This is such a different focus from doing the Kander and Ebb show," Ziémba says. "In *World Goes 'Round* I run offstage, change character, and I'm back on. There's no time to think. In *Happy Fella*, there's too much time to think. I'm on and I'm off and I have to stay in character to go back on an hour later. I come limping off after singing 'Poor Feet' and continue limping around my dressing room.

"This cast is a mixture of opera and theatre performers, and that makes it difficult. The training is different. Opera folks are more focused on vocal prowess. Theatre buffs focus on interacting with the other performers. The two styles don't always mesh."

In the second act, Cleo is summoned to the farm to support Amy, renamed Rosabella by her Italian suitor. Ziémba enters with red hair and dressed all in lime green amid "Happy to Make Your Acquaintance," in which Tony and Rosabella begin to connect. Later, dressed more casually, she meets a hick of a farmhand named Herman, who, like Cleo, happens to be from Dallas. In "Big D," the kind of in-your-face production number that was a staple of the musicals of this show's period, she polkas and hoofs with the tall Lara Teeter, well matched with Ziémba as Herman, and then with about thirty-five other dancers. Throughout Dan Siretta's spirited choreography, Ziémba is a little firefly flitting all around the stage, her purple skirt flying and great joy filling the auditorium.

At intermission, a young press agent named John Barlow stands out by the fountain in the courtyard, smiling from what he has seen, and says, "Karen Ziémba and Nathan Lane [who will be cast in the upcoming revival of *Guys and Dolls*] are the two hottest people in town. Everyone knows it. They're headed right through the stratosphere."

In the third act, Ziémba gets to strut her stuff with Herman again in "Smile, Smile, Smile." She's in green polka dots this time. Her exit is a joke as Herman puts her over his shoulder and she reaches down his back upside down to embrace him. Meanwhile, Joe leaves town, and Tony expresses his love for Rosabella by accepting as his own child the baby that Joe has fathered. The curtain falls, then rises again for the bows that are appreciative—until Ziémba appears and is greeted with a roar that won't be repeated for her costars.

Equipped with her Equity card after her debut at the North Shore Music Theatre, Ziémba got a job in the chorus of a production of *Carousel*, starring Ron Holgate and Judy Kaye at the Carousel Dinner Theatre in Nanuet, New York. "I was so naïve then," she says. "I went up to Ron and said, 'You're kissing Judy awfully stiff up there.' He must've thought I was strange. Four years later, I had to kiss him in *42nd Street*."

She was in the chorus of *The King and I* in Nanuet, then got her first New York City job in the chorus of *Seesaw* at the Equity Library Theatre. The male lead in that show was an actor named Bill Tatum, who was seeing another woman at the time. Nevertheless, Ziémba took a liking to him.

She did a version of the Gershwins' *Funny Face* at the Goodspeed Opera House in East Haddam, Connecticut, where she met Dan Siretta, the choreographer of *Happy Fella*. While appearing in the fiftieth anniversary show for Radio City Music Hall, she was invited to audition for the bus-and-truck company of *A Chorus Line*. On the stage of the Shubert Theatre she sang André and Dory Previn's song "You're Gonna Hear from Me," which Natalie Wood first sang in the film *Inside Daisy Clover*, and was cast as Maggie. She joined the line in Minneapolis and traveled with the company to Fargo, Grand Rapids, and later Pittsburgh, where that company closed. Then she was invited to join the international company, which was playing in Las Vegas at the time, as an understudy.

Her relationship with Tatum had intensified, but his affections were still divided, and she thought it might be wise to get away. Vegas was difficult for her and she missed Bill. But he called her there and said he wanted to have a life together with her. So Ziémba returned to New York, married Bill, and was put into the Broadway company of *A Chorus Line*. Ziémba was still in her mid-twenties, and her career took a leap now—she participated in the finale of the unforgettable gala performance of *A Chorus Line*, celebrating the show's achievement of becoming the longest-running Broadway show of all time. She was cast in the lead role in *42nd Street* as Peggy Sawyer, the chorus girl who gets to go on for the injured star, first played by Ruby Keeler on film and by Wanda Richert onstage. From there she went on to play a featured role in the short-lived Broadway musical *Teddy and Alice*, five roles in the Los Angeles company of *Jerome Robbins' Broadway*, and returned to *A Chorus Line* five years after she left.

So what we have here is a working musical-theatre actress who's in the small pool of women you want to see at every audition for the leading lady. There is usually a job somewhere for this select group, if not on Broadway, then in regional theatre. Yet Ziémba remains frustrated.

"What I'm frustrated about is that what I do best, there isn't necessarily a market for anymore—at least not in the new shows," she says over a beer at the Saloon, across Broadway from Lincoln Center, as she winds down from her doubleheader. "I mean, you can always do the old shows in stock and in occasional Broadway revivals. But that's not what we get in this for. It's creating roles in new shows that is the plum.

"Sure, I'm part of a pool that works, but there are so many good people in that pool, many who you would think of ahead of me for roles that don't emphasize dancing. And how many shows have much dancing today? So what I need to do is move up in that pool, and the only way to make that leap is to accept jobs that are not primarily dancing." And that's a loss to all of us.

She's got the buzz now, the adrenaline rush that lingers following the nervousness and the concentration and the dancing and the music and the excitement of the crowd and its applause.

"I won't get to sleep for a while," she says as she hails a cab on Broadway just after midnight. "Not after all this. It's been a really neat day.

"What I accomplished today, doing the two shows and all, it'll probably strike me in the middle of the night tonight when I can't sleep and I'm up worrying about something. But I hope not. I've got a matinee tomorrow."

The John F. Kennedy Center for the Performing Arts

JAMES D. WOLFENSOHN, *Chairman*

OPERA HOUSE

CAMERON MACKINTOSH and
THE REALLY USEFUL THEATRE COMPANY, INC.

present

The
PHANTOM
of the
OPERA.

starring

KEVIN GRAY ★

TERI BIBB

KEITH BUTERBAUGH

RICK HILSABECK   DAVID HUNERYAGER   PATRICIA HURD
OLGA TALYN   DONN COOK   PATRICIA WARD

At certain performances
SARAH PFISTERER
plays the role of "Christine"

Music by
ANDREW LLOYD WEBBER

Lyrics by CHARLES HART

Additional lyrics by RICHARD STILGOE

Book by RICHARD STILGOE & ANDREW LLOYD WEBBER

Based on the novel 'Le Fantôme de L'Opéra' by GASTON LEROUX

Production Design by MARIA BJÖRNSON   Lighting by ANDREW BRIDGE

Sound by MARTIN LEVAN   Musical Director JACK GAUGHAN   Production Supervisor MITCHELL LEMSKY

Musical Supervision & Direction DAVID CADDICK   DAVID CULLEN & ANDREW LLOYD WEBBER

Orchestrations by DAVID CULLEN & ANDREW LLOYD WEBBER

Casting by JOHNSON-LIFF & ZERMAN   General Management ALAN WASSER

Musical Staging & Choreography by GILLIAN LYNNE

Directed by HAROLD PRINCE

The taking of photographs and the use of recording equipment are not allowed in this auditorium.
The Filene Memorial Organ in the Concert Hall contributed by Mrs. Jouett Shouse.
Baldwin is the official piano and electronic organ of the Kennedy Center.

12

LEADING MAN

"Close Your Eyes, Let Your Spirit Start to Soar"

★

KEVIN GRAY (*The Phantom of the Opera*) comes directly from the Broadway production of *The Phantom of the Opera*, where he played The Phantom, after having played the role of Raoul for more than a year. He created the role of Valentin opposite John Rubinstein in the Harold Prince/Terrence McNally/John Kander/Fred Ebb musical version of *Kiss of the Spider Woman* for the New Musicals series at Purchase, New York. Mr. Gray first came to the attention of New York theatre-goers in the 1985 revival of Stephen Sondheim's *Pacific Overtures*, in which he received rave reviews for his portrayal of Kayama. Subsequently, he has been seen on Broadway in *Chu Chem* (as the Prince); off-Broadway in *The Baker's Wife;* at the New York Shakespeare Festival in *The Knife* and *The Death of Garcia Lorca;* and in the Young Playwrights Festival at Playwrights Horizons. In 1987 he sang the lead in Villa-Lobos's *Magdalena* at Alice Tully Hall, opposite George Rose, Judy Kaye, Faith Evsham, and John Raitt. Among Mr. Gray's other musical credits is Lun Tha in a national tour of *The King and I* with Stacy Keach. Mr. Gray was a recipient of the 1988–89 National Institute for Music Theatre Award.

Practice the art of doing without doing.

To be simple is to be great—EMERSON.

Wait patiently. Don't flinch.

*Can you do the whole show without your mind drifting?
If not, why not? When is your attention going?
Where should it be?*

This actor's graffiti and much more, some typed neatly on file cards, others scribbled on scraps of paper, are taped on the mirror above the dressing table in this two-room dressing suite in the basement of the Kennedy Center in Washington, D.C. In the adjoining room, Kevin Gray is doing push-ups. He is an exotically handsome young man—the son of a Jewish father and Chinese mother, though he prefers not to discuss these roots, fearing they might pigeonhole him in the eyes of those people who cast—now in his mid-thirties, though he could still pass for a college kid if anyone's producing *Good News*.

Those looks and that youth are not assets for the role he will play on this Thursday evening in September. At a little before 7, Gray walks across the hall into a makeup room where Janice Innella will distort his features and age him considerably to convince the 2,100 people fortunate enough to have obtained tickets that he is the Phantom of the Opera.

At an age in life and a stage in his career when many of his contemporaries are fortunate to win a featured role on Broadway and must head for the stock or Civic Light Opera circuits to have a shot at the biggies, Gray has landed himself the central role in a show that is among the greatest phenomena in the history of not only Broadway, but also American entertainment. The Phantom is a role that makes whoever plays it much in demand by fans, reporters, and assorted hangers-on in each city the show visits. Such prominence is new and somewhat startling to Kevin Gray—after all, he has but one other appearance in a Broadway show to his credit. That show, *Chu Chem*, was a flop. Gray was fired. He seriously considered searching for a new occupation afterward. Then, less than two years later, this.

The saga of how he got here is a credit to his own talent; it's also the story of how timing and breaks kick in in an occupation where the only certainty is uncertainty.

Gray sits in the kind of rotating chair that might be found in a hair salon. Innella begins her magic by covering his face with aloe moisturizer to create a layer between his skin and the makeup. She then takes a thin latex cap, cuts out places for his ears, and glues it to his head with spirit gum.

"Makeup is a chance for you to escape into the character," Gray says. "In this role, you share your time with everyone. But this is private time. Michael Crawford [who originated the role on Broadway] got into his makeup very early and spent time in character. But I need that time to warm up."

Innella puts mustache wax on Gray's eyebrows to serve as a medicinal adhesive. Makeup artist Chris Tucker designs a different face for each actor who plays the Phantom, based on his facial features. For Gray, Tucker has created a large purple latex scar that Innella affixes over the actor's right eye. Under the eye, another piece gives him a purple, swollen mouth slightly off-center.

"My vision is that this character has been deformed from birth," Gray says. "He has no hair, and his skin is uneven probably because of the way he was delivered with clamps. I prefer the natural interpretation to the acid-disfigurement interpretation." He laughs beneath the latex. "People who have these things happen in their lives are different from people born with afflictions. People born this way are more apt to overcome the deformity."

Innella then applies liquid latex paint on the part of Gray's face not covered with the rubber scars. She puts a hair cap on him, then dries the latex with a hair dryer. Then she takes a palette of gels and paints additional and deeper scars. Gray's microphone is set on his bald cap, and then an alopecia with a few scattered head hairs is placed on top. Now he looks wonderfully horrible. Now he is the Phantom.

"As the show gets closer, I start putting my head into the situation," he says. "I don't talk about what motivates me, because when I do, I lose it. And I keep changing my conception of the Phantom's history all the time. It's a game you play with yourself to keep you going eight times a week. I'll meditate down here to get the day out of my mind. Then I go up to the deck and prepare my imagination. I get myself into the first scene. I've been doing this role for ten months now, but I haven't set anything yet. This role requires you to be effortlessly flawless. It's a very stylistic piece, and if it isn't true, it can descend into melodrama.

"So acting it, your choices have to be life and death."

In a twist of fate not unlike Christine's getting the opportunity to replace the Paris opera diva in the *Phantom* plot, Kevin Gray was on the verge of leaving the theatre for another profession, but was then cast to replace Steve Barton as Raoul, Christine's love interest, in the Broadway production of this show in October 1989. But Gray did not have the Phantom behind him as his "angel of mercy" to instigate the opportunity, as Christine does. Instead, what he had preceding this was the embarrassment of having been fired from his first Broadway show.

In mid-1988, Gray opened at the Walter Kerr Theatre in a musical called *Chu Chem*. This Zen Buddhist Jewish musical was originally created by composer Mitch Leigh and director Albert Marre in 1966, coming right off their success with *Man of La Mancha*. It began a pre-Broadway tryout in Philadelphia, starring Molly Picon, who decided she'd rather be unemployed than in *Chu Chem* in Philadelphia, and jumped ship before the critics had any chance to see her. One of those critics, Ernie Schier of the *Philadelphia Daily News*, labeled what he did see as "The King and Oy." The producers folded their tent and spared the New York critics and audiences the task of seeing the debacle—for twenty-two years, anyway.

In 1988, a little resident theatre located in a Fourteenth Street Y in New York called the Jewish Repertory Theatre presented a modest production of the show (which Gray was not in), and Leigh immodestly moved it to Broadway, where Gray assumed the lead. The reviewer for *USA Today* wrote that Kevin Gray was the only thing in the show worth seeing—and he couldn't understand why the actor had taken this job. The producers saved Gray from needing to explain by replacing him.

"I was devastated," Gray says. "I thought my career was over. It's one thing to be fired from *Sunday in the Park with George*, but *Chu Chem*? People couldn't even pronounce it. They thought the title was clearing your throat.

"I then got a call from my agents about replacing in *Into the Woods*. I was told Stephen Sondheim [for whom Gray had appeared in *Pacific Overtures* at the York and Promenade theatres off-Broadway] liked the idea, but James Lapine, the book writer and director, didn't. I figured if Sondheim was now working with Lapine, and Lapine didn't like me, what was the sense of doing musicals? I'd never get to do Sondheim's work. The signs just seemed to be everywhere that I should quit. I looked into applying to an opera training program to be in the chorus."

Gray received an offer to tour as the male "young lover" in a production of *The King and I* starring Stacy Keach. He decided to take this one last job and then hang up his Capezios. While rehearsing the show, he received a phone call from his agent, Alan Willig, reporting that the *Phantom* company wanted to see him as a replacement for Raoul. Gray had already sung for director Hal Prince a year earlier while in San Francisco playing a different Phantom in a version of the story written by Ken Hill. "I said, Forget it," Gray says. "I appreciated that casting agents Vinnie Liff and Andy Zerman were looking out for me. They had gotten me seven auditions for

Les Misérables and I never got hired. I didn't want to get my hopes up and have my heart broken again. But Alan pushed me and I went to audition.

"The audition was at a weird time—like six forty-five—and I got to the Majestic Theatre and smoke was pouring out on the street. Cris Groenendaal, who was then the Phantom, was outside in a towel. It seemed that a pipe had broken in the theatre and the audition was going to be rescheduled. But as I left, I looked around and saw that every man in New York who had won a Tony Award the last few years was there to audition. And I thought, What am I doing here? These guys are actors. I just got fired.

"But Alan pushed me again and I went to audition. I was so distraught I was sure I didn't have a chance. I had this long hair and wore my oldest jeans, with holes in them, and cowboy boots. Everyone else showed up in these Armani suits with their hair slicked back to look the part. My attitude was, If they want me, they're going to have to take me. I sang and then David Caddick, the musical director, came up to me and said, 'We're gonna want you to meet with Hal Prince.' I told him I was heading to Atlanta with a show and I appreciated this opportunity, but, no, thanks, this was my last Broadway audition. Then I went to meet some friends for coffee and I told them the story and said, 'You know what was really great about today? I was just me. For the first time I was just me, instead of trying to be a Broadway actor.'

"Somehow, they must've responded to that. Two days later I was home in Connecticut and Alan calls about noon and says, 'Stop whatever you're doing. You have to be at Hal Prince's office at four. Hal's in rehearsal for *Don Giovanni* and he's taking a half-hour and seeing you and one other actor and making a decision.' Vinnie Liff faxed me the script pages I needed and the song. I pasted them all over the inside of my car, and I'm driving down I-95 and singing, 'That's all I ask of you.' I walk into Hal's office and he's sitting at his desk. My knees are knocking so hard you could hear them. I mean, these are the moments that decide your life. You could take classes and do workshops forever, but he was going to pick right there. Either I was going to pull it off or I wasn't.

"I read the dressing-room scene with Jan Horvath, who was the understudy for Christine. I understood the scene because I had done the other *Phantom*. When I finished, Hal said, 'That was a very intelligent reading.'

"Well, kiss of death for an actor. What you want to hear is: That was emotional, that was passionate, that was inspired. But *intelligent*? That's like saying, She's a real nice girl and you'll like her.

"The next day I was at a *King and I* rehearsal and I was called to the phone. It was Alan, and he said, 'Are you alone?' 'Yeah,' I said. 'You just got *Phantom*,' he said. I hung up the phone and stood in the hall and cried."

Gray went out with *The King and I* tour for a few stops, then returned to New York to begin rehearsals for *Phantom*. "On my first day, Fred Hanson, the production stage manager, said to me, 'So how do you want to start?' And I said, 'I think the first thing to do is see the show.' He was shocked that I had never seen it. So I went out and sat on the steps in the Majestic and I reacted just like the audience did. It was so beautiful. I'd never seen anything like it. The stage looked like glass to me. And the costumes looked as new as they must have opening night. Then, Steve Barton, who originated the role, started dancing, and I panicked. Steve's a wonderful dancer. He was doing pirouettes up there. And I thought, Oh, God, they're gonna fire me. When they find out I can't dance, they'll fire me.

"I began rehearsal with the stage managers and the dance captain, Denny Berry, putting me into the role. Denny said, 'How well do you dance?' I said, 'Pretty well, for a guy with a high C.' She knew she had her hands full. But I worked my ass off for the next three weeks and didn't get fired.

"I have a vivid memory of going to the wardrobe room for the first time and putting on Steve Barton's coat. It fit perfectly. And I thought, Well, maybe this is going to be all right."

Six months later, in March 1990, Prince took Gray out of the show and cast him as the revolutionary opposite John Rubinstein's window dresser in the New Musicals production of *Kiss of the Spider Woman*. With the future of that show uncertain, Gray returned to *Phantom* during the summer. He auditioned for a role in the upcoming American production of *Miss Saigon* and was told he was in contention. Then Steve Barton, who had become the Phantom when Kevin became Raoul, injured his knee. Suddenly, the plum was available.

With Cris Groenendaal and Barton each getting a stint in playing the part, it was clear that Prince liked replacing from within the company. Gray was thirty-one at the time, much younger than anyone else who had played the role, but with the encouragement of the show's staff he decided to give it a shot. Fearing that Prince would dismiss the notion out of hand because of Kevin's age, the staff did not inform the director that Gray would be auditioning.

On the day of the audition, each of the other actors took his turn. Then Gray walked onto the stage of the Majestic, in street clothes and unannounced, and sang "Music of the Night." "I stood perfectly still and just sang it," Gray says. "It was an unusual choice, but I wanted Hal to see the inner life. With Hal, it's often, 'How's your family? Great to see you. 'Bye.' But then I was asked to sing the first-act finale. 'Music of the Night' is the bare minimum for the role. It's the end of the act that really counts.

"Out in the audience were all the people I had been working with for a year, my theatre family. When I finished singing they broke out in spontaneous applause. I don't think I ever felt better in my life. Then Hal said, 'Well, that's it.' And I knew I had it.

"I played the role on Broadway for three months. Then Hal came to me and said Mark Jacoby, the Phantom in the national company, had just become a father and wanted to come home to New York. Would I go on the road? And I thought, Why not? Maybe someone would do something like that for me someday."

Gray joined the national company in March 1991 to open the brand-new Broward County Center for the Arts in Fort Lauderdale, Florida. He was joined by his live-in girlfriend, Dodie Pettit, whom he had met in the New York company and who now became part of the ensemble and understudied Christine on the road. Suddenly he was the leading man in a show that was so highly anticipated that all the tickets for the run were sold before it got to town. The role he was playing was romantic, tragic, and, most of all, mysterious. All that makeup hid his face for the entire evening. Whatever his past history, the fact that he was playing this role in this show made him very much in demand by the local press, fans, and lots of people who wanted something from him. Whoever opens in an American city—or foreign city, for that matter—as The Phantom instantly becomes one of the most sought-after celebrities in town.

"There are usually two reasons to go on the road," Gray says. "To make money, or to play a role you can't play in New York. But I already played the role, and I wasn't going to get paid any more. But there are other advantages for a young actor.

"I spent two years studying at the Neighborhood Playhouse learning to act, and hundreds of hours learning how to sing. But there's no course that teaches you how to be an actor. And there's no way to learn how to be a leading man when you take over a role that's the centerpiece of a show like this, except to do it. They just give you the job and you're expected to do the rest.

"In New York, once a show opens, that pressure is gone. But on the road you're traveling to different cities, opening and being reviewed over and over again. So you must learn how to deal with the pressure, the critics, the interviews, the fanaticism.

"I'm a very different interview than I used to be. I remember when Enid Nemy of *The New York Times* interviewed me for the 'New Faces' column when I opened in the 1985 revival of *Pacific Overtures*. At the end she said, 'You're such a great interview. You just talk.' But that can become a problem. People in this business are sensitive. You have to be careful and realize that your relationship with the artists is finally much more important in your career than any publicity.

"You also have to learn how to deal with a company that's traveling together. I'm young and ebullient, and as the leading man I wanted to take care of people. One of my mistakes was trying to do it for people who didn't need it or didn't want it. I thought I had to be the pylon. People would depend on me. I'd be the company's spokesperson. But a lot of the company resented that, especially from someone younger and someone who just joined the cast. I was told, Who do you think you are?—not by one actor, but by many.

"Then there are tremendous opportunities for publicity in a role like this—and lots of people who want to use you. Everybody wants you to come to some function. Even the Bushes came and invited us to lunch at the White House. A show like this can easily take over your life. So you learn how to be gracious. You learn when to leave and how to say no. You try to use the celebrity for something positive, to help charities. There are tremendous opportunities for that."

One invitation Gray did accept came faxed to the Kennedy Center from a stranger. The children of a Washington woman named Estelle Sullivan wrote that the family had purchased tickets as soon as the show was announced and were eagerly anticipating seeing it. But Mrs. Sullivan was suffering from cancer, her condition had worsened, and she was no longer well enough to attend the show. So Kevin and Dodie went to visit Mrs. Sullivan at her home and performed Christine and Raoul's romantic rooftop scene from the end of Act I and "Music of the Night" for the ailing woman in her living room.

One night in the mid-1960s, young Kevin Gray was asleep in his grandparents' Connecticut home when his grandfather awakened him and said, "Shh! Don't wake up your grandmother. I want you to see something." He walked into the living room, where the motion picture *Shane* was just beginning on the television. "That was a great gift he gave me," Gray says. "Talk about being captivated. And it wasn't by the fact that there was a kid in it and I was a kid. What I wanted to be was Alan Ladd. Now there's a leading man with a conflict."

But in his adolescence and teens, Gray's devotion was to sports; acting was something he watched other people do. He played baseball, basketball, and football in junior high school. Then the other boys continued to grow and he stopped. In high school he suddenly wasn't one of the best athletes anymore. As a junior, he performed in his first play, as a walking minstrel in *A Comedy of Errors*. Then as a senior, he was cast in a production of the four-person musical revue *Jacques Brel Is Alive and Well and Living in Paris.*

"I felt that I was never more correctly placed on this planet," he says. "The girls in the show were the girls I wanted to date. The guys involved were the guys I wanted to hang out with. It all just seemed so right."

But acting was not a serious pursuit for a smart kid. Accepted at Duke University, he entered with a double major, in history and English. In 1976, there was a knock on his dorm-room door and a fellow student said, "My girlfriend saw you do *Jacques Brel* in high school. I'm doing a production of *The Fantasticks* and I need a leading man."

"I had not followed theatre and I didn't even know what the show was," Gray says. "But I went out and bought the album and I loved it and I wanted to do it. That had to be when I started thinking, Maybe this is something I could do. But since I hadn't followed theatre as a kid, I was so far behind everyone. I had no awareness of the repertoire. I remember I was at a fraternity party one night and heard this great music and I asked, What's that? And I was told it was *A Chorus Line*. When I went home, I went to see it. Then I went to see it five more times. Then I saw *Sweeney Todd* and that was it. Here was a guy acting like it was *Macbeth* and singing like it was opera. That really appealed to me.

"You see, it's always the extreme characters like that who I'm attracted to. The actors whose movies I liked watching when I was a kid were Paul Muni, John Garfield, Montgomery Clift. Their intensity appealed to me.

"I'm different-looking because of my background. And my voice is not a traditionally heavy baritone. When I was younger, this all upset me. I thought they were disadvantages. But I've learned that I'm not like anyone, and that's good. That's what gives you opportunities.

"You might think of me for Lancelot, which I've played, but I want to play Arthur. You would think of me for Raoul, which of course I've played, but I want to be the Phantom.

"I always want the ball. I want the role that's traumatic. Someday, I have to play Sweeney."

You first hear him when he's behind the mirror in Christine's dressing room, belittling the "boy" he has just seen his beloved talking to. The voice is intense. It's not a voice you want to hear in a small nightclub singing the cocktail music of Cole Porter or Irving Berlin. There's a grandeur to the voice that demands a big hall and emotions as big as the hall.

With a sweeping gesture that shows off his athlete's coordination, he whisks Christine off with him and reappears in the boat heading toward his lair. (The boat runs on infrared light and is controlled by a stagehand.

The candelabras that emerge from beneath the floor on Broadway move on from the wings in this traveling production, opening like accordions and spewing the smoke that fills the stage.)

In his boat, he sings the work's hypnotic title song—he has power over her, he is in her mind, she is the mask he wears. From the opening moments of this show, when the white wrapping covering the proscenium arch disappears to reveal gold friezes, masks and curtains are the dominant images.

It is an evening of revelations, building to the climactic point when The Phantom removes his mask. Like that mask, which covers a part of The Phantom's face, curtains cover parts of settings until director Prince is willing to show the entirety to us. Hal Prince, above everyone else, is the master of mood. In production designer Maria Björnson and lighting designer Andrew Bridge, he has found clever co-conspirators to create this haunted house of a musical. They have taken their cue from the Andrew Lloyd Webber–Charles Hart score and tried to conjure up a method of storytelling that gets under your skin. But for all the smoke and mirrors (quite literally, in this instance), the eeriness that lingers in the darkness outside the theatre after an evening performance must finally be provided by an actor who plays the pained, mysterious, and obsessed Phantom. Since you see so little of his face, the emotion must come from the one-two combination of the voice and the body. Gray is blessed with the unusual tools to perform this task. When he hangs in a gold angel above the stage spying on Christine and Raoul at the end of Act I, his voice cries and you feel as if he is about to leap from the scenery in pain. The mask, in this case, is hiding not just the latex scars, but also the youth and attractiveness of the man beneath the latex. And of all the evening's stage tricks, this may be the most effective.

In the production's climax, Christine rips off the white mask to reveal all the physical scars. In a surprise gesture of his own invention, Gray straightens his few strands of hair, a touch of vanity that makes the monster so like the rest of us. Then, as Christine goes to kiss him, there is an incredible stillness in this opera house. No coughing. No rustling of programs. And if anyone's breathing, they're hiding it.

It's fifteen minutes after the performance has ended, and all the actors in the company gather in the yellow-brick hallway outside their dressing rooms. Hal Prince has come to Washington to check on the condition of his production this evening. Dressed, as is his style, in plaids and stripes and paisley all in conflict with one another and glasses atop his head, Prince sits with the actors on the tiled floor directly across from Gray and Dodie Pettit.

"The show's hot," Prince says. "It's really, really good. Just some things I can remind you of. This show works only if it's always threatening. It must put on the spooky cloak from the beginning. There must be something dangerous in the air all through the show.

"Kevin, you're pulling back at the end of some musical phrases. In the second half of the lair scene, you're upstage too far. You're denying yourself contact with the audience. Just take the scene and say, Okay, I have an operatic here. Take the scene and make it a moment for yourself." And then Prince asks, "Who's the shadow?"

He's looking for the actor who has a moment doubling for The Phantom behind a scrim, flailing his cape around. An actor who could be fresh out of college raises his hand. He looks frightened, as if he's been caught cheating.

"It's the best it's ever been," Prince says. The whole company breaks into applause.

Walking back to his hotel, Prince is giddy. A director opens a show and then goes on to other projects while the show continues. Catching up with it is like a visit with your children at college—you give a little advice, but it's a relief to know that all is well. "Kevin just keeps growing as an actor," he says. "I never would've thought of him for this. It was a complete surprise. He won me over. And he's one of the smartest, least neurotic, most cooperative actors you'll ever work with."

When informed of Prince's remarks, Gray is surprised. "I look at myself as very difficult," he says. "I don't know. One of the things you have to learn as an actor is when to fight for something and when not to. You have to fight for the right reasons, when it's an artistic matter. But it's a very fine line.

"God, there's so much to learn. I still have big holes in my technique. I'm not able to tap into certain emotions—pain and fear—that I know are inside me. So I act those abstractly. Stanislavsky said, Don't squeeze it. But I'm a squeezer.

"Like when the Phantom's up in the angel at the end of the act—the realization of pain should be so naked and honest. You don't rip yourself open—you just open. But I don't trust that yet.

"So I've got all that to learn. Then all this offstage stuff. I don't know. I sometimes wonder if I'm just another one of those actors who replaces someone, and then someday people sit around and ask, Whatever happened to . . . ? Or am I an actor bringing something really special to people? I don't know."

ST. JAMES THEATRE

JUJAMCYN THEATERS   **ROCCO LANDESMAN**
PRESIDENT

JAMES H. BINGER
CHAIRMAN

PAUL LIBIN
PRODUCING DIRECTOR

JACK VIERTEL
CREATIVE DIRECTOR

Heidi Landesman

Rick Steiner, Frederic H. Mayerson, Elizabeth Williams,
Jujamcyn Theaters / TV ASAHI and Dodger Productions

present

Book and Lyrics by
Marsha Norman

Music by
Lucy Simon

based on the novel by Frances Hodgson Burnett

with

(in alphabetical order)

Alison Fraser   Rebecca Luker | Howard McGillin
John Cameron Mitchell   Lydia Ooghe   Barbara Rosenblat
Diedrich Stelljes   Tom Toner   Robert Westenberg

Elizabeth Acosta   Michael De Vries   Paul Jackel
Nancy Johnston   Rebecca Judd   Lee Alison Marino
Peter Marinos   Peter Samuel   Drew Taylor   Kay Walbye

Frank Di Pasquale   Betsy Friday   Brian Quinn   Laurie Gayle Stephenson

Costumes by
Theoni V. Aldredge

Lighting by
Tharon Musser

Scenery by
Heidi Landesman

Sound by
Otts Munderloh

Orchestrations by
William D. Brohn

Musical Direction and
Vocal Arrangements
Michael Kosarin

Dance
Arrangements
Jeanine Levenson

Choreography by
Michael Lichtefeld

Casting
Wendy Ettinger

Production Stage Manager
Perry Cline

Musical Coordinator
John Miller

Hair and Makeup Design by
Robert DiNiro

General Management
David Strong Warner, Inc.

Production Manager
Peter Fulbright

Press Representation
Adrian Bryan-Brown

Directed by
Susan H. Schulman

Senior Associate Producer
Greg C. Mosher
Associate Producers

Rhoda Mayerson   Dentsu, Inc., New York   Dorothy and Wendell Cherry
Margo Lion   126 Second Ave. Corp.   Playhouse Square Center

Originally produced by Virginia Stage Company
The Producers and Theatre Management are members of The League of American Theaters and Producers, Inc.
The Producers wish to express their appreciation to Theatre Development Fund for its support of this production.

13

CHILD ACTORS

"A Place Where I Can Hide"

LYDIA OOGHE (*Mary Lennox*) made her Broadway debut last spring in *Les Misérables*, opening as Young Cosette on her eleventh birthday. The previous spring she played Young Cosette in *Les Misérables* (first national tour) in Washington, D.C. She has appeared on "Candid Camera," and has done commercials and jingles. A native of Charlottesville, Virginia, Lydia made her stage debut at age seven in a Children's Community Theatre production of *Peter Pan* (as a lost boy and Jane). Lydia attends the Professional Children's School in Manhattan. She enjoys riding, swimming, reading, playing with her two hamsters, and watching musicals, "90210," and "Avonlea." She misses her dog, Darwin, and guinea pig, Twitch, but they wanted to stay in Virginia. To be in *The Secret Garden* is a dream come true for Lydia. She thanks her brother, Robert (her first director); family; Elaine Brown (her hometown singing teacher); R.J.A.; and many friends for their love and support.

It's after 11 on a school night but the eyes of the twenty-four twelve-year-old kids scattered among the first few rows of the St. James Theatre are wide open and filled with a combination of awe and envy. This seventh-grade class from the Carlyle Middle School in Carlyle, Massachusetts, has just seen a performance of *The Secret Garden*. Now—in what has to be absolutely the coolest part of their class trip to New York—they are having a private conversation with the show's star. And get this: The star, Lydia Ooghe, who sits on the edge of the stage before them in blue jeans and a floppy denim hat, is now celebrating the last hour of her eleventh year. She's almost the same age as all of them!

"Is your family here with you?" she's asked.

"Just my mom," Lydia says. "My dad and my brother are home in Charlottesville, Virginia."

"How did you get started?"

"I used to sing a lot—especially in the car," Lydia says. "So my mother found me a singing teacher when I was seven. I now have one voice teacher and one vocal coach."

"Do you like your role?"

"Oh, I wanted this part really badly," Lydia says. "And I've grown to really know the character of Mary Lennox."

Through all this, a portly boy, wearing a knit crew shirt that won't stay in his pants and a tie, has been waving his hand for attention but hasn't been called on. Finally, he shouts out, "How much money do you make?"

The show's stage manager steps in and says, "Lydia's done two shows today and she has to go to school in the morning, so we'd better get her home."

As Lydia leaves through the stage door with her mother, June, you know this is one scene that will be included in every single essay about this class trip.

So now you've reached the chapter about the kid, and you're expecting it to be Mama Rose time. You think you're going to read about those Killer-Stage-Mothers-from-Theatre-Hell who possess the souls of their children and infuse them with their own pent-up anger and frustrations at the unfairness of life; the evil women who fill malleable minds with their own desperate need for a little attention.

Sorry, folks. That's okay for some people—but it's not our story. In fact, our tale is at the extreme opposite end of the neuroses spectrum from the psychic waste dump where the Killer-Stage-Mothers dwell: it is that of a sweet and lovable young girl from a tightly knit, well-to-do family who happened to get the chance to open on Broadway on the night of her eleventh birthday. How can that be, you say? We've heard all the melancholy sagas of the struggle to get to and remain on Broadway: It took Faith Prince ten years of hard work, *and* she's Faith Prince. It took Margo Lion eleven years to produce one show. Susan Stroman had to wait until she was almost forty. And this little fifty-inch tall, sixty-pound cherub was singing in *Les Misérables* at eleven? And she did it without her father pulling any strings, or her mother doing "favors" for some overweight, undersexed smelly old producer?

Well, the truth is, the avenue of Lydia Ooghe's precocious ascent to Broadway is quite simple: She has a lovely voice and she did a great audition.

Lydia Ooghe was born the week of the Tony Awards ceremony in 1980 (*Evita* won Best Musical that year). She was the younger of two children of June and Bob Ooghe. Her father was an internist in Charlottesville, Virginia, home of the university founded by Thomas Jefferson. When Lydia was two and a half, June took her daughter to see *Peter Pan* at her son's school and the child was fascinated. That summer, the family made its first trip to Hilton Head Island, South Carolina—which is now an annual vacation site. When they visited a favorite outdoor spot, a stage called the Singing Tree, little Lydia got up on the stage at her brother Robert's urging and sang for the crowd.

It was at this same venue five years later, when Bob Ooghe watched his now seven-year-old daughter win a talent contest and a T-shirt singing "Chantilly Lace," that he suggested to his wife that their daughter might have significant talent. One of Dr. Ooghe's patients was a singing teacher named Elaine Brown. He told Elaine that his daughter loved to sing and always seemed to be on key, and invited her to his home to evaluate Lydia's abilities. Brown was impressed with the child's sweet soprano and suggested they start formal lessons immediately.

"She taught me how to breathe," Lydia says. "She told me to pretend there's a glass belt around my waist and I couldn't move without breaking the belt. And she taught me how to connect different words so the sounds flow like a stream from one to the other, instead of breaking up into little bits."

Within a month, Lydia was singing "The Good Ship Lollipop" to audition for a community-theatre production of *Peter Pan*, in which she was cast as both a lost boy and Wendy's daughter Jane.

"We never pushed her," Dr. Ooghe says. "She always pulled us."

Soon Lydia added dance and riding lessons to her busy after-school schedule. She continued to act in her hometown's active and well-supported community-theatre program. Her roles included playing (don't choke!) Baby Louise in *Gypsy* and the lead in *Pinocchio*.

"When she was in *Gypsy* I guess she heard all about Broadway," June says. "She came home and said she wanted to be an actress and a singer as her life's work. I told Lydia, There are thousands of people who work all their lives and never make it to Broadway. If when you say you want to be an actress and a singer you mean that if community theatre is all that you'll ever get to do, you still want to do it, then that's fine. But you can't think about Broadway because that's something very rare. Lydia said she would be happy to act and sing in community theatre for the rest of her life."

A review of Lydia's Pinocchio in a local newspaper, *The Daily Progress*, said, "If eight-year-old Lydia Ooghe's mom isn't already a stage mother, she may be tempted to become one after this production."

At that point, the thought had not crossed June Ooghe's mind. Yet it would be as an indirect result of that production that Lydia and June would end up in the land of agents and auditions.

A friend of Lydia's named John Fulmer played Gepetto to Lydia's Pinocchio. When he ran into some family problems at home, he was taken in to live with the Ooghes. Among the possessions John brought to his new home was his CD collection. "I was just sort of in my room and he was in his," Lydia says. "I heard this beautiful music and I just kind of wandered in and we listened quietly without talking. And then John told me I was listening to the score to *Les Misérables*. I didn't understand the story very much, but I just loved that music and couldn't stop listening to the CD."

The next year, when Lydia was nine, one of the *Les Misérables* national touring companies performed in Richmond, and the Ooghes took their children to see the show. It was the first Broadway-size show Lydia had ever seen.

Less than a year later, in May 1990, a voice teacher mentioned in passing that there was going to be an open-call audition for children for the Washington, D.C., stop of the first national tour of *Les Misérables* at the end of that week. "Just one person mentioned it to me on a Tuesday, and the audition was Friday," June Ooghe says. "If she hadn't mentioned it, I never would have thought to come to Washington."

Lydia wanted to try out for the show. To lessen any possible pressure on their daughter, Bob and June Ooghe decided to make the whole experience a family outing. They rented a room at the Crystal City Marriott in Alexandria, Virginia, packed the family in the car, and drove the two and a half hours to Washington.

The audition took place in the lobby of the National Theatre, around the corner from the White House. When Lydia arrived in her pink-and-white striped culottes outfit, there were already more than fifty girls lined up. She was given number fifty-six and told it would be a couple of hours until she was called. So the family went shopping in the mall built into the Marriott hotel that surrounds the theatre.

When Lydia returned to the theatre lobby, she sat for a while among the girls. "That was the first time I ever had an encounter with a stage mother," she says. "This one girl's mother had her sing her song over and over and over until the girl couldn't sing anymore—right there in the lobby in front of us all. It was just awful."

Lydia was called into the upstairs lobby with four other girls. There she sang "Maybe" from *Annie* for Richard Jay-Alexander, the show's executive producer who restages the road companies; and for Tara Jayne Rubin, from the Johnson, Liff, Zerman casting office. Then Lydia was asked to sing a little of "Castle on a Cloud," the song sung by Cosette, the role she was auditioning for and the inspiration for the face that is the show's popular logo.

"I wasn't nervous until she went up there," says June Ooghe. "But then I felt, My God, she's up there all by herself. Will she be all right?"

After Lydia sang, Alexander asked her if she would bring her parents upstairs. Lydia went down to the lobby where her mother and brother were sitting. But her father was not there. He had sneaked up another staircase to try to eavesdrop on his daughter's audition. June sent her son to find her husband and went with Lydia to meet Alexander.

"Richard said, You know, your daughter is extremely talented," June says. "He said, If I were to use her, how would you handle it? It would be three and a half months in Washington, and you live in Charlottesville. At that point, my husband appeared at the door and said, 'We'll do anything we have to do.'"

"We were all in a daze. Like zombies. We never expected this. And I said to the stage manager, Do we just walk downstairs now and act like nothing happened? And he told me, Nothing has happened, not until you get a call."

The family returned to their hotel. While June waited by the phone, Bob took his daughter swimming to try to keep her mind occupied. At 5:20 the phone rang. It was Tara Rubin, who informed June the contract would arrive the next week.

"I do volunteer work at the school library on Monday mornings," June says. "A mother came up to me and said, So what is Lydia going to be doing this summer? I said, Well, she's going to be in *Les Misérables* You should've seen the look on her face."

Lydia told her closest friends, but was reluctant to talk too much about her good fortune, afraid it would cause some resentment among her peers. But soon it was reported on the front page of the Charlottesville *Daily Progress* that a local girl was going to be appearing in *Les Misérables*.

In July, Lydia, accompanied by her mother, joined the touring company at the Colonial Theatre in Boston to learn her role. The show has two parts for girls and one for a boy. One girl and one boy travel with the show, while two additional girls and one additional boy are cast locally in each city where the show is running; all the children divide up the performances. Lydia spent a week trailing the local girl who played Cosette in Boston, learning the staging, how and where to put on her costume, and how to "smudge up my face," she says. Then the company moved on to Washington. Lydia and June, as well as the other kids in the show, moved into an apartment in a complex across the Potomac in Fairfax, Virginia. Lydia soon learned that she would be playing the performances on Monday and Wednesday nights, and the Saturday matinee.

"The first night I went on—it was a Wednesday—when I was waiting backstage I was so jittery," Lydia says. "I went on when I was told to, and I just did it and I didn't even think about it. I did the whole thing and I came off from the first scene and I thought, Wow! I did this and I'm going to finish it. And I finished and it was great. After you finish, they send the kids home, so I didn't get to do the curtain call. That's not true on Broadway, but that's how they do it on the road."

"The only seat I could get on Lydia's opening night had an obstructed view," June says. She sat there leaning left and right to get a glance of her daughter, with the anxiety any parent has watching his or her kid's first at-bat in Little League or first dance recital. "It was like a white-knuckle plane flight for me. My fear was not how it was going to affect me, but how it might affect Lydia. I wouldn't want her to get scared and never want to do this again. But she did just fine."

Lydia was paid an Actors' Equity minimum salary, which was about $800 per week at the time, plus travel expenses and benefits. Her mother put half the money toward the rent of the apartment in Fairfax, and the other half in the bank.

School-age children in shows are required by their Actors' Equity contract to have tutors supplied by the production. Lydia's fourth-grade teacher in Charlottesville sent lesson plans to the tutor. Classes were held on a daily basis, but because of the children's night performance schedule, they did not begin until 11 A.M. and ended at 4 P.M.

The Equity rulebook also requires that children have a chaperone to look after them and help them get to and from the theatre. Lydia grew close with her chaperone, Bobby Wilson, who not only watched after the children but also took it upon himself to make sure they were constantly entertained. When the engagement ended in Washington, Lydia and her mom gave Wilson a VCR. "When I gave it to him I said, Well, I won't see you tomorrow," Lydia says. "I was really upset and everything. So he said, Well, that's show business."

In the fall, the *Les Misérables* company moved on to Philadelphia, where another young girl would get the opportunity to play Cosette. Lydia and her mom returned to Charlottesville. There the Ooghes found themselves with a depressed daughter, which was unusual for Lydia. "She missed the show a lot," June says. "She would just get weepy about it." Lydia auditioned for a community-theatre production of *Tom Sawyer* and was offered the role of Tom's sister, but turned it down.

"We knew she had some talent, but not in comparison to others," June says. "The stage managers on *Les Misérables* told us she really did have exceptional talent and gave us a list of talent agents who represented children. I thought maybe in the future we would call them. But then when Lydia was so sad, I told her we would go to New York during spring break and find her an agent."

The first agent they met with was Nancy Carson, whom they liked so much they canceled all their other appointments. On the trip, Lydia saw *The Phantom of the Opera*, her first Broadway show. The next time she would enter a Broadway theatre, she'd be a performer there.

In March 1991, Lydia was at an awards ceremony in Charlottesville where she was to receive a commendation in a writing competition. While awaiting her turn, her father's beeper went off. Bob Ooghe went off to find a phone, then came back and pulled Lydia aside into a room. There he told her the call was from the *Les Misérables* casting directors. If Lydia was still under fifty inches in height, they wanted her for the play on Broadway.

"We forgot about the award and drove to my father's office, where he measured me," Lydia says. "And I was like the thickness of a piece of paper under fifty inches."

On May 29, 1991, her eleventh birthday, Lydia made her Broadway debut. This time she got to stay for the curtain call. Lydia and her mom moved to New York, into an apartment that was being vacated by the girl Lydia was replacing in the show. It was right next door to the Professional Children's School, on West Sixtieth Street, the private school Lydia would attend.

The walls of the entrance lobby at P.C.S. are lined with head shots of the students. As you enter the school, on one wall there is a call-board with listings of various job opportunities, including for the Nora Ephron movie *Sleepless in Seattle* and a "Geraldo!" show on professional children. On an adjacent wall is a telephone-message board, and there is always a kid on the pay phone talking with an agent. The hallway that leads to the administrative offices is decorated with the photos and accomplishments of noted alumni, including Marvin Hamlisch, Leslie Uggams, Amy Irving, Carol Kane, and Janine Turner. The school opened in 1914, when the kids playing in *Daddy Long Legs*, starring Ruth Chesterton at the Gaiety Theatre, were backstage playing cards for money and cursing. So a school was started in Times Square that would adjust its scheduling to meet the needs of children employed in the arts.

"I think for these kids who have busy, busy lives, this grounds them," says Janice Aubrey of the school's public relations office. "Here they're not stars. Nobody stares at them. They're just kids.

"Of course, some kids come here and think they're going to meet stars or make connections. And we have to be prepared to deal with those parents who may want to take any show-business frustrations out on us.

"But this is strictly an academic school. We have a rolling enrollment to accommodate the flow of children in and out of New York. We work closely with the tutors for the kids in shows. When the schoolday ends, the kids shoot out of here to go on to their professional activities."

Wandering through the classroom hallways—which are lined with show posters—I find Danny Gerard of *Lost in Yonkers* and the television series "Brooklyn Bridge" sitting on the floor studying French; and Macaulay Culkin of . . . oh, you know . . . in the all-purpose room being bawled out by a teacher, while a boy nearly twice his size stands by holding his nose and crying. (I didn't ask.)

Lydia is in a class that combines fourth- and fifth-grade students, and her schoolmates include Laura Bundy, from the off-Broadway musical *Ruthless*; Eliza Harris, who is in *Les Misérables*; Lance Robinson, from *The Secret Garden*; Eden Riegel, who is one of the kids in *The Will Rogers Follies*; and Lauren Gaffney, who is out on the road playing in *Annie Warbucks*. If show business is evident throughout the school (including on the magazine rack in the library, where *Variety* and *The Hollywood Reporter* sit side by side with *Sports Illustrated* and *People*), it disappears when you walk into Lydia's third-floor classroom. There the homework assignment is written on the blackboard ("Finish the math workbook pretest"), and resting on the twelve desks arranged in a semicircle are a Madeleine L'Engle title and *Problem Solving in Math*.

Lunch on this sunny spring day is a barbecue out in the schoolyard. One table is all Asians, music students at Juilliard. Another table is all boys. Lydia sits at a picnic table with five of her girlfriends. "We're all Southern girls and we're all in New York," Lydia says.

They talk about show business. ("Did anyone see *Nick and Nora?*" "I did. Terrible." "When's Lauren coming home?" "She's not. She's staying with the tour.") And they talk a lot about Jason Priestly and Luke Perry. ("I just wish they didn't have those sideburns." "They don't matter to me.")

After lunch, the school starts to empty out. Some kids head for auditions. Others go out on commercial shoots. Lydia's off to a photo session for a new ad campaign for *The Secret Garden*.

There are shows with children, and then there are shows about children. Among those preteen girls with dreams of growing up to be Broadway performers instead of rock stars (which must be a very small club), Mary Lennox in *The Secret Garden* is the biggest plum to come along since *Annie*. The Frances Hodgson Burnett novel on which the musical is based seems to be a rite of female adolescence, a book that is passed on as a very special gift from mothers to daughters in the same way that fathers give their sons baseball.

Heidi Landesman, the savvy producer and designer who initiated the project, has, with her husband, Rocco, and the marketing expertise of Dodger Productions, found success by doing musicals that appeal to a family audience (*Big River* and *Into the Woods* among them). As soon as the Burnett novel became available to the public domain a few years back, Heidi set out to musicalize it. The production that opened in the spring of 1990 received decidedly mixed reviews from the critics. But at that year's Tony Awards presentation, Daisy Eagan, who originated the role of Mary Lennox, won for Best Featured Actress in a Musical, and she also won the hearts of the theatre audience when her emotional response to the honor resulted in a stream of sweet tears. Knowing a special moment when they saw it, the producers of the show soon made that nationally televised occurrence their television commercial. It gave a prolonged life to the show and endowed the role of Mary with a certain aura among those with the qualifications to play it.

Replacing the actors who originate roles in Broadway shows is akin to replacing Richard Burton as Elizabeth Taylor's husband: There are pleasures to be had for sure—but who's going to notice? Yet somehow this role became bigger than all that.

Daisy Eagan's original contract was up in September, and Lydia was first asked to audition in August. At that point June Ooghe assumed the producers were hedging their bet and giving themselves a backup position that would permit them to negotiate with Daisy with the confidence that they could survive her departure. Daisy renewed for another six months, and in January Lydia was called in again. In all, Lydia did four auditions, the maximum number permitted by Actors' Equity without payment. She prepared an English accent for her auditions in private sessions with an acting coach and got a better understanding of the Mary character by reading the Burnett novel.

"The book made you think of Mary more as someone who needed to be loved rather than someone who was a brat," Lydia says. "I mean, she was a brat, but because she needed to be loved rather than someone who is just abrupt. I mean she was abrupt, but only because she needed to be loved."

"We had planned to go home at the end of the school year, or certainly by the end of the summer," June Ooghe says. "But Lydia really wanted that part and we decided it was certainly something worth staying for."

In early February, Lydia was offered the chance to replace Daisy Eagan—at more than three times the union minimum she was making in *Les Misérables*. She went right into rehearsals with Perry Cline, the show's stage manager, worked for a month, and trailed Daisy through a few performances. Lydia left *Les Misérables* on February 29 and went home to Charlottesville to fulfill a long-standing commitment to appear in a fund-raiser for the renovation of an old vaudeville house called the Movie Palace, which was being converted into a new home for the local community theatre. The advance publicity for the event in both local newspapers, as well as in the University of Virginia newspaper, used the homecoming for Lydia, local child become Broadway sensation, as the hook to sell the event. She performed five numbers in that show, including "Castle on a Cloud," her song from *Les Misérables*. Then she returned to New York to assume the pivotal role in *The Secret Garden*.

"When I'm doing the show I don't feel as if I'm carrying the whole story," Lydia says. "Maybe I shouldn't think about it. I just do my role from one minute to the next."

Lydia is the first to arrive at the loft on Thirtieth Street, the photographer's studio where the *Secret Garden* cast is gathering to shoot a new ad campaign. As she waits for the others she sits peacefully and reads *Which Way to the Beach*, a "Beverly Hills 90210" book. Soon the pampering crew shows up. Lydia is passed from the hairdresser, who trims her pageboy; to the dresser, who helps her into a purple jumper; to the makeup artist, who finishes what Lydia has started on her own; then back to the hairdresser for a final once-over; and finally to the photographer and his assistants. The attention she receives is right out of a 1930s Hollywood movie about a Hollywood movie. She stands up on a pedestal constructed of milk crates against a white background, her hands clasped, with an angelic look on her face—a face from another era, a face you might find on a cameo.

"Okay, we're going for the family look here," the man from the advertising agency says. "Sell it as the family show—not the sour Mary, not the Mary after she inherits the house, buys a Ferrari, and meets Jason Priestly." That causes a big grin to spread across Lydia's little face, and the motor-driven camera begins to flash away.

June Ooghe sits on a couch toward the back of the loft far from where her daughter is being fussed over. "When she's through with *Secret Garden* we'll just go back home," she says. "That's not to say she won't come back if she gets a part that she really wants. But we're not going to stay here just looking for another part. Nancy will let us know if there are any auditions to come up for."

June is told that other producers seem to have finally caught on to the Landesman success scheme, and there are a slew of family musicals in the works. In fact, with *Annie Warbucks* and *The Goodbye Girl* on their way to town and a musical based on the film *Paper Moon* in the wings, they may have to create a special Tony Award category for Best Twelve-Year-Old Girl in a Musical.

"But they're all cast," June says.

"The first cast. But there's always replacements," she's told.

"Well," she says, "what Lydia really wants to do is originate a role."

THE BOOTH THEATRE

A Shubert Organization Theatre

Gerald Schoenfeld, *Chairman*

Bernard B. Jacobs, *President*

The Goodspeed Opera House
The Shubert Organization

Center Theatre Group/Ahmanson Theatre
Japan Satellite Broadcasting/Stagevision
present

Lincoln Center Theater
Suntory International Corp.

The Most Happy Fella

book, music, and lyrics by
FRANK LOESSER

based on Sidney Howard's *They Knew What They Wanted*

starring

★ SPIRO MALAS   SOPHIE HAYDEN

also starring (in alphabetical order)   TAD INGRAM   LIZ LARSEN
BUDDY CRUTCHFIELD   SCOTT WAARA
CHARLES PISTONE

CLAUDIA CATANIA   BILL NABEL   and   BILL BADOLATO
MARK LOTITO   ROBERT ASHFORD   BOB FRESCHI
                     ANNE ALLGOOD   MARY HELEN FISHER   KEN NAGY
JOHN ALLER   KYLE CRAIG   T. DOYLE LEVERETT   JOHN SOROKA
MOLLY BROWN   KERI LEE   JANE SMULYAN
RAMON GALINDO   ED ROMANOFF   MELANIE VAUGHAN
GAIL PENNINGTON   THOMAS TITONE
       LAURA STREETS

costumes
JESS GOLDSTEIN

lighting
CRAIG MILLER

artistic associate
JO SULLIVAN

sets
JOHN LEE BEATTY

duo piano arrangements
ROBERT PAGE
under the supervision of
FRANK LOESSER

musical direction
TIM STELLA

casting director
WARREN PINCUS, C.S.A.

poster art
JAMES McMULLAN

general press agent
MERLE DEBUSKEY

producing associate
SUE FROST

production manager
JEFF HAMLIN

general manager
STEVEN C. CALLAHAN

choreography by
LIZA GENNARO

entire production directed by
GERALD GUTIERREZ

pianos by STEINWAY & SONS

THIS PRODUCTION WAS ORIGINALLY PRODUCED BY THE GOODSPEED OPERA HOUSE,
MICHAEL P. PRICE, EXECUTIVE PRODUCER.

SPONSORED BY THE LILA ACHESON AND DEWITT WALLACE FUND FOR LINCOLN CENTER,
ESTABLISHED BY THE FOUNDERS OF READER'S DIGEST.

SPECIAL THANKS TO BARCLAYS BANK FOR GENEROUSLY SUPPORTING
LINCOLN CENTER THEATER'S MUSIC THEATER PROGRAM.

14

VISITOR FROM ANOTHER WORLD

"I Dunno Nothin' About You"

SPIRO MALAS (*Tony*). Regional. *The Most Happy Fella* (Goodspeed Opera House and Doolittle Theatre; Dramalogue Award), *Fanny* (Goodspeed), *Fiddler on the Roof* (Tevye), *South Pacific* (Emile). Metropolitan Opera: debut in *La Fille Du Regiment* (Sgt. Sulpice with Dame Joan Sutherland and Alfredo Kraus), *Il Barbiere Di Siviglia, L'Elisir d'Amore, Tosca, Werther, Don Giovanni*. Concerts and opera: New York City Opera, Lyric Opera of Chicago, San Francisco and Canadian operas; Vienna, Salzburg, Florence, Edinburgh festivals. TV: *La Fille* with Beverly Sills (PBS), "Ryan's Hope," "Kojak," "Spenser: for Hire." Albums: *Tosca* with Kiri Te Kanawa for Decca, *La Fille* and *L'Elisir* with Sutherland and Pavarotti, *Guilio Cesare* with Sills.

Frank Loesser sure knew how to write star entrances. Take *The Most Happy Fella*, for instance. All the people who work at the Napa Valley vineyard are singing about Tony; then, suddenly, here's Tony. Ed McMahon couldn't do the table setting any better. You don't have any questions about whose story this show is. Tony sings that he's "the most happy fella in the whole Napa valley." He's happy because today's the day his mail-order bride is arriving. He's not your usual musical-comedy hero, this Tony. He's no hunk like Curly or Billy Bigelow or the other leading-man Tony. This particular Tony now at the Booth Theatre is an oversize teddy bear in a striped tweed jacket, striped shirt, tie that can't get over his midsection, and cap. He's got a receding hairline, a strong profile, a cleft in his chin, prominent eyebrows that look painted on like the shoe polish under a ball player's eyes on a sunny day, and hands so large they look as if they could palm a medicine ball.

His name is Spiro Malas, his broken English is totally believable, and his big bass-baritone voice can probably be heard in the Music Box Theatre, which is across the street. He may think he's happy, but his sister Marie seems to strike a chord in him when she tells him, "You're not good-looking, you're not smart, and you're not young." And later, when she sings to him that "young people gotta dance, dance, dance," a refrain he picks up, you know this Tony feels like a fish out of water dabbling in the world of romantic illusions.

The man portraying this Tony is also out of his realm in his own way. After a successful thirty-year career in opera, Malas is making his Broadway debut at the age of fifty-seven. As is the case for more conventional fields of employment, the worlds of Broadway and opera have both developed their own self-contained subcultures, with their unique styles and habits and traditions. The two worlds may share storytelling via music, but that is about all they have in common (except for occasional talent).

If Malas is swimming in strange waters on Broadway in the second *Most Happy Fella* of the season (a season in which Loesser is more), he is at home in the role he is playing. In both demeanor and history he shares much with Loesser's Tony, even this: "About a month ago my aunt Diane came to see the show," Malas says. "She was my uncle Pete's mail-order bride. He lived in Baltimore and she was in Greece. They sent a picture of her here. When he sent over enough money, she came over and they got married, whether they liked each other or not. They had one of the greatest marriages there's ever been."

Spiro Malas's parents, Sam and Lillian, met and married in the little Greek town of Karitza, "about a two-hour donkey ride from Sparta," he says. They migrated to Baltimore, where they ran a lunch counter at a drugstore on the corner of Baltimore and Gilmore streets.

"My parents only spoke Greek in our house, and worked very hard. As soon as I could wash dishes I was working in the restaurant.

"The only music I ever heard as a child was the Greek dances with bazouki music," Malas says. "There was never any classical or show music playing. One day my best friend played me a record of Robert Merrill singing, and this sound came out and I thought, That's a beautiful sound. But I didn't think too much about it."

Malas's Baltimore teen years were right out of Barry Levinson's film *Diner*, and he played football for Forest Park High, the same school Levinson would graduate from a few years later. "In fact, you know that famous scene in the movie with the girl reaching into the popcorn box and the guy has his thing in there?" Malas says. "That actually happened to me. At the Crest Theatre. I was there with our quarterback and we were sharing popcorn. I kept reaching into the box and there it was. I told everybody this story and I always wondered if Barry got it from me."

After attending Baltimore Junior College for two years, the nineteen-year-old Malas enlisted in the army. "Because of my size, I became an MP," he says. "I was stationed at a prison camp in Harrisburg, Pennsylvania. You had to have a five-year-to-life sentence to be in there. The job really preyed on your mind. It was so difficult being around those guys, we only had to work every third day, and then it took two to recover. I finally went to the company commander and said, Sir, I'm a gentle soul. I'd rather be a prisoner myself than have to listen to this stuff. He transferred me to the Athletic and Recreation section. Every morning I would screen a movie to see if we could present it to the prisoners that night. One night I screened *Tonight We Sing*, an opera movie with Ezio Pinza, Jan Peerce, and Roberta Peters. And the prisoners made such a ruckus I had to shut it off.

"Then a few days later, I looked at *The Great Caruso*, with Mario Lanza. I don't know why, but I was getting goose bumps and I was getting thrilled and excited. I didn't know the human voice could do this to somebody. Later I would find out that Lanza was a big influence on Luciano Pavarotti and José Carreras, and a whole group of tenors who grew up in the fifties. After seeing that, I would walk around and sing 'Pagliacci.' I didn't know what the words meant, I didn't know a thing about it. All I knew was that the human voice was exciting the hell out of me."

When Malas's army stint was up, he returned to Baltimore Junior College and headed right to the office of Mrs. Bolsby, who ran the school choir. "I said, Mrs. Bolsby, I don't know anything about singing," he recalls, "but I have a feeling that something is inside of me. I sang for her and she said, Maybe there's something there, but you have to study voice. I said, I don't know what that means. She said, You have to find a teacher and learn how to vocalize and study voice. She told me to go to a different church every Sunday. Go and listen and see what voices you like, and they will all probably study with the same teacher.

"We went to the Greek church, but one Christmas I went to the Methodist church to hear Elwood Gary singing. He sang 'O Holy Night' and went for that high note, it was a B flat, and I almost died. Just goose bumps. I went 'Ooh, aaahhh,' and people looked at me like I was a nut.

"As it turned out, Mrs. Bolsby was right. All the singers I liked studied with a teacher named Elsa Baklor.

"So I went to my father and said to him, Tata, you know I want to study voice. And with his accent—the same accent I use in the show—he says, What means this study voice? So I started to vocalize a little. And he says, I don't know nothing about to sing, but if you want to study, you study, and I pay, but I don't want you to tell none of the relatives because I don't want nobody to laugh at my boy. That's the way the Greeks are.

"My sister has a beautiful voice and is very musical. When I told her I wanted to study singing, she went to the piano and banged out a note and said, Hum that note for me. I couldn't find the note for ten minutes. She said, Spiro, you have to train your ear. Two days later, bong, bong, bong, every note I played I could hum. It was there, but I never knew I had it.

"I began my lessons with Elsa Baklor. She came in one day and said she had been to New York that weekend because a friend named Robert Weede, whom she shared a voice teacher with, was starring in this new musical called *Most Happy Fella*. That was the first I heard of this show.

"About a year and a half into my studies, I was doing this exercise we did, working on the *e* vowel, and suddenly it started to ring. I got chills. I started to cry. The voice took on this resonance that it never had before. And my teacher said, Now we've got a tone and we can start to build.

"I never could get the *ah*. But most tenors, Placido Domingo included, don't like the *ah*, and they change it to an *e* sound. Pavarotti was the only tenor I've seen who can sing every vowel on every pitch of his voice. Later, when I was working with Richard Bonynge, Joan Sutherland's husband, he said to me, 'Just give me your best sound, I don't give a damn about the word. Three people are gonna know you sang the wrong word, but three thousand are going to know you made an ugly sound.'

"Then in 1959 I was working in the restaurant with my father and he said to me, Spiro, what do you think about the singing? And I said, I think I'm good. He said, How are we going to find out? So he paid five hundred dollars for me to go to this place at Lake George one summer called Diamond Point. We studied all week, and on Tuesdays and Thursdays we sang at different resort hotels. I started singing 'Some Enchanted Evening.' The first week, I was third on the program. By the third or fourth week, I started to get pushed back to the end. I went to complain that they were pushing me back and was told, Spiro, don't you know they save the best for last? I called my father and said, Tata, I'm good. I'm last on the program.

"One night I was singing, 'Once you have found her, never let her go,' and I finish and this man comes up to me and says, 'Buddy, you might sound like Ezio Pinza, but you don't wear white socks with a dark suit.' I just didn't know. I never wore white socks again after that.

"In January of 1960, they were holding the Metropolitan Opera auditions at the National Gallery and I said to myself, You know, I should just go there and see what they say. Who knows? Elsa Baklor did not stress the repertory, she stressed sound, and I had learned just one Verdi aria. So I went there and sang this aria for the five judges, who were all hidden behind screens. The aria ended on this low note, and I went for the low note and every head popped out. I couldn't believe it.

"Then John Guttman from the Met says to me, Mr. Malas, what else can you sing? I said, That's it. He said, You don't know any other arias? I said, No, I just learned this one to see how I would do. They gave me second place and told me to call when I learned a few more arias and they would bring me to New York.

"My picture was in the Baltimore newspaper for finishing second. When my father saw it, he said, Now we tell everybody Spiro sings."

Encouraged by the Met audition, Malas entered and won two more competitions in 1960, including one that sent him on a singing tour of Italy. When he was away on that tour, his father, Sam, died, without ever having the chance to hear his son sing.

Malas returned to the States and hooked up with a traveling opera company. He played Leporello in an English-language production of *Don Giovanni* that included Sherrill Milnes.

"I had taken one acting class with a director named Elmer Nadge, who gave me four basic rules," Malas says. "To this day it's what I use as my approach to the acting. The first thing is, you think of the theatre as being divided into nine points. The highest people are one, two, three; the middle people are four, five, six; and those closest to the stage are seven, eight, nine. You sing to all those points. The second rule is you think of yourself as a bus driver and you have all these things to do—put the money in the slot, give change, give transfers—but you keep your concentration on the road and everything else is just natural. The third rule is, you think of yourself as a tank—the gun is the eye, the turret is the head, and you are just rolling through the battle naturally, not stopping and starting, just natural movements. And the fourth was always to listen, not to be concentrating on everything else so you can't listen and you find yourself reacting onstage before the question even comes."

Malas studied Italian during his year on the road and then came to New York, where he was invited to join the New York City Opera in 1961. He would remain there for the next twenty years. He began with character roles in *The Mikado* and *La Bohème*. Shortly into the season, Julius Rudel, the director of the company, called Malas into his office and said, "You know, I think you're talented, but nothing's coming across."

"In a room studying with someone it's one thing," Malas says. "But putting it across in a big theatre like the City Center was something else that I had to learn."

Malas spent the following summer at the Santa Fe Opera, where he performed in *Tosca* and met a soprano named Marlene Kleiner, originally from Mott Street on New York's Lower East Side. He was Greek and she was Jewish, which caused some problems with both of their families, but Kleiner also won a contract with City Opera and in 1963 they married.

Now with the added responsibility of marriage, Malas needed to get beyond the lowest-paying choral roles. He requested an appointment with Rudel. Half an hour after it was scheduled, Rudel came out of his office and said, "You still here?" Malas walked into the office and sang three or four arias for Rudel, then said, "Who can sing these as well? Who?"

Malas says, "I thought, Oh, my God, I'm killing myself. I'm going to end up with no job at all. But Rudel said to me, 'You made your point.'" Rudel went to director William Ball and suggested he cast Malas as Bottom in *A Midsummer Night's Dream*. But Ball had never seen Malas in anything. "I said to Julius," Malas says, "Just ask him to give me a half-an-hour rehearsal and if he doesn't like me, I'll cover or do whatever he wants." Ball came and listened to the bass baritone and then said, "Let's get to work."

"I went out for the first performance," Malas says, "and when it finished I was hit by this response, this applause, this wall of sound that knocked me back against the curtain. And I said to myself, This is good. I can really do this."

By the time he was in his thirties, Malas had put together a significant career in opera, spending part of the year under contract to City Opera playing the most important bass/baritone roles, and the rest of the time touring the world with the likes of Joan Sutherland and Luciano Pavarotti.

"In 1965, Richard Bonynge, who played a very important role in getting many of the less-popular operas heard, asked me to join his wife, Joan Sutherland, in a three-month tour of Australia," Malas says. "Of course I went. I would do anything with Joan anyplace. After all these years I am still like a little boy and she is the star when I'm in her presence. But on this tour we were going to do *L'Elisir d'Amore*, and my wife and I are walking up the steps to rehearsal and we hear this singing. It's so beautiful my wife turns to me crying, and I say, 'There's our tenor.' We walked in and met this man, who had the exact same frame as me. He was two hundred twenty-five pounds. And not yet thirty years old. His name was Luciano Pavarotti. I say, 'I can't believe we look alike, we're the same size, and you're a tenor and I'm a bass baritone.' And he says, 'You will do fine, monkey.' From that day he calls me Monkey. We became brothers, very close. I taught him so many things that summer. He'd never eaten an avocado, and I took the pit out for him. He had never seen a V-neck undershirt before. When he went home to Italy, he took all my sport jackets because he was so big and didn't have money to have any made for him.

"No one knew him yet, and at the first performance there were maybe three hundred people. By the second performance word had gotten around and the place was sold out. I watched two hundred people come backstage to touch the tenor. His reviews were not so good. He would read them and say, 'Strange, only the people like me. So maybe not so bad.' "

In 1969, Malas was rehearsing *Figaro* for City Opera while auditions for a summer-season production of *Oklahoma!* were being held across the hall. "I was thinner then and I happened to be wearing blue jeans and a work shirt that day," he says, "so I sneaked in and wrote my name down to audition for the role of Jud. I was told that when you audition for Richard Rodgers you never sing his music, you sing something else. But I wasn't prepared and the music was there, so I learned Jud's song. I went in and Richard Rodgers was sitting there with three or four guys on each side. I knew I couldn't make as much noise as those Broadway guys, so I just sang it as beautifully as I could. I finished and someone said, 'Thank you very much.' Then Mr. Rodgers said, 'Wait a second.' And I knew I had gotten it. When we were doing the show, Richard Rodgers said to me, 'I never heard it sung so well,' and we became good friends."

Over the years, Malas was offered some roles in Broadway-bound musicals, including the 1969 adaptation of Federico Fellini's *La Strada*, starring Bernadette Peters; and the 1975 *The Baker's Wife*, starring Topol, which never made it to town. But successful opera singers like Malas are booked two to three years in advance, and Broadway shows rarely have such lead time, so he could never make himself available.

Though he seemed so right physically for *The Most Happy Fella*, it was never really a consideration for him. "I would listen to Robert Weede singing on the record and say, God, I wish I could do that," he says. "But it's written too high for me. It was for a high baritone. A Verdi baritone. Guys who could sing *Rigoletto*. Like Weede. He could sing a high C anytime he wanted. But I'm a bass baritone—with the emphasis on the bass. I sing from F to F, two octaves. Once in a while I throw in a high G if I'm singing with Sutherland or Sills or Luciano.

"If you look at the score for *Most Happy Fella*, it has high G's all over the place. In order to sing high G's all night long, you have to have a high A above that. It's best to have an extra note. Like Placido has this heavier voice. He's not really a super-high tenor. He can splat out a high note. He does it like he's trying to give his all for the audience. One time we were doing *Tosca* and he cracked on his high B flat through the whole night, and the audience kept breaking into applause like it was the greatest thing they ever heard. They were thanking him for trying.

"But the first thing out of Tony's mouth is a high F, and then at the end of the song a high G. I couldn't get past the first thing he sings.

"Every two or three years, I would get a call from someone asking me to do *Most Happy Fella*, and I had to say, I can't do it. It's too high.

"Then Alan Willig, who represents me for some theatre and knows opera and voices as well as anyone, called me and said Goodspeed was doing the show and I should go in and audition. He said that the run there was long enough that they might be willing to transpose some of it. I had filled in in *Fanny* at Goodspeed a couple of years ago, so they knew me. 'What key should I sing it in?' I asked. Alan said, 'Sing it in the key you want to sing it in.' "

In January 1991, when he was performing in *Die Fledermaus* in Toronto, Malas came to New York and went down to the 890 Studios to sing for director Gerald Gutierrez and Goodspeed's producing director, Michael Price, then returned to Canada. A few weeks later, Willig called and asked if he'd sing for them again. "My voice hasn't gone up in this time," Malas said. "I still can't sing it. And I don't want to spend my own money to fly down again for something I'm not right for."

But when the Toronto run ended and Malas returned to New York, the role still had not been cast.

"So I went in to sing again," Malas says, "and Tim Stella, the musical director, keeps trying to make me sing higher. I said, 'Wait a second. This is my voice. I can't sing it that high. I'm sorry. That's the end of it. I'll sing a high E where the baritone sings a high G. It's a third lower, and the bass voice is a third lower than the baritone voice. That's what I can give you. But that means throughout the whole piece we'll have to change everything.' Michael Price grabbed me and took me aside and said, 'They really want you.' He asked about my availability and I told him my Met contract ended on May 15. They were starting rehearsals May 17. I told him it would have to be in my contract that they would adjust it to fit Spiro's voice. I was not going to kill myself.

"So we agreed that it would be transposed into my key and that I could have a copy of the transpositions. I figured, This is good because now I would be able to do the show anyplace. We also agreed that I would only have to sing six performances a week instead of the usual eight.

"We got together for the first read-through of the material and, of course, everything was still in the high key. So I just sang it down an octave. The rest of the cast is just looking at me like, Who is this guy? What's he up to? I said, Sorry, people. Not my key.

"Then Tim made an adjustment with the pianist and I heard him say, Look, it's not about the high G's. It's about heart. Then I knew I had him. I think if Frank Loesser were around, he would've agreed and maybe written it in my key.

"Then Gerry Gutierrez sits down to describe his approach to the cast and he says, 'I want to approach this like a play, as a story, and we're going to do it with two pianos.' Well, my heart sank. I thought I was going to walk away with a complete score that I could use to do the show anywhere. But then I thought, There's no problem here. If it's only two pianos, I can do it in any key I want to do it in.

"One day in rehearsal Sophie Hayden [who played Rosabella] and I are singing 'My Heart Is So Full of You,' and I'm singing in my light voice. Gutierrez says to me, What's that? I said, That's my soft singing. Some people call it marking, but for me it's legit because I open up on all the sounds. It's just a gift I have that most basses don't. And he says, 'Wow! If you can sing like that, we can really tell this story.' Then a few weeks later he says to me, 'Well, we've made it easier on you with the soft singing, and it's not a great strain, so you can do all eight performances.' And I think, Wait a minute! The whole rehearsal period they're not rehearsing anybody else. And I kept thinking, I'm being took! I'm always being took. I'm working for a thousand bucks a week here, when at the Met I make twice that just for standing by. There I just have to call in, and here I'm expected to do eight shows a week.

"Then in the third week we had a run-through, and Jo Sullivan came and she says to me, 'You're fantastic. You have the chance to be the best

Tony there ever was.' Then Michael Price says to me, 'You're the best thing we've had on this stage in twenty years. With you we can travel. We can travel big-time.' And I don't know if they're lying to me, or if there really is an opportunity for something here. That's how I get took.

"It wasn't so hard for me to find the character. My father was Tony. He came from Greece, and whether you're Greek or Italian, when you come here all you do is work. He established himself in a restaurant, like Tony did with his business. The accent I use is my father's. The way Tony says things is the same way I would. I didn't have trouble saying one line that I wouldn't phrase in exactly the same way. You know, sometimes you do a show and you're trying to memorize a line, but it's not anywhere near the way you would've said it. But Frank Loesser wrote it the way I'd like to say it.

"Tony's a simple man with a good heart. So was my father. My father never asked me questions. He paid for my voice lessons for three and a half years without questioning me. It takes quite a person to do something like that, to have that kind of trust. With Rosabella, she's gotten herself into trouble and I trust her. I say, 'I want to get married. I don't care about this. I don't care about that.'

"I cry easily. I'm very emotional. And I think Tony would've cried, too. That's not hard for me. It's part of me. The only thing in there I didn't like is when at the end he says, 'She could make me feel like a dumb, ugly, old wop.' I can't say that. That's the only thing I backed out on. I say, 'She makes me feel like a dumb, ugly, old nothing.'

"Gerry Gutierrez would say to me, 'Spiro, tell the story. The singing is secondary.' But I said, With me, singing can't be secondary. I've got to represent the Metropolitan Opera and what I've been for thirty years. I said, If my voice was shot, it wouldn't matter. But my voice is in pretty damn good shape for my age. I said, Once in a while I need to be operatic. Tony would be that way, too.

"When we opened at Goodspeed, as far as I was concerned, I was there for the nine weeks and then I was going to London to do an opera. The first review came out—in a Hartford paper—and it was not that good. Then came the New York press, and it was love letters. The only review I remember is *Time* magazine, which said, '. . . and all that remains is ageless art.' That's something you'd say for Vivaldi or Joan Sutherland.

"Then Michael Price grabbed me and said, 'Where are you going?' I said, 'I'm going to London to do *Tosca*.' He said, 'You're going to leave this success to go to London?' I said I had a commitment. I could make a whole year out of doing that. And Michael is telling me we might go to Broadway, we might do this, we might do that. And Gerry Gutierrez says to me, If you leave, I don't have a show.

"Well, I didn't know what to do. In opera, you have a group of people who are known—Pavarotti, Sutherland, Beverly Sills, maybe Placido—but half of the people are out there because it's a social thing. But here you come out of the theatre and people would say, 'Tony, Tony, the man with the heart.' 'The feelings you gave me, this and that.' The response was very emotional, very immediate. It's not just, 'You're a great singer.' It's, 'I saw you and you are in my living room, you are with me in my life. You're my Tony.' It's hard to leave.

"So I started to cancel everything. I was going to go back to Baltimore to sing. But I had to cancel that. I had to cancel doing *Daughter of the Regiment* in Israel, *Cinderella* at the Metropolitan Opera. And they don't like it when you cancel. Now for the first time in my life, I have no plans beyond this show, because I canceled so much. And you never know how the show will do.

"In opera, if you go out of town and do a production of *Fledermaus*, like I did in Toronto, you're singing two, maybe three, performances a week. You gear yourself up for that performance and then you think to yourself at the end of the week: Was that performance better than this performance? I sang this note a little better in that one than this one. But when you're doing eight a week on Broadway, you sort of aim in a curve, you find an even way of performing them rather than aiming for this performance or that one.

"I tape myself a lot and then I go back to the dressing room to listen to see how I am singing. Kids in the show would say, What are you doing? But a lot of opera people do that. When I listen I don't care what anyone says about whether it's good or it's bad. I'm my own worst critic. And I can hear how I'm singing.

"In opera, the bass is usually the supporting person. If you're Samuel Ramey and you're doing *Faust*, you really have the chance to bring the house down. I'm not a possessor of the frame or the voice to do that. I'm always the nice guy or the bad guy who doesn't really have the central role in the opera. But here, as Tony, you know you're the heart of the show. And the people stand up and cheer—Bravo, Spiro!

"One day a woman came backstage to see me and she said, 'I'm a drama teacher and I love your performing, but could you tell me who taught you to use your hands like that?' I said, 'I don't know what you're talking about.' She said, 'Your hands are so beautiful and they say so much.' And I said, 'The hands are connected to the heart. Extra large.'"

WINTER GARDEN

ⓢ A Shubert Organization Theatre

Gerald Schoenfeld, *Chairman*

Bernard B. Jacobs, *President*

CATS

MUSIC BY ANDREW LLOYD WEBBER

BASED ON 'OLD POSSUM'S BOOK OF PRACTICAL CATS' BY T. S. ELIOT

PRESENTED BY CAMERON MACKINTOSH, THE REALLY USEFUL COMPANY
AND THE SHUBERT ORGANIZATION
DAVID GEFFEN
LIMITED,

THE "CATS" COMPANY: (IN ALPHABETICAL ORDER)

BRIAN ANDREWS, LAURIE BEECHMAN, JANE BODLE, NORA BRENNAN,
JOE ANTONY CAVISE, RENÉ CLEMENTE, CHARLOTTE d'AMBOISE,
PAIGE DANA, MARLÈNE DANIELLE, ERICK DEVINE, DENISE DiRENZO,
MARK FRAWLEY, RAMON GALINDO, STEVEN GELFER, MICHAEL
SCOTT GREGORY, STEVEN HACK, JANENE LOVULLO, DEBORAH HENRY,
TIMOTHY JEROME, SUNDY LEIGH LEAKE, ANNA McNEELY, DODIE PETTIT, JACK
MAGRADEY, KEVIN MARCUM, JOEL ROBERTSON, JAMIE ROCCO,
JAY POINDEXTER, SUSAN POWERS, CLAUDE R. TESSIER,
BONNIE SIMMONS, BRIAN SUTHERLAND, VALERIE C. WRIGHT
JAMIE TORCELLINI, SCOTT WISE, LILY-LEE WONG,

EXECUTIVE PRODUCERS R. TYLER GATCHELL, JR., PETER NEUFELD,
CASTING BY JOHNSON / LIFF ASSOCIATES ORCHESTRATIONS BY
DAVID CULLEN AND ANDREW LLOYD WEBBER, PRODUCTION MUSICAL
DIRECTOR STANLEY LEBOWSKY, MUSICAL DIRECTOR RENÉ WIEGERT,
SOUND DESIGN BY MARTIN LEVAN, LIGHTING DESIGN BY DAVID HERSEY,
DESIGNED BY JOHN NAPIER, ASSOCIATE DIRECTOR
AND CHOREOGRAPHER GILLIAN LYNNE, DIRECTED BY TREVOR NUNN.

ORIGINAL CAST ALBUM ON GEFFEN RECORDS & TAPES

15

LONG RUNS

"And I Once Understudied Dick Whittington's Cat"

★

MARLENE DANIELLE (*Bombalurina*) was seen on Broadway in *Sarava, Marlowe,* and as Anita in *West Side Story*. Off-Broadway, she was Chiffon in *Little Shop of Horrors,* and was featured in *Damn Yankees* at Jones Beach. Other credits include the movies *Fort Apache* and *Tootsie;* and choreographer/principal of her latest national commercial. Among her many achievements, one of the most rewarding was collaborating with Andre DeShields on *Black by Popular Demand*.

The first real chill of autumn sneaked into town this first Monday evening in October. But the outdoor café at Rockefeller Center is jammed with men in suits and women in body-hugging black cocktail dresses with shoulders and more exposed to the crisp air. A large society band glides easily from Kern to Berlin to Porter as couples fox-trot around the floor where others will be ice-skating any day now. Large bunches of black and white balloons decorate the tables. All around, young attractive men and women, most of them sinfully slender, in clothes that you'd kill to look good in, embrace and kiss like long-lost friends do. You don't need a *Playbill* to know that these are the "Cats." Almost 200 of them. These are all the actors who over the past nine years have taken their turns slithering into the painted leotards to become the twenty-six felines that composer Andrew Lloyd Webber and director Trevor Nunn created from T. S. Eliot's poems. The occasion for this feline reunion is that today is the show's ninth anniversary.

Why hold such a blowout after nine years rather than, say, ten? Well, the thematic justification is, of course, that cats have nine lives. The practical concern is that the show might not survive to see another October. With tonight's 3,758th performance, which preceded this party, *Cats* has already surpassed *Fiddler on the Roof* to become the third-longest-running Broadway musical of all time, trailing only *A Chorus Line* and *Oh, Calcutta!* Each of those shows had considerably lower weekly running costs than this sizable production, which permitted them to break even with smaller audiences, thereby protracting their runs. So Cameron Mackintosh (who presented this Broadway *Cats* along with the Shubert Organization, David Geffen, and Webber's Really Useful Company) cannily chose to throw a bash now that both humbly concedes the end is in sight and attracts enough media attention to build audiences and delay the final curtain. Such is the promotional skill of Mackintosh, the savviest marketer of our current producers. He also throws some of the best parties.

This gathering of 1,000 or more has brought together an unusual combination of people connected with the production being honored, and others who are not and wander around slightly lost, like wallflowers at their spouse's high-school reunion.

(This evening does provide an opportunity to clear up one of the great mysteries about this musical: A motif of the show is the concept of "Jellicle" cats. The opening number is about them, and the Act I finale is the

"Jellicle" ball. We also hear about "Pollicle" dogs. Well, you no longer have to feel like an idiot, like the rest of us, for not knowing what they are. According to Andrew Lloyd Webber, when T. S. Eliot was a little boy, his grandma would talk about "dear little cats" and "poor little dogs"—but to his young ears it sounded as if she was saying "jellicle cats" and "pollicle dogs.")

Though *Cats* looks good on any actor's résumé (especially as a credit for dancers who have survived Gillian Lynne's gymnastic choreography), it is not exactly a career booster. It's an ensemble piece. The actors' features are masked behind heavy paint and headpieces. And playing an animal in a nearly storyless evening provides little sense of the performers' acting abilities. So when you spot faces of ex-Cats scattered around the plaza, you recognize them from previous or subsequent work: Terrence Mann, the original Rum Tum Tugger, who went on to garner a Tony nomination for his performance as Javert in *Les Misérables*; Scott Wise and Charlotte D'Amboise, who were both featured in *Jerome Robbins' Broadway*; Harry Groener, who would follow a four-year stint on television's "Dear John" by starring in the upcoming *Crazy for You*; Ken Page from *Ain't Misbehavin'*; and Gregg Edelman, who originated the role of the writer Stine (or was it Stone?) in *City of Angels*.

Cats was once a pit stop for each of them. It was a hit, and it was fun, and they worked with some interesting people, surely. But it was these other shows that truly made the difference in the careers of these *Cats* alumni; and it is these other roles that writers, directors, and producers recall when they are in casting.

The job of acting, by its very nature, breeds opportunism. It is a freelance occupation, and even the best situation is only temporary. So a show is not viewed as just a job; it's also an audition to audition for the next job. Most actors tend to stay in a show as long as they feel they are benefiting from the exposure. Then they leave in search of the next opportunity. A part is not thought of as just a payday; it's also evaluated as a "career move." In an earlier era of musical theatre, performers were proud to stay with a show for years and, in some cases, for the run of the show. Today, most agents try to get their clients an "out" after just six months. And for the better-known stars, even six months has become too long for them to be in New York and out of the movie market. Checking the records, we find that eighteen of the original twenty-six Cats were gone by the end of the second season of the run.

Standing inside the glass doors of the American Café, on the periphery of the plaza, we find a kitten with different stripes. There Marlene Danielle, glamorous this evening in a brocaded dress, with lovely cocoa skin and waves of dark, flowing hair, is approached by a radio reporter who holds a tape recorder in front of her full mouth and asks, "So how are you able to keep this fresh every night after nine years?"

In a polite and soft voice that belies the fiery growl she lets out when strutting her stuff through the Winter Garden junkyard as the sensual Bombalurina each night, Marlene says, "A long time ago, my acting teacher taught me that it's not acting—it's *re*acting. You've got to get in a frame of mind so that you're seeing and hearing things for the first time. I don't anticipate that crash that's coming. I forget it. I never heard it before. Then—*pow!*" Her eyes flash with surprise. Then she smiles. "That's what makes it fun every night."

As Bombalurina, Marlene (pronounced Mar-leh-na) Danielle is often in the background as other cats tell their stories stage center. Yet throughout the evening she remains a mysterious and seductive presence, sashaying slowly in and out of focus with a ballerina's grace. Although her smooth elegance blends into the corps, her body stands out. Painted in orange and red and black, with a full head of orange fur, she is eminently noticeable as all-woman in a show of neuter characters. She's the sex kitten, so to speak.

"She's a cat who can mix with any kind of crowd," Danielle says. "She can fit in with the kittens as well as with the adult cats. She moves easily in and out of situations. She's the good-time girl. She makes light of things and she's not afraid of anything." When she's given the chance to grab the stage in a hard-driving solo describing the elusive Macavity the Mystery Cat, she flaunts her wares like Mick Jagger performing "Honky-Tonk Woman," which at this evening's hot performance won her a roar both at the number's end and at Marlene's curtain call.

Of the 3,758 performances of *Cats* on Broadway, Marlene Danielle has done about 3,500. Along with featured actress Bonnie Simmons and chorus member Susan Powers, Marlene has been at this one job for nine years tonight.

But Marlene's is not another sad theatre story—the frustrations of a performer stuck in a job who can't find an opportunity that will rescue her. Instead, Marlene's is a positive theatre story—one of a woman who realized early into the run of her show that it was going to be around for a long while, and that that presented an opportunity. It could provide her with things in life that gypsies don't often have: financial security and a family life, both rare entities in show business. The chance to be present to watch a child grow up. The chance to lay down real roots.

Marlene is accompanied this evening by her seventeen-year-old son, Benjamin Bernouy; by her mother, Dorothy Epps; and by her sister, Aelise. This is only fitting since this show has been a catalyst to improve all of their lives. This impressive family may have just a little bit more to celebrate this evening than anyone else at the festive gathering.

Marlene Epps spent her early childhood in St. Albans, Queens. Her mother, Dorothy, worked at the Bulova watch company. Her father, Lawrence, waited tables at the Steak Joynt in Greenwich Village and at Lundy's in Brooklyn's Sheepshead Bay. When Marlene was seven, her father left for good and her mother decided that an outerborough environment was not an appropriate one for her two growing daughters. So she moved her family into a railroad flat on West Third Street in Greenwich Village, diagonally across the street from the Blue Note jazz club. "We had a bathroom in the hallway and a bathtub in the kitchen and one bedroom with a triple bunk bed," Danielle says. "The rent was only thirty-three dollars per month, so my mother worked only when she wanted to or needed to. And it was the happiest time in our lives.

"Richie Havens was playing next door at the Night Owl. Bob Dylan and the Lovin' Spoonful were running up and down the block. And Jimi Hendrix. It felt like we were right at the center of pop culture.

"We were pretty wild kids, me and my sister. We were three girls living alone and our door was always open. People hung out at our house all hours of the night. My mother got a lot of criticism because of the freedom she gave us. But she didn't care. She felt like she was doing the right thing, and she was."

Danielle attended Public School 41 on Greenwich Avenue, where "a lot of the kids were from broken homes. We'd hang out in the halls after school and harmonize. The echo was great in those hallways." The school's music teacher, Mr. Feldman, heard Marlene sing in the halls. He invited her into the chorus and encouraged her talents. The students voted for Marlene to play Dorothy in their production of *The Wizard of Oz*, performed with no script and made up as it went along.

"Our house was filled with music," she says. "Ray Charles, Nat King Cole, Bessie Smith. Tough songs, one about a woman going to the electric chair, which went right to my gut. Then one day I remember seeing Tina Turner on television, when she was still with Ike. Short skirt, blond wig, all that dancing. I remember thinking, Wow! That's entertainment. I want to be that."

When Marlene was twelve, her mother met a man who worked in the music business in Philadelphia, wanted to be near him, and moved her family there.

"I had culture shock after living in the Village, in what I thought was the center of everything that existed," Danielle says. "I was having a hard time adjusting so my mother suggested I get involved in some cultural activity. She insisted I get some classical training, and at fourteen I started dance school at the Pennsylvania Ballet.

"I also got selected in a lottery to attend an experimental high school that had no building. To study we went to houses and museums and jobs. It was good for me because I was brought up with such freedom. I worked in a boutique sewing appliqués so I could pay for dancing school."

When Marlene was fifteen, an art student from France named Daniel Bernouy came to Philadelphia to study and lived in a spare room in the Eppses' house. Marlene fell in love with Daniel, graduated from high school early at sixteen, and went with him to France to live and continued to pursue ballet.

While studying in Paris, Marlene was invited to go to London to audition for the school of the Royal Ballet. "At that audition, I realized for the first time that before anything, ballet was about body type," she says. "They wanted a certain neck, shape, butt. I knew I didn't have the parts to become the kind of technician they wanted. I saw how different my body was, compared to the frail white English girls. I came back to France with my heart sunk."

A year later, when Marlene was eighteen, she and Daniel married. Then son Benjamin came along. When they returned to the States, she accepted an apprenticeship with the Dance Theatre of Harlem.

"I figured now I was with my people," she says. "But even here they wanted a different type of body. I was thicker and bigger-boned. I had this teacher there named Alice Elliot. She had this great air about her. And one day she put her hands on her hips and said, 'Marlene, you know what you have to do? Get yourself a pair of long eyelashes and go dance.' I knew what she was saying. There were other kinds of dancing I would be more suited to. That made me realize I could still dance, even if it wasn't going to be in a ballet company."

Marlene was determined to give her son the same experience growing up in Greenwich Village that she had treasured. The family moved to a railroad flat on Carmine Street, just a few blocks from where Marlene had spent her grade-school years. Daniel painted and Marlene mothered. Then one day she received a phone call from a former Katharine Dunham dancer named Walter Nicks who had a modern-dance troupe of eight that toured Europe performing and teaching. He was one girl short, and was leaving the next day. Daniel and Marlene's mom said they would take care of Benjamin, and they encouraged Marlene to take advantage of the opportunity. So the nineteen-year-old Marlene went off to France for her first professional job.

"One night we were sitting around the dinner table in France," Danielle says, "and Walter talked about this script someone had sent him for a Broadway musical set in Brazil. When I came home, I bought a copy of *Backstage*—first time I ever bought it—and I saw a casting announcement for this show called *Sarava*, based on the novel *Doña Flor and Her Two Husbands*. I said, Hey, that's the one Walter was telling us about. I know this one. I gotta go for this audition.

"I had never gone to a theatre audition before. I didn't know the process. I walked in wearing a unitard, tights, and heels, and walked to the back of the room. I watched what the choreographer was doing. There were conga players. And it was hot! I knew exactly what he wanted. It was the same stuff I was doing with Walter Nicks's company. When my turn came, I started in the back row and the choreographer saw me and said, Girl, get down here in front. I had the hair and the movement, and he wanted me to show everyone. I got hired to do the workshop—I think it was the first workshop that Equity endorsed—for twenty-five dollars a week.

"I had no sense of theatre. The other dancers would talk about these other productions and I was completely ignorant. I didn't know the repertory. I didn't know about regional theatres. I just had this kind of attitude toward the material that was right on, so I got hired.

"I could never do that audition now. I was a wild woman. The movement just came naturally to me and I just had fun."

She did the workshop, went out of town with the production to Boston, then in 1979 came to the Mark Hellinger Theatre with the show.

Sarava was a musical based on a Jorge Amado novel about a love triangle among a Brazilian widow, her suitor, and the ghost of her late husband. It had a book and lyrics by N. Richard Nash and music by Mitch Leigh, but it is most remembered as a show that was doing such good business in previews as a result of an energetic television commercial that it kept postponing its opening until the critics decided to purchase tickets and review the show without being invited.

"Working in that show, I noticed different levels of professionalism," Danielle says. "My training in ballet had been very intense. I had Russian teachers and a lot of discipline. But a lot of Broadway dancers were less disciplined. They almost seemed nonchalant. There were singers who were really trained and then those who just had talent and used it instead of honing it. Theatre was a very American, very New York culture, different from what I had grown up around. I sensed that a lot of the people were unhappy. They thought they should be doing better. And they complained a lot. They complained that the music should be better. That Doña Flor (played by Tovah Feldshuh) should be more ethnic. But I didn't care. Hey, I was on Broadway! And I was getting paid more than anyone in my family ever had."

The 1978–79 Broadway season had an artistic success in the Harold Prince–Stephen Sondheim collaboration *Sweeney Todd* and a commercial success in the Neil Simon–Marvin Hamlisch–Carol Bayer Sager collaboration *They're Playing Our Song*. But it is primarily remembered as a season of expensive flops, many by the creative A-team including Michael Bennett (*Ballroom*), Gower Champion (*A Broadway Musical*), Jerry Herman (*The Grand Tour*), Alan Jay Lerner (*Carmelina*), and Richard Rodgers (*I Remember Mama*). Amid all this expensive rubble, *Sarava* managed to stay alive for almost five months.

One day, Marlene saw a notice on the backstage call-board announcing an open casting call for a revival of *West Side Story*. "This was the one show I knew because I had loved the movie," she says. "So I said to myself, I'm gonna get this job! The dance call was at the Hellinger, and the dancing was a piece of cake for me. I got called back for an audition at the Minskoff Theatre. I went downstairs to the bathroom, and when I came out, there were all these girls sitting around a piano singing, 'Happy birthday to you, happy birthday to you . . .' So I asked in this little voice, 'Do I have to sing "Happy Birthday"?' The musical director said, 'What else can you do?' I said, 'How about this?' And I turned my back toward him and put my hands on my hips, spun around, and sang:

" 'Puerto Rico, you lovely island . . .'

"Then I said, 'And how about . . .'

" 'A boy like that, he kill your brother . . .'

"The other girls are now saying, Shoo! Where she come off doing that? Then I get a call to come in and read for the role for Anita. And I think, Now this is really gonna be cool. I'm gonna get Anita. So I go to the call all cocky and I hear this squeaky voice say, 'Hello. I'm here.' In comes this woman in a tight dress with her hair up. I didn't know she was Debbie Allen or who Debbie Allen was, but just by the way she entered I knew she was it, and I was here to read for her understudy. I did get into the show and to cover her. When Barry Moss, the casting director, told me to come in and sign a contract, I just said, Okay. No excitement. I expected it to happen because I didn't know any better.

"Watching Debbie Allen every night, I learned how to be a leading lady. She was so gracious with everyone, making them feel a part of her success. And she gave one hundred percent every single night.

"Then she got a part in the *Ragtime* movie and she came right to me and said, These are the days I'll be out and you're going on. That was perfect. It gave me the chance to invite everyone to see me. The night she left, she took me onstage after the performance and walked me through it—said things like, Watch that trap; you can get a heel caught. Watch the scenery coming in from there.

"The next night, after my debut in the role, I come back to my dressing room and there's a dozen roses there with a card that says 'Read your reviews. You were wonderful. Love, Debbie.'

"She even sent her agent to see me. He became a good and helpful friend."

Meanwhile, Benjamin attended P.S. 41 in the Village, just like his mom had. Daniel continued to paint, without any commercial success. And Dorothy Epps began working as an investigator for the Workmen's Compensation Board and moved into a 3,000-square-foot loft on West Forty-sixth Street next door to the Lyceum Theatre, where Marlene and her family soon joined her mother.

Each summer, Benjamin would vacation with Daniel in France. At six he had already developed a faculty for imitating accents. He liked to put on his father's hat and imitate Maurice Chevalier singing "Louise." Dorothy Epps saw an ad in the trade papers for a casting call for young boys for a musical about Charlie Chaplin. So she decided to take Benjamin to it. He had no training at all, but he brought his father's hat, made up his own choreography, and did his Maurice Chevalier impersonation. He got hired as the understudy. So Dorothy gave up her job and joined the child on the road as his chaperone. Benjamin soon signed on as a client of Debbie Allen's agent. He went on to a production of *Member of the Wedding* in Nashville and the television movie *Evergreen*, which was filmed in Toronto. "My mother and Benjamin had a ball on the road, living in hotels and on those per diems," Marlene says.

Marlene spent a year in *West Side Story*. "Now I was starting to learn the ropes of theatre," she says. "I went to a lot of auditions and started to see that everything wasn't going to be like *Sarava* and *West Side Story* for me. There were a lot of places where I didn't feel comfortable. And I saw a lot of people who were better than me. I started to become like the rest of the people. I realized I was a certain type, that I have a certain coloration, and I'm not right for everything.

"I auditioned for Bob Fosse for the *All That Jazz* film. He was very kind to me and appreciated my style and technique, but it wasn't his. I realized there was a difference between the tall show girls and the ballet people like myself. Now that I'm older and more experienced, I'm closer to what he was looking for. But I was very naïve at the time.

"Then I was doing *Damn Yankees* with Joe Namath at the Jones Beach amphitheater and I got a call to audition for Michael Bennett for *Dreamgirls*. I made the callbacks, but when I got there I saw all the girls were darker. And they didn't have my hair. I saw I was in a situation I wasn't going to fit into. The girls were great. They were great at soul. I never developed that. My training had been more classical. But after I auditioned, Michael and everyone at his table fell back in their chairs with laughter and applauded. Then I got a call from Vinnie Liff, the casting director, who said Michael asked him to call and tell me that if he was ever doing a show I was right for, he was going to use me. That's all I needed.

"It made me realize I wasn't always going to be right for situations I wanted to be in. To perform on Broadway, there are so many things that count. But what comes first is the package. First it's the impression you make, and only then is it what you can do."

Marlene danced in the chorus of an oddity called *Marlowe*, which spent six weeks at the Rialto Theatre in the fall of 1981.

Early the next year, she was called by Vinnie Liff and invited to audition for the American company of *Cats*, which was already a sensation in London.

At her first audition, she sang and danced "America" from *West Side Story*, as well as a ballad called "Home." She was called back to the old Broadway Arts Studios at Fifty-fifth Street and Broadway to learn part of the "Jellicle Ball" sequence. "At the next audition, Trevor Nunn came up to me," she says. "Complimented me on my hairstyle and asked me why I spoke French—which was on my résumé. I told him my husband was French, and that was it."

Marlene was called in one more time, on Easter Sunday, to audition on the stage of the Lyceum, right downstairs from the loft in which she was living. By the third audition for a show, actors assume they are under serious consideration. It's at that point that many of them start telling friends they are "up for" a role in a show. That can be true. But sometimes what "up for" means is that the director and his or her creative staff are seeing a lot of different types to help them sort out precisely what they are looking for.

After three auditions for *Cats*—and all the mounting anticipation accompanying the protracted process—Marlene Danielle was not offered a role.

That summer, inspired by her *Dreamgirls* audition to cram up on pop music, she learned fast enough to be asked to sub for Leilani Jones (who had a commitment to do an industrial show) during the opening week of

Little Shop of Horrors off-Broadway at the Orpheum Theatre on lower Second Avenue. Marlene performed for the show and got good reviews; then Leilani was back and she was gone.

Then in August, she received a phone call from Vinnie Liff. *Cats* was already a few weeks into rehearsal, and a job had become available to understudy Cassandra, Tantomile, Demeter, and Bombalurina.

"I wasn't sure I wanted it," Danielle says. "I had always been onstage, and I didn't know if I could handle standing by. But I had a child, and my husband was having trouble selling his art. I had gotten used to getting that weekly paycheck doing *Sarava* and *West Side Story*, and it sure made life easier. This was a job in New York, where I could be with my family.

"Somewhere along the way, I had lost some of that wildness I grew up with. I realized that the security looked good to me. Practically, I knew I needed that job."

Cats is a physically demanding show, and the dancers sustain frequent injuries. Even during previews, Marlene found herself subbing in most performances. Then, about six months into the run, Wendy Edmead, who opened as Demeter, started missing performances, claiming an injury, and Marlene went on frequently. But at a dance call for Francis Ford Coppola's motion picture *The Cotton Club*, "I saw Wendy right there in front, dancing her little buns off," Marlene says. "So I talked to management and said, Get me in here." Edmead was let go and Marlene became the regular Demeter. A year later, Donna King, who had originated the role of Bombalurina, left to marry the production's English scenic designer, John Napier, and Marlene assumed the role she has played ever since.

At about the same time, Daniel Bernouy's fruitless struggle to succeed as an artist was taking its toll on their marriage. "I never minded that he wasn't doing well," Marlene says. "I was doing what I liked doing and making things work for the family. But he was very frustrated and we decided it was best if we parted."

Marlene had been in *Cats* for more than two years by that time. When opportunities for new shows came along, she auditioned. "I didn't get cast," she says. "But I don't know what I would've done if I had. This show was giving me the life I wanted. It was allowing me to be here in New York while my son was growing up. So I wasn't thinking like an actress who had been in a show for a long time and felt she just had to get out. It was quite the opposite. I knew this show was going to be here and it was going to give me the opportunity to make money for a long time.

"When you're in this business as a Gypsy, you never plan. You just live day to day. But then I began to realize, Hey, since this show is going to be here, maybe I can make some plans.

"One day I was sitting home reading and the television was on and this show called something like 'How to Make Money from Real Estate' came on. And it's like a bell went off in my head. We had moved around a lot from rental to rental, and I didn't want to rent anymore. The only things I ever really wanted were to own a house in the city and a house in the country.

"So my mom and I decided we'd find a property together. We found a HUD house up for auction in Philadelphia. I bid twenty-five-thousand dollars and found out by mail that I had made the highest bid. It was a rental property, and it brought me some income and started a relationship with lenders.

"Then the loft we were all living in up above the Lyceum was no longer available. I was gung-ho on real estate by now and I wasn't going to pay rent anymore. My sister, Aelise, who works in the fashion industry, decided to go in with me now. We looked all over the city, but couldn't find the right place. Then we found a brownstone in Jersey City that was perfect. So Aelise and I bought it together and we all moved in there. Here we were, the three girls who had shared the one bedroom in the thirty-three-dollar-a-month railroad flat in the Village, owning our own place, each with a unit of her own. That felt good. And we weren't finished.

"Then we started to look for a piece of property in the country. We found a forty-acre lot three hours upstate. It was perfect. It had an old farmhouse and a barn, a little cottage and a pond. And we bought it.

"Benjamin had worked straight through as an actor until he was eleven. Then he lost that little-boy cuteness. It was time to focus on school. So he and my mom moved up to the farm and I would go up there every chance I got. We have a lot of animals running around up there, including six cats, whom I study all the time. They each have their own personality. We don't have a Bombalurina.

"Then, in November 1989, we were in the house and a neighbor comes running up the driveway shouting, 'Your house is on fire!' We had done some work on the house, but had not yet replaced the old roof. Some ashes from the fireplace caught and there were flames all through the house. I ran around like a madwoman and tried to save things. It's amazing the strength you summon up under extraordinary circumstances. I dragged a sideboard full of china out of the house by myself. But this is the country, and the fire department didn't get there for twenty minutes. By then we had lost nearly everything.

"We've been rebuilding the house little by little ever since. We make a little progress and I run out of money and then I save a little money and we make some more progress. We should be ready to get back inside within a year. I just hope the show plays long enough for me to finish. I think it will.

"And then? Well, Benjamin's graduating from high school this year. And I do have one more dream. I want a place in the islands . . . and the means to get there.

"Then I'll have everything."

SUNDAY EVENING, MAY 31, 1992

GERSHWIN THEATRE

UNDER THE DIRECTION OF THE MESSRS. NEDERLANDER

THE LEAGUE OF AMERICAN THEATRES AND PRODUCERS

and

THE AMERICAN THEATRE WING

The Founder of the Tony® Awards

present

1992 TONY AWARDS

Executive Producer
JOSEPH CATES

Produced and Directed by
WALTER C. MILLER

Written by
PETER STONE

Coordinating Producer
KAREN FERLITO

Associate Producer
ALFREDA D. ALDRIDGE

Musical Direction by
ELLIOT LAWRENCE

Costumes by
DAVID TOSER

Lighting by
BILL KLAGES

Scenery by
JOHN FALABELLA

Production Executive
DEBRA DAVIS

Exec. in Charge of Production
EMILY COHEN

National Public Relations
**KEITH SHERMAN &
ASSOCIATES**

Production Supervisor
BEVERLEY RANDOLPH

Talent Executive
CATHY VASAPOLI

For The League of American Theatres and Producers and The American Theatre Wing

Artistic Consultant
ROBERT WHITEHEAD

Managing Producer
ROY A. SOMLYO

THE TONYS

"A Barrel and a Heap and I'm Talking in My Sleep"

FAITH PRINCE (*Miss Adelaide*). Earlier this season, Ms. Prince was featured as the lovable murder victim, Lorraine Bixby, in *Nick & Nora*. Last year she originated the role of Trina in the William Finn–James Lapine musical *Falsettoland*. She was nominated for Tony and Drama Desk awards for her dual role in *Jerome Robbins' Broadway*. Her other New York credits include *Bad Habits, Urban Blight, Groucho, Little Shop of Horrors, Olympus on My Mind, Scrambled Feet, Philco Blues,* and *Living Color*. She was featured as Carrie Pipperidge in the revival of *Carousel* at the Kennedy Center in Washington, D.C. On television Ms. Prince was a regular on the HBO children's series "Encyclopedia." She costarred as Angela in the feature film *The Last Dragon*.

Would you like some pancakes?" Faith Prince asks as I enter her ground-floor apartment.

"Oh, you don't have to do that," I say.

"No, please. Have some," she says. "When I'm nervous I make pancakes."

So Faith goes off into her phone-booth-size kitchen to make blueberry-walnut pancakes. She uses a small frying pan and makes one large pancake that fills the circumference. She's making pancakes so that she's not just sitting around waiting for the phone to ring. On the television set, Joan Rivers is interviewing Richard Grieco and Melissa Gilbert Brinkman. In the backyard outside the one-bedroom first-floor apartment, Faith's husband, Larry Lunetta, is admiring the planting he recently completed in their small garden. And thirty or so blocks downtown in the conference room of the League of American Theatres and Producers, the Tony nominating committee is in session.

I won't pretend it's a coincidence that I'm sitting among the antique-wood end tables and chairs and writing desk in Faith Prince's quaint yellow living room on this May 4 morning while the committee is making its selections. When I was researching the Jerry Zaks chapter of this book in March 1992, the director invited me to a run-through of his production of *Guys and Dolls* at the 890 Studios. The show was just four weeks into rehearsal at the time and still finding its legs. But it was already apparent that what was outstanding about this version of the Frank Loesser–Abe Burrows–Jo Swerling classic was Faith Prince's portrayal of Miss Adelaide, the lead singer in the girlie show at the Hot Box nightclub who has been engaged to gambler Nathan Detroit for fourteen years. This fourteen-year engagement, by the way, is a masterful comic stroke, for it leads directly to two pieces of funny business that make Adelaide such an original and beloved heroine: her fabrication of fourteen years of family bliss for her mother, and her perdurable cold. Adelaide is a bubbling brew of humor and sadness, and Faith Prince just happens to have all of Adelaide inside her. As is the case for all memorable musical-comedy performances, she inhabits the character, as if they've known each other intimately for a long time. And, in fact, Faith played Adelaide twice before—at the Seattle Rep, and at the Wagon Wheel Theatre in Warsaw, Indiana, when she was just twenty years old (which meant she had been engaged since first grade).

In addition to her Adelaide, Prince gave the one unanimously praised performance in *Nick & Nora* earlier in the season, playing Lorraine, the victim of the murder that both Nick and Nora Charles tried to solve.

If the world were fair, it seemed likely that the thirty-five-year-old actress would be nominated for Tony Awards in two categories at season's end—both Best Performance by an Actress in a Leading Role, and in a Featured Role.

About ten days after I saw the run-through, Zaks invited me back to watch a technical rehearsal of the show at the Martin Beck Theatre. While the lighting was being set for the crap-game sequence in the auditorium, I happened upon Faith Prince taking a break in the lobby. I told her about this book and asked if I could shadow her for the month of May to record her Tony Award experience. "I'd love to do it . . . if I'm nominated," she said.

And so here we are eating pancakes together at her home, surrounded by the kind of simple, relaxed domesticity Adelaide would kill for, eagerly awaiting the news. This past year has been a dream time for Prince, whatever may happen today. In addition to her star turns in *Guys and Dolls* and *Nick & Nora*, she started out the year finishing a sustained run as Trina in the off-Broadway production of *Falsettoland*, a role she could have re-created on Broadway were it not for the other two commitments. You can hear her on the *Falsettoland* cast album, as well as on the albums for *Nick & Nora*, recorded in New York just last weekend, and *Guys and Dolls*, which she recorded yesterday at BMG Studios in a session that was filmed for a PBS "Great Performances" documentary. And in January, after a relationship going back a few seasons, she married Larry, a handsome and talented trumpet player she spotted in the pit one night when she was onstage playing Daisy Gamble in *On a Clear Day You Can See Forever* at the Sacramento Light Opera Association.

Despite all this, and despite a set of reviews for her Adelaide that not only praised the performance but hailed her as a genuine new Broadway star, reviews that have kept her phone ringing with offers and electrified her career, she says she did not sleep last night, and her face is now filled with fear. It's a face of someone who knows things can go wrong, someone who expects unpleasant surprises.

"I'll be nervous until I hear the news," she says. No words of comfort will change that.

The press conference at Sardi's, where the list of nominations will be read, is scheduled for noon. But as it gets well past twelve and then past one, there is no news. Her mother, Tootie Prince, calls from her office at a travel agency in Lynchburg, Virginia, and Faith tells her, "Nothing yet." Her father, Keith, a nuclear physicist, calls from his office and she tells him the same. Larry can't take the tension and goes out to run some errands.

Then, at 1:17 P.M., the phone rings. It is Peter Strain, Faith's agent since she first arrived in New York twelve years ago. The committee is still deliberating, but word has already leaked out that Faith has been nominated for best actress along with her *Guys and Dolls* costar, Josie de Guzman; Sophie Hayden from *The Most Happy Fella*; and Jodi Benson from *Crazy for You*. She's got one in the bag. But there is no word yet on the Featured Actress category. Prince doesn't want to call anybody until she has all the news. But her first response is that she's thrilled for Josie. Josie was originally cast as Faith's lesbian lover in *Nick & Nora* and was fired from that role in previews, a move that the rest of the cast found unwarranted. She was then hired as Carolyn Mignini's understudy for *Guys and Dolls*, but assumed the role of Sarah Brown, the mission doll, when Mignini was let go, also in previews.

A spot opened up for Josie to receive a nomination when it was decided by the Tony eligibility committee (administering the Tonys requires many committees) that Barbara Walsh, who took Faith's old role as Trina when *Falsettos* came to Broadway, would be entered in the Featured Actress category rather than that of Leading Actress. That decision may well end up costing Faith her second nomination—and for a role that Faith originated. She can be knocked out of the running by an actress playing the role she could have played. (But if she played it, she wouldn't have been able to play Adelaide. Unless, of course, she played both roles at once, running back and forth between the Martin Beck and Golden theatres. Go from one man who's strung her along for fourteen years to another who left her for another man. Sing "A person could develop a cold," then run across the street and sing "I'm breaking down." In which case she would have been assured both nominations. This still might have resulted in her losing out on a nomination for *Nick & Nora*—but to herself for *Falsettos*.)

At 1:40 the phone rings again. This time it's Chris Boneau, the *Guys and Dolls* press agent. Sure enough, all the little ironies come into play. Faith is not nominated for Featured Actress. Barbara Walsh is—along with Liz Larsen for *The Most Happy Fella*; Tonya Pinkins for *Jelly's Last Jam*; and, in a surprise, Vivian Reed for *High Rollers Social and Pleasure Club*, a revue of Allen Toussaint's New Orleans music that stopped by the Helen Hayes Theatre in April for a cup of coffee.

You can never predict the dynamics in a room full of fifteen theatre professionals trying to settle on a consensus of subjective opinions. This was an unusual year in which, in addition to Faith, there were four designers whose work might have netted two nominations each—Tony Walton, for his sets for *Guys and Dolls* and *Four Baboons Facing the Sun*; Robin Wagner, for his sets for *Crazy for You* and *Jelly's Last Jam*; William Ivey

Long, for his costumes for *Crazy for You* and *Guys and Dolls*; and Paul Gallo, for his lighting design for *Crazy for You* and *Guys and Dolls*. Of these five artists, only Gallo received a double nomination, and lighting is an area that most people on the committee and most people in theatre know as little about as they know about quoits. But it would appear as if there were a tacit agreement among the committee members to try to allot only one nomination per person.

"Now that it's over I feel great," Faith says as she lifts the phone to call her parents. "It's the waiting that makes you so nervous, and all the things you hear from other people that builds your expectations. But I really feel great about getting nominated for this role. And I'm glad that Josie got one. And Barbara. And it's all good."

This is not just lip service. You can see the genuine relief in her face. The fear of major disappointment is gone. She doesn't have to struggle to find the smile anymore. Faith, you see, is a worrier by nature. She worries like anyone who is obsessed with details. She lays awake at night making lists in her mind. She expects a lot of herself. These are her little demons. And they have driven her to create the superb string of performances she has delivered on the New York stage in the past decade—not just in *Guys and Dolls*, *Nick & Nora*, and *Falsettoland*, but also in *Groucho*, *Olympus on My Mind*, and *Jerome Robbins' Broadway*, for which she received her first Tony nomination.

During the month between the announcement of the Tony nominations and the actual awards ceremony, Faith Prince will go through a period of incredible demands on her time and her energy, unlike anything she has ever known or imagined. She will devote the same effort and anxiety to each task asked of her that she gives in her performances. This will be her first month as not just an actress, but a star. She spent most of her life training to be an actress—but this star thing is a whole other occupation.

"My parents each have a terrific sense of humor, and I think that's where it all probably started," Faith says. "My dad was always great at telling jokes. He has terrific timing. When I was a child growing up in Lynchburg, whenever we had people over, he was the center of attention. I really liked that power that I saw he had over people, making them laugh, so I think I cultivated a similar thing. When I was in the first grade I came home and asked my mother if I could be in the school talent show. I said the teacher had this poem I could do and it was about Raggedy Ann. So my mother made up this costume with white tights and she put red strips of material on, so I had these candy-cane legs. She took an old pair of tennis shoes and cut a hole in one and put sawdust in the toe, so at the end I could shake my foot and the sawdust would come out. I don't recall any fear at the time. None. I couldn't wait to get in front of the class. I was a natural ham. I won third prize.

"Even before that, when I was three, my mother says I stood up in front of my church during a ceremony and someone asked me something and I said, 'My bowels moved three times today.' The person said, What did you say? And my mother stood up and shouted, 'Don't ask her again!' I was just very presentational.

"When I got to junior high school I played some piano for the chorale. But I wasn't very good, and mostly what I did was turn the pages for my friend Jeanne Wood. Then in ninth grade the teacher, Carl Harris, asked me to get up and audition for a solo, and I did. He said, You never told me you could really sing. And I said, I didn't know I could. Then when I got to eleventh grade at E. C. Glass High School I got cast as Laurie in *Oklahoma!* The next year Mr. Harris gave me Nellie Forbush in *South Pacific*, and that was when he went to my mom and dad and said, 'I've never said this to any parents before, but I really think Faith should go to Broadway. I think she has raw talent.' He told my parents they should do whatever they could to get me into the Cincinnati Conservatory of Music. But the weekend I was supposed to go to audition I had laryngitis, so Mr. Harris rigged together a tape of some of my performances and sent it to the school with a letter, and I got in based on that. But that made me feel as if I had gotten in some way under the rug and I shouldn't really be there. I remember in the middle of my first year I went to see Worth Gardner, who was the head of the department. I got up my courage and I went into his office and I just said, I want to know if I should be here. He said, Do you really think you could've lasted here three months if you really weren't supposed to be here? But I tell you my first year was really hard. They gave me warnings when I did my performing boards that I was funny, but I didn't do other things that showed them different sides of me. I kept the results of those boards under my pillow for a year and I was really determined. I knew I was up against the wall and I had to really go for this or get out. That was the turning point in my life, because I learned how hard you had to work.

"The summer after my sophomore year, this was 1977, I auditioned for and got cast at the Wagon Wheel, a tent theatre in Warsaw, the Bible Belt part of Indiana. That was a really big thing for the kids from Northwestern, Catholic U., the American Drama Academy, and Cincinnati. We did seven shows that summer for two weeks each. And my roles included Adelaide.

"I didn't know anything about Adelaide when I auditioned. But I knew when I performed it that summer that I had a real thing for her. I really was her. It just felt as if I wasn't acting. It's tough to be engaged for fourteen years when you're twenty. But I've always said I'm an old soul. That's why I never worry about my age. I've always played women who are older than I am. And when people ask me how old I am, they're surprised. I think that's just something that will precede me my whole life.

"In some ways my Adelaide then was very similar to now. I've grown up a lot, so I am a little stronger in some areas. And, having the experiences I've had, I know how certain things really feel. Like disappointment. I think at that time I'd never really been in love before. But I just substituted with what I knew. I feel more like an adult with this Adelaide. I feel this Adelaide is not a victim; she's very strong. But I'd say my sense of humor has not changed that much. My timing and things like that. I think all that was just innately there."

In her senior year at the conservatory, Faith was cast as Ann in a production of *A Little Night Music*, directed by Word Baker, who had directed the original production of *The Fantasticks* off-Broadway. "Word invited me to New York after that," she says. "It was my first time here, and he took me down Fifth Avenue and to the Oak Room at the Plaza. He suggested that I go see a couple of shows, and so I stood on the TKTS line and went to see Michael Bennett's *Ballroom*, and Whoopi Goldberg's show. Those were my first Broadway shows. And I remember in *Ballroom*, Dorothy Loudon got entrance applause when she came in and I thought, She must really feel incredible. I still think about that when I get entrance applause for *Guys and Dolls*. It's overwhelming."

When she graduated, Faith was selected as most talented in her senior class, "and that was really something because I don't think my peers expected me to make it through the first year," she says. She went back to Wagon Wheel for one more summer, then planned to head right for New York, where she had already sublet an apartment on West Ninety-third Street with a school chum, Kim Criswell. But Faith received a phone call from a choreographer who had worked at the summer-stock theatre and was now staging the Broadway Revue at the International Hotel in Washington, D.C. The actress doing the comic role in the show had dropped out, and Faith was offered the job and the chance to get her Equity card. When the show closed in February 1980, Faith finally arrived in New York to discover her landlord had rented the apartment to two sets of tenants and was collecting money from both. So she and Kim found another place on Ninety-eighth Street.

"Kim had already gotten cast in the national tour of *Annie*," Prince says. "And that really pissed me off at the time. I felt as if I had to get off my butt and get out there and be something—which was ridiculous, since

I'd been out of school only a few months and worked the whole time. My own drive sometimes surprised me.

"I started going to all these cattle-call auditions. I bought *Backstage* and if the producers wanted a six-foot-four black woman, I was there. I didn't care.

"At the conservatory we were all groomed to audition. You could spot us the minute we walked in because we were so used to being grilled and performing under the gun. By the time I got to New York I had my audition songs, I knew how to go in, I had my stuff planned, I knew what type of role I was right for, I knew how to market myself."

One weekend Faith's mom came to New York to visit her. A friend of Faith's from the conservatory, James Walton, was understudying in an off-Broadway revue called *Scrambled Feet*, at the Village Gate. He phoned Faith to report that he was going on, and she brought her mom down there to see the show. "At intermission my mother leans over to me and says, 'You know, you'd be great in this show,'" Faith says. "There was one woman, three men, a piano, and a duck. The woman played the piano, and I could do that, and in the second act I began to look at it in a whole new way."

After the show that night, the actors stayed for a discussion with a drama class visiting from Colorado. Faith and her mom stayed also. "I don't know what possessed me," Faith says. "But I raised my hand, and Jeffrey Haddow, one of the writers and performers, called on me and I said, I have one question: Do you need another girl? Jimmy was crawling under the tables by this time. But Haddow said, Do you sing? And I said, Of course. And he said, Well, why don't you talk to our stage manager and he'll set up an audition for you. So I auditioned and I got cast in the Boston company and then came to do it in New York."

Soon after leaving *Scrambled Feet*, Faith was cast in a new sitcom developed for Suzanne Somers in which the star played an airline stewardess and Prince was a lawyer, her roommate, and her female straight man.

"I did not like L.A. at all," she says. "I probably should have stayed there. I could have had a television career at that point. I was only twenty-two years old. But I just didn't like it and something inside me said to go back. L.A. was very tough and I didn't feel ready for it personally.

"So I went back to New York and I started to take anything that came along. Regional jobs. Summer stock. Civic Light Opera shows." Soon she was on a roll in New York: *Olympus on My Mind* and *Groucho* off-Broadway, *Urban Blight* and *Bad Habits* at the Manhattan Theatre Club, her Broadway debut in *Jerome Robbins' Broadway* at the age of thirty-two after nearly ten years in New York, *Falsettoland*, and *Nick & Nora*. Good performance after good performance. A reputation as a hard worker and a cooperative one. Big voice, great comic timing, kind of quirky-looking and off center. An actress who seemed to have a lot in common with Lucille Ball and Carol Burnett and Judy Holliday—all of whom, not coincidentally, were her idols—and with a better singing voice than any of them. But what had been written in the twelve years since she'd been working in the theatre that could show off the talents of a daffy belter who brought a strong sense of reality to offbeat characters and elevate her to the headliner level? Bette Midler's *Divine Madness*, maybe—but that's all. Oddly enough, she had probably played every role she was right for in that period.

Then the decision was made to revive *Guys and Dolls*. And actress and character collided like atoms.

By the time a musical reaches opening night everyone is exhausted and needs a vacation. For more than a week before previews begin, you're rehearsing ten-out-of-twelve hour workdays, usually a noon-to-midnight schedule, with no day off. Once previews begin, you're rehearsing during the day and playing the show at night. Generally, shows limp toward opening night, then get an adrenaline boost for the three or four previews that the critics are invited to attend. That carries you through the opening-night celebration and, if the reviews are positive, into the next week. If the reviews are negative, all the air can go out of the balloon.

Faith Prince came out of this period with as good a set of reviews as any actor or actress has ever had in a musical, and her adrenaline was pumping. In the remainder of April following the *Guys and Dolls* opening, she gave up her one day off a week to record the albums for *Nick & Nora* and then for *Guys and Dolls*.

Then very quickly she was into May, the closing month of the theatre season that has become a dizzying roller-coaster ride of social events and awards ceremonies. It's fun to celebrate success in a field in which it is difficult to come by. But the month-long bacchanalia soon becomes a strain on all of the actors and creators of the year's more successful shows. Faith, as the most-praised star of the biggest hit of the most successful season of musical theatre in many years, was at the center of the celebrating. In addition to being required to attend all the usual season-ending events, she would be called upon to fulfill an endless flurry of media requests to help publicize her show. And she would have to field the avalanche of offers from creators and producers of theatre shows, television shows, and motion pictures who wanted to be the first to hook their wagons to the new star. Sure, it sounds exactly like what every young actress dreams about. You don't get to these heights by being reserved. But it's also overwhelming: a textbook case of the admonition to be careful what you wish for. . . .

First and foremost, there were the eight performances each six-day week. (*Guys and Dolls* plays a Monday-through-Saturday schedule.) And no actor with an eye on the ball is going to miss any show in May, since that's when the 650 Tony voters are given their complimentary seats to see the nominated shows and make their selections.

There was a steady stream of interviewers flowing through Faith and Larry's tiny home, filling those days when she did not have matinees to play. Jan Stuart came for *Newsday*. David Patrick Stearns visited her for *USA Today*. David Richards profiled her for *The New York Times*, a piece she liked very much. "I think I was more myself with him than I have been to date," she says. "I was tired, for one thing, and I couldn't help but be totally honest. I thought he really appreciated the wacky side of me. But then he started to dig out what's underneath that, that very dark side that exists for all actors and comedians."

People magazine filled her apartment with photographers. "NBC Nightly News" sent a crew that spent two days at the house for a piece that ran three minutes, Faith says. She did an interview for *Parade* magazine, the national Sunday newspaper supplement, that included a two-hour photo shoot that was physically exhausting. The CBS documentary program "48 Hours" sent a crew to trail her on the day of the Tony Awards for a fifteen-minute segment in a program about Times Square. Faith's family was in town for the event, and between them and the large crew, the apartment seemed like the Marx Brothers' packed stateroom scene in *A Night at the Opera*. (They all ate pancakes, by the way.)

Then there was a fashion shoot to accompany an interview in *Mirabella*. "I had never done a fashion shoot before and I was very scared," Faith says. "There were two outfits—a Bob Mackie gown and a series of pieces put together by some young SoHo designers. They kept talking about how the clothes hung, and I kept looking at my lines and thought, What am I going to look like? The clothes were very 'high chic,' and the Bob Mackie gown was very low-cut. It didn't seem to be me. So I just said, I'll do my hair and makeup and get the feel of what you do, and then we'll just start from there. They did my hair away from my face, with these large curls, and they used this waxing thing. It was a look I never thought of before, but I looked very chic and wonderful and it was what I used again for the Tonys. After years of paging through Sears Roebuck catalogs, I was in awe. This was unleashing another side of me, and that was exciting. I'd do it again in a heartbeat."

Prince was concerned about how she came off in the interviews and approached each one with great care. "I wanted to make each one interesting and different," she says. "Not as if I was just repeating the same things methodically. I was scared when I was doing each one that I was running out of time and wondering how people were going to see me. I think that's important. Those interviews become your résumé. But I like the way I came off. I wanted to be seen as someone other than Adelaide. I mean, she's certainly a part of me. But when I meet someone whom I see in a particular part and see how different the person really is, to me that's the highest compliment you can receive as an actor, because you are truly throwing yourself into someone else. I wanted the interviewers and readers to know that I certainly use humor to cope with certain aspects of life, but that I'm just as serious as I am humorous. I think you can fly for a really long time on one kind of part, but the role of Adelaide's just a little piece of me.

Then there were the job offers. Jerry Herman contacted Prince after seeing *Guys and Dolls* to say he wanted to write a show for her. They batted around some ideas and agreed to meet in July. Lynn Ahrens and Steve Flaherty, for whom Prince had participated in a reading of their work in progress, the *My Favorite Year* musical, also had an idea they wanted to discuss with her. Movie producers showed up backstage after the show on a regular basis and told Prince they had something for her. Some followed up with calls to her agent, and she signed to play Kevin Kline's colleague in the motion picture *Dave* that she would go to L.A. to shoot in October. Not surprisingly, given the role she was playing, the most aggressive pursuit came from the television producers. Nine different production companies made offers to pay her a holding fee and develop a sitcom for her. "I'm going to deal with that in October when I have a clear head," she says. "But I have to do this television thing. You can't live in New York and just do theatre. It's too hard. Doing it each and every night, each and every week, is too hard. I'm not saying I don't love it. I do, and I'll keep doing it. But to get some acclaim doing something else and get some power so that people start developing things for me, that would balance it out."

The only offers Prince dismissed out of hand were the calls from just about every agent in town, usually suggesting they take her out for a drink after the show. She would not entertain any thoughts of leaving Peter Strain; she relies now more than ever upon his guidance to wade through whatever comes her way.

Chris Boneau, the *Guys and Dolls* press agent, introduced Prince to a shopper named Liz Burpoe, to help the actress find a wardrobe for the dizzying circuit of social functions she would attend. Burpoe put together two outfits from Donna Karan's company, which wanted the actress to be seen in its clothes. She selected a green-and-white suit with a lace bustier, and an ankle-length double-breasted blue dress with a pinched waist and brass buttons. "The last thing I wanted to have to worry about was what I looked like and having to pay attention to that," Prince says. "I just wanted something I could put on and feel comfortable all night."

Prince won the Best Actress in a Musical honor from both the Outer Critics Circle and the Drama Desk. She attended both organizations' ceremonies to accept her awards and make a speech, "which is something I'm not very good at and that makes me very nervous," she says. She attended the annual Tony nominees' brunch at Sardi's the week after the nominations, which is a press event to help build an audience for the telecast. She attended the annual season-ending luncheon of the Drama League, a group of society women who support the theatre, at the Plaza Hotel.

It seemed that life couldn't get more hectic. But it did on Sunday, May 31, the day of the Tony Awards presentation and national telecast. After doing two shows the day before, Prince had little sleep and was out of bed early that morning preparing for the arrival of her family and the "48 Hours" crew. She did an hour of on-camera interviewing with Dan Rather, then headed uptown to the Gershwin Theatre for the Tony show preparations.

The Tony rehearsal, which goes on all afternoon until showtime, is one of the biggest star-ogling events of the year in New York City. The orchestra section of the theatre and the green room backstage are filled with the casts of the Broadway musicals, there to run through their numbers, and with the evening's presenters, in most cases movie stars who have had some association with the theatre world. So you find Sigourney Weaver standing in an aisle joking with Gene Hackman and Richard Dreyfuss. And Michael Douglas onstage introducing his father, Kirk, to his fatal attraction, Glenn Close. Peter Stone, who wrote the show, looks on as Joe Cates, the producer, and the presenters rewrite his lines on the spot and cracks, "They've just changed my credit from 'written by' to 'not a word by.'" Large sheets of oaktag sit on the aisle seats in the orchestra section, each with the name of the nominee who will occupy the seat written on it so the CBS crew can pick out camera angles. The show is rehearsed in running order, and after the performers do their segments they linger in the house to socialize.

Shortly after 2 P.M., the *Guys and Dolls* company is called to the stage to perform "Sit Down, You're Rockin' the Boat," the number that the producers have selected to showcase. Prince was hoping that would be the choice so she would not have to worry about performing this evening. But since the number does not feature the show's stars, a coda has been added, the final scene of the show: a double wedding for Adelaide and Nathan and Sarah and Sky, with a reprise of the title song. The company, all in street clothes—though a few of the men have brought along their fedoras—finishes "Sit Down," the orchestra segues into "Guys and Dolls," and Faith comes out onto the stage in her wedding-dress costume. What she is here to rehearse, it turns out, is a costume change. Her show's segment will fall late in the evening, and it is to be followed immediately by the presentation of the award for Best Actress in a Musical. She has but a few minutes to get offstage, down the stairs to the dressing room, change into her own clothes, then return to her designated seat. The number ends, director Walter Miller shouts, "Applause! Applause! Applause!" Then Faith takes off for the dressing room. In less than two minutes she's back onstage in her Donna Karan, huffing and puffing. "You look just gorgeous," a dresser says to her. And she rolls those big brown eyes.

She returns home for an hour, then is back at the Gershwin at 4 P.M. for the dress rehearsal. It ends at 6. Rather than heading back uptown, she goes to her dressing room six blocks downtown at the Martin Beck to prepare for the evening. She does her makeup, has her hair done for her as it was for the *Mirabella* shoot, puts on her blue dress, with no jewelry, but there's a red AIDS awareness ribbon on the collar. She is picked up in a limousine by her husband, Larry, and her parents, Tootie and Keith. The broadcast is scheduled for 9, and everyone is asked to be in their seats in the theatre by 7:45. But all those present resist taking their seats because the gathering in the lobby is the year's single largest and most elegant display of theatre folk. Faith enters, stops, and takes the time to introduce her parents proudly to all those who greet her.

When the glitzy ceremony finally does get started, there is a palpable tension in the auditorium. As the theatre audience has shrunk over the years, it has become increasingly difficult for a show to get a large enough share of that audience to support itself, and this nationally televised showcase, always a good marketing tool, has become a critical marketing opportunity. Every show wants to outdo the others, both in the way it presents itself and in the awards it collects. This year's competition is particularly important in the minds of the factions representing the two seriously themed musicals, *Jelly's Last Jam* and *Falsettos*. Both camps feel that it will require some award recognition to keep those shows healthy—maybe even prevent them from closing. As the awards are divvied up, rather than being witness to a community cheering on its own for their achievements, you hear tepid applause and are less aware of the happy few than the disappointed many. There are two exceptions, two award recipients whose work this season cuts through the self-interest and gains a loud ovation of consent: The first is Susan Stroman, for her choreography for *Crazy for You*. The second occurs at 10:47, when, to no one's surprise, Faith Prince is announced as the Best Actress in a Musical.

When Prince takes the stage, she is not a funny woman. It is that other side she has talked about that she presents tonight. Her speech is a gracious list of thank-yous in an evening full of gracious lists of thank-yous. After speaking, Faith waits in the wings as Gregory Hines is honored as Best Actor in a Musical. Then they are whisked off together to the Les Pyrénées restaurant across the street, where the representatives of the press view the show and interview the winners.

On the way there Hines sees that Prince is in a kind of stupor and says, "It's all right now. You won."

Prince responds, "What did I just say out there? Did I speak okay?"

"You were great. Stop worrying," Hines says.

After answering a few questions for the press, Faith heads for the Tony Ball in the ballroom of the Marriott Marquis hotel. There she spends most of her time posing for photos, with Glenn Close, who won Best Actress in a Play for *Death and the Maiden*, and then with Hines, Close, and Judd Hirsch, who has won Best Actor in a Play for *Conversations with My Father*. Good company all.

By 12:30, Tootie Prince is pacing in the lobby waiting for her daughter to arrive at the Copacabana, where Dodger Productions is throwing its own party for the cast and crew and friends of *Guys and Dolls*. Tootie is concerned about what the recent breakneck pace is doing to her already winded daughter. Faith arrives and hugs her mother. Then they come down the stairs, where the rock-and-roll is good and loud and the dance floor is full. But Faith never gets to the dance floor or even to the table where both parents now sit, along with her brother and sister-in-law. Everyone in the crowded room wants the chance to congratulate her. Patiently she accepts a nonstop barrage of hugs and kisses.

A few weeks later Faith and I meet for lunch at Sarabeth's Kitchen in her neighborhood. The "May Madness" is over, but she still looks tired, less sprightly than she was when we first met, more conscious that the people filling the restaurant at lunchtime recognize her, and not yet completely at ease with that reality.

"The responsibility that I have now is hard—extremely hard," she says. "I don't know how people with kids do it. I would have had no time for my children. I would not have been a very good mother. I haven't even been a very good dog owner.

"I never gave much thought to the glamour part of this business and I had no preconception of what it would feel like. I remember getting good results from being funny and talented, and I just thought about getting the chance to do shows. I always find the world does me a lot better if I don't try to imagine certain things and just keep going toward a goal. And if I don't have any preconceived notions, it always turns out better than I could have hoped or dreamed up anyway.

"It takes everything I've got to pour the kind of energy I do into the show every night. When I have to do all these other things on top of it, it's extremely hard for me.

"Now, what concerns me is how far behind I am in keeping up with people. I've received cards and letters from more people than I ever knew I knew in my life, who want to come to New York and see me. Best friends from the third grade whom I haven't seen since then. But I'm getting more tired and I have to protect myself and my family. So I feel kind of like stone, but I think it will get easier now that I know I don't have to say yes to everything and I can be very clear about what I need.

"I need to keep the level of my performance up there. I would say it's characteristic of me to be good when I'm exhausted. Certainly there are days when I think I could've done better, but I don't think I've fallen below a certain point. I talk to the stage manager a lot, and Jerry Zaks comes by, so I can be sure of this. I have a lot of energy, there's a natural funniness about me. When I have that extra energy, it's effortless for me. When I don't, I really have to tough it out. And I don't like that feeling anymore. I really need my day off on Sunday. I just can't accept engagements on my day off anymore. If they just gave you two days off a week in this business, then it would be a breeze.

"It's been an amazing period of time, and I don't think it will ever be this way again. I don't think I quite understand what's happened or what it's all about. I don't get it. But I'm glad I have all these articles. I'm glad I was chosen for them. Because a month or so down the line, I think I'll really be able to sit down and enjoy them. Maybe then I'll be able to get it."

CURTAIN CALL

". . . And so It Begins"

★

My favorite curtain-call story: Just a few years back, Debbie Reynolds was the star and a producer of a revival of the Meredith Wilson musical *The Unsinkable Molly Brown* that ventured out on a national tour. You may recall that Ms. Reynolds was nominated for an Oscar for her portrayal of Molly Brown on the screen, but until now she had not played the role on the stage. She was joined in this production by Harve Presnell, who was also her costar in the motion picture.

The tour began at, and was co-produced by, the Theatre Under the Stars in Houston, Texas. In rehearsals the show was running well over three hours, which upset Frank Young, the executive producer of that institution. After 11 P.M., you see, Young, by stipulation of his union contract, was forced to pay his pit musicians the overtime rate, which was not an expense he had anticipated or relished. In the kind of battle of wills that has been known to occur sometimes between producers and stars, Young threatened that the curtain would come down at one minute to eleven, wherever the show might be at that point.

On opening night, the show ended at precisely 11 P.M.—whereupon Young jumped into the pit and grabbed the baton from his conductor. Ms. Reynolds then asked for the curtain to be raised. She announced to the audience that the company had staged an elaborate curtain call filled with song and dance, but that the producer would allow no more music to be played this evening. She told the members of the audience to contribute more money to the theatre the following year so that it could afford to pay its musicians. Then she said the company would now perform their bows as staged but without musical accompaniment. And they did.

Despite this tale, the curtain call is one of the more civil traditions of the theatre, a favorite of both the performers and their audience. After you've spent the evening on a journey with the characters, it provides you with one more opportunity to see and acknowledge them all.

It will not surprise you, I'm sure, that it has taken me some time beyond the end of the season of musicals chronicled in these pages to record it. As I write this, it is in fact June 1993, and another theatre season has come and gone. While I've been writing, the people whose stories you have read have continued to practice their craft.

City of Angels closed on Broadway in the winter of 1993, after nearly a two-year run. David Zippel's next show, *The Goodbye Girl*, on which he collaborated with Marvin Hamlisch and Neil Simon, opened at the Marriott Marquis Theatre on Broadway in March to some disappointing reviews. But it continues there, thanks largely to the appeal of its stars, Martin Short and Bernadette Peters.

Stephen Bogardus continued to play Whizzer in *Falsettos* at the John Golden Theatre in New York until late spring this year. He doesn't know whether William Finn has decided if there is still more to tell us about Marvin.

My Favorite Year had a difficult time growing into the cavernous Vivian Beaumont Theatre, which resulted in a disappointing critical reception. The show closed on January 10. Lynn Ahrens and Stephen Flaherty's score will continue to live on, courtesy of the cast album recorded by RCA. The team is now beginning work on a new project.

Margo Lion has managed as of this writing to return ninety percent of the five-million-dollar investment in *Jelly's Last Jam*, and the show continues to run at the Virginia Theatre, with Brian Mitchell having replaced Gregory Hines, and with Ben Vereen and Phylicia Rashad joining the cast. Lion went on to co-produce Tony Kushner's play *Angels America*, which arrived at the Walter Kerr Theatre in April and won the Tony for Best Play. It was directed by George C. Wolfe, who was also awarded a Tony for his work.

Jerry Zaks staged the national tour of *Guys and Dolls*, starring Lorna Luft. Then he had his first Broadway flop with a new play called *Face Value*, by David Henry Hwang, who'd previously scored a hit with *M. Butterfly*. The show played an engagement in Boston, began previews at the Cort Theatre on Broadway in the spring, but closed without an official opening.

Five Guys Named Moe ran at the O'Neill until May, and Milton Craig Nealy will now be joining it for a national tour. This will delay his catching up with an *Ain't Misbehavin'* or *Dreamgirls* production someplace.

Susan Stroman reunited with director Scott Ellis to choreograph a reworked version of the 1963 musical *110 in the Shade*, by Tom Jones and Harvey Schmidt, at New York City Opera, as well as a national tour and Toronto production of *And the World Goes 'Round* and a tribute to Stephen Sondheim at Carnegie Hall. She re-created her choreography for *Crazy for You* for both the London production and the U.S. national tour. In autumn 1993, she will choreograph a new production of *Showboat*, to be directed by Harold Prince, and open a new theatre complex in Toronto. On a weekend off in September, she served as a judge at the Miss America Pageant.

In addition to working on the London production of *Grand Hotel* and the national tour of *The Will Rogers Follies*, Peter Stone has been writing the books for two new musicals. One, a small contemporary farce called *Love Me, Love My Dog*, will feature a score by Jimmy Webb. The other, a large spectacle about the sinking of the *Titanic*, will have a score by Maury Yeston, and be produced by Mike Nichols and directed by Tommy Tune. In both scripts, Stone continues to fiddle with both time and space.

Kay McClelland considered chucking it all and going home to Atlanta for about five minutes last fall. In the interim she played Lois Lane in a production of the 1966 musical *It's a Bird . . . It's a Plane . . . It's Superman!* at the Goodspeed Opera House and appeared in a revue of Jule Styne songs at the Rainbow and Stars venue in Manhattan. She is now in the national touring company of *Crazy for You*.

Graciela Daniele choreographed the dances to David Zippel and Marvin Hamlisch's tunes for *The Goodbye Girl*. Prior to that, she directed and choreographed the national tour of *Once on This Island* and the premiere of a musical based on the novel *Captains Courageous* at Ford's Theatre in Washington, D.C. In her spare time she staged a pair of ballets for the Ballet Hispanico, of which she is the resident choreographer. She has also recently been awarded a fellowship that will provide her with a two-year residency at the Lincoln Center Theater.

Karen Ziémba continued her collaboration with Ellis and Stroman, delivering a critically acclaimed performance as Lizzie in *110 in the Shade* at the New York City Opera and starring in the national tour of *And the World Goes 'Round*. She is now appearing as Polly, the female lead, in the national company of *Crazy for You*—the role that she was upset about losing to Jodi Benson on Broadway.

Kevin Gray remained with the national tour of *Phantom of the Opera* for extended runs in Philadelphia, Boston, and Detroit. He used his vacation time last summer to grab the opportunity to play one of the great leading-male roles in the musical-theatre repertoire, Billy Bigelow in *Carousel*, in a well-received production at the Pittsburgh Civic Light Opera. He is now starring as The Engineer in a production of *Miss Saigon* in Toronto.

The Secret Garden ended a twenty-month run on Broadway in December, and, after a short visit to her home in Charlottesville, Lydia Ooghe assumed the role of Mary in the national touring company.

The Most Happy Fella ended its run at the Booth Theatre last August. Spiro Malas went out on the road performing his one-man show while he waited for a promised national tour of *Happy Fella* to materialize. It never did.

Last October, Marlene Danielle celebrated the tenth anniversary of *Cats*, and it appears as if she and it will be together for an eleventh. The basement and top floor of her country home have been rebuilt and she is now saving up to finish the two floors in between.

Faith Prince remains with *Guys and Dolls*, following a hiatus to play Kevin Kline's colleague in the motion picture *Dave*. She will soon shoot the pilot episode for her own television situation comedy.

After spending my own favorite year hanging out safely backstage at everyone else's musicals, I am, of course, champing at the bit to be back in rehearsal with one of my own.

INDEX

★

Waara, Scott, 12
Wagner, Robin, 10, 12–13, 66, 117, 131, 151, 260
Waldman, Robert, 182
Waller, Fats, 53, 54
Walsh, Barbara, 29, 30, 260, 261
Walsh, Elizabeth, 203
Walton, James, 264
Walton, Tony, 78, 80–81, 82, 91, 134, 142, 143, 260
Warner, Sherman, 76
Weaver, Sigourney, 95, 268
Webb, Jimmy, 275
Webber, Andrew Lloyd, 121, 158, 197, 216, 244, 225
Weede, Robert, 234, 238
Weegee (photographer), 41
Weidman, John, 33, 75, 79, 80
Weissler, Barry, 28, 29, 53
Weissler, Fran, 28, 29, 53
Weitzman, Ira, 35, 40, 43, 189
Wenceslas Square, 75, 95
Werther, 231
Wesley, Richard, 54
West Side Story, 17, 21, 23, 72, 108, 121, 161, 167, 181, 185, 190, 200, 243, 250, 251, 252, 253
What Makes Sammy Run?, 182
Whitehead, Robert, 52
Who Cares?, 131
Whoopee, 126
Wildcat, 3
Wilder, Billy, 151, 163
Willard, Charlie, 125
Williams, Elizabeth, 52–53, 57
Willig, Lan, 210, 211, 238

Will Rogers Follies, The, 3, 134, 152–55, 160, 226, 275
Wilson, August, 56
Wilson, Billy, 109
Wilson, Bobby, 225
Wilson, Lanford, 193
Wilson, Meredith, 273
Winer, Linda, 69, 131, 171
Wise, Scott, 245
Witchel, Alex, 63, 171
Wits End Players, 157, 166, 167
Wolfe, George C., 29, 43, 50, 55, 57–62, 65–67, 72, 73, 74
Woman of the Year, 133, 139
Wonderful Town, 78, 86, 88, 97
Wood, Natalie, 204
Wopat, Tom, 160–61
Wright, Robert, 135–36, 137, 146

Yeston, Maury, 137–38, 275
York, Rachel, 11
Young, Frank, 273–74

Zakreski, Paul, 5
Zaks, Jerry, 31, 56, 57, 72, 75, 77–101, 119, 258, 259, 271, 275
Zanuck, Darryl F., 144
Zerman, Andy, 210
Ziegfeld, Florenz, 126
Ziegfeld Follies, 152
Ziémba, Karen, 119, 124, 193, 194–205, 276
Zien, Chip, 18, 19–20, 24, 25, 27, 28, 29, 30–31
Zippel, David, 1, 2–15, 198, 274, 275
Zippel, Martin, 4, 5
Zorba, 56, 150, 175, 185